THE DATA PROTECTION GUIDEBOOK

A Survey of U.S. Federal and State Laws, Statutes, and Regulations Governing Data Breach Notification, Biometric Information, Cybersecurity, and Data Privacy

January 1, 2023
[Second Edition]

ISBN 9798367777871

Thompson Hine LLP. Printed in the United States of America.

Discounts are available for books ordered in bulk.
Special consideration is given to state bars, CLE programs, and other bar-related organizations.
Inquire at https://www.thompsonhine.com/contactus/ or at
Thompson Hine LLP, ATTN: Marketing Operations, 127 Public Square # 3900, Cleveland, OH 44114.

https://www.thompsonhine.com

Book Design by Michelle Benjamin

TABLE OF CONTENTS

INTRODUCTION

Welcome to *The Data Protection Guidebook.*

In the United States, complex systems of federal and state laws and regulations govern the collection, use, disclosure, retention, security, and disposal of personal information. For instance, U.S. federal data protection laws specifically apply to certain industries and organizations, such as health care, education, and financial institutions. Given that the U.S. does not have a comprehensive data protection law governing all business sectors or all types and categories of information at all times, state and local governments have independently developed and implemented their own unique privacy and cybersecurity requirements applicable to a broad range of sectors, industries, and businesses. Many states have enacted, at a minimum, privacy legislation that mirrors the laws adopted at the federal level, such as in electronic and telephonic marketing, the confidentiality of student records, and privacy representations and consumer protections.

In addition, as described in greater detail below, every state government has enacted a data breach notification law. Each requires organizations to make affirmative disclosures under defined circumstances in which personal information in their custody or control, or in the custody or control of a third party acting on their behalf, has been compromised and/or subject to an unauthorized use, acquisition, or disclosure. Several states have also enacted laws and regulations imposing affirmative obligations on businesses to implement and maintain certain technical, physical, and administrative security measures to protect and safeguard personal information from a data security breach.

Separately, a growing number of state legislatures are enacting consumer data protection laws, which grant individuals certain rights with respect to the collection and use of their personal information. They also impose obligations on the businesses and service providers that collect and retain such data. Additionally, some of these states have enacted biometric data protection laws that focus on an organization's ability to collect, retain, sell, disclose, or otherwise process biometric data, including in the employment context.

Data Breach Notification Laws

Cyberattacks, ransomware, and other data breaches now commonly occur across all major business sectors. The theft, loss, or unauthorized disclosure of personal information or other sensitive data can lead to revenue loss, reputation damage, fines, regulatory enforcement action, litigation, and legal fees. A variety of factors contribute to data breaches, including human error or accident and illegal or malicious activity by individuals and criminal enterprises. In the event of a data breach, organizations need to both remediate the damage and harm caused by the incident and be prepared to comply with data breach notification laws.

Each U.S. state, and the District of Columbia, has enacted laws, statutes, or regulations that require organizations to provide notice to consumers, regulatory authorities, and credit protection bureaus, in the event they suffer a data breach. The federal government has also enacted similar laws and rules governing data breach notification, although these legal frameworks are sector-specific (e.g., health care, financial institutions, and defense contractors). These laws generally require an organization to alert individuals when personal information is subject to unauthorized acquisition and/or access. They have many similarities. For instance, many state data breach notification laws do not apply to personal information that has been lawfully made available to the general public from federal, state, or local government records. These laws, however, contain important distinctions and requirements, including with respect to the following:

- The definition of "personal information."
- The scope of what constitutes a data "breach" or "incident."
- The applicability of "good-faith" exceptions and safe harbors.
- Certain "risk-of-harm" requirements.
- Breach notification timelines and exemptions.
- Engaging government authorities and credit monitoring agencies.
- The content of data breach notifications.
- How breach notices may be delivered.

The Data Protection Guidebook describes each of these legal requirements and categories based on individual state legal frameworks to help you better understand and respond to an actual or reasonably suspected data breach. The guidebook primarily focuses on general requirements applicable to private-sector organizations and excludes government agencies and businesses subject to specialized regulations (e.g., state health care laws, financial institutions, and insurance).

Consumer Data Protection Laws and Biometric Data

As noted above, some U.S. states have enacted comprehensive data protection laws and regulations that afford consumers, employees, business contacts, customers, job applicants, and others a broad range of data privacy rights and privileges, including the following:

- The right to be informed with respect to how their personal information is collected, used, disclosed, retained, and processed.
- The right to request access to specific pieces of their personal information, and to the categories of personal information about them, that have been collected.
- The right to request their personal information be deleted from a business's custody and control.
- The right to request their personal information be transferred to third parties.
- The right to opt out of having their personal information sold for profit or for monetary or other valuable considerations, or used for certain marketing and targeted advertising purposes.

These data privacy rights are not absolute, and each state has created its own unique exceptions and exemptions to its law's scope and applicability. In addition, each state imposes its own rules regulating how businesses must receive, process, and respond to individuals exercising their data privacy rights. Such rules address, among other issues, how businesses must notify individuals of their privacy rights. They also limit the ways personal information may be collected and retained and outline instances in which businesses must obtain express consent from an individual in order to process their personal information.

Similarly, a growing number of states and municipalities are enacting laws governing how private sector businesses may collect and use biometric data. These laws often have similar definitions of "biometric data" or "biometric information." They most often include a retina or iris scan, a fingerprint or voiceprint, a scan a person's hand or face geometry, or similar biological identifying characteristic. Such biometric data is sensitive and can cause significant harm to an individual if it's subject to a breach or compromise. For example, unlike traditional usernames and passwords, biometric data cannot be easily changed, updated, or altered once compromised. In addition, some U.S. state biometric laws allow for individuals to pursue legal action if an organization collects their biometric information without first obtaining proper consent or violates other aspects of the law. The terms "biometric data" and "biometric information" are often included in the definitions of "personal information" for purposes of data breach notification laws and therefore impose additional obligations on organizations to affirmatively notify individuals when such data and information is subject to unauthorized access and/or use. *The Data Protection Guidebook* summarizes or otherwise sets forth the most significant and comprehensive consumer privacy and biometric protection laws, statutes, and regulations.

Information Security and Data Disposal

Except with respect to health care, financial institutions, defense contractors, and other specific business sectors, the federal government has not enacted a law requiring all organizations, in all circumstances, to implement security controls designed to protect personal information from a data breach. On the other hand, several state and local governments have implemented requirements that mandate organizations to implement such security controls. Often, these legal frameworks require organizations to implement "reasonable" security measures to protect personal information in their custody or control from unauthorized access, acquisition, or disclosure. However, some state governments have enacted legislation that more specifically delineates the technical, physical, and administrative security controls that organizations must adopt. An important aspect of data security is ensuring that personal information is properly deleted and destroyed so as to not allow its recovery and use in an unauthorized manner. Accordingly, several state governments have enacted laws and regulations that require organizations to dispose of personal information through specific techniques, such as burning or shredding. *The Data Protection Guidebook* sets forth these information security and data disposal legal requirements.

* *

Steven G. Stransky

Partner, Thompson Hine LLP

Co-Chair, Privacy & Cybersecurity Practice Group

216.566.5646 | 202.263.4126

Steve.Stransky@ThompsonHine.com

Certified Information Privacy Professional/Government (CIPP/G)

Certified Information Privacy Professional/United States (CIPP/US)

https://www.thompsonhine.com/services/privacy-and-cybersecurity

DATA BREACH RESPONSE PLAN

Organizations must protect the privacy and security of the personal information and confidential information in their custody and control. In today's dynamic threat environment, however, businesses face ever-evolving risks to their information technology (IT) systems and networks. To mitigate these risks, businesses should build data protection programs tailored to their unique concerns and threats.

A key aspect of developing an optimal data protection program is to create, implement, and maintain a clear and concise data incident response plan (IRP) that outlines the measures and tools needed to prepare for and respond to an actual or reasonably suspected data breach, including the following:

- **Governance and responsibilities.** The IRP must identify the key individuals who have roles in the security incident response process.
- **Incident Response Coordinator.** The business should delegate authority to one person, an Incident Response Coordinator, to oversee data breach response efforts.
- **Incident Response Team (IRT).** An IRT is a predetermined group of employees, contractors, and other resources responsible for responding to data security incidents.
- **Incident response procedures.** The IRP should include procedures and protocols that address detection and discovery of security incidents; assessment and escalation of the incident; IRT investigation and analysis; and, containment, remediation, and recovery.
- **Evidence preservation.** The IRT should direct appropriate internal or external resources to capture and preserve evidence during the investigation, analysis, and response activities, which should include properly developed and scoped litigation holds.
- **Communications and notifications.** In coordination and consultation with legal counsel, the IRT should consider developing a communication plan for both internal and external stakeholders, including consumers, law enforcement, insurance carriers, regulatory authorities, and the media.
- **Post-incident response.** Following a security incident or data breach, a business should reconvene the IRT to assess the incident, the effectiveness of the response, and any remedial measures needed to mitigate gaps and shortcomings in the same.

Full access to the Thompson Hine LLP data breach response plan checklist is available at the following: https://www.thompsonhine.com/uploads/1135/doc/Data_Breach_Checklist.pdf

DATA BREACH NOTIFICATION, INFORMATION SECURITY, AND DATA DISPOSAL

ALABAMA

Data Breach Requirements: Ala. Code 1975 § 8-38-1 et seq.

The numbering and internal citations herein are derived from the applicable state statute.

	Alabama (Data Breach Requirements)
Personal Information	(6) The term "sensitive personally identifying information" means: a. Except as provided in paragraph b., an Alabama resident's first name or first initial and last name in combination with one or more of the following with respect to the same Alabama resident: 1. A non-truncated Social Security number or tax identification number. 2. A non-truncated driver's license number, state-issued identification card number, passport number, military identification number, or other unique identification number issued on a government document used to verify the identity of a specific individual. 3. A financial account number, including a bank account number, credit card number, or debit card number, in combination with any security code, access code, password, expiration date, or PIN, that is necessary to access the financial account or to conduct a transaction that will credit or debit the financial account. 4. Any information regarding an individual's medical history, mental or physical condition, or medical treatment or diagnosis by a health care professional. 5. An individual's health insurance policy number or subscriber identification number and any unique identifier used by a health insurer to identify the individual. 6. A username or email address, in combination with a password or security question and answer that would permit access to an online account affiliated with the covered entity that is reasonably likely to contain or is used to obtain sensitive personally identifying information.
Security Breach Definition	The term "breach of security" or "breach" means the unauthorized acquisition of data in electronic form containing sensitive personally identifying information. Acquisition occurring over a period of time committed by the same entity constitutes one breach.
Good Faith Exception	A "breach of security" or "breach" does not include any of the good faith acquisition of sensitive personally identifying information by an employee or agent of a covered entity, unless the information is used for a purpose unrelated to the business or subject to further unauthorized use.
Risk of Harm Analysis	A covered entity that determines that sensitive personally identifying information has been acquired or is reasonably believed to have been acquired by an unauthorized person, and is reasonably likely to cause substantial harm to the individuals to whom the information relates, must give notice of the breach to each impacted individual.
Notification Timeline	A breach notice shall be made as expeditiously as possible and without unreasonable delay, taking into account the time necessary to allow the covered entity to conduct an investigation. The breach notification must be provided within 45 days of identifying that a breach has occurred and is reasonably likely to cause substantial harm to the individuals to whom the information relates.
Security and Investigation Exceptions	If a federal or state law enforcement agency determines that a breach notice to individuals would interfere with a criminal investigation or national security, the notice shall be delayed upon the receipt of written request of the law enforcement agency for a period that the law enforcement agency determines is necessary. A law enforcement agency, by a subsequent written request, may revoke the delay as of a specified date or extend the period set forth in the original request made under this section if further delay is necessary.

	Alabama (Data Breach Requirements)
Notification Content Requirements	The breach notice shall include, at a minimum, all of the following: (1) The date, estimated date, or estimated date range of the breach. (2) A description of the sensitive personally identifying information that was acquired by an unauthorized person as part of the breach. (3) A general description of the actions taken by a covered entity to restore the security and confidentiality of the personal information involved in the breach. (4) A general description of steps an affected individual can take to protect himself or herself from identity theft. (5) Information that the individual can use to contact the covered entity to inquire about the breach.
Delivery Methods	A breach notice shall be given in writing and sent to the mailing address of the individual in the records of the covered entity or sent to the email address of the individual in the records of the covered entity. - - - A covered entity required to provide a breach notice to any individual may provide substitute notice in lieu of direct notice, if direct notice is not feasible due to any of the following: a. Excessive cost: (1) Excessive cost to the covered entity relative to the resources of the covered entity. (2) The cost to the covered entity exceeds $500,000. b. Lack of sufficient contact information for the individual required to be notified. c. The affected individuals exceed 100,000 persons.
Substitute Notice	Substitute notice shall include both of the following: 1. A conspicuous notice on the internet website of the covered entity, if the covered entity maintains a website, for a period of 30 days. 2. Notice in print and in broadcast media, including major media in urban and rural areas where the affected individuals reside. b. An alternative form of substitute notice may be used with the approval of the attorney general.
Notice to Government Agencies	If the number of individuals a covered entity is required to notify of a breach exceeds 1,000, the entity shall provide written notice of the breach to the attorney general as expeditiously as possible and without unreasonable delay, and within 45 days of identifying a breach has occurred and is reasonably likely to cause substantial harm to the individuals to whom the information relates. Written notice to the attorney general shall include all of the following: (1) A synopsis of the events surrounding the breach at the time that notice is provided. (2) The approximate number of individuals in the state who were affected by the breach. (3) Any services related to the breach being offered or scheduled to be offered, without charge, by the covered entity to individuals and instructions on how to use the services. (4) The name, address, telephone number, and email address of the employee or agent of the covered entity from whom additional information may be obtained about the breach. - - - A covered entity may provide the attorney general with supplemental or updated information regarding a breach at any time.

	Alabama (Data Breach Requirements)
Consumer Reporting Agencies	If a covered entity discovers circumstances requiring notice of the breach to more than 1,000 individuals at a single time, the entity shall also notify, without unreasonable delay, all consumer reporting agencies and provide the timing, distribution, and content of the breach notices.
Preemption and Compliance	An entity subject to or regulated by federal laws, rules, regulations, procedures, or guidance on data breach notification established or enforced by the federal government is exempt from this law, as long as the entity does all of the following: (1) Maintains procedures pursuant to those laws, rules, regulations, procedures, or guidance. (2) Provides notice to affected individuals pursuant to those laws, rules, regulations, procedures, or guidance. (3) Provides a copy of the notice to the attorney general in a timely manner when the number of individuals the entity notified exceeds 1,000.
Data Processor Obligations	In the event a third-party agent has experienced a breach of security in the system maintained by the agent, the agent shall notify the covered entity of the breach of security as expeditiously as possible and without unreasonable delay, but no later than 10 days following the determination of the breach of security or reason to believe the breach occurred. - - - A third-party agent, in cooperation with a covered entity, shall provide information in the possession of the third-party agent so that the covered entity can comply with its notice requirements. - - - A covered entity may enter into a contractual agreement with a third-party agent whereby the third-party agent agrees to handle notifications required under this law.

	Alabama (Data Breach Requirements)
Other Information	If a covered entity determines that a breach of security has or may have occurred in relation to sensitive personally identifying information that is accessed, acquired, maintained, stored, utilized, or communicated by, or on behalf of, the covered entity, the covered entity shall conduct a good faith and prompt investigation that includes all of the following: (1) An assessment of the nature and scope of the breach. (2) Identification of any sensitive personally identifying information that may have been involved in the breach and the identity of any individuals to whom that information relates. (3) A determination of whether the sensitive personally identifying information has been acquired or is reasonably believed to have been acquired by an unauthorized person and is reasonably likely to cause substantial harm to the individuals to whom the information relates. (4) Identification and implementation of measures to restore the security and confidentiality of the systems compromised in the breach. - - - In determining whether sensitive personally identifying information has been acquired or is reasonably believed to have been acquired by an unauthorized person without valid authorization, the following factors may be considered: (1) Indications that the information is in the physical possession and control of a person without valid authorization, such as a lost or stolen computer or other device containing information. (2) Indications that the information has been downloaded or copied. (3) Indications that the information was used by an unauthorized person, such as fraudulent accounts opened or instances of identity theft reported. (4) Whether the information has been made public. - - - If a covered entity determines that notice is not required under this section, the entity shall document the determination in writing and maintain records concerning the determination for no less than five years.

ALABAMA

<u>Data Disposal and Security</u>: Ala. Code 1975 § 8-38-2, -3, -10.

The numbering and internal citations herein are derived from the applicable state statute. See statute for any applicable exceptions or exemptions.

	Alabama (Data Disposal and Security)
Key Terms	The term "sensitive personally identifying information" means a. Except as provided in paragraph b, an Alabama resident's first name or first initial and last name in combination with one or more of the following with respect to the same Alabama resident: 1. A non-truncated Social Security number or taxpayer identification number. 2. A non-truncated driver's license number, state-issued identification card number, passport number, military identification number, or other unique identification number issued on a government document used to verify the identity of a specific individual. 3. A financial account number, including a bank account number, credit card number, or debit card number, in combination with any security code, access code, password, expiration date, or PIN, that is necessary to access the financial account or to conduct a transaction that will credit or debit the financial account. 4. Any information regarding an individual's medical history, mental or physical condition, or medical treatment or diagnosis by a health care professional. 5. An individual's health insurance policy number or subscriber identification number and any unique identifier used by a health insurer to identify the individual. 6. A username or email address, in combination with a password or security question and answer that would permit access to an online account affiliated with the covered entity that is reasonably likely to contain or is used to obtain sensitive personally identifying information. b. The term does not include either of the following: 1. Information about an individual which has been lawfully made public by a federal, state, or local government record or a widely distributed media. 2. Information that is truncated, encrypted, secured, or modified by any other method or technology that removes elements that personally identify an individual or that otherwise renders the information unusable, including encryption of the data, document, or device containing the sensitive personally identifying information, unless the covered entity knows or has reason to know that the encryption key or security credential that could render the personally identifying information readable or useable has been breached together with the information.

	Alabama (Data Disposal and Security)
Security Requirements	Each covered entity and third-party agent shall implement and maintain reasonable security measures to protect sensitive personally identifying information against a breach of security. - - - (b) Reasonable security measures means security measures practicable for the covered entity subject to subsection (c), to implement and maintain, including consideration of all of the following: (1) Designation of an employee or employees to coordinate the covered entity's security measures to protect against a breach of security. An owner or manager may designate himself or herself. (2) Identification of internal and external risks of a breach of security. (3) Adoption of appropriate information safeguards to address identified risks of a breach of security and assess the effectiveness of such safeguards. (4) Retention of service providers, if any, that are contractually required to maintain appropriate safeguards for sensitive personally identifying information. (5) Evaluation and adjustment of security measures to account for changes in circumstances affecting the security of sensitive personally identifying information. (6) Keeping the management of the covered entity, including its board of directors, if any, appropriately informed of the overall status of its security measures; provided, however, that the management of a government entity subject to this subdivision may be appropriately informed of the status of its security measures through a properly convened executive session under the Open Meetings Act pursuant to Section 36-25A-7. - - - An assessment of a covered entity's security shall be based upon the entity's reasonable security measures as a whole and shall place an emphasis on data security failures that are multiple or systemic, including consideration of all the following: (1) The size of the covered entity. (2) The amount of sensitive personally identifying information and the type of activities for which the sensitive personally identifying information is accessed, acquired, maintained, stored, utilized, or communicated by, or on behalf of, the covered entity. (3) The covered entity's cost to implement and maintain the reasonable security measures to protect against a breach of security relative to its resources.
Data Disposal	A covered entity or third-party agent shall take reasonable measures to dispose, or arrange for the disposal, of records containing sensitive personally identifying information within its custody or control when the records are no longer to be retained pursuant to applicable law, regulations, or business needs. Disposal shall include shredding, erasing, or otherwise modifying the personal information in the records to make it unreadable or undecipherable through any reasonable means consistent with industry standards.

ALASKA

Data Breach Requirements: Alaska Stat. Ann. § 45.48.010 et seq.

The numbering and internal citations herein are derived from the applicable state statute.

	Alaska (Data Breach Requirements)
Personal Information	(7) The term "personal information" means information in any form on an individual that is not encrypted or redacted, or is encrypted and the encryption key has been accessed or acquired, and that consists of a combination of (A) An individual's name; and (B) one or more of the following information elements: (i) The individual's Social Security number; (ii) The individual's driver's license number or state identification card number; (iii) Except as provided in (iv) of this subparagraph, the individual's account number, credit card number, or debit card number; (iv) If an account can only be accessed with a personal code, the number in (iii) of this subparagraph and the personal code; in this sub-subparagraph, "personal code" means a security code, an access code, a personal identification number, or a password; (v) Passwords, personal identification numbers, or other access codes for financial accounts.
Security Breach Definition	The term "breach of the security" means unauthorized acquisition, or reasonable belief of unauthorized acquisition, of personal information that compromises the security, confidentiality, or integrity of the personal information maintained by the information collector. - - - The term "acquisition" includes acquisition by (A) photocopying, facsimile, or other paper-based method; (B) a device, including a computer, that can read, write, or store information that is represented in numerical form; or (C) a method not identified by (A) or (B) of this paragraph.
Good Faith Exception	The good faith acquisition of personal information by an employee or agent of an information collector for a legitimate purpose of the information collector is not a breach of the security of the information system if the employee or agent does not use the personal information for a purpose unrelated to a legitimate purpose of the information collector and does not make further unauthorized disclosure of the personal information.
Risk of Harm Analysis	A data breach notification is not required if, after an appropriate investigation and after written notification to the state attorney general, the covered person determines that there is not a reasonable likelihood that harm to the consumers whose personal information has been acquired has resulted or will result from the breach. The determination shall be documented in writing, and the documentation shall be maintained for five years. The notification required by this subsection may not be considered a public record open to inspection by the public.
Notification Timeline	An information collector shall make the breach notification disclosure in the most expeditious time possible and without unreasonable delay and as necessary to determine the scope of the breach and restore the reasonable integrity of the information system.

	Alaska (Data Breach Requirements)
Security and Investigation Exceptions	An information collector may delay disclosing the breach if an appropriate law enforcement agency determines that disclosing the breach will interfere with a criminal investigation. However, the information collector shall disclose the breach to the state resident in the most expeditious time possible and without unreasonable delay after the law enforcement agency informs the information collector in writing that disclosure of the breach will no longer interfere with the investigation.
Notification Content Requirements	N/A
Delivery Methods	An information collector shall make the breach notification disclosure (1) by a written document sent to the most recent address the information collector has for the state resident; (2) by electronic means if the information collector's primary method of communication with the state resident is by electronic means or if making the disclosure by the electronic means is consistent with the provisions regarding electronic records and signatures required for notices legally required to be in writing under 15 U.S.C. § 7001 (The Electronic Signatures in Global and National Commerce Act); or (3) if the information collector demonstrates that the cost of providing notice would exceed $150,000, that the affected class of state residents to be notified exceeds 300,000, or that the information collector does not have sufficient contact information to provide notice, by (A) electronic mail if the information collector has an electronic mail address for the state resident; (B) conspicuously posting the disclosure on the internet website of the information collector if the information collector maintains an internet website; and (C) providing a notice to major statewide media.
Substitute Notice	See Delivery Methods.
Notice to Government Agencies	See Risk of Harm Analysis.
Consumer Reporting Agencies	(a) If an information collector is required notify more than 1,000 state residents of a breach, the information collector shall also notify without unreasonable delay all consumer credit reporting agencies and provide the agencies with the timing, distribution, and content of the notices to state residents. (b) This section may not be construed to require the information collector to provide the consumer reporting agencies identified under (a) of this section with the names or other personal information of the state residents whose personal information was subject to the breach. (c) This section does not apply to an information collector who is subject to the Gramm-Leach-Bliley Act.
Preemption and Compliance	N/A
Data Processor Obligations	Immediately after the information recipient discovers the breach, the information recipient shall give notification of the breach to the information distributor who owns the personal information or who licensed the use of the personal information to the information recipient. The information recipient shall cooperate with the information distributor as necessary to allow the information distributor to comply with its legal obligations. In this subsection "cooperate" means sharing with the information distributor information relevant to the breach, except for confidential business information or trade secrets.

ALASKA

Data Disposal and Security: Alaska Stat. Ann. § 45.48.500 et seq.

The numbering and internal citations herein are derived from the applicable state statute. See statute for any applicable exceptions or exemptions.

	Alaska (Data Disposal and Security)
Key Terms	The term "dispose" means: (A) the discarding or abandonment of records containing personal information; (B) the sale, donation, discarding, or transfer of (i) any medium, including computer equipment or computer media, that contains records of personal information; (ii) non-paper media, other than that identified under (i) of this subparagraph, on which records of personal information are stored; and (iii) equipment for non-paper storage of information. - - - The term "personal information" means: (A) an individual's passport number, driver's license number, state identification number, bank account number, credit card number, debit card number, other payment card number, financial account information, or information from a financial application; or (B) a combination of an individual's (i) name; and (ii) medical information, insurance policy number, employment information, or employment history.
Written Policies	A business or governmental agency shall adopt written policies and procedures that relate to the adequate destruction and proper disposal of records containing personal information. - - - <u>See</u> Data Disposal (implementing and monitoring compliance with policies and procedures).
Data Disposal	When disposing of records that contain personal information, a business and a governmental agency shall take all reasonable measures necessary to protect against unauthorized access to or use of the records. - - - The measures that may be taken to comply with the data disposal requirements include: (1) implementing and monitoring compliance with policies and procedures that require the burning, pulverizing, or shredding of paper documents containing personal information so that the personal information cannot practicably be read or reconstructed; (2) implementing and monitoring compliance with policies and procedures that require the destruction or erasure of electronic media and other non-paper media containing personal information so that the personal information cannot practicably be read or reconstructed; (3) after due diligence, entering into a written contract with a third party engaged in the business of record destruction to dispose of records containing personal information in a manner consistent with AS 45.48.500-45.48.590. The term "due diligence" ordinarily includes performing one or more of the following: (i) reviewing an independent audit of the third party's operations and its compliance with AS 45.48.500-45.48.590; (ii) obtaining information about the third party from several references or other reliable sources and requiring that the third party be certified by a recognized trade association or similar organization with a reputation for high standards of quality review; or (iii) reviewing and evaluating the third party's information security policies and procedures, or taking other appropriate measures to determine the competency and integrity of the third party.

	Alaska (Data Disposal and Security)
Other Information	If a business or governmental agency has otherwise complied with the provisions of AS 45.48.500-45.48.590 in the selection of a third party engaged in the business of record destruction, the business or governmental agency is not liable for the disposal of records under AS 45.48.500-45.48.590 after the business or governmental agency has relinquished control of the records to the third party for the destruction of the records. - - - A business or governmental agency is not liable for the disposal of records under AS 45.48.500-45.48.590 after the business or governmental agency has relinquished control of the records to the individual to whom the records pertain.

ARIZONA

Data Breach Requirements: Ariz. R.S. § 18-551 et seq.

The numbering and internal citations herein are derived from the applicable state statute.

	Arizona (Data Breach Requirements)
Personal Information	(7) The term "personal information" (a) means any of the following: (i) An individual's first name or first initial and last name in combination with one or more specified data elements. (ii) An individual's username or email address, in combination with a password or security question and answer, that allows access to an online account. - - - 11. The term "specified data element" means any of the following: (a) An individual's Social Security number. (b) The number on an individual's driver's license issued pursuant to § 28-3166 or nonoperating identification license issued pursuant to § 28-3165. (c) A private key that is unique to an individual and that is used to authenticate or sign an electronic record. (d) An individual's financial account number or credit or debit card number in combination with any required security code, access code, or password that would allow access to the individual's financial account. (e) An individual's health insurance identification number. (f) Information about an individual's medical or mental health treatment or diagnosis by a health care professional. (g) An individual's passport number. (h) An individual's taxpayer identification number or an identity protection personal identification number issued by the United States Internal Revenue Service. (i) Unique biometric data generated from a measurement or analysis of human body characteristics to authenticate an individual when the individual accesses an online account.
Security Breach Definition	The term "breach" or "security system breach": (a) means an unauthorized acquisition of and unauthorized access that materially compromises the security or confidentiality of unencrypted and unredacted computerized personal information maintained as part of a database of personal information regarding multiple individuals. - - - A "security incident" means an event that creates reasonable suspicion that a person's information systems or computerized data may have been compromised or that measures put in place to protect the person's information systems or computerized data may have failed.
Good Faith Exception	A "breach" or "security system breach" does not include a good faith acquisition of personal information by a person's employee or agent for the purposes of the person if the personal information is not used for a purpose unrelated to the person and is not subject to further unauthorized disclosure.
Risk of Harm Analysis	A person is not required to make a breach notification if the person, an independent third-party forensic auditor, or a law enforcement agency determines after a reasonable investigation that a security system breach has not resulted in or is not reasonably likely to result in substantial economic loss to affected individuals.

	Arizona (Data Breach Requirements)
Notification Timeline	If a person that conducts business in this state and who owns, maintains, or licenses unencrypted and unredacted computerized personal information becomes aware of a security incident, the person shall conduct an investigation to promptly determine whether there has been a security system breach. If the investigation results in a determination that there has been a security system breach, the person that owns or licenses the computerized data shall provide the breach notification within forty-five days after the determination.
Security and Investigation Exceptions	The breach notification may be delayed if a law enforcement agency advises the person that the notifications will impede a criminal investigation. On being informed by the law enforcement agency that the notifications no longer compromise the investigation, the person shall make the required notifications, as applicable, within forty-five days
Notification Content Requirements	The breach notification shall include at least the following: 1. The approximate date of the breach. 2. A brief description of the personal information included in the breach. 3. The toll-free numbers and addresses for the three largest nationwide consumer reporting agencies. 4. The toll-free number, address, and website address for the Federal Trade Commission or any federal agency that assists consumers with identity theft matters.
Delivery Methods	The breach notification shall be provided by one of the following methods: 1. Written notice. 2. An email notice if the person has email addresses for the individuals who are subject to the notice. 3. Telephonic notice, if telephonic contact is made directly with the affected individuals and is not through a prerecorded message. 4. Substitute notice if the person demonstrates that the cost of providing notice pursuant to paragraphs 1, 2, or 3 would exceed $50,000, that the affected class of subject individuals to be notified exceeds one hundred thousand (100,000) individuals, or that the person does not have sufficient contact information.
Substitute Notice	Substitute notice consists of all of the following: (a) A written letter to the attorney general that demonstrates the facts necessary for substitute notice. (b) Conspicuous posting of the notice for at least orty-five days on the website of the person if the person maintains one.
Notice to Government Agencies	If the breach requires notification of more than 1,000 individuals, the affected person must notify the attorney general, in writing, in a form prescribed by rule or order of the attorney general or by providing the attorney general with a copy of the notification provided pursuant to paragraph 1 of this subsection.
Consumer Reporting Agencies	If the breach requires notification of more than one thousand individuals, the affected person must notify the three largest nationwide consumer reporting agencies.

	Arizona (Data Breach Requirements)
Preemption and Compliance	A person who complies with the notification requirements or security system breach procedures pursuant to the rules, regulations, procedures, guidance, or guidelines established by the person's primary or functional federal regulator is deemed to be in compliance with these breach notification requirements. - - - The breach notification requirements do not apply to either of the following: 1. A person that is subject to Title V of the Gramm-Leach-Bliley Act. 2. A covered entity or business associates as defined under regulations implementing the Health Insurance Portability and Accountability Act of 1996 (HIPAA), 45 Code of Federal Regulations section 160.103 (2013), or a charitable fund-raising foundation or nonprofit corporation whose primary purpose is to support a specified covered entity, if the charitable fund-raising foundation or nonprofit corporation complies with any applicable provision of the Health Insurance Portability and Accountability Act of 1996 (HIPAA) and its implementing regulations.
Data Processor Obligations	A person that maintains unencrypted and unredacted computerized personal information that the person does not own or license shall notify, as soon as practicable, the owner or licensee of the information on discovering any security system breach and cooperate with the owner or the licensee of the personal information, including sharing information relevant to the breach with the owner or licensee. The person that maintains the data under an agreement with the owner or licensee is not required to provide the notifications required by subsection B of this section unless the agreement stipulates otherwise.
Other Information	If a breach involves personal information as prescribed in § 18-551, paragraph 7, subdivision (a), item (ii) for an online account (i.e., an individual's username or email address, in combination with a password or security question and answer, that allows access to an online account) and does not involve personal information as defined in § 18-551, paragraph 7, subdivision (a), item (i), the person may comply with this law by providing the notification in an electronic or other form. The notification should direct the individual whose personal information has been breached to promptly change the individual's password and security question or answer, as applicable, or to take other steps that are appropriate to protect the online account of the person and all other online accounts for which the individual whose personal information has been breached uses the same username and email address and password or security question or answer. - - - If the breach of personal information as prescribed in § 18-551, paragraph 7, subdivision (a), item (ii) is for login credentials of an email account furnished by the person, the person is not required to comply with this section by providing the notification to that email address, but may comply with this section by providing notification by another method described in this subsection or by providing clear and conspicuous notification delivered to the individual online when the individual is connected to the online account from an internet protocol address or online location from which the person knows the individual customarily accesses the account. The person satisfies the notification requirement with regard to the individual's account by requiring the individual to reset the individual's password or security question and answer for that account if the person also notifies the individual to change the same password or security question and answer for all other online accounts for which the individual uses the same username or email address and password or security question or answer.

ARIZONA

Data Disposal and Security: Ariz. R.S. § 44-7601.

The numbering and internal citations herein are derived from the applicable state statute. See statute for any applicable exceptions or exemptions.

	Arizona (Data Disposal and Security)
Key Terms	See Data Disposal.
Data Disposal	A. An entity shall not knowingly discard or dispose of records or documents without redacting the information or destroying the records or documents if the records or documents contain an individual's first and last name or first initial and last name in combination with a corresponding complete: 1. Social Security number. 2. Credit card, charge card, or debit card number. 3. Retirement account number. 4. Savings, checking, or securities entitlement account number. 5. Driver's license number or nonoperating identification license number. - - - An entity that maintains and complies with the entity's own procedures for the discarding or disposing of records or documents containing the information listed in Subsection A of this section that is consistent with the requirements of this section shall be deemed to be in compliance with this section.
Other Information	The data disposal requirements only apply to paper records and paper documents.

ARKANSAS

Data Breach Requirements: Ark. Code Ann. § 4-110-101 et seq.

The numbering and internal citations herein are derived from the applicable state statute.

	Arkansas (Data Breach Requirements)
Personal Information	(7) The term "personal information" means an individual's first name or first initial and his or her last name in combination with any one or more of the following data elements when either the name or the data element is not encrypted or redacted: (A) Social Security number; (B) Driver's license number or Arkansas identification card number; (C) Account number, credit card number, or debit card number in combination with any required security code, access code, or password that would permit access to an individual's financial account; (D) Medical information; and (E)(i) Biometric data. (ii) As used in this subdivision (7)(E), "biometric data" means data generated by automatic measurements of an individual's biological characteristics, including without limitation: (a) Fingerprints; (b) Faceprint; (c) A retinal or iris scan; (d) Hand geometry; (e) Voiceprint analysis; (f) Deoxyribonucleic acid (DNA); or (g) Any other unique biological characteristics of an individual if the characteristics are used by the owner or licensee to uniquely authenticate the individual's identity when the individual accesses a system or account;
Security Breach Definition	The term "breach of the security of the system" means unauthorized acquisition of computerized data that compromises the security, confidentiality, or integrity of personal information maintained by a person or business.
Good Faith Exception	A "breach of the security of the system" does not include the good faith acquisition of personal information by an employee or agent of the person or business for the legitimate purposes of the person or business if the personal information is not otherwise used or subject to further unauthorized disclosure.
Risk of Harm Analysis	A breach notification is not required if, after a reasonable investigation, the person or business determines that there is no reasonable likelihood of harm to customers.
Notification Timeline	Any person or business that acquires, owns, or licenses computerized data that includes personal information shall disclose any breach of the security of the system following discovery or notification of the breach of the security of the system to any Arkansas resident whose unencrypted personal information was, or is reasonably believed to have been, acquired by an unauthorized person. The disclosure shall be made in the most expedient time and manner possible and without unreasonable delay, consistent with the legitimate needs of law enforcement, or any measures necessary to determine the scope of the breach and to restore the reasonable integrity of the data system
Security and Investigation Exceptions	The breach notification may be delayed if a law enforcement agency determines that the notification will impede a criminal investigation. The breach notification required shall be made after the law enforcement agency determines that it will not compromise the investigation.
Notification Content Requirements	N/A

	Arkansas (Data Breach Requirements)
Delivery Methods	A breach notice may be provided by one of the following methods: (1) Written notice; (2) Electronic mail notice if the notice provided is consistent with the provisions regarding electronic records and signatures set forth in 15 U.S.C. § 7001 (The Electronic Signatures in Global and National Commerce Act), as it existed on January 1, 2005; or (3)(A) Substitute notice if the person or business demonstrates that: (i) The cost of providing notice would exceed $250,000; (ii) The affected class of persons to be notified exceeds 500,000; or (iii) The person or business does not have sufficient contact information.
Substitute Notice	Substitute notice shall consist of all of the following: (i) Electronic mail notice when the person or business has an electronic mail address for the subject persons; (ii) Conspicuous posting of the notice on the website of the person or business if the person or business maintains a website; and (iii) Notification by statewide media.
Notice to Government Agencies	If a breach affects the personal information of more than one thousand individuals, the person or business required to make a breach notification shall, at the same time the security breach is disclosed to an affected individual or within 45 days after the person or business determines that there is a reasonable likelihood of harm to customers, whichever occurs first, disclose the security breach to the attorney general.
Consumer Reporting Agencies	N/A
Preemption and Compliance	The law does not apply to a person or business that is regulated by a state or federal law that provides greater protection to personal information and at least as thorough disclosure requirements for breaches of the security of personal information than that provided by this law. Compliance with the state or federal law shall be deemed compliance with this chapter with regard to the subjects covered by this law.
Data Processor Obligations	A person or business that maintains computerized data that includes personal information that the person or business does not own shall notify the owner or licensee that there has been a breach of the security of the system immediately following discovery if the personal information was, or is reasonably believed to have been, acquired by an unauthorized person.
Other Information	A person or business shall retain a copy of the written determination of a breach of the security of a system and supporting documentation for five (5) years from the date of determination of the breach of the security of the system. If the attorney general submits a written request for the written determination of the breach of the security of the system, the person or business shall send a copy of the written determination of the breach of the security of the system and supporting documentation to the Attorney General no later than thirty (30) days after the date of receipt of the request.

ARKANSAS

Data Disposal and Security: Ark. Code Ann. §§ 4-110-103, 4-110-104, 4-110-106.

The numbering and internal citations herein are derived from the applicable state statute. See statute for any applicable exceptions or exemptions.

	Arkansas (Data Disposal and Security)
Key Terms	The term "personal information" means an individual's first name or first initial and his or her last name in combination with any one or more of the following data elements when either the name or the data element is not encrypted or redacted: (A) Social Security number; (B) Driver's license number or Arkansas identification card number; (C) Account number, credit card number, or debit card number in combination with any required security code, access code, or password that would permit access to an individual's financial account; (D) Medical information; and (E)(i) Biometric data. - - - The term "biometric data" means data generated by automatic measurements of an individual's biological characteristics, including without limitation: (a) Fingerprints; (b) Faceprint; (c) A retinal or iris scan; (d) Hand geometry; (e) Voiceprint analysis; (f) Deoxyribonucleic acid (DNA); or (g) Any other unique biological characteristics of an individual if the characteristics are used by the owner or licensee to uniquely authenticate the individual's identity when the individual accesses a system or account.
Security Requirements	A person or business that acquires, owns, or licenses personal information about an Arkansas resident shall implement and maintain reasonable security procedures and practices appropriate to the nature of the information to protect the personal information from unauthorized access, destruction, use, modification, or disclosure.
Data Disposal	A person or business shall take all reasonable steps to destroy or arrange for the destruction of a customer's records within its custody or control containing personal information that is no longer to be retained by the person or business by shredding, erasing, or otherwise modifying the personal information in the records to make it unreadable or undecipherable through any means.

CALIFORNIA

Data Breach Requirements: Cal. Civ. Code § 1798.82.

The numbering and internal citations herein are derived from the applicable state statute.

	California (Data Breach Requirements)
Personal Information	(h) The term "personal information" means either of the following: (1) An individual's first name or first initial and last name in combination with any one or more of the following data elements, when either the name or the data elements are not encrypted: (A) Social Security number. (B) Driver's license number, California identification card number, taxpayer identification number, passport number, military identification number, or other unique identification number issued on a government document commonly used to verify the identity of a specific individual. (C) Account number or credit or debit card number, in combination with any required security code, access code, or password that would permit access to an individual's financial account. (D) Medical information. (E) Health insurance information. (F) Unique biometric data generated from measurements or technical analysis of human body characteristics, such as a fingerprint, retina, or iris image, used to authenticate a specific individual. Unique biometric data does not include a physical or digital photograph, unless used or stored for facial recognition purposes. (G) Information or data collected through the use or operation of an automated license plate recognition system, as defined in Section 1798.90.5. (H) Genetic data. (2) A username or email address, in combination with a password or security question and answer that would permit access to an online account. - - - The term "genetic data" means any data, regardless of its format, that results from the analysis of a biological sample of an individual, or from another source enabling equivalent information to be obtained, and concerns genetic material. Genetic material includes, but is not limited to, deoxyribonucleic acids (DNA), ribonucleic acids (RNA), genes, chromosomes, alleles, genomes, alterations or modifications to DNA or RNA, single nucleotide polymorphisms (SNPs), uninterpreted data that results from analysis of the biological sample or other source, and any information extrapolated, derived, or inferred therefrom.
Security Breach Definition	The term "breach of the security of the system" means unauthorized acquisition of computerized data that compromises the security, confidentiality, or integrity of personal information maintained by the person or business.
Good Faith Exception	Good faith acquisition of personal information by an employee or agent of the person or business for the purposes of the person or business is not a breach of the security of the system, provided that the personal information is not used or subject to further unauthorized disclosure.
Risk of Harm Analysis	N/A
Notification Timeline	The data breach notification shall be made in the most expedient time possible and without unreasonable delay, consistent with the legitimate needs of law enforcement, or any measures necessary to determine the scope of the breach and restore the reasonable integrity of the data system.

	California (Data Breach Requirements)
Security and Investigation Exceptions	The breach notification may be delayed if a law enforcement agency determines that the notification will impede a criminal investigation. The notification shall be made promptly after the law enforcement agency determines that it will not compromise the investigation.
Notification Content Requirements	(d) A person or business that is required to issue a security breach notification shall meet all of the following requirements: (1) The security breach notification shall be written in plain language, shall be titled "Notice of Data Breach," and shall present the information described in paragraph (2) under the following headings: "What Happened," "What Information Was Involved," "What We Are Doing," "What You Can Do," and "For More Information." Additional information may be provided as a supplement to the notice. (A) The format of the notice shall be designed to call attention to the nature and significance of the information it contains. (B) The title and headings in the notice shall be clearly and conspicuously displayed. (C) The text of the notice and any other notice provided shall be no smaller than 10-point type. (D) For a written notice described in paragraph (1) of subdivision (j), use of the model security breach notification form prescribed below or use of the headings described in this paragraph with the information described in paragraph (2), written in plain language, shall be deemed to be in compliance with this subdivision. [NAME OF INSTITUTION / LOGO] Date: [insert date] NOTICE OF DATA BREACH What Happened? What Information Was Involved? What We Are Doing. What You Can Do. Other Important Information. [insert other important information] Call [telephone number] or go to [internet website] For More Information. (E) For an electronic notice described in paragraph (2) of subdivision (j), use of the headings described in this paragraph with the information described in paragraph (2), written in plain language, shall be deemed to be in compliance with this subdivision. (2) The security breach notification described in paragraph (1) shall include, at a minimum, the following information: (A) The name and contact information of the reporting person or business subject to this section. (B) A list of the types of personal information that were or are reasonably believed to have been the subject of a breach. (C) If the information is possible to determine at the time the notice is provided, then any of the following: (i) the date of the breach, (ii) the estimated date of the breach, or (iii) the date range within which the breach occurred. The notification shall also include the date of the notice. (D) Whether notification was delayed as a result of a law enforcement investigation, if that information is possible to determine at the time the notice is provided.

	California (Data Breach Requirements)
	(E) A general description of the breach incident, if that information is possible to determine at the time the notice is provided. (F) The toll-free telephone numbers and addresses of the major credit reporting agencies if the breach exposed a Social Security number or a driver's license or California identification card number. (G) If the person or business providing the notification was the source of the breach, an offer to provide appropriate identity theft prevention and mitigation services, if any, shall be provided at no cost to the affected person for not less than 12 months, along with all information necessary to take advantage of the offer to any person whose information was or may have been breached if the breach exposed or may have exposed personal information defined in subparagraphs (A) and (B) of paragraph (1) of subdivision (h). (3) At the discretion of the person or business, the security breach notification may also include any of the following: (A) Information about what the person or business has done to protect individuals whose information has been breached. (B) Advice on steps that people whose information has been breached may take to protect themselves. (C) In breaches involving biometric data, instructions on how to notify other entities that used the same type of biometric data as an authenticator to no longer rely on data for authentication purposes.
Delivery Methods	(j) For purposes of this section, "notice" may be provided by one of the following methods: (1) Written notice. (2) Electronic notice, if the notice provided is consistent with the provisions regarding electronic records and signatures set forth in 15 U.S.C. § 7001 (The Electronic Signatures in Global and National Commerce Act). (3) Substitute notice, if the person or business demonstrates that the cost of providing notice would exceed $250,000, or that the affected class of subject persons to be notified exceeds 500,000, or the person or business does not have sufficient contact information.
Substitute Notice	Substitute notice shall consist of all of the following: (A) Email notice when the person or business has an email address for the subject persons. (B) Conspicuous posting, for a minimum of 30 days, of the notice on the internet website page of the person or business, if the person or business maintains one. For purposes of this subparagraph, conspicuous posting on the person's or business' internet website means providing a link to the notice on the home page or first significant page after entering the internet website that is in larger type than the surrounding text, or in contrasting type, font, or color to the surrounding text of the same size, or set off from the surrounding text of the same size by symbols or other marks that call attention to the link. (C) Notification to major statewide media.
Notice to Government Agencies	A person or business that is required to issue a breach notification to more than 500 California residents as a result of a single breach of the security system shall electronically submit a single sample copy of that security breach notification, excluding any personally identifiable information, to the Attorney General. A single sample copy of a security breach notification shall not be deemed to be within subdivision (f) of Section 6254 of the Government Code.

	California (Data Breach Requirements)
Consumer Reporting Agencies	N/A
Preemption and Compliance	A covered entity under the Health Insurance Portability and Accountability Act of 1996 (HIPAA), will be deemed to have complied with the breach notice requirements if it has complied completely with Section 13402(f) of the federal Health Information Technology for Economic and Clinical Health Act (Public Law 111-5). However, nothing in this subdivision shall be construed to exempt a covered entity from any other provision of this section.
Data Processor Obligations	A person or business that maintains computerized data that includes personal information that the person or business does not own shall notify the owner or licensee of the information of the breach of the security of the data immediately following discovery, if the personal information was, or is reasonably believed to have been, acquired by an unauthorized person.
Other Information	In the case of a breach of the security of the system involving personal information defined in paragraph (2) of subdivision (h) for an online account, and no other personal information defined in paragraph (1) of subdivision (h), the person or business may comply with this section by providing the security breach notification in electronic or other form. The notification should direct the person whose personal information has been breached promptly to change the person's password and security question or answer, as applicable, or to take other steps appropriate to protect the online account with the person or business and all other online accounts for which the person whose personal information has been breached uses the same username or email address and password or security question or answer. - - - In the case of a breach of the security of the system involving personal information defined in paragraph (2) of subdivision (h) for login credentials of an email account furnished by the person or business, the person or business shall not comply with this section by providing the security breach notification to that email address, but may, instead, comply with this section by providing notice by another method described in this subdivision or by clear and conspicuous notice delivered to the resident online when the resident is connected to the online account from an internet protocol address or online location from which the person or business knows the resident customarily accesses the account.

CALIFORNIA

Data Disposal and Security: Cal. Civ. Code § 1798.80 et seq.

The numbering and internal citations herein are derived from the applicable state statute. See statute for any applicable exceptions or exemptions.

	California (Data Disposal and Security)
Key Terms	The terms "own" and "license" include personal information that a business retains as part of the business' internal customer account or for the purpose of using that information in transactions with the person to whom the information relates. - - - The term "maintain" includes personal information that a business maintains but does not own or license. - - - (1) The term "personal information" means either of the following: (A) An individual's first name or first initial and the individual's last name in combination with any one or more of the following data elements, when either the name or the data elements are not encrypted or redacted: (i) Social Security number. (ii) Driver's license number, California identification card number, taxpayer identification number, passport number, military identification number, or other unique identification number issued on a government document commonly used to verify the identity of a specific individual. (iii) Account number or credit or debit card number, in combination with any required security code, access code, or password that would permit access to an individual's financial account. (iv) Medical information. (v) Health insurance information. (vi) Unique biometric data generated from measurements or technical analysis of human body characteristics, such as a fingerprint, retina, or iris image, used to authenticate a specific individual. Unique biometric data does not include a physical or digital photograph, unless used or stored for facial recognition purposes. (vii) Genetic data. (B) A username or email address in combination with a password or security question and answer that would permit access to an online account. - - - (2) "Medical information" means any individually identifiable information, in electronic or physical form, regarding the individual's medical history or medical treatment or diagnosis by a health care professional. - - - (3) "Health insurance information" means an individual's insurance policy number or subscriber identification number, any unique identifier used by a health insurer to identify the individual, or any information in an individual's application and claims history, including any appeals records. - - - (5) "Genetic data" means any data, regardless of its format, that results from the analysis of a biological sample of an individual, or from another source enabling equivalent information to be obtained, and concerns genetic material. Genetic material includes, but is not limited to, deoxyribonucleic acids (DNA), ribonucleic acids (RNA), genes, chromosomes, alleles, genomes, alterations or modifications to DNA or RNA, single nucleotide polymorphisms (SNPs), uninterpreted data that results from analysis of the biological sample or other source, and any information extrapolated, derived, or inferred therefrom.

	California (Data Disposal and Security)
Security Requirements	A business that owns, licenses, or maintains personal information about a California resident shall implement and maintain reasonable security procedures and practices appropriate to the nature of the information, to protect the personal information from unauthorized access, destruction, use, modification, or disclosure. - - - A business that discloses personal information about a California resident pursuant to a contract with a nonaffiliated third party that is not subject to these security requirements shall require by contract that the third party implement and maintain reasonable security procedures and practices appropriate to the nature of the information, to protect the personal information from unauthorized access, destruction, use, modification, or disclosure.
Data Disposal	A business shall take all reasonable steps to dispose, or arrange for the disposal, of customer records within its custody or control containing personal information when the records are no longer to be retained by the business by (a) shredding, (b) erasing, or (c) otherwise modifying the personal information in those records to make it unreadable or undecipherable through any means.
Other Information	<u>See</u> the California Consumer Privacy Act, as amended.

COLORADO

Data Breach Requirements: Colo. Rev. Stat. § 6-1-716.

The numbering and internal citations herein are derived from the applicable state statute.

	Colorado (Data Breach Requirements)
Personal Information	(g)(I)(A) The term "personal information" means a Colorado resident's first name or first initial and last name in combination with any one or more of the following data elements that relate to the resident, when the data elements are not encrypted, redacted, or secured by any other method rendering the name or the element unreadable or unusable: Social Security number; student, military, or passport identification number; driver's license number or identification card number; medical information; health insurance identification number; or biometric data; (B) A Colorado resident's username or email address, in combination with a password or security questions and answers, that would permit access to an online account; or (C) A Colorado resident's account number or credit or debit card number in combination with any required security code, access code, or password that would permit access to that account.
Security Breach Definition	The term "security breach" means the unauthorized acquisition of unencrypted computerized data that compromises the security, confidentiality, or integrity of personal information maintained by a covered entity.
Good Faith Exception	Good faith acquisition of personal information by an employee or agent of a covered entity for the covered entity's business purposes is not a security breach if the personal information is not used for a purpose unrelated to the lawful operation of the business or is not subject to further unauthorized disclosure.
Risk of Harm Analysis	A covered entity that maintains, owns, or licenses computerized data that includes personal information about a resident of Colorado shall, when it becomes aware that a security breach may have occurred, conduct in good faith a prompt investigation to determine the likelihood that personal information has been or will be misused. The covered entity shall give notice to the affected Colorado residents unless the investigation determines that the misuse of information about a Colorado resident has not occurred and is not reasonably likely to occur.
Notification Timeline	Notice of the security breach must be made in the most expedient time possible and without unreasonable delay, but not later than thirty days after the date of determination that a security breach occurred, consistent with the legitimate needs of law enforcement and consistent with any measures necessary to determine the scope of the breach and to restore the reasonable integrity of the computerized data system.
Security and Investigation Exceptions	Notice of a data breach may be delayed if a law enforcement agency determines that the notice will impede a criminal investigation and the law enforcement agency has notified the covered entity that conducts business in Colorado not to send the breach notice. The breach notice must be made in good faith, in the most expedient time possible, and without unreasonable delay, but not later than thirty days after the law enforcement agency determines that notification will no longer impede the investigation and has notified the covered entity that conducts business in Colorado that it is appropriate to send the breach notice.

	Colorado (Data Breach Requirements)
Notification Content Requirements	In the case of a breach of personal information, notice to affected Colorado residents must include, but need not be limited to, the following information: (I) The date, estimated date, or estimated date range of the security breach; (II) A description of the personal information that was acquired or reasonably believed to have been acquired as part of the security breach; (III) Information that the resident can use to contact the covered entity to inquire about the security breach; (IV) The toll-free numbers, addresses, and websites for consumer reporting agencies; (V) The toll-free number, address, and website for the Federal Trade Commission; and (VI) A statement that the resident can obtain information from the Federal Trade Commission and the credit reporting agencies about fraud alerts and security freezes.
Delivery Methods	A breach notice may be provided by one of the following methods: (I) Written notice to the postal address listed in the records of the covered entity; (II) Telephonic notice; (III) Electronic notice, if a primary means of communication by the covered entity with a Colorado resident is by electronic means or the notice provided is consistent with the provisions regarding electronic records and signatures set forth in 15 U.S.C. § 7001 (The Electronic Signatures in Global and National Commerce Act); or (IV) Substitute notice, if the covered entity required to provide notice demonstrates that the cost of providing notice will exceed $250,000, the affected class of persons to be notified exceeds 250,000 Colorado residents, or the covered entity does not have sufficient contact information to provide notice.
Substitute Notice	Substitute notice consists of all of the following: (A) Email notice if the covered entity has email addresses for the members of the affected class of Colorado residents; (B) Conspicuous posting of the notice on the website page of the covered entity if the covered entity maintains one; and (C) Notification to major statewide media.
Notice to Government Agencies	The covered entity that must notify Colorado residents of a data breach shall provide notice of any security breach to the Colorado attorney general in the most expedient time possible and without unreasonable delay, but not later than 30 days after the date of determination that a security breach occurred, if the security breach is reasonably believed to have affected 500 Colorado residents or more, unless the investigation determines that the misuse of information about a Colorado resident has not occurred and is not likely to occur. The Colorado attorney general shall designate a person or persons as a point of contact for these functions and shall make the contact information for the person or persons public on the attorney general's website and by any other appropriate means.
Consumer Reporting Agencies	If a covered entity is required to notify more than 1,000 Colorado residents of a security breach, the covered entity shall also notify, in the most expedient time possible and without unreasonable delay, all consumer reporting agencies of the anticipated date of the notification to the residents and the approximate number of residents who are to be notified. Nothing in this subsection (2)(d) requires the covered entity to provide to the consumer reporting agency the names or other personal information of security breach notice recipients. This subsection (2)(d) does not apply to a covered entity who is subject to Title V of the Gramm-Leach-Bliley Act.

	Colorado (Data Breach Requirements)
Preemption and Compliance	A covered entity that is regulated by state or federal law and that maintains procedures for a security breach pursuant to the laws, rules, regulations, guidances, or guidelines established by its state or federal regulator is in compliance with this section; notice to the attorney general is still required pursuant to subsection (2)(f) of this section. In the case of a conflict between the time period for notice to individuals that is required pursuant to law and the applicable state or federal law or regulation, the law or regulation with the shortest time frame for notice to the individual controls. - - - The law's content requirements shall not be interpreted to prohibit data breach notifications from containing additional information, including any information that may be required by state or federal law.
Data Processor Obligations	If a covered entity uses a third-party service provider to maintain computerized data that includes personal information, then the third-party service provider shall give notice to and cooperate with the covered entity in the event of a security breach that compromises such computerized data, including notifying the covered entity of any security breach in the most expedient time possible, and without unreasonable delay following discovery of a security breach, if misuse of personal information about a Colorado resident occurred or is likely to occur. Cooperation includes sharing with the covered entity information relevant to the security breach; except that such cooperation does not require the disclosure of confidential business information or trade secrets.
Other Information	If an investigation by the covered entity into the security breach determines that the type of personal information described in subsection (1)(g)(I)(B) of this section has been misused or is reasonably likely to be misused, then the covered entity shall, in addition to the notice otherwise required by subsection (2)(a.2) of this section and in the most expedient time possible and without unreasonable delay, but not later than thirty days after the date of determination that a security breach occurred, consistent with the legitimate needs of law enforcement and consistent with any measures necessary to determine the scope of the breach and to restore the reasonable integrity of the computerized data system: (I) Direct the person whose personal information has been breached to promptly change his or her password and security question or answer, as applicable, or to take other steps appropriate to protect the online account with the covered entity and all other online accounts for which the person whose personal information has been breached uses the same username or email address and password or security question or answer. (II) For log-in credentials of an email account furnished by the covered entity, the covered entity shall not comply with this section by providing the security breach notification to that email address, but may instead comply with this section by providing notice through other methods, as defined in subsection (1)(f) of this section, or by clear and conspicuous notice delivered to the resident online when the resident is connected to the online account from an internet protocol address or online location from which the covered entity knows the resident customarily accesses the account. - - - A covered entity that is required to provide a breach notification to affected Colorado residents is prohibited from charging the cost of providing such notice to such residents.

COLORADO

Data Disposal and Security: Colo. Rev. Stat. § 6-1-713 and 713.5.

The numbering and internal citations herein are derived from the applicable state statute. See statute for any applicable exceptions or exemptions.

	Colorado (Data Disposal and Security)
Key Terms	The term "personal identifying information" means a Social Security number; a personal identification number; a password; a pass code; an official state or government-issued driver's license or identification card number; a government passport number; biometric data, as defined in Section 6-1-716(1)(a); an employer, student, or military identification number; or a financial transaction device, as defined in Section 18-5-701(3). The term "biometric data" means unique biometric data generated from measurements or analysis of human body characteristics for the purpose of authenticating the individual when he or she accesses an online account. - - - The term "financial transaction device" means any instrument or device whether known as a credit card, banking card, debit card, electronic fund transfer card, or guaranteed check card, or account number representing a financial account or affecting the financial interest, standing, or obligation of or to the account holder, that can be used to obtain cash, goods, property, or services or to make financial payments, but shall not include a "check," a "negotiable order of withdrawal," and a "share draft" as defined in Section 18-5-205. - - - The term "third-party service provider" means an entity that has been contracted to maintain, store, or process personal identifying information on behalf of a covered entity.
Security Requirements	To protect personal identifying information from unauthorized access, use, modification, disclosure, or destruction, a covered entity that maintains, owns, or licenses personal identifying information of an individual residing in the state shall implement and maintain reasonable security procedures and practices that are appropriate to the nature of the personal identifying information and the nature and size of the business and its operations. - - - Unless a covered entity agrees to provide its own security protection for the information it discloses to a third-party service provider, the covered entity shall require that the third-party service provider implement and maintain reasonable security procedures and practices that are: (a) appropriate to the nature of the personal identifying information disclosed to the third-party service provider; and (b) reasonably designed to help protect the personal identifying information from unauthorized access, use, modification, disclosure, or destruction. A disclosure of personal identifying information does not include disclosure of information to a third party under circumstances where the covered entity retains primary responsibility for implementing and maintaining reasonable security procedures and practices appropriate to the nature of the personal identifying information and the covered entity implements and maintains technical controls that are reasonably designed to: (a) Help protect the personal identifying information from unauthorized access, use, modification, disclosure, or destruction; or (b) Effectively eliminate the third party's ability to access the personal identifying information, notwithstanding the third party's physical possession of the personal identifying information.
Written Policy	Yes (See Data Disposal).

	Colorado (Data Disposal and Security)
Data Disposal	Each covered entity in the state that maintains paper or electronic documents during the course of business that contain personal identifying information shall develop a written policy for the destruction or proper disposal of those paper and electronic documents containing personal identifying information. Unless otherwise required by state or federal law or regulation, the written policy must require that, when such paper or electronic documents are no longer needed, the covered entity shall destroy or arrange for the destruction of such paper and electronic documents within its custody or control that contain personal identifying information by shredding, erasing, or otherwise modifying the personal identifying information in the paper or electronic documents to make the personal identifying information unreadable or indecipherable through any means.
Other Information	A covered entity that is regulated by state or federal law and that maintains procedures for disposal of personal identifying information pursuant to the laws, rules, regulations, guidances, or guidelines established by its state or federal regulator is in compliance with this section. - - - Unless an entity specifically contracts with a recycler or disposal firm for destruction of documents that contain personal identifying information, nothing in the law shall require a recycler or disposal firm to verify that the documents contained in the products it receives for disposal or recycling have been properly destroyed or disposed of as required by this section. - - - A covered entity that is regulated by state or federal law and that maintains procedures for protection of personal identifying information pursuant to the laws, rules, regulations, guidances, or guidelines established by its state or federal regulator is in compliance with this section.
	See Colorado Privacy Act (Appendix 2).

CONNECTICUT

Data Breach Requirements: Conn. Gen. Stat. § 36a-701b.

The numbering and internal citations herein are derived from the applicable state statute.

	Connecticut (Data Breach Requirements)
Personal Information	The term "personal information" means an individual's (A) first name or first initial and last name in combination with any one, or more, of the following data: (i) Social Security number; (ii) Taxpayer identification number; (iii) Identity protection personal identification number issued by the Internal Revenue Service; (iv) Driver's license number, state identification card number, passport number, military identification number, or other identification number issued by the government that is commonly used to verify identity; (v) Credit or debit card number; (vi) Financial account number in combination with any required security code, access code, or password that would permit access to such financial account; (vii) Medical information regarding an individual's medical history, mental or physical condition, or medical treatment or diagnosis by a health care professional; (viii) Health insurance policy number or subscriber identification number, or any unique identifier used by a health insurer to identify the individual; or, (ix) Biometric information consisting of data generated by electronic measurements of an individual's unique physical characteristics used to authenticate or ascertain the individual's identity, such as a fingerprint, voice print, retina or iris image; or (B) Username or electronic mail address, in combination with a password or security question and answer that would permit access to an online account.
Security Breach Definition	The term "breach of security" means unauthorized access to or unauthorized acquisition of electronic files, media, databases or computerized data, containing personal information when access to the personal information has not been secured by encryption or by any other method or technology that renders the personal information unreadable or unusable.
Good Faith Exception	N/A
Risk of Harm Analysis	A breach notification is not required if, after an appropriate investigation, the person reasonably determines that the breach will not likely result in harm to the individuals whose personal information has been acquired or accessed.
Notification Timeline	A breach notification shall be made without unreasonable delay but not later than sixty (60) days after the discovery of such breach, unless a shorter time is required under federal law.
Security and Investigation Exceptions	A breach notification shall be delayed for a reasonable period of time if a law enforcement agency determines that the notification will impede a criminal investigation and such law enforcement agency has made a request that the notification be delayed. Any such delayed notification shall be made after such law enforcement agency determines that notification will not compromise the criminal investigation and so notifies the person of such determination.
Notification Content Requirements	See Other Information.

	Connecticut (Data Breach Requirements)
Delivery Methods	A breach notice may be provided by one of the following methods: (1) Written notice; (2) Telephone notice; (3) Electronic notice, provided such notice is consistent with the provisions regarding electronic records and signatures set forth in 15 U.S.C. § 7001 (The Electronic Signatures in Global and National Commerce Act); (4) substitute notice, provided such person demonstrates that the cost of providing notice in accordance with subdivision (1), (2), or (3) of this subsection would exceed $250,000, that the affected class of subject persons to be notified exceeds 500,000 persons, or that the person does not have sufficient contact information.
Substitute Notice	Substitute notice shall consist of the following: (A) Electronic mail notice when the person has an electronic mail address for the affected persons; (B) Conspicuous posting of the notice on the website of the person if the person maintains one; and (C) Notification to major state-wide media, including newspapers, radio, and television.
Notice to Government Agencies	The person who owns, licenses, or maintains computerized data that includes personal information, shall, not later than the time when notice is provided to the resident, also provide notice of the breach of security to the Attorney General.
Consumer Reporting Agencies	N/A
Preemption and Compliance	Any person that maintains such a security breach procedure pursuant to the rules, regulations, procedures or guidelines established by the primary or functional regulator, as defined in 15 USC 6809(2), shall be deemed to be in compliance with the security breach notification requirements of this section, provided (1) such person notifies, as applicable, such residents of this state, owners, and licensees required to be notified under and in accordance with the policies or the rules, regulations, procedures, or guidelines established by the primary or functional regulator in the event of a breach of security, and (2) if notice is given to a resident of this state in accordance with subdivision (1) of this subsection regarding a breach of security, such person also notifies the attorney general not later than the time when notice is provided to the resident. - - - Any person that is subject to and in compliance with the privacy and security standards under the Health Insurance Portability and Accountability Act of 1996 (HIPAA) and the Health Information Technology for Economic and Clinical Health Act (HITECH) shall be deemed to be in compliance with this section, provided that (1) any person required to provide notification to Connecticut residents pursuant to HITECH shall also provide notice to the attorney general not later than the time when notice is provided to such residents if notification to the attorney general would otherwise be required under the law, and (2) the person otherwise complies with the other requirements of the law (i.e., identify theft protection).
Data Processor Obligations	Any person that maintains computerized data that includes personal information that the person does not own shall notify the owner or licensee of the information of any breach of the security of the data immediately following its discovery, if the personal information of a resident of this state was breached or is reasonably believed to have been breached.

	Connecticut (Data Breach Requirements)
Other Information	The person who owns or licenses computerized data that includes personal information shall offer to each resident whose personal information under clause (i) or (ii) of subparagraph (A) of subdivision (2) of subsection (a) of this section (i.e., Social Security number; taxpayer identification number) was breached or is reasonably believed to have been breached, appropriate identity theft prevention services and, if applicable, identity theft mitigation services. Such service or services shall be provided at no cost to such resident for a period of not less than twenty-four (24) months. Such person shall provide all information necessary for such resident to enroll in such service or services and shall include information on how such resident can place a credit freeze on such resident's credit file. - - - In the event of a breach of login credentials, notice to a resident may be provided in electronic or other form that directs the resident whose personal information was breached or is reasonably believed to have been breached to promptly change any password or security question and answer, as applicable, or to take other appropriate steps to protect the affected online account and all other online accounts for which the resident uses the same username or email address and password or security question and answer. - - - Any person that furnishes an electronic mail account shall not comply with this section by providing notification to the email account that was breached or reasonably believed to have been breached if the person cannot reasonably verify the affected resident's receipt of such notification. In such an event, the person shall provide notice by another method described in this section or by clear and conspicuous notice delivered to the resident online when the resident is connected to the online account from an internet protocol address or online location from which the person knows the resident customarily accesses the account.

CONNECTICUT

Data Disposal and Security: Conn. Gen. Stat. § 42-471, 42-471a.

The numbering and internal citations herein are derived from the applicable state statute. See statute for any applicable exceptions or exemptions.

	Connecticut (Data Disposal and Security)
Key Terms	The term "personal information" means information capable of being associated with a particular individual through one or more identifiers, including, but not limited to, a Social Security number, a driver's license number, a state identification card number, an account number, a credit or debit card number, a passport number, an alien registration number, a health insurance identification number, or any military identification information, and does not include publicly available information that is lawfully made available to the general public from federal, state, or local government records or widely distributed media, and (2) "military identification information" means information identifying a person as a member of the armed forces, as defined in Section 27-103, or a veteran, as defined in said section, including, but not limited to, a selective service number, military identification number, discharge document, military identification card, or military retiree identification card. - - - The term "publicly displayed" includes, but is not limited to, posting on an Internet web page.
Security Requirements	Any person in possession of personal information of another person shall safeguard the data, computer files, and documents containing the information from misuse by third parties.
Written Policy	Any person who collects Social Security numbers in the course of business shall create a privacy protection policy which shall be published or publicly displayed. The policy shall: (1) protect the confidentiality of Social Security numbers, (2) prohibit unlawful disclosure of Social Security numbers, and (3) limit access to Social Security numbers.
Data Disposal	Any person in possession of personal information of another person shall destroy, erase, or make unreadable such data, computer files, and documents prior to disposal.
Other Information	Each employer shall obtain and retain employment applications in a secure manner and shall employ reasonable measures to destroy or make unreadable such employment applications upon disposal. Such measures shall, at a minimum, include the shredding or other means of permanent destruction of such employment applications in a secure setting. For purposes of this section, "employer" has the meaning provided in Section 31-128a ("Employer" means an individual, corporation, partnership, or unincorporated association).

DELAWARE

Data Breach Requirements: 6 Del. C. § 12B-101 et seq.

The numbering and internal citations herein are derived from the applicable state statute.

	Delaware (Data Breach Requirements)
Personal Information	(7) a. The term "personal information" means a Delaware resident's first name or first initial and last name in combination with any one or more of the following data elements that relate to that individual: 1. Social Security number. 2. Driver's license number or state or federal identification card number. 3. Account number, credit card number, or debit card number, in combination with any required security code, access code, or password that would permit access to a resident's financial account. 4. Passport number. 5. A username or email address, in combination with a password or security question and answer that would permit access to an online account. 6. Medical history, medical treatment by a health care professional, diagnosis of mental or physical condition by a health care professional, or deoxyribonucleic acid (DNA) profile. 7. Health insurance policy number, subscriber identification number, or any other unique identifier used by a health insurer to identify the person. 8. Unique biometric data generated from measurements or analysis of human body characteristics for authentication purposes. 9. An individual taxpayer identification number.
Security Breach Definition	A "breach of security" means the unauthorized acquisition of computerized data that compromises the security, confidentiality, or integrity of personal information. The unauthorized acquisition of computerized data that compromises the security, confidentiality, or integrity of personal information is not a breach of security to the extent that personal information contained therein is encrypted, unless such unauthorized acquisition includes, or is reasonably believed to include, the encryption key and the person that owns or licenses the encrypted information has a reasonable belief that the encryption key could render that personal information readable or useable.
Good Faith Exception	Good faith acquisition of personal information by an employee or agent of any person for the purposes of such person is not a breach of security, provided that the personal information is not used for an unauthorized purpose or subject to further unauthorized disclosure.
Risk of Harm Analysis	Any person who conducts business in this state and who owns or licenses computerized data that includes personal information shall provide notice of any breach of security following determination of the breach of security to any resident of this state whose personal information was breached or is reasonably believed to have been breached, unless, after an appropriate investigation, the person reasonably determines that the breach of security is unlikely to result in harm to the individuals whose personal information has been breached.

	Delaware (Data Breach Requirements)
Notification Timeline	A breach notification must be made without unreasonable delay but not later than 60 days after determination of the breach of security, unless a shorter time is required under federal law or an exception applies. When a person could not, through reasonable diligence, identify within 60 days that the personal information of certain residents of this state was included in a breach of security, such person must provide the breach notice to such residents as soon as practicable after the determination that the breach of security included the personal information of such residents, unless such person provides or has provided substitute notice in accordance with § 12B-101(5)d. of this title.
Security and Investigation Exceptions	A breach notification may be delayed if a law enforcement agency determines that the notice will impede a criminal investigation and such law enforcement agency has made a request of the person that the notice be delayed. Any such delayed notice must be made after such law enforcement agency determines that notice will not compromise the criminal investigation and so notifies the person of such determination.
Notification Content Requirements	<u>See</u> Other Information.
Delivery Methods	A breach notice may be provided by one of the following methods: a. Written notice. b. Telephonic notice. c. Electronic notice, if the notice provided is consistent with the provisions regarding electronic records and signatures set forth in 15 U.S.C. § 7001 (The Electronic Signatures in Global and National Commerce Act) or if the person's primary means of communication with the resident is by electronic means. d. Substitute notice, if the person required to provide notice under this chapter demonstrates that the cost of providing notice will exceed $75,000, or that the affected number of Delaware residents to be notified exceeds 100,000 residents, or that the person does not have sufficient contact information to provide notice.
Substitute Notice	Substitute notice consists of all of the following: 1. Electronic notice if the person has email addresses for the members of the affected class of Delaware residents. 2. Conspicuous posting of the notice on a website page of the person if the person maintains one or more website pages. 3. Notice to major statewide media, including newspapers, radio, and television and publication on the major social media platforms of the person providing notice.
Notice to Government Agencies	If the affected number of Delaware residents to be notified exceeds 500 residents, the person required to provide notice shall, not later than the time when notice is provided to the resident, also provide notice of the breach of security to the attorney general.
Consumer Reporting Agencies	N/A
Preemption and Compliance	A person that is regulated by state or federal law, including the Health Insurance Portability and Accountability Act of 1996 (HIPAA) and the Gramm-Leach-Bliley Act and that maintains procedures for a breach of security pursuant to the laws, rules, regulations, guidance, or guidelines established by its primary or functional state or federal regulator is deemed to be in compliance with this law if the person notifies affected Delaware residents in accordance with the maintained procedures when a breach of security occurs.

	Delaware (Data Breach Requirements)
Data Processor Obligations	A person that maintains computerized data that includes personal information that the person does not own or license shall give notice to and cooperate with the owner or licensee of the information of any breach of security immediately following determination of the breach of security. For purposes of this subsection, "cooperation" includes sharing with the owner or licensee information relevant to the breach.
Other Information	If the breach of security includes a Social Security number, the person shall offer to each resident, whose personal information, including Social Security number, was breached or is reasonably believed to have been breached, credit monitoring services at no cost to such resident for a period of one year. Such person shall provide all information necessary for such resident to enroll in the services and shall include information on how such resident can place a credit freeze on such resident's credit file. Such services are not required if, after an appropriate investigation, the person reasonably determines that the breach of security is unlikely to result in harm to the individuals whose personal information has been breached. - - - In the case of a breach of security involving personal information defined in § 12B-101(7)a.5. of this title for login credentials of an email account, if the person cannot comply with this section by providing the security breach notification to such email address, the person may instead comply with this section by providing notice by another method described in § 12B-101(5) of this title or by clear and conspicuous notice delivered to the resident online when the resident is connected to the online account from an internet protocol address or online location from which the person knows the resident customarily accesses the account.

DELAWARE

Data Disposal and Security: 6 Del. C. §§ 5001C to 5004C; § 12B-100.

The numbering and internal citations herein are derived from the applicable state statute. See statute for any applicable exceptions or exemptions.

	Delaware (Data Disposal and Security)
Key Terms	The term "personal information" means a Delaware resident's first name or first initial and last name in combination with any one or more of the following data elements that relate to that individual: 1. Social Security number. 2. Driver's license number or state or federal identification card number. 3. Account number, credit card number, or debit card number, in combination with any required security code, access code, or password that would permit access to a resident's financial account. 4. Passport number. 5. A username or email address, in combination with a password or security question and answer that would permit access to an online account. 6. Medical history, medical treatment by a health care professional, diagnosis of mental or physical condition by a health care professional, or deoxyribonucleic acid (DNA) profile. 7. Health insurance policy number, subscriber identification number, or any other unique identifier used by a health insurer to identify the person. 8. Unique biometric data generated from measurements or analysis of human body characteristics for authentication purposes. 9. An individual taxpayer identification number. - - - The term "personal identifying information" means a consumer's first name or first initial and last name in combination with any one of the following data elements that relate to the consumer, when either the name or the data elements are not encrypted: Social Security number; passport number; driver's license or state identification card number; insurance policy number; financial services account number; bank account number; credit card number; debit card number; tax or payroll information; or confidential health-care information, including all information relating to a patient's health care history, diagnosis, condition, and treatment, or evaluation obtained from a health care provider who has treated the patient, that explicitly or by implication identifies a particular patient. - - - The term "record" means information that is inscribed on a tangible medium, or that is stored in an electronic or other medium and is retrievable in perceivable form on which personal identifying information is recorded or preserved. "Record" does not include publicly available directories or sources containing information a consumer has voluntarily consented to have publicly disseminated or listed, or that is disseminated as provided for by applicable law or regulation, such as name, address, or telephone number, or other directories or sources as are derived solely from such directories or sources.
Security Requirements	Any person who conducts business in Delaware and owns, licenses, or maintains personal information shall implement and maintain reasonable procedures and practices to prevent the unauthorized acquisition, use, modification, disclosure, or destruction of personal information collected or maintained in the regular course of business.

	Delaware (Data Disposal and Security)
Data Disposal	In the event that a commercial entity seeks permanently to dispose of records containing consumers' personal identifying information within its custody or control, such commercial entity shall take reasonable steps to destroy or arrange for the destruction of each such record by shredding, erasing, or otherwise destroying or modifying the personal identifying information in those records to make it unreadable or indecipherable.

DISTRICT OF COLUMBIA

Data Breach Requirements: D.C. Code § 28-3851 et seq.

The numbering and internal citations herein are derived from the applicable state statute.

	District of Columbia (Data Breach Requirements)
Personal Information	(3)(A) The term "personal information" means: (i) An individual's first name, first initial and last name, or any other personal identifier, which, in combination with any of the following data elements, can be used to identify a person or the person's information: (I) Social Security number, individual taxpayer identification number, passport number, driver's license number, District of Columbia identification card number, military identification number, or other unique identification number issued on a government document commonly used to verify the identity of a specific individual; (II) Account number, credit card number or debit card number, or any other number or code or combination of numbers or codes, such as an identification number, security code, access code, or password, that allows access to or use of an individual's financial or credit account; (III) Medical information; (IV) Genetic information and deoxyribonucleic acid (DNA) profile; (V) Health insurance information, including a policy number, subscriber information number, or any unique identifier used by a health insurer to identify the person that permits access to an individual's health and billing information; (VI) Biometric data of an individual generated by automatic measurements of an individual's biological characteristics, such as a fingerprint, voice print, genetic print, retina or iris image, or other unique biological characteristic, that is used to uniquely authenticate the individual's identity when the individual accesses a system or account; or (VII) Any combination of data elements included in sub-sub-subparagraphs (I) through (VI) of this sub-subparagraph that would enable a person to commit identity theft without reference to a person's first name or first initial and last name or other independent personal identifier. (ii) A username or email address in combination with a password, security question and answer, or other means of authentication, or any combination of data elements included in sub-sub-subparagraphs (I) through (VI) of sub-subparagraph (i) that permits access to an individual's email account.
Security Breach Definition	The term "breach of the security of the system" means unauthorized acquisition of computerized or other electronic data or any equipment or device storing such data that compromises the security, confidentiality, or integrity of personal information maintained by the person or entity who conducts business in the District of Columbia.
Good Faith Exception	A "breach of the security of the system" does not include a good-faith acquisition of personal information by an employee or agency of the person or entity for the purposes of the person or entity if the personal information is not used improperly or subject to further unauthorized disclosure.
Risk of Harm Analysis	A "breach of the security of the system" does not include acquisition of personal information of an individual that the person or entity reasonably determines, after a reasonable investigation and consultation with the Office of the Attorney General for the District of Columbia and federal law enforcement agencies, will likely not result in harm to the individual.

	District of Columbia (Data Breach Requirements)
Notification Timeline	The breach notification shall be made in the most expedient time possible and without unreasonable delay, consistent with the legitimate needs of law enforcement, and with any measures necessary to determine the scope of the breach and restore the reasonable integrity of the data system.
Security and Investigation Exceptions	The breach notification may be delayed if a law enforcement agency determines that the notification will impede a criminal investigation but shall be made as soon as possible after the law enforcement agency determines that the notification will not compromise the investigation.
Notification Content Requirements	The breach notification shall include: (1) To the extent possible, a description of the categories of information that were, or are reasonably believed to have been, acquired by an unauthorized person, including the elements of personal information that were, or are reasonably believed to have been, acquired; (2) Contact information for the person or entity making the notification, including the business address, telephone number, and toll-free telephone number if one is maintained; (3) The toll-free telephone numbers and addresses for the major consumer reporting agencies, including a statement notifying the resident of the right to obtain a security freeze free of charge pursuant to 15 U.S.C. § 1681c-1 and information on how a resident may request a security freeze; and (4) The toll-free telephone numbers, addresses, and website addresses for the following entities, including a statement that an individual can obtain information from these sources about steps to take to avoid identity theft: (A) The Federal Trade Commission; and (B) The Office of the Attorney General for the District of Columbia.
Delivery Methods	A breach notice may be provided by one of the following methods: (A) Written notice; (B) Electronic notice, if the customer has consented to receipt of electronic notice consistent with the provisions regarding electronic records and signatures set forth in 15 U.S.C. § 7001 (The Electronic Signatures in Global and National Commerce Act); or (C)(i) Substitute notice, if the person or entity demonstrates that the cost of providing notice to persons subject to this subchapter would exceed $50,000, that the number of persons to receive notice under this subchapter exceeds 100,000, or that the person or entity does not have sufficient contact information.
Substitute Notice	Substitute notice shall consist of all of the following: (I) Email notice when the person or entity has an email address for the subject persons; (II) Conspicuous posting of the notice on the website page of the person or entity if the person or entity maintains one; and (III) Notice to major local and, if applicable, national media.

	District of Columbia (Data Breach Requirements)
Notice to Government Agencies	In addition to giving the breach notification required under subsection (a) of this section, and subject to subsection (d) of this section (security and investigation exceptions), the person or entity required to give notice shall promptly provide written notice of the breach of the security of the system to the Office of the Attorney General for the District of Columbia if the breach affects 50 or more District residents. This notice shall be made in the most expedient manner possible, without unreasonable delay, and in no event later than when notice is provided under subsection (a) of this section. The written notice shall include: (1) The name and contact information of the person or entity reporting the breach; (2) The name and contact information of the person or entity that experienced the breach; (3) The nature of the breach of the security of the system, including the name of the person or entity that experienced the breach; (4) The types of personal information compromised by the breach; (5) The number of District residents affected by the breach; (6) The cause of the breach, including the relationship between the person or entity that experienced the breach and the person responsible for the breach, if known; (7) The remedial action taken by the person or entity to include steps taken to assist District residents affected by the breach; (8) The date and time frame of the breach, if known; (9) The address and location of corporate headquarters, if outside of the District; (10) Any knowledge of foreign country involvement; and (11) A sample of the notice to be provided to District residents. - - - This notice shall not be delayed on the grounds that the total number of District residents affected by the breach has not yet been ascertained.
Consumer Reporting Agencies	If any person or entity is required by subsection (a) or (b) of this section to notify more than 1,000 persons of a breach, the person shall also notify, without unreasonable delay, all consumer reporting agencies of the timing, distribution and content of the notices. Nothing in this subsection shall be construed to require the person to provide to the consumer reporting agency the names or other personal identifying information of breach notice recipients. This subsection shall not apply to a person or entity who is required to notify consumer reporting agencies of a breach pursuant to Title V of the Gramm-Leach-Bliley Act.
Preemption and Compliance	A person or entity that maintains procedures for a breach notification system under Title V of the Gramm-Leach-Bliley Act, or the breach notification rules issued pursuant to the Health Insurance Portability Accountability Act of 1996 (HIPAA), or the Health Information Technology for Economic and Clinical Health Act (HITECH), and provides notice in accordance with such acts, and any rules, regulations, guidance, and guidelines thereto, to each affected resident in the event of a breach, shall be deemed to be in compliance with this section with respect to the notification of residents whose personal information is included in the breach. The person or entity shall, in all cases, provide written notice of the breach of the security of the system to the Office of the Attorney General for the District of Columbia.
Data Processor Obligations	Any person or entity who maintains, handles, or otherwise possesses computerized or other electronic data that includes personal information that the person or entity does not own shall notify the owner or licensee of the information of any breach of the security of the system in the most expedient time possible following discovery.

	District of Columbia (Data Breach Requirements)
Other Information	Notwithstanding subsection (a-1) of this section, in the case of a breach of the security of the system that only involves personal information as defined in § 28-3851 (3)(A)(ii), the person or entity may comply with this section by providing the notification in electronic format or other form that directs the person to change the person's password and security question or answer, as applicable, or to take other steps appropriate to protect the email account with the person or entity and all other online accounts for which the person whose personal information has been breached uses the same username or email address and password or security question or answer. - - - When a person or entity experiences a breach of the security of the system and such breach includes or is reasonably believed to include a Social Security number or taxpayer identification number, the person or entity shall offer to each District resident whose Social Security number or taxpayer identification number was released identity theft protection services at no cost for a period of not less than 18 months. The person or entity that experienced the breach of the security of its system shall provide all information necessary for District residents to enroll in the services.

DISTRICT OF COLUMBIA

Data Disposal and Security: D.C. Code § 28-3852.01

The numbering and internal citations herein are derived from the applicable state statute. See statute for any applicable exceptions or exemptions.

	District of Columbia (Data Disposal and Security)
Key Terms	The term "personal information" means: (i) An individual's first name, first initial, and last name, or any other personal identifier, which, in combination with any of the following data elements, can be used to identify a person or the person's information: (I) Social security number, individual taxpayer identification number, passport number, driver's license number, District of Columbia identification card number, military identification number, or other unique identification number issued on a government document commonly used to verify the identity of a specific individual; (II) Account number, credit card number, or debit card number, or any other number or code or combination of numbers or codes, such as an identification number, security code, access code, or password, that allows access to or use of an individual's financial or credit account; (III) Medical information; (IV) Genetic information and deoxyribonucleic acid (DNA) profile; (V) Health insurance information, including a policy number, subscriber information number, or any unique identifier used by a health insurer to identify the person that permits access to an individual's health and billing information; (VI) Biometric data of an individual generated by automatic measurements of an individual's biological characteristics, such as a fingerprint, voice print, genetic print, retina or iris image, or other unique biological characteristic, that is used to uniquely authenticate the individual's identity when the individual accesses a system or account; or (VII) Any combination of data elements included in sub-sub-subparagraphs (I) through (VI) of this sub-subparagraph that would enable a person to commit identity theft without reference to a person's first name or first initial and last name or other independent personal identifier. (ii) A username or email address in combination with a password, security question and answer, or other means of authentication, or any combination of data elements included in sub-sub-subparagraphs (I) through (VI) of sub-subparagraph (i) that permits access to an individual's email account.
Security Requirements	To protect personal information from unauthorized access, use, modification, disclosure, or a reasonably anticipated hazard or threat, a person or entity that owns, licenses, maintains, handles, or otherwise possesses personal information of an individual residing in the District shall implement and maintain reasonable security safeguards, including procedures and practices that are appropriate to the nature of the personal information and the nature and size of the entity or operation. - - - A person or entity that uses a nonaffiliated third party as a service provider to perform services for a person or entity and discloses personal information about an individual residing in the District under a written agreement with the third party shall require by the agreement that the third party implement and maintain reasonable security procedures and practices that: (1) Are appropriate to the nature of the personal information disclosed to the nonaffiliated third party; and (2) Are reasonably designed to protect the personal information from unauthorized access, use, modification, and disclosure.

	District of Columbia (Data Disposal and Security)
Data Disposal	When a person or entity is destroying records, including computerized or electronic records and devices containing computerized or electronic records, that contain personal information of a consumer, employee, or former employee of the person or entity, the person or entity shall take reasonable steps to protect against unauthorized access to or use of the personal information, taking into account: (1) The sensitivity of the records; (2) The nature and size of the business and its operations; (3) The costs and benefits of different destruction and sanitation methods; and (4) Available technology.

FLORIDA

Data Breach Requirements: Fla. Stat. § 501.171.

The numbering and internal citations herein are derived from the applicable state statute.

	Florida (Data Breach Requirements)
Personal Information	(g)1. The term "personal information" means either of the following: a. An individual's first name or first initial and last name in combination with any one or more of the following data elements for that individual: (I) A Social Security number; (II) A driver's license or identification card number, passport number, military identification number, or other similar number issued on a government document used to verify identity; (III) A financial account number or credit or debit card number, in combination with any required security code, access code, or password that is necessary to permit access to an individual's financial account; (IV) Any information regarding an individual's medical history, mental or physical condition, or medical treatment or diagnosis by a health care professional; or (V) An individual's health insurance policy number or subscriber identification number and any unique identifier used by a health insurer to identify the individual. b. A username or email address, in combination with a password or security question and answer that would permit access to an online account.
Security Breach Definition	The term a "breach of security" or "breach" means unauthorized access of data in electronic form containing personal information.
Good Faith Exception	Good faith access of personal information by an employee or agent of the covered entity does not constitute a breach of security, provided that the information is not used for a purpose unrelated to the business or subject to further unauthorized use.
Risk of Harm Analysis	A breach notice to the affected individuals is not required if, after an appropriate investigation and consultation with relevant federal, state, or local law enforcement agencies, the covered entity reasonably determines that the breach has not and will not likely result in identity theft or any other financial harm to the individuals whose personal information has been accessed. Such a determination must be documented in writing and maintained for at least five years. The covered entity shall provide the written determination to the department within 30 days after the determination.
Notification Timeline	A breach notice shall be made as expeditiously as practicable and without unreasonable delay, taking into account the time necessary to allow the covered entity to determine the scope of the breach of security, to identify individuals affected by the breach, and to restore the reasonable integrity of the data system that was breached. A breach notice shall be made no later than 30 days after the determination of a breach or reason to believe a breach occurred unless subject to a delay authorized under paragraph (b) (security and investigation exceptions) or waiver under paragraph (c) (risk of harm analysis).
Security and Investigation Exceptions	If a federal, state, or local law enforcement agency determines that notice to individuals required under this subsection would interfere with a criminal investigation, the notice shall be delayed upon the written request of the law enforcement agency for a specified period that the law enforcement agency determines is reasonably necessary. A law enforcement agency may, by a subsequent written request, revoke such delay as of a specified date or extend the period set forth in the original request made under this paragraph to a specified date if further delay is necessary.

	Florida (Data Breach Requirements)
Notification Content Requirements	The notice to an individual with respect to a breach of security shall include, at a minimum: 1. The date, estimated date, or estimated date range of the breach of security. 2. A description of the personal information that was accessed or reasonably believed to have been accessed as a part of the breach of security. 3. Information that the individual can use to contact the covered entity to inquire about the breach of security and the personal information that the covered entity maintained about the individual.
Delivery Methods	A breach notice may be provided by one of the following methods: 1. Written notice sent to the mailing address of the individual in the records of the covered entity; or 2. Email notice sent to the email address of the individual in the records of the covered entity. 3. A covered entity required to provide notice to an individual may provide substitute notice in lieu of direct notice if such direct notice is not feasible because the cost of providing notice would exceed $250,000, because the affected individuals exceed 500,000 persons, or because the covered entity does not have an email address or mailing address for the affected individuals.
Substitute Notice	The substitute notice shall include the following: 1. A conspicuous notice on the internet website of the covered entity if the covered entity maintains a website; and 2. Notice in print and to broadcast media, including major media in urban and rural areas where the affected individuals reside.
Notice to Government Agencies	(a) A covered entity shall provide notice to the department of any breach of security affecting 500 or more individuals in this state. Such notice must be provided to the department as expeditiously as practicable, but no later than 30 days after the determination of the breach or reason to believe a breach occurred. A covered entity may receive 15 additional days to provide notice as required in subsection (4) if good cause for delay is provided in writing to the department within 30 days after determination of the breach or reason to believe a breach occurred. (b) The written notice to the department must include: 1. A synopsis of the events surrounding the breach at the time notice is provided. 2. The number of individuals in this state who were or potentially have been affected by the breach. 3. Any services related to the breach being offered or scheduled to be offered, without charge, by the covered entity to individuals, and instructions as to how to use such services. 4. A copy of the notice required under subsection (4), or an explanation of the other actions taken pursuant to subsection (4). 5. The name, address, telephone number, and email address of the employee or agent of the covered entity from whom additional information may be obtained about the breach. (c) The covered entity must provide the following information to the department upon its request: 1. A police report, incident report, or computer forensics report. 2. A copy of the policies in place regarding breaches. 3. Steps that have been taken to rectify the breach. (d) A covered entity may provide the department with supplemental information regarding a breach at any time.

	Florida (Data Breach Requirements)
Consumer Reporting Agencies	If a covered entity discovers circumstances requiring a breach notice to more than 1,000 individuals at a single time, the covered entity shall also notify, without unreasonable delay, all consumer reporting agencies of the timing, distribution, and content of the notices.
Preemption and Compliance	Notice provided pursuant to rules, regulations, procedures, or guidelines established by the covered entity's primary or functional federal regulator is deemed to be in compliance with the notice requirement in this subsection if the covered entity notifies affected individuals in accordance with the rules, regulations, procedures, or guidelines established by the primary or functional federal regulator in the event of a breach of security. Under this paragraph, a covered entity that provides a copy of such notice to the department in a timely manner is deemed to be in compliance with the notice requirement herein.
Data Processor Obligations	In the event of a breach of security of a system maintained by a third-party agent, such third-party agent shall notify the covered entity of the breach of security as expeditiously as practicable, but no later than 10 days following the determination of the breach of security or reason to believe the breach occurred. A third-party agent shall provide a covered entity with all information that the covered entity needs to comply with its notice requirements.
Other Information	The "Department" means the Department of Legal Affairs.

FLORIDA

Data Disposal and Security: Fla. Stat. § 501.171.

The numbering and internal citations herein are derived from the applicable state statute. See statute for any applicable exceptions or exemptions.

	Florida (Data Disposal and Security)
Key Terms	The term "personal information" means either of the following: a. An individual's first name or first initial and last name in combination with any one or more of the following data elements for that individual: (I) A Social Security number; (II) A driver's license or identification card number, passport number, military identification number, or other similar number issued on a government document used to verify identity; (III) A financial account number or credit or debit card number, in combination with any required security code, access code, or password that is necessary to permit access to an individual's financial account; (IV) Any information regarding an individual's medical history, mental or physical condition, or medical treatment or diagnosis by a health care professional; or (V) An individual's health insurance policy number or subscriber identification number and any unique identifier used by a health insurer to identify the individual. b. A username or email address, in combination with a password or security question and answer that would permit access to an online account.
Security Requirements	Each covered entity, governmental entity, or third-party agent shall take reasonable measures to protect and secure data in electronic form containing personal information.
Data Disposal	Each covered entity or third-party agent shall take all reasonable measures to dispose, or arrange for the disposal, of customer records containing personal information within its custody or control when the records are no longer to be retained. Such disposal shall involve shredding, erasing, or otherwise modifying the personal information in the records to make it unreadable or undecipherable through any means.

GEORGIA

Data Breach Requirements: O.C.G.A. § 10-1-910 et seq.

The numbering and internal citations herein are derived from the applicable state statute.

	Georgia (Data Breach Requirements)
Personal Information	(6) The term "personal information" means an individual's first name or first initial and last name in combination with any one or more of the following data elements, when either the name or the data elements are not encrypted or redacted: (A) Social Security number; (B) Driver's license number or state identification card number; (C) Account number, credit card number, or debit card number, if circumstances exist wherein such a number could be used without additional identifying information, access codes, or passwords; (D) Account passwords or personal identification numbers or other access codes; or (E) Any of the items contained in subparagraphs (A) through (D) of this paragraph when not in connection with the individual's first name or first initial and last name, if the information compromised would be sufficient to perform or attempt to perform identity theft against the person whose information was compromised.
Security Breach Definition	The term "breach of the security of the system" means unauthorized acquisition of an individual's electronic data that compromises the security, confidentiality, or integrity of personal information of such individual maintained by an information broker or data collector.
Good Faith Exception	Good faith acquisition or use of personal information by an employee or agent of an information broker or data collector for the purposes of such information broker or data collector is not a breach of the security of the system, provided that the personal information is not used or subject to further unauthorized disclosure.
Risk of Harm Analysis	N/A
Notification Timeline	The breach notice shall be made in the most expedient time possible and without unreasonable delay, consistent with the legitimate needs of law enforcement, or with any measures necessary to determine the scope of the breach and restore the reasonable integrity, security, and confidentiality of the data system.
Security and Investigation Exceptions	The breach notification may be delayed if a law enforcement agency determines that the notification will compromise a criminal investigation. The notification shall be made after the law enforcement agency determines that it will not compromise the investigation.
Notification Content Requirements	N/A

	Georgia (Data Breach Requirements)
Delivery Methods	A breach notice may be provided by one of the following methods: (A) Written notice; (B) Telephone notice; (C) Electronic notice, if the notice provided is consistent with the provisions regarding electronic records and signatures set forth in 15 U.S.C. § 7001 (The Electronic Signatures in Global and National Commerce Act); or (D) Substitute notice, if the information broker or data collector demonstrates that the cost of providing notice would exceed $50,000, that the affected class of individuals to be notified exceeds 100,000, or that the information broker or data collector does not have sufficient contact information to provide written or electronic notice to such individuals.
Substitute Notice	Substitute notice shall consist of all of the following: (i) Email notice, if the information broker or data collector has an email address for the individuals to be notified; (ii) Conspicuous posting of the notice on the information broker's or data collector's website page, if the information broker or data collector maintains one; and (iii) Notification to major state-wide media.
Notice to Government Agencies	N/A
Consumer Reporting Agencies	In the event that an information broker or data collector discovers circumstances requiring notification of more than 10,000 residents of this state at one time, the information broker or data collector shall also notify, without unreasonable delay, all consumer reporting agencies that compile and maintain files on consumers on a nation-wide basis of the timing, distribution, and content of the notices.
Preemption and Compliance	No express provision.
Data Processor Obligations	Any person or business that maintains computerized data on behalf of an information broker or data collector that includes personal information of individuals that the person or business does not own shall notify the information broker or data collector of any breach of the security of the system within 24 hours following discovery, if the personal information was, or is reasonably believed to have been, acquired by an unauthorized person.
Other Information	The term "information broker" means any person or entity who, for monetary fees or dues, engages in whole or in part in the business of collecting, assembling, evaluating, compiling, reporting, transmitting, transferring, or communicating information concerning individuals for the primary purpose of furnishing personal information to nonaffiliated third parties, but does not include any governmental agency whose records are maintained primarily for traffic safety, law enforcement, or licensing purposes.

GEORGIA

Data Disposal and Security: O.C.G.A. § 10-15-1 et seq.

The numbering and internal citations herein are derived from the applicable state statute. See statute for any applicable exceptions or exemptions.

	Georgia (Data Disposal and Security)
Key Terms	The term "discard" means to throw away, get rid of, or eliminate. - - - The term "dispose" means the sale or transfer of a record for value to a company or business engaged in the business of record destruction. - - - The term "personal information" means: (A) Personally identifiable data about a customer's medical condition, if the data are not generally considered to be public knowledge; (B) Personally identifiable data which contain a customer's account or identification number, account balance, balance owing, credit balance, or credit limit, if the data relate to a customer's account or transaction with a business; (C) Personally identifiable data provided by a customer to a business upon opening an account or applying for a loan or credit; or (D) Personally identifiable data about a customer's federal, state, or local income tax return. - - - The term "personally identifiable" means capable of being associated with a particular customer through one or more identifiers, including, but not limited to, a customer's fingerprint, photograph, or computerized image, Social Security number, passport number, driver identification number, personal identification card number, date of birth, medical information, or disability information. A customer's name, address, and telephone number shall not be considered personally identifiable data unless one or more of them are used in conjunction with one or more of the identifiers listed here. - - - The term "record" means any material on which written, drawn, printed, spoken, visual, or electromagnetic information is recorded or preserved, regardless of physical form or characteristics.
Data Disposal	A business may not discard a record containing personal information unless it: (1) Shreds the customer's record before discarding the record; (2) Erases the personal information contained in the customer's record before discarding the record; (3) Modifies the customer's record to make the personal information unreadable before discarding the record; or (4) Takes actions that it reasonably believes will ensure that no unauthorized person will have access to the personal information contained in the customer's record for the period between the record's disposal and the record's destruction.

HAWAII

Data Breach Requirements: HRS § 487N-1 et seq.

The numbering and internal citations herein are derived from the applicable state statute.

	Hawaii (Data Breach Requirements)
Personal Information	The term "personal information" means an individual's first name or first initial and last name in combination with any one or more of the following data elements, when either the name or the data elements are not encrypted: (1) Social Security number; (2) Driver's license number or Hawaii identification card number; or (3) Account number, credit or debit card number, access code, or password that would permit access to an individual's financial account.
Security Breach Definition	The term "security breach" means an incident of unauthorized access to and acquisition of unencrypted or unredacted records or data containing personal information where illegal use of the personal information has occurred or is reasonably likely to occur and that creates a risk of harm to a person. Any incident of unauthorized access to and acquisition of encrypted records or data containing personal information along with the confidential process or key constitutes a security breach.
Good Faith Exception	Good faith acquisition of personal information by an employee or agent of the business for a legitimate purpose is not a security breach, provided that the personal information is not used for a purpose other than a lawful purpose of the business and is not subject to further unauthorized disclosure.
Risk of Harm Analysis	See Security Breach Definition (creates a risk of harm to a person).
Notification Timeline	The breach notification shall be made without unreasonable delay, consistent with the legitimate needs of law enforcement, and consistent with any measures necessary to determine sufficient contact information, determine the scope of the breach, and restore the reasonable integrity, security, and confidentiality of the data system.
Security and Investigation Exceptions	The breach notice shall be delayed if a law enforcement agency informs the business or government agency that notification may impede a criminal investigation or jeopardize national security and requests a delay, provided that such request is made in writing, or the business or government agency documents the request contemporaneously in writing, including the name of the law enforcement officer making the request and the officer's law enforcement agency engaged in the investigation. The breach notice shall be provided without unreasonable delay after the law enforcement agency communicates to the business or government agency its determination that notice will no longer impede the investigation or jeopardize national security.
Notification Content Requirements	(d) The breach notice shall be clear and conspicuous. The notice shall include a description of the following: (1) The incident in general terms; (2) The type of personal information that was subject to the unauthorized access and acquisition; (3) The general acts of the business or government agency to protect the personal information from further unauthorized access; (4) A telephone number that the person may call for further information and assistance, if one exists; and (5) Advice that directs the person to remain vigilant by reviewing account statements and monitoring free credit reports.

	Hawaii (Data Breach Requirements)
Delivery Methods	A breach notice may be provided by one of the following methods: (1) Written notice to the last available address the business or government agency has on record; (2) Electronic mail notice, for those persons for whom a business or government agency has a valid email address and who have agreed to receive communications electronically if the notice provided is consistent with the provisions regarding electronic records and signatures for notices legally required to be in writing set forth in 15 U.S.C. § 7001 (The Electronic Signatures in Global and National Commerce Act); (3) Telephonic notice, provided that contact is made directly with the affected persons; and (4) Substitute notice, if the business or government agency demonstrates that the cost of providing notice would exceed $100,000 or that the affected class of subject persons to be notified exceeds 200,000, or if the business or government agency does not have sufficient contact information or consent to satisfy paragraph (1), (2), or (3), for only those affected persons without sufficient contact information or consent, or if the business or government agency is unable to identify particular affected persons, for only those unidentifiable affected persons.
Substitute Notice	Substitute notice shall consist of all the following: (A) Email notice when the business or government agency has an email address for the subject persons; (B) Conspicuous posting of the notice on the website page of the business or government agency, if one is maintained; and (C) Notification to major statewide media.
Notice to Government Agencies	N/A
Consumer Reporting Agencies	In the event a business provides a breach notice to more than 1,000 persons at one time, the business shall notify in writing, without unreasonable delay, the State of Hawaii's Office of Consumer Protection and all consumer reporting agencies of the timing, distribution, and content of the notice.
Preemption and Compliance	The following businesses shall be deemed to be in compliance with this section: (1) A financial institution that is subject to the federal Interagency Guidance on Response Programs for Unauthorized Access to Customer Information and Customer Notice; and (2) Any health plan or health care provider that is subject to and in compliance with the standards for privacy or individually identifiable health information and the security standards for the protection of electronic health information of the Health Insurance Portability and Accountability Act of 1996 (HIPAA).
Data Processor Obligations	Any business located in Hawaii or any business that conducts business in Hawaii that maintains or possesses records or data containing personal information of residents of Hawaii that the business does not own or license, or any government agency that maintains or possesses records or data containing personal information of residents of Hawaii shall notify the owner or licensee of the information of any security breach immediately following discovery of the breach, consistent with the legitimate needs of law enforcement.

HAWAII

Data Disposal and Security: HRS §§ 487R-1 to 487R-3.

The numbering and internal citations herein are derived from the applicable state statute. See statute for any applicable exceptions or exemptions.

	Hawaii (Data Disposal and Security)
Key Terms	The term "disposal" means the discarding or abandonment of records containing personal information or the sale, donation, discarding, or transfer of any medium, including computer equipment or computer media, containing records of personal information, or other non-paper media upon which records of personal information are stored, or other equipment for non-paper storage of information. - - - The term "personal information" means an individual's first name or first initial and last name in combination with any one or more of the following data elements, when either the name or the data elements are not encrypted: (1) Social Security number; (2) Driver's license number or Hawaii identification card number; or (3) Account number, credit or debit card number, access code, or password that would permit access to an individual's financial account.
Security Requirements	Any business or government agency that conducts business in Hawaii and any business or government agency that maintains or otherwise possesses personal information of a resident of Hawaii shall take reasonable measures to protect against unauthorized access to or use of the information in connection with or after its disposal.
Written Policy	See Data Disposal (official written policies; implementing and monitoring compliance with policies and procedures).
Data Disposal	The reasonable security requirements in connection with disposal include: (1) Implementing and monitoring compliance with policies and procedures that require the burning, pulverizing, recycling, or shredding of papers containing personal information so that information cannot be practicably read or reconstructed; (2) Implementing and monitoring compliance with policies and procedures that require the destruction or erasure of electronic media and other non-paper media containing personal information so that the information cannot practicably be read or reconstructed; and (3) Describing procedures relating to the adequate destruction or proper disposal of personal records as official policy in the writings of the business entity. - - - A business or government agency may satisfy its obligation hereunder by exercising due diligence and entering into a written contract with, and thereafter monitoring compliance by, another party engaged in the business of records destruction to destroy personal information in a manner consistent with this section. Due diligence should ordinarily include one or more of the following: (1) Reviewing an independent audit of the disposal business' operations or its compliance with this chapter; (2) Obtaining information about the disposal business from several references or other reliable sources and requiring that the disposal business be certified by a recognized trade association or similar third party with a reputation for high standards of quality review; or (3) Reviewing and evaluating the disposal business' information security policies or procedures, or taking other appropriate measures to determine the competency and integrity of the disposal business. - - -

	Hawaii (Data Disposal and Security)
	A disposal business that conducts business in Hawaii or disposes of personal information of residents of Hawaii shall take reasonable measures to dispose of records containing personal information by implementing and monitoring compliance with policies and procedures that protect against unauthorized access to, or use of, personal information during or after the collection, transportation, and disposing of such information.

IDAHO

Data Breach Requirements: Idaho Code § 28-51-104 et seq.

The numbering and internal citations herein are derived from the applicable state statute.

	Idaho (Data Breach Requirements)
Personal Information	The term "personal information" means an Idaho resident's first name or first initial and last name in combination with any one or more of the following data elements that relate to the resident, when either the name or the data elements are not encrypted: (a) Social Security number; (b) Driver's license number or Idaho identification card number; or (c) Account number, or credit or debit card number, in combination with any required security code, access code, or password that would permit access to a resident's financial account.
Security Breach Definition	The term "breach of the security of the system" means the illegal acquisition of unencrypted computerized data that materially compromises the security, confidentiality, or integrity of personal information for one or more persons maintained by an agency, individual, or a commercial entity.
Good Faith Exception	Good faith acquisition of personal information by an employee or agent of an agency, individual or a commercial entity for the purposes of the agency, individual, or the commercial entity is not a breach of the security of the system, provided that the personal information is not used or subject to further unauthorized disclosure.
Risk of Harm Analysis	When an individual or commercial entity becomes aware of a breach of the security of the system, it must conduct in good faith a reasonable and prompt investigation to determine the likelihood that personal information has been or will be misused. If the investigation determines that the misuse of information about an Idaho resident has occurred or is reasonably likely to occur, the individual or the commercial entity shall provide notice of the breach.
Notification Timeline	A breach notification must be made in the most expedient time possible and without unreasonable delay, consistent with the legitimate needs of law enforcement and consistent with any measures necessary to determine the scope of the breach, to identify the individuals affected, and to restore the reasonable integrity of the computerized data system.
Security and Investigation Exceptions	A data breach notice may be delayed if a law enforcement agency advises the individual or commercial entity that the notice will impede a criminal investigation. The breach notice must be made in good faith, without unreasonable delay, and as soon as possible after the law enforcement agency advises the agency, individual, or commercial entity that notification will no longer impede the investigation.
Notification Content Requirements	N/A

	Idaho (Data Breach Requirements)
Delivery Methods	A breach notice may be provided by one of the following methods: (a) Written notice to the most recent address the agency, individual, or commercial entity has in its records; (b) Telephonic notice; (c) Electronic notice, if the notice provided is consistent with the provisions regarding electronic records and signatures set forth in 15 U.S.C. § 7001 (The Electronic Signatures in Global and National Commerce Act); or (d) Substitute notice, if the agency, individual, or the commercial entity required to provide notice demonstrates that the cost of providing notice will exceed $25,000, or that the number of Idaho residents to be notified exceeds 50,000, or that the agency, individual, or the commercial entity does not have sufficient contact information to provide notice.
Substitute Notice	Substitute notice consists of all of the following: (i) Email notice if the agency, individual, or the commercial entity has email addresses for the affected Idaho residents; and (ii) Conspicuous posting of the notice on the website page of the agency, individual, or the commercial entity if the agency, individual, or the commercial entity maintains one; and (iii) Notice to major statewide media.
Notice to Government Agencies	N/A
Consumer Reporting Agencies	N/A
Preemption and Compliance	(2) An individual or a commercial entity that is regulated by state or federal law and that maintains procedures for a breach of the security of the system pursuant to the laws, rules, regulations, guidances, or guidelines established by its primary or functional state or federal regulator is deemed to be in compliance with section 28-51-105, Idaho Code, if the individual or the commercial entity complies with the maintained procedures when a breach of the security of the system occurs.
Data Processor Obligations	An agency, individual, or a commercial entity that maintains computerized data that includes personal information that the agency, individual, or the commercial entity does not own or license shall give notice to and cooperate with the owner or licensee of the information of any breach of the security of the system immediately following discovery of a breach if misuse of personal information about an Idaho resident occurred or is reasonably likely to occur. Cooperation includes sharing with the owner or licensee information relevant to the breach.

ILLINOIS

Data Breach Requirements: 815 ILCS § 530/1 et seq.

The numbering and internal citations herein are derived from the applicable state statute.

	Illinois (Data Breach Requirements)
Personal Information	The term "personal information" means either of the following: (1) An individual's first name or first initial and last name in combination with any one or more of the following data elements, when either the name or the data elements are not encrypted or redacted or are encrypted or redacted but the keys to unencrypt or unredact or otherwise read the name or data elements have been acquired without authorization through the breach of security: (A) Social Security number. (B) Driver's license number or state identification card number. (C) Account number or credit or debit card number, or an account number or credit card number in combination with any required security code, access code, or password that would permit access to an individual's financial account. (D) Medical information. (E) Health insurance information. (F) Unique biometric data generated from measurements or technical analysis of human body characteristics used by the owner or licensee to authenticate an individual, such as a fingerprint, retina or iris image, or other unique physical representation or digital representation of biometric data. (2) Username or email address, in combination with a password or security question and answer that would permit access to an online account, when either the username or email address or password or security question and answer are not encrypted or redacted or are encrypted or redacted but the keys to unencrypt or unredact or otherwise read the data elements have been obtained through the breach of security.
Security Breach Definition	The term "breach of the security of the system data" or "breach" means unauthorized acquisition of computerized data that compromises the security, confidentiality, or integrity of personal information maintained by the data collector.
Good Faith Exception	A breach does not include good faith acquisition of personal information by an employee or agent of the data collector for a legitimate purpose of the data collector, provided that the personal information is not used for a purpose unrelated to the data collector's business or subject to further unauthorized disclosure.
Risk of Harm Analysis	N/A
Notification Timeline	A data breach notification shall be made in the most expedient time possible and without unreasonable delay, consistent with any measures necessary to determine the scope of the breach and restore the reasonable integrity, security, and confidentiality of the data system.
Security and Investigation Exceptions	The breach notification may be delayed if an appropriate law enforcement agency determines that notification will interfere with a criminal investigation and provides the data collector with a written request for the delay. However, the data collector must notify the Illinois resident as soon as notification will no longer interfere with the investigation.

	Illinois (Data Breach Requirements)
Notification Content Requirements	The disclosure notification to an Illinois resident shall include, but need not be limited to, information as follows: (1) With respect to personal information as defined in Section 5 in paragraph (1) of the definition of "personal information": (A) The toll-free numbers and addresses for consumer reporting agencies; (B) The toll-free number, address, and website address for the Federal Trade Commission; and (C) A statement that the individual can obtain information from these sources about fraud alerts and security freezes. (2) With respect to personal information defined in Section 5 in paragraph (2) of the definition of "personal information," notice may be provided in electronic or other form directing the Illinois resident whose personal information has been breached to promptly change his or her username or password and security question or answer, as applicable, or to take other steps appropriate to protect all online accounts for which the resident uses the same username or email address and password or security question and answer.
Delivery Methods	A breach notice may be provided by one of the following methods: (1) Written notice; (2) Electronic notice, if the notice provided is consistent with the provisions regarding electronic records and signatures for notices legally required to be in writing as set forth in 15 U.S.C. § 7001 (The Electronic Signatures in Global and National Commerce Act); or (3) Substitute notice, if the data collector demonstrates that the cost of providing notice would exceed $250,000, or that the affected class of subject persons to be notified exceeds 500,000, or the data collector does not have sufficient contact information.
Substitute Notice	Substitute notice shall consist of all of the following: (i) email notice if the data collector has an email address for the subject persons; (ii) conspicuous posting of the notice on the data collector's website page if the data collector maintains one; and (iii) notification to major statewide media or, if the breach impacts residents in one geographic area, to prominent local media in areas where affected individuals are likely to reside if such notice is reasonably calculated to give actual notice to persons whom notice is required.
Notice to Government Agencies	Any data collector required to issue a data breach notice to more than 500 Illinois residents as a result of a single breach of the security system shall provide notice to the attorney general of the breach, including: (A) A description of the nature of the breach of security or unauthorized acquisition or use. (B) The number of Illinois residents affected by such incident at the time of notification. (C) Any steps the data collector has taken or plans to take relating to the incident. Such notification must be made in the most expedient time possible and without unreasonable delay, but in no event later than when the data collector provides notice to consumers. If the date of the breach is unknown at the time the notice is sent to the attorney general, the data collector shall send the attorney general the date of the breach as soon as possible.
Consumer Reporting Agencies	N/A to private sector.

	Illinois (Data Breach Requirements)
Preemption and Compliance	Any covered entity or business associate that is subject to and in compliance with the privacy and security standards for the protection of electronic health information established pursuant to Health Insurance Portability and Accountability HIPAA and the Health Information Technology for Economic and Clinical Health Act (HITECH) shall be deemed to be in compliance with the provisions of this act, provided that any covered entity or business associate required to provide notification of a breach to the secretary of Health and Human Services pursuant to HITECH also provides such notification to the attorney general within five business days of notifying the secretary of Health and Human Services. - - - The notification "delivery" requirements to consumers do not apply to data collectors that are covered entities or business associates and are in compliance with the above.
Data Processor Obligations	Any data collector that maintains or stores, but does not own or license, computerized data that includes personal information that the data collector does not own or license shall notify the owner or licensee of the information of any breach of the security of the data immediately following discovery, if the personal information was, or is reasonably believed to have been, acquired by an unauthorized person. In addition to providing such notification to the owner or licensee, the data collector shall cooperate with the owner or licensee in matters relating to the breach. That cooperation shall include, but need not be limited to, (i) informing the owner or licensee of the breach, including giving notice of the date or approximate date of the breach and the nature of the breach, and (ii) informing the owner or licensee of any steps the data collector has taken or plans to take relating to the breach. The data collector's cooperation shall not, however, be deemed to require either the disclosure of confidential business information or trade secrets or the notification of an Illinois resident who may have been affected by the breach.
Other Information	A data breach notification must be given at no charge. - - - The breach notification to Illinois residents must not include information concerning the number of Illinois residents affected by the breach - - - Upon receiving notification from a data collector of a breach of personal information, the attorney general may publish the name of the data collector that suffered the breach, the types of personal information compromised in the breach, and the date range of the breach.

ILLINOIS

Data Disposal and Security: 815 ILCS §§ 530/5, 530/40, and 530/45.

The numbering and internal citations herein are derived from the applicable state statute. See statute for any applicable exceptions or exemptions.

	Illinois (Data Disposal and Security)
Key Terms	The term "person" means: a natural person; a corporation, partnership, association, or other legal entity; a unit of local government or any agency, department, division, bureau, board, commission, or committee thereof; or the State of Illinois or any constitutional officer, agency, department, division, bureau, board, commission, or committee thereof. - - - The term "personal information" means either of the following: (1) An individual's first name or first initial and last name in combination with any one or more of the following data elements, when either the name or the data elements are not encrypted or redacted or are encrypted or redacted but the keys to unencrypt or unredact or otherwise read the name or data elements have been acquired without authorization through the breach of security: (A) Social Security number. (B) Driver's license number or state identification card number. (C) Account, credit, or debit card number, or an account number or credit card number in combination with any required security code, access code, or password that would permit access to an individual's financial account. (D) Medical information. (E) Health insurance information. (F) Unique biometric data generated from measurements or technical analysis of human body characteristics used by the owner or licensee to authenticate an individual, such as a fingerprint, retina or iris image, or other unique physical representation or digital representation of biometric data. (2) Username or email address, in combination with a password or security question and answer that would permit access to an online account, when either the username, email address, password, or security question and answer are not encrypted or redacted or are encrypted or redacted but the keys to unencrypt or unredact or otherwise read the data elements have been obtained through the breach of security.
Security Requirements	A data collector that owns, licenses, maintains, or stores but does not own or license records that contain personal information concerning an Illinois resident shall implement and maintain reasonable security measures to protect those records from unauthorized access, acquisition, destruction, use, modification, or disclosure. - - - A contract for the disclosure of personal information concerning an Illinois resident that is maintained by a data collector must include a provision requiring the person to whom the information is disclosed to implement and maintain reasonable security measures to protect those records from unauthorized access, acquisition, destruction, use, modification, or disclosure.
Written Policy	See Data Disposal (third parties must implement and monitor compliance with policies and procedures).

	Illinois (Data Disposal and Security)
Data Disposal	A person must dispose of the materials containing personal information in a manner that renders the personal information unreadable, unusable, and undecipherable. Proper disposal methods include, but are not limited to, the following: (1) Paper documents containing personal information may be either redacted, burned, pulverized, or shredded so that personal information cannot practicably be read or reconstructed. (2) Electronic media and other non-paper media containing personal information may be destroyed or erased so that personal information cannot practicably be read or reconstructed. - - - (c) Any person disposing of materials containing personal information may contract with a third party to dispose of such materials. Any third party that contracts with a person to dispose of materials containing personal information must implement and monitor compliance with policies and procedures that prohibit unauthorized access to or acquisition of or use of personal information during the collection, transportation, and disposal of materials containing personal information.
Other Information	If a state or federal law requires a data collector to provide greater protection to records that contain personal information concerning an Illinois resident that are maintained by the data collector and the data collector is in compliance with the provisions of that state or federal law, the data collector shall be deemed to be in compliance with the provisions herein.

INDIANA

Data Breach Requirements: Ind. Code § 24-4.9-1-1 et seq.

The numbering and internal citations herein are derived from the applicable state statute.

	Indiana (Data Breach Requirements)
Personal Information	The term "personal information" means: (1) A Social Security number that is not encrypted or redacted; or (2) An individual's first and last names, or first initial and last name, and one or more of the following data elements that are not encrypted or redacted: (A) A driver's license number. (B) A state identification card number. (C) A credit card number. (D) A financial account number or debit card number in combination with a security code, password, or access code that would permit access to the person's account.
Security Breach Definition	The term "breach of the security of data" means unauthorized acquisition of computerized data that compromises the security, confidentiality, or integrity of personal information maintained by a person. The term includes the unauthorized acquisition of computerized data that have been transferred to another medium, including paper, microfilm, or a similar medium, even if the transferred data are no longer in a computerized format.
Good Faith Exception	A breach does not include the good faith acquisition of personal information by an employee or agent of the person for lawful purposes of the person, if the personal information is not used or subject to further unauthorized disclosure.
Risk of Harm Analysis	A data breach notification must be provided if the database owner knows, should know, or should have known that the unauthorized acquisition constituting the breach has resulted in or could result in identity deception (as defined in IC 35-43-5-3.5), identity theft, or fraud affecting the Indiana resident.
Notification Timeline	A person required to make a disclosure or notification under this chapter shall make the disclosure or notification without unreasonable delay, but not more than forty-five (45) days after the discovery of the breach.
Security and Investigation Exceptions	For purposes of this section, a delay is reasonable if the delay is: (1) necessary to restore the integrity of the computer system; (2) necessary to discover the scope of the breach; or (3) if in response to a request from the attorney general or a law enforcement agency to delay disclosure because disclosure will: (A) impede a criminal or civil investigation; or (B) jeopardize national security. A person required to make a breach disclosure or notification shall make the disclosure or notification as soon as possible after: (1) delay is no longer necessary to restore the integrity of the computer system or to discover the scope of the breach; or (2) the attorney general or a law enforcement agency notifies the person that delay will no longer impede a criminal or civil investigation or jeopardize national security.
Notification Content Requirements	N/A

	Indiana (Data Breach Requirements)
Delivery Methods	(a) Except as provided in subsection (b), a database owner required to make a disclosure under this chapter shall make the disclosure using one (1) of the following methods: (1) Mail. (2) Telephone. (3) Facsimile (fax). (4) Electronic mail, if the database owner has the electronic mail address of the affected Indiana resident. (5) Substitute Notice.
Substitute Notice	(b) If a database owner required to make a disclosure under this chapter is required to make the disclosure to more than five hundred thousand (500,000) Indiana residents, or if the database owner required to make a disclosure under this chapter determines that the cost of the disclosure will be more than two hundred fifty thousand dollars ($250,000), the database owner required to make a disclosure under this chapter may elect to make the disclosure by using both of the following methods: (1) Conspicuous posting of the notice on the website of the database owner, if the database owner maintains a website. (2) Notice to major news reporting media in the geographic area where Indiana residents affected by the breach of the security of a system reside.
Notice to Government Agencies	If a database owner makes a data breach disclosure, the database owner shall also disclose the breach to the attorney general.
Consumer Reporting Agencies	A database owner required to make a breach disclosure to more than 1,000 consumers shall also disclose to each consumer reporting agency information necessary to assist the consumer reporting agency in preventing fraud, including personal information of an Indiana resident affected by the breach.
Preemption and Compliance	(a) Except as provided in subsection (b), this section does not apply to a database owner that maintains its own data security procedures as part of an information privacy, security policy, or compliance plan under: (1) The federal USA PATRIOT Act (P.L. 107-56); (2) Executive Order 13224; (3) The federal Driver's Privacy Protection Act (18 U.S.C. 2721 et seq.); (4) The federal Fair Credit Reporting Act (15 U.S.C. 1681 et seq.); (5) The Gramm-Leach-Bliley Act; or (6) The Health Insurance Portability and Accountability Act of 1996 (HIPAA). (b) This section applies to a current or former health care provider (as defined by IC 4-6-14-2) who is a database owner or former database owner: (1) to which an exemption under subsection (a)(6) applies or applied; and (2) whose information privacy, security policy, or compliance plan: (A) does not require the database owner or former database owner to maintain and implement reasonable procedures; or (B) is not implemented by the database owner or former database owner; to ensure that the personal information described in subsection (a), including health records (as defined by IC 4-6-14-2.5), is protected and safeguarded from unlawful use or disclosure after the database owner or former database owner ceases to be a covered entity under the Health Insurance Portability and Accountability Act.

	Indiana (Data Breach Requirements)
	A financial institution that complies with the disclosure requirements prescribed by the Federal Interagency Guidance on Response Programs for Unauthorized Access to Customer Information and Customer Notice or the Guidance on Response Programs for Unauthorized Access to Member Information and Member Notice, as applicable, is not required to make a disclosure under this chapter.
Data Processor Obligations	A person that maintains computerized data but that is not a database owner shall notify the database owner if the person discovers that personal information was or may have been acquired by an unauthorized person.
Other Information	A database owner that maintains its own disclosure procedures as part of an information privacy, security policy, or compliance plan under: (1) The federal USA PATRIOT Act (P.L. 107-56); (2) Executive Order 13224; (3) The federal Driver's Privacy Protection Act (18 U.S.C. 2781 et seq.); (4) The federal Fair Credit Reporting Act (15 U.S.C. 1681 et seq.); (5) The Gramm-Leach-Bliley Act; or (6) The Health Insurance Portability and Accountability Act of 1996 (HIPAA); is not required to make a disclosure under this chapter if the database owner's information privacy, security policy, or compliance plan requires that Indiana residents be notified of a breach of the security of data without unreasonable delay and the database owner complies with the database owner's information privacy, security policy, or compliance plan.

INDIANA

Data Disposal and Security: Ind. Code §§ 24-4.9-2-3, 24-4.9-2-10, and 24-4.9-3-3.5.

The numbering and internal citations herein are derived from the applicable state statute. See statute for any applicable exceptions or exemptions.

	Indiana (Data Disposal and Security)
Key Terms	The term "database owner" means a person that owns or licenses computerized data that includes personal information. - - - The term "personal information" means: (1) A Social Security number that is not encrypted or redacted; or (2) An individual's first and last names, or first initial and last name, and one (1) or more of the following data elements that are not encrypted or redacted: (A) A driver's license number. (B) A state identification card number. (C) A credit card number. (D) A financial account or debit card number in combination with a security code, password, or access code that would permit access to the person's account.
Security Requirements	A database owner shall implement and maintain reasonable procedures, including taking any appropriate corrective action, to protect and safeguard from unlawful use or disclosure any personal information of Indiana residents collected or maintained by the database owner.
Data Disposal	A database owner shall not dispose of or abandon records or documents containing unencrypted and unredacted personal information of Indiana residents without shredding, incinerating, mutilating, erasing, or otherwise rendering the personal information illegible or unusable.

IOWA

Data Breach Requirements: Iowa Code Ann. § 715C.1 et seq.

The numbering and internal citations herein are derived from the applicable state statute.

	Iowa (Data Breach Requirements)
Personal Information	The term "personal information" means an individual's first name or first initial and last name in combination with any one or more of the following data elements that relate to the individual if any of the data elements are not encrypted, redacted, or otherwise altered by any method or technology in such a manner that the name or data elements are unreadable or are encrypted, redacted, or otherwise altered by any method or technology but the keys to unencrypt, unredact, or otherwise read the data elements have been obtained through the breach of security: (1) Social Security number. (2) Driver's license number or other unique identification number created or collected by a government body. (3) Financial account number, credit card number, or debit card number in combination with any required expiration date, security code, access code, or password that would permit access to an individual's financial account. (4) Unique electronic identifier or routing code, in combination with any required security code, access code, or password that would permit access to an individual's financial account. (5) Unique biometric data, such as a fingerprint, retina or iris image, or other unique physical representation or digital representation of biometric data.
Security Breach Definition	The term "breach of security" means unauthorized acquisition of personal information maintained in computerized form by a person that compromises the security, confidentiality, or integrity of the personal information. A "breach of security" also means unauthorized acquisition of personal information maintained by a person in any medium, including on paper, that was transferred by the person to that medium from computerized form and that compromises the security, confidentiality, or integrity of the personal information.
Good Faith Exception	Good faith acquisition of personal information by a person or that person's employee or agent for a legitimate purpose of that person is not a breach of security, provided that the personal information is not used in violation of applicable law or in a manner that harms or poses an actual threat to the security, confidentiality, or integrity of the personal information.
Risk of Harm Analysis	A breach notification is not required if, after an appropriate investigation or after consultation with the relevant federal, state, or local agencies responsible for law enforcement, the person determined that no reasonable likelihood of financial harm to the consumers whose personal information has been acquired has resulted or will result from the breach. Such a determination must be documented in writing and the documentation must be maintained for five years.
Notification Timeline	A breach notification shall be made in the most expeditious manner possible and without unreasonable delay, consistent with the legitimate needs of law enforcement, and consistent with any measures necessary to sufficiently determine contact information for the affected consumers, determine the scope of the breach, and restore the reasonable integrity, security, and confidentiality of the data.
Security and Investigation Exceptions	The breach notification requirements may be delayed if a law enforcement agency determines that the notification will impede a criminal investigation and the agency has made a written request that the notification be delayed. The breach notification shall be made after the law enforcement agency determines that the notification will not compromise the investigation and notifies the person required to give notice in writing.

	Iowa (Data Breach Requirements)
Notification Content Requirements	The breach notification shall include, at a minimum, all of the following: a. A description of the breach of security. b. The approximate date of the breach of security. c. The type of personal information obtained as a result of the breach of security. d. Contact information for consumer reporting agencies. e. Advice to the consumer to report suspected incidents of identity theft to local law enforcement or the attorney general.
Delivery Methods	A breach notice may be provided by one of the following methods: a. Written notice to the last available address the person has in the person's records. b. Electronic notice if the person's customary method of communication with the consumer is by electronic means or is consistent with the provisions regarding electronic records and signatures set forth in 15 U.S.C. § 7001 (The Electronic Signatures in Global and National Commerce Act). c. Substitute notice, if the person demonstrates that the cost of providing notice would exceed $250,000, that the affected class of consumers to be notified exceeds 350,000 persons, or if the person does not have sufficient contact information to provide notice.
Substitute Notice	Substitute notice shall consist of the following: (1) Email notice when the person has an email address for the affected consumers. (2) Conspicuous posting of the notice or a link to the notice on the internet site of the person if the person maintains an internet site. (3) Notification to major statewide media.
Notice to Government Agencies	Any person who was subject to a breach requiring notification to more than 500 residents of this state shall give written notice of the breach of security to the director of the Consumer Protection Division of the Office of the Attorney General within five business days after giving notice of the breach of security to any consumer.
Consumer Reporting Agencies	N/A
Preemption and Compliance	The breach notification requirements do not apply to any of the following: a. A person who complies with notification requirements or breach of security procedures that provide greater protection to personal information and at least as thorough disclosure requirements than that provided by this section pursuant to the rules, regulations, procedures, guidance, or guidelines established by the person's primary or functional federal regulator. b. A person who complies with a state or federal law that provides greater protection to personal information and at least as thorough disclosure requirements for breach of security or personal information than that provided by this section. c. A person who is subject to and complies with regulations promulgated pursuant to Title V of the Gramm-Leach-Bliley Act. d. A person who is subject to and complies with regulations promulgated pursuant to the Health Insurance Portability and Accountability Act of 1996 (HIPAA), and Health Information Technology for Economic and Clinical Health Act of 2009.
Data Processor Obligations	Any person who maintains or otherwise possesses personal information on behalf of another person shall notify the owner or licensor of the information of any breach of security immediately following discovery of such breach of security if a consumer's personal information was included in the information that was breached.

KANSAS

Data Breach Requirements: Kansas S.A. § 50-7a01 et seq.

The numbering and internal citations herein are derived from the applicable state statute.

	Kansas (Data Breach Requirements)
Personal Information	The term "personal information" means a consumer's first name or first initial and last name linked to any one or more of the following data elements that relate to the consumer, when the data elements are neither encrypted nor redacted: (1) Social Security number; (2) Driver's license number or state identification card number; or (3) Financial account number, or credit or debit card number, alone or in combination with any required security code, access code, or password that would permit access to a consumer's financial account.
Security Breach Definition	The term "security breach" means the unauthorized access and acquisition of unencrypted or unredacted computerized data that compromises the security, confidentiality, or integrity of personal information maintained by an individual or a commercial entity and that causes, or such individual or entity reasonably believes has caused or will cause, identity theft to any consumer.
Good Faith Exception	Good faith acquisition of personal information by an employee or agent of an individual or a commercial entity for the purposes of the individual or the commercial entity is not a breach of the security of the system, provided that the personal information is not used for or is not subject to further unauthorized disclosure.
Risk of Harm Analysis	A person that conducts business in this state who owns or licenses computerized data that includes personal information shall, when he or she becomes aware of any breach of the security of the system, conduct in good faith a reasonable and prompt investigation to determine the likelihood that personal information has been or will be misused.
Notification Timeline	A breach notification must be made in the most expedient time possible and without unreasonable delay, consistent with the legitimate needs of law enforcement and consistent with any measures necessary to determine the scope of the breach and to restore the reasonable integrity of the computerized data system.
Security and Investigation Exceptions	A breach notification may be delayed if a law enforcement agency determines that the notice will impede a criminal investigation. Notice shall be made in good faith, without unreasonable delay, and as soon as possible after the law enforcement agency determines that notification will no longer impede the investigation.
Notification Content Requirements	N/A
Delivery Methods	A breach notice may be provided by one of the following methods: (1) Written notice; (2) Electronic notice, if the notice provided is consistent with the provisions regarding electronic records and signatures set forth in 15 U.S.C. § 7001 (The Electronic Signatures in Global and National Commerce Act); or (3) Substitute notice, if the individual or the commercial entity required to provide notice demonstrates that the cost of providing notice will exceed $100,000, or that the affected class of consumers to be notified exceeds 5,000, or that the individual or the commercial entity does not have sufficient contact information to provide notice.

	Kansas (Data Breach Requirements)
Substitute Notice	Substitute notice means: (1) Email notice if the individual or the commercial entity has email addresses for the affected class of consumers; (2) conspicuous posting of the notice on the website page of the individual or the commercial entity if the individual or the commercial entity maintains a website; and (3) notification to major statewide media.
Notice to Government Agencies	N/A
Consumer Reporting Agencies	In the event that a person discovers circumstances requiring breach notification to more than 1,000 consumers at one time, the person shall also notify, without unreasonable delay, all consumer reporting agencies of the timing, distribution, and content of the notices.
Preemption and Compliance	An individual or a commercial entity that is regulated by state or federal law and that maintains procedures for a breach of the security of the system pursuant to the laws, rules, regulations, guidances, or guidelines established by its primary or functional state or federal regulator is deemed to be in compliance with this section. This section does not relieve an individual or a commercial entity from a duty to comply with other requirements of state and federal law regarding the protection and privacy of personal information.
Data Processor Obligations	An individual or a commercial entity that maintains computerized data that includes personal information that the individual or the commercial entity does not own or license shall give notice to the owner or licensee of the information of any breach of the security of the data following discovery of a breach, if the personal information was, or is reasonably believed to have been, accessed and acquired by an unauthorized person.

KANSAS

Data Disposal and Security: Kansas S.A. § 50-6,139b.

The numbering and internal citations herein are derived from the applicable state statute. See statute for any applicable exceptions or exemptions.

	Kansas (Data Disposal and Security)
Key Terms	The term "holder of personal information" or "holder" means a person who, in the ordinary course of business, collects, maintains, or possesses, or causes to be collected, maintained, or possessed, the personal information of any other person. - - - The term "personal information" means personal information as defined by K.S.A. 50-7a01(g), and amendments thereto, and any other information which identifies an individual for which an information security obligation is imposed by federal or state statute or regulation. - - - K.S.A. 50-7a01(g) defines personal information as a consumer's first name or first initial and last name linked to any one or more of the following data elements that relate to the consumer, when the data elements are neither encrypted nor redacted: (1) Social security number; (2) Driver's license number or state identification card number; or (3) Financial account, credit, or debit card number, alone or in combination with any required security code, access code, or password that would permit access to a consumer's financial account. The term "personal information" does not include publicly available information that is lawfully made available to the general public from federal, state, or local government records.
Security Requirements	A holder of personal information shall implement and maintain reasonable procedures and practices appropriate to the nature of the information, and exercise reasonable care to protect the personal information from unauthorized access, use, modification, or disclosure.
Data Disposal	A holder of personal information shall, unless otherwise required by federal law or regulation, take reasonable steps to destroy or arrange for the destruction of any records within such holder's custody or control containing any person's personal information when such holder no longer intends to maintain or possess such records. Such destruction shall be by shredding, erasing, or otherwise modifying the personal identifying information in the records to make it unreadable or undecipherable through any means.
Other Information	If federal or state law or regulation governs the procedures and practices of the holder of personal information for such protection of personal information, then compliance with such federal or state law or regulation shall be deemed compliance with this paragraph and failure to comply with such federal or state law or regulation shall be prima facie evidence of a violation of this law.

KENTUCKY

Data Breach Requirements: Kentucky R.S. § 365.732.

The numbering and internal citations herein are derived from the applicable state statute.

	Kentucky (Data Breach Requirements)
Personal Information	The term "personally identifiable information" means an individual's first name or first initial and last name in combination with any one or more of the following data elements, when the name or data element is not redacted: 1. Social Security number; 2. Driver's license number; or 3. Account number or credit or debit card number, in combination with any required security code, access code, or password to permit access to an individual's financial account.
Security Breach Definition	The term "breach of the security of the system" means unauthorized acquisition of unencrypted and unredacted computerized data that compromises the security, confidentiality, or integrity of personally identifiable information maintained by the information holder as part of a database regarding multiple individuals that actually causes or leads the information holder to reasonably believe has caused or will cause, identity theft or fraud against any resident of the Commonwealth of Kentucky.
Good Faith Exception	Good-faith acquisition of personally identifiable information by an employee or agent of the information holder for the purposes of the information holder is not a breach of the security of the system if the personally identifiable information is not used or subject to further unauthorized disclosure.
Risk of Harm Analysis	See Security Breach Definition.
Notification Timeline	A breach notification shall be made in the most expedient time possible and without unreasonable delay, consistent with the legitimate needs of law enforcement or any measures necessary to determine the scope of the breach and restore the reasonable integrity of the data system.
Security and Investigation Exceptions	A breach notification may be delayed if a law enforcement agency determines that the notification will impede a criminal investigation. The breach notification shall be made promptly after the law enforcement agency determines that it will not compromise the investigation.
Notification Content Requirements	N/A
Delivery Methods	A breach notice may be provided by one of the following methods: (a) Written notice; (b) Electronic notice, if the notice provided is consistent with the provisions regarding electronic records and signatures set forth in 15 U.S.C. § 7001 (The Electronic Signatures in Global and National Commerce Act); or (c) Substitute notice, if the information holder demonstrates that the cost of providing notice would exceed $250,000, or that the affected class of subject persons to be notified exceeds 500,000, or the information holder does not have sufficient contact information.

	Kentucky (Data Breach Requirements)
Substitute Notice	Substitute notice shall consist of all of the following: 1. Email notice, when the information holder has an email address for the subject persons; 2. Conspicuous posting of the notice on the information holder's internet website page, if the information holder maintains a website page; and 3. Notification to major statewide media.
Notice to Government Agencies	N/A
Consumer Reporting Agencies	If a person discovers circumstances requiring breach notification to more than 1,000 persons at one time, the person shall also notify, without unreasonable delay, all consumer reporting agencies and credit bureaus that compile and maintain files on consumers on a nationwide basis of the timing, distribution, and content of the notices.
Preemption and Compliance	The provisions of this section and the requirements for nonaffiliated third parties in KRS Chapter 61 shall not apply to any person who is subject to the provisions of Title V of the Gramm-Leach-Bliley Act, or the Health Insurance Portability and Accountability Act of 1996 (HIPAA), as amended, or any agency of the Commonwealth of Kentucky or any of its local governments or political subdivisions.
Data Processor Obligations	Any information holder that maintains computerized data that includes personally identifiable information that the information holder does not own shall notify the owner or licensee of the information of any breach of the security of the data as soon as reasonably practicable following discovery, if the personally identifiable information was, or is reasonably believed to have been, acquired by an unauthorized person.

KENTUCKY

Data Disposal and Security: Kentucky R.S. §§ 365.720 and 365.725.

The numbering and internal citations herein are derived from the applicable state statute. See statute for any applicable exceptions or exemptions.

	Kentucky (Data Disposal and Security)
Key Terms	The term "personally identifiable information" means data capable of being associated with a particular customer through one (1) or more identifiers, including but not limited to a customer's name, address, telephone number, electronic mail address, fingerprints, photographs or computerized image, Social Security number, passport number, driver identification number, personal identification card number or code, date of birth, medical information, financial information, tax information, and disability information.
Data Disposal	When a business disposes of, other than by storage, any customer's records that are not required to be retained, the business shall take reasonable steps to destroy, or arrange for the destruction of, that portion of the records containing personally identifiable information by shredding, erasing, or otherwise modifying the personal information in those records to make it unreadable or indecipherable through any means.

LOUISIANA

Data Breach Requirements: La. R.S. § 51:3073 et seq.

The numbering and internal citations herein are derived from the applicable state statute.

	Louisiana (Data Breach Requirements)
Personal Information	The term "personal information" means the first name or first initial and last name of an individual resident of this state in combination with any one or more of the following data elements, when the name or the data element is not encrypted or redacted: (i) Social Security number. (ii) Driver's license number or state identification card number. (iii) Account number, credit or debit card number, in combination with any required security code, access code, or password that would permit access to an individual's financial account. (iv) Passport number. (v) Biometric data, which means data generated by automatic measurements of an individual's biological characteristics, such as fingerprints, voice print, eye retina or iris, or other unique biological characteristic that is used by the owner or licensee to uniquely authenticate an individual's identity when the individual accesses a system or account.
Security Breach Definition	The term "breach of the security of the system" means the compromise of the security, confidentiality, or integrity of computerized data that results in, or has a reasonable likelihood to result in, the unauthorized acquisition of and access to personal information maintained by an agency or person.
Good Faith Exception	Good faith acquisition of personal information by an employee or agent of an agency or person for the purposes of the agency or person is not a breach of the security of the system, provided that the personal information is not used for, or is subject to, unauthorized disclosure.
Risk of Harm Analysis	A breach notification shall not be required if, after a reasonable investigation, the person or business determines that there is no reasonable likelihood of harm to the residents of this state. The person or business shall retain a copy of the written determination and supporting documentation for five years from the date of discovery of the breach of the security system. If requested in writing, the person or business shall send a copy of the written determination and supporting documentation to the attorney general no later than 30 days from the date of receipt of the request. The provisions of R.S. 51:1404(A)(1)(c) shall apply to a written determination and supporting documentation sent to the attorney general pursuant to this law.
Notification Timeline	A breach notification shall be made in the most expedient time possible and without unreasonable delay, but not later than 60 days from the discovery of the breach, consistent with the legitimate needs of law enforcement, or any measures necessary to determine the scope of the breach, prevent further disclosures, and restore the reasonable integrity of the data system.
Security and Investigation Exceptions	If a law enforcement agency determines that the breach notification would impede a criminal investigation, such notification may be delayed until such law enforcement agency determines that the notification will no longer compromise such investigation.
Notification Content Requirements	N/A

	Louisiana (Data Breach Requirements)
Delivery Methods	A breach notice may be provided by one of the following methods: (1) Written notification. (2) Electronic notification, if the notification provided is consistent with the provisions regarding electronic records and signatures set forth in 15 U.S.C. § 7001 (The Electronic Signatures in Global and National Commerce Act). (3) Substitute notification, if an agency or person demonstrates that the cost of providing notification would exceed $100,000, or that the affected class of persons to be notified exceeds 100,000, or the agency or person does not have sufficient contact information.
Substitute Notice	Substitute notification shall consist of all of the following: (a) Email notification when the agency or person has an email address for the subject persons. (b) Conspicuous posting of the notification on the internet site of the agency or person, if an internet site is maintained. (c) Notification to major statewide media.
Notice to Government Agencies	<u>See</u> Louisiana Breach Notice Regulation (16 LA Code ch 7, § 701) A. When notice to Louisiana citizens is required pursuant to R.S. 51:3074, the person or agency shall provide written notice detailing the breach of the security of the system to the Consumer Protection Section of the Attorney General's Office. Notice shall include the names of all Louisiana citizens affected by the breach. B. Failure to provide timely notice may be punishable by a fine not to exceed $5,000 per violation. Notice to the attorney general shall be timely if received within 10 days of distribution of notice to Louisiana citizens. Each day notice is not received by the attorney general shall be deemed a separate violation. C. Written notification shall be mailed to: Louisiana Department of Justice Office of the Attorney General Consumer Protection Section 1885 N. Third Street Baton Rouge, LA 70802
Consumer Reporting Agencies	N/A
Preemption and Compliance	A financial institution that is subject to and in compliance with the Federal Interagency Guidance on Response Programs for Unauthorized Access to Customer Information and Customer Notice shall be deemed to be in compliance with this law.
Data Processor Obligations	Any agency or person that maintains computerized data that includes personal information that the agency or person does not own shall notify the owner or licensee of the information if the personal information was, or is reasonably believed to have been, acquired by an unauthorized person through a breach of security of the system containing such data, following discovery by the agency or person of a breach of security of the system.

	Louisiana (Data Breach Requirements)
Other Information	When a breach notification is delayed because of the security and investigation exceptions, or due to a determination by the person or agency that measures are necessary to determine the scope of the breach, prevent further disclosures, and restore the reasonable integrity of the data system, the person or agency shall provide the attorney general the reasons for the delay in writing within the 60-day notification period provided in this subsection. Upon receipt of the written reasons, the attorney general shall allow a reasonable extension of time to provide the breach notification.

LOUISIANA

Data Disposal and Security: La. R.S. §§ 51:3073 and 51:3074.

The numbering and internal citations herein are derived from the applicable state statute. See statute for any applicable exceptions or exemptions.

	Louisiana (Data Disposal and Security)
Key Terms	The term "personal information" means the first name or first initial and last name of an individual resident of this state in combination with any one or more of the following data elements, when the name or the data element is not encrypted or redacted: (i) Social Security number. (ii) Driver's license number or state identification card number. (iii) Account, credit, or debit card number, in combination with any required security code, access code, or password that would permit access to an individual's financial account. (iv) Passport number. (v) Biometric data, which means data generated by automatic measurements of an individual's biological characteristics, such as fingerprints, voice print, eye retina or iris, or other unique biological characteristic that is used by the owner or licensee to uniquely authenticate an individual's identity when the individual accesses a system or account.
Security Requirements	Any person that conducts business in the state or that owns or licenses computerized data that includes personal information, or any agency that owns or licenses computerized data that includes personal information, shall implement and maintain reasonable security procedures and practices appropriate to the nature of the information to protect the personal information from unauthorized access, destruction, use, modification, or disclosure.
Data Disposal	Any person that conducts business in the state or that owns or licenses computerized data that includes personal information, or any agency that owns or licenses computerized data that includes personal information shall take all reasonable steps to destroy or arrange for the destruction of the records within its custody or control containing personal information that is no longer to be retained by the person or business by shredding, erasing, or otherwise modifying the personal information in the records to make it unreadable or undecipherable through any means.

MAINE

Data Breach Requirements: 10 M.R.S.A § 1346 et seq.

The numbering and internal citations herein are derived from the applicable state statute.

	Maine (Data Breach Requirements)
Personal Information	The term "personal information" means an individual's first name, or first initial, and last name in combination with any one or more of the following data elements, when either the name or the data elements are not encrypted or redacted: A. Social Security number; B. Driver's license number or state identification card number; C. Account number, credit card number, or debit card number, if circumstances exist wherein such a number could be used without additional identifying information, access codes, or passwords; D. Account passwords or personal identification numbers or other access codes; or E. Any of the data elements contained in paragraphs A to D when not in connection with the individual's first name, or first initial, and last name, if the information if compromised would be sufficient to permit a person to fraudulently assume or attempt to assume the identity of the person whose information was compromised.
Security Breach Definition	The term "breach of the security of the system" or "security breach" means unauthorized acquisition, release, or use of an individual's computerized data that includes personal information that compromises the security, confidentiality, or integrity of personal information of the individual maintained by a person.
Good Faith Exception	Good faith acquisition, release, or use of personal information by an employee or agent of a person on behalf of the person is not a breach of the security of the system if the personal information is not used for or subject to further unauthorized disclosure to another person.
Risk of Harm Analysis	See Other Information (a "misuse" standard for non-information brokers).
Notification Timeline	A breach notification must be made as expediently as possible and without unreasonable delay, consistent with the legitimate needs of law enforcement, or with measures necessary to determine the scope of the security breach and restore the reasonable integrity, security, and confidentiality of the data in the system. If there is no delay of notification due to law enforcement investigation, the notices must be made no more than 30 days after the person becomes aware of a breach of security and identifies its scope.
Security and Investigation Exceptions	If, after the completion of an investigation (see Other Information), a breach notification is required, the notification may be delayed for no longer than seven business days after a law enforcement agency determines that the notification will not compromise a criminal investigation.
Notification Content Requirements	See Consumer Reporting Agencies.

	Maine (Data Breach Requirements)
Delivery Methods	A breach notice may be provided by one of the following methods: A. Written notice; B. Electronic notice, if the notice provided is consistent with the provisions regarding electronic records and signatures set forth in 15 U.S.C. § 7001 (The Electronic Signatures in Global and National Commerce Act); or C. Substitute notice, if the person maintaining personal information demonstrates that the cost of providing notice would exceed $5,000, that the affected class of individuals to be notified exceeds 1,000, or that the person maintaining personal information does not have sufficient contact information to provide written or electronic notice to those individuals.
Substitute Notice	Substitute notice must consist of all of the following: (1) Email notice, if the person has email addresses for the individuals to be notified; (2) Conspicuous posting of the notice on the person's publicly accessible website, if the person maintains one; and (3) Notification to major statewide media.
Notice to Government Agencies	When notice of a breach is required by this law, the person shall notify the appropriate state regulators within the Department of Professional and Financial Regulation, or if the person is not regulated by the department, the attorney general.
Consumer Reporting Agencies	If a person discovers a breach of the security of the system that requires notification to more than 1,000 persons at a single time, the person shall also notify, without unreasonable delay, consumer reporting agencies. Notification must include the date of the breach, an estimate of the number of persons affected by the breach, if known, and the actual or anticipated date that persons were or will be notified of the breach.
Preemption and Compliance	A person that complies with the security breach notification requirements of rules, regulations, procedures, or guidelines established pursuant to federal law or the law of this state is deemed to be in compliance with the requirements of section 1348 as long as the law, rules, regulations, or guidelines provide for notification procedures at least as protective as the notification requirements of section 1348.
Data Processor Obligations	A third-party entity that maintains, on behalf of a person, computerized data that includes personal information that the third-party entity does not own, shall notify the person maintaining personal information of a breach of the security of the system immediately following discovery if the personal information was, or is reasonably believed to have been, acquired by an unauthorized person.

	Maine (Data Breach Requirements)
Other Information	An "information broker" means a person who, for monetary fees or dues, engages in whole or in part in the business of collecting, assembling, evaluating, compiling, reporting, transmitting, transferring, or communicating information concerning individuals for the primary purpose of furnishing personal information to nonaffiliated third parties. "Information broker" does not include a governmental agency whose records are maintained primarily for traffic safety, law enforcement, or licensing purposes. - - - If an information broker that maintains computerized data that includes personal information becomes aware of a breach of the security of the system, the information broker shall conduct in good faith a reasonable and prompt investigation to determine the likelihood that personal information has been or will be misused and shall give notice of a breach of the security of the system following discovery or notification of the security breach to a resident of this state whose personal information has been, or is reasonably believed to have been, acquired by an unauthorized person. - - - If any other person who maintains computerized data that includes personal information becomes aware of a breach of the security of the system, the person shall conduct in good faith a reasonable and prompt investigation to determine the likelihood that personal information has been or will be misused and shall give notice of a breach of the security of the system following discovery or notification of the security breach to a resident of this state if misuse of the personal information has occurred or if it is reasonably possible that misuse will occur.

MARYLAND

Data Breach Requirements: Md. Code Ann., Com. Law § 14-3501 et seq.

The numbering and internal citations herein are derived from the applicable state statute.

	Maryland (Data Breach Requirements)
Personal Information	The term "personal information" means: (i) An individual's first name or first initial and last name in combination with any one or more of the following data elements, when the name or the data elements are not encrypted, redacted, or otherwise protected by another method that renders the information unreadable or unusable: 1. A Social Security number, an individual taxpayer identification number, a passport number, or other identification number issued by the federal government; 2. A driver's license number or state identification card number; 3. An account number, a credit card number, or a debit card number, in combination with any required security code, access code, or password, that permits access to an individual's financial account; 4. Health information, including information about an individual's mental health; 5. A health insurance policy or certificate number or health insurance subscriber identification number, in combination with a unique identifier used by an insurer or an employer that is self-insured, that permits access to an individual's health information; or 6. Biometric data of an individual generated by automatic measurements of an individual's biological characteristics such as a fingerprint, voice print, genetic print, retina or iris image, or other unique biological characteristic, that can be used to uniquely authenticate the individual's identity when the individual accesses a system or account; or (ii) A username or email address in combination with a password or security question and answer that permits access to an individual's email account.
Security Breach Definition	The term "breach of the security of a system" means the unauthorized acquisition of computerized data that compromises the security, confidentiality, or integrity of the personal information maintained by a business.
Good Faith Exception	A breach of the security of a system does not include the good faith acquisition of personal information by an employee or agent of a business for the purposes of the business, provided that the personal information is not used or subject to further unauthorized disclosure.
Risk of Harm Analysis	A business that owns, licenses, or maintains computerized data that includes personal information of an individual residing in the state, when it discovers or is notified that it incurred a breach of the security of a system, shall conduct in good faith a reasonable and prompt investigation to determine the likelihood that personal information of the individual has been or will be misused as a result of the breach. Unless the business reasonably determines that the breach of the security of the system does not create a likelihood that personal information has been or will be misused, the owner or licensee of the computerized data shall notify the individual of the breach.
Notification Timeline	The breach notification shall be given as soon as reasonably practicable, but not later than 45 days after the business discovers or is notified of the breach of the security of a system.

	Maryland (Data Breach Requirements)
Security and Investigation Exceptions	The breach notification may be delayed: (i) If a law enforcement agency determines that the notification will impede a criminal investigation or jeopardize homeland or national security; or (ii) To determine the scope of the breach of the security of a system, identify the individuals affected, or restore the integrity of the system. (2) If notification is delayed under paragraph (1)(i) of this subsection, notification shall be given as soon as reasonably practicable, but not later than 30 days after the law enforcement agency determines that it will not impede a criminal investigation and will not jeopardize homeland or national security
Notification Content Requirements	The breach notification shall include: (1) To the extent possible, a description of the categories of information that were, or are reasonably believed to have been, acquired by an unauthorized person, including which of the elements of personal information were, or are reasonably believed to have been, acquired; (2) Contact information for the business making the notification, including the business' address, telephone number, and toll-free telephone number if one is maintained; (3) The toll-free telephone numbers and addresses for the major consumer reporting agencies; and (4)(i) The toll-free telephone numbers, addresses, and website addresses for: the Federal Trade Commission; and the Office of the Attorney General; and (ii) a statement that an individual can obtain information from these sources about steps the individual can take to avoid identity theft.
Delivery Methods	A breach notice shall be provided by one of the following methods: (1) By written notice sent to the most recent address of the individual in the records of the business; (2) By email to the most recent email address of the individual in the records of the business, if: (i) the individual has expressly consented to receive electronic notice; or (ii) the business conducts its business primarily through internet account transactions or the internet; (3) By telephonic notice, to the most recent telephone number of the individual in the records of the business; or (4) By substitute notice if the business does not have sufficient contact information to give notice in accordance with item (1), (2), or (3) of this subsection.
Substitute Notice	Substitute notice shall consist of: (1) Emailing the notice to an individual entitled to notification under subsection (b) of this section, if the business has an email address for the individual to be notified; (2) Conspicuous posting of the notice on the website of the business, if the business maintains a website; and (3) Notification to major print or broadcast media in geographic areas where the individuals affected by the breach likely reside.
Notice to Government Agencies	Prior to giving the breach notification (and subject to subsection to the timeline delay exceptions), a business shall provide notice of a breach of the security of a Prior to giving the breach notification (and subject to subsection to the timeline delay exceptions), a business shall provide notice of a breach of the security of a system to the Office of the Attorney General. The notice required under paragraph (1) of this subsection shall include, at a minimum: (i) the number of affected individuals residing in the state; (ii) a description of the breach of the security of a system, including when and how it occurred; (iii) any steps the business has taken or plans to take relating to the breach of the security of a system; and (iv) the form of notice that will be sent to affected individuals and a sample notice.

	Maryland (Data Breach Requirements)
Consumer Reporting Agencies	If a business is required to give notice of a breach of the security of a system to 1,000 or more individuals, the business also shall notify, without unreasonable delay, each consumer reporting agency that compiles and maintains files on consumers on a nationwide basis of the timing, distribution, and content of the notices. This does not require the inclusion of the names or other personal identifying information of recipients of notices of the breach of the security of a system.
Preemption and Compliance	A business that complies with the requirements for notification procedures, the protection or security of personal information, or the destruction of personal information under the rules, regulations, procedures, or guidelines established by the primary or functional federal or state regulator of the business shall be deemed to be in compliance with this subtitle. - - - A business that is subject to and in compliance with § 501(b) of the federal Gramm-Leach-Bliley Act, § 216 of the federal Fair and Accurate Credit Transactions Act, 15 U.S.C. § 1681w, the federal Interagency Guidelines Establishing Information Security Standards, and the federal Interagency Guidance on Response Programs for Unauthorized Access to Customer Information and Customer Notice, and any revisions, additions, or substitutions, shall be deemed to be in compliance with this subtitle. An affiliate that complies with § 501(b) of the federal Gramm-Leach-Bliley Act, 15 U.S.C. § 6801, § 216 of the federal Fair and Accurate Credit Transactions Act, 15 U.S.C. § 1681w, the federal Interagency Guidelines Establishing Information Security Standards, and the federal Interagency Guidance on Response Programs for Unauthorized Access to Customer Information and Customer Notice, and any revisions, additions, or substitutions, shall be deemed to be in compliance with this subtitle. - - - A business that is subject to and in compliance with the Health Insurance Portability and Accountability Act of 1996 (HIPAA) shall be deemed to be in compliance with this subtitle. An affiliate that is in compliance with HIPAA shall be deemed to be in compliance with this subtitle.
Data Processor Obligations	(c)(1) A business that maintains computerized data that includes personal information of an individual residing in the state that the business does not own or license, when it discovers or is notified of a breach of the security of a system, shall notify, as soon as practicable, the owner or licensee of the personal information of the breach of the security of a system. (2) Except as provided in subsection (d) of this section, the notification required under paragraph (1) of this subsection shall be given as soon as reasonably practicable, but not later than 10 days after the business discovers or is notified of the breach of the security of a system. (3) A business that is required to notify an owner or licensee of personal information of a breach of the security of a system under paragraph (c)(1) of this subsection shall share with the owner or licensee information relative to the breach.

	Maryland (Data Breach Requirements)
Other Information	In the case of a breach of the security of a system involving personal information that permits access to an individual's email account under § 14-3501(e)(1)(ii) of this subtitle and no other personal information under § 14-3501(e)(1)(i) of this subtitle, the business may comply with the breach notification requirement by providing the notification in electronic or other form that directs the individual whose personal information has been breached promptly to: (i) change the individual's password and security question or answer, as applicable; or (ii) take other steps appropriate to protect the email account with the business and all other online accounts for which the individual uses the same username or email and password or security question or answer. Notwithstanding, the breach notification provided here may be given to the individual by any method, except the notification may not be given to the individual by sending notification by email to the email account affected by the breach. The breach notification described here may be given by a clear and conspicuous notice delivered to the individual online while the individual is connected to the affected email account from an internet protocol address or online location from which the business knows the individual customarily accesses the account. - - - (4)(i) If the business that incurred the breach of the security of a system is not the owner or licensee of the computerized data, the business may not charge the owner or licensee of the computerized data a fee for providing information that the owner or licensee needs to make a notification under subsection (b)(2) of this section. (ii) The owner or licensee of the computerized data may not use information relative to the breach of the security of a system for purposes other than: 1. Providing notification of the breach; 2. Protecting or securing personal information; or 3. Providing notification to national information security organizations created for information-sharing and analysis of security threats, to alert and avert new or expanded breaches.

MARYLAND

Data Disposal and Security: Md. Code Ann., Com. Law §§ 14-3501 to 14-3503.

The numbering and internal citations herein are derived from the applicable state statute. See statute for any applicable exceptions or exemptions.

	Maryland (Data Disposal and Security)
Key Terms	The term "personal information" means: (i) An individual's first name or first initial and last name in combination with any one or more of the following data elements, when the data elements are not encrypted, redacted, or otherwise protected by another method that renders the information unreadable or unusable: 1. A Social Security number, an individual taxpayer identification number, a passport number, or other identification number issued by the federal government; 2. A driver's license number or state identification card number; 3. An account, credit, or a debit card number, in combination with any required security code, access code, or password, that permits access to an individual's financial account; 4. Health information, including information about an individual's mental health; 5. A health insurance policy or certificate number or health insurance subscriber identification number, in combination with a unique identifier used by an insurer or an employer that is self-insured, that permits access to an individual's health information; 6. Biometric data of an individual generated by automatic measurements of an individual's biological characteristics such as a fingerprint, voice print, genetic print, retina or iris image, or other unique biological characteristic that can be used to uniquely authenticate the individual's identity when the individual accesses a system or account; or 7. For purposes of the notifications required under section 14-3504(b)(2), (c), (d), (e), (f), and (g) of this subtitle, genetic information with respect to an individual; (ii) A username or email address in combination with a password or security question and answer that permits access to an individual's email account; or (iii) For the purposes of the requirements of this title other than the notifications required under section 14-3504(b)(2), (c), (d), (e), (f), and (g) of this subtitle, genetic information with respect to an individual when the genetic information is not encrypted, redacted, or otherwise protected by another method that renders the information unreadable or unusable.
Security Requirements	To protect personal information from unauthorized access, use, modification, or disclosure, a business that owns, maintains, or licenses personal information of an individual residing in the state shall implement and maintain reasonable security procedures and practices that are appropriate to the nature of the personal information owned, maintained, or licensed and the nature and size of the business and its operations. - - - A business that uses a nonaffiliated third party as a service provider to perform services for the business and discloses personal information about an individual residing in the state under a written contract with the third party shall require by contract that the third party implement and maintain reasonable security procedures and practices that: (i) Are appropriate to the nature of the personal information disclosed to the nonaffiliated third party; and (ii) Are reasonably designed to help protect the personal information from unauthorized access, use, modification, disclosure, or destruction.

	Maryland (Data Disposal and Security)
Data Disposal	When a business is destroying a customer's, an employee's, or a former employee's records that contain personal information of the customer, employee, or former employee, the business shall take reasonable steps to protect against unauthorized access to or use of the personal information, taking into account: (1) The sensitivity of the records; (2) The nature and size of the business and its operations; (3) The costs and benefits of different destruction methods; and (4) Available technology.

MASSACHUSETTS

Data Breach Requirements: M.G.L. c. 93H, § 1 et seq.

The numbering and internal citations herein are derived from the applicable state statute.

	Massachusetts (Data Breach Requirements)
Personal Information	The term "personal information" means a resident's first name and last name or first initial and last name in combination with any one or more of the following data elements that relate to such resident: (a) Social Security number; (b) Driver's license number or state-issued identification card number; or (c) Financial account number, or credit or debit card number, with or without any required security code, access code, personal identification number, or password, that would permit access to a resident's financial account.
Security Breach Definition	The term "breach of security" means the unauthorized acquisition or unauthorized use of unencrypted data or, encrypted electronic data and the confidential process or key that is capable of compromising the security, confidentiality, or integrity of personal information, maintained by a person or agency that creates a substantial risk of identity theft or fraud against a resident of the commonwealth.
Good Faith Exception	A good faith but unauthorized acquisition of personal information by a person or agency, or employee or agent thereof, for the lawful purposes of such person or agency, is not a breach of security unless the personal information is used in an unauthorized manner or subject to further unauthorized disclosure.
Risk of Harm Analysis	See Security Breach Definition (a substantial risk of identity theft of fraud standard).
Notification Timeline	A person or agency shall provide the breach notice as soon as practicable and without unreasonable delay, when such person or agency (1) knows or has reason to know of a breach of security or (2) when the person or agency knows or has reason to know that the personal information of such resident was acquired or used by an unauthorized person or used for an unauthorized purpose.
Security and Investigation Exceptions	A breach notice may be delayed if a law enforcement agency determines that provision of such notice may impede a criminal investigation and has notified the attorney general in writing thereof and informs the person or agency of such determination. If notice is delayed due to such determination and as soon as the law enforcement agency determines and informs the person or agency that notification no longer poses a risk of impeding an investigation, notice shall be provided, as soon as practicable and without unreasonable delay. The person or agency shall cooperate with law enforcement in its investigation of any breach of security or unauthorized acquisition or use, which shall include the sharing of information relevant to the incident, provided, however, that such disclosure shall not require the disclosure of confidential business information or trade secrets. - - - A breach notice shall not be delayed on grounds that the total number of residents affected is not yet ascertained. In such case, and where otherwise necessary to update or correct the information required, a person or agency shall provide additional notice as soon as practicable and without unreasonable delay upon learning such additional information.

	Massachusetts (Data Breach Requirements)
Notification Content Requirements	The notice to be provided to the resident shall include, but shall not be limited to: (i) the resident's right to obtain a police report; (ii) how a resident may request a security freeze and the necessary information to be provided when requesting the security freeze; (iii) that there shall be no charge for a security freeze; and (iv) mitigation services to be provided under the law, provided, however, that said notice shall not include the nature of the breach of security or unauthorized acquisition or use, or the number of residents of the commonwealth affected by said breach of security or unauthorized access or use. - - - If the person or agency that experienced a breach of security is owned by another person or corporation, the notice to the consumer shall include the name of the parent or affiliated corporation.
Delivery Methods	A breach notice may be provided by one of the following methods: (i) Written notice; (ii) Electronic notice, if notice provided is consistent with the provisions regarding electronic records and signatures set forth in 15 U.S.C. § 7001 (The Electronic Signatures in Global and National Commerce Act); or (iii) Substitute notice, if the person or agency required to provide notice demonstrates that the cost of providing written notice will exceed $250,000, or that the affected class of Massachusetts residents to be notified exceeds 500,000 residents, or that the person or agency does not have sufficient contact information to provide notice.
Substitute Notice	Substitute notice shall consist of all of the following: (i) Email notice, if the person or agency has email addresses for the members of the affected class of Massachusetts residents; (ii) Clear and conspicuous posting of the notice on the home page of the person or agency if the person or agency maintains a website; and (iii) Publication in or broadcast through media or medium that provides notice throughout the commonwealth.
Notice to Government Agencies	A person or agency that owns or licenses data that includes personal information about a resident of the commonwealth, shall provide the breach notice to the attorney general, and the director of the Office of Consumer Affairs and Business Regulation. The notice to be provided to the attorney general and said director, and consumer reporting agencies or state agencies if any, shall include, but not be limited to: (i) the nature of the breach of security or unauthorized acquisition or use; (ii) the number of residents of the commonwealth affected by such incident at the time of notification; (iii) the name and address of the person or agency that experienced the breach of security; (iv) name and title of the person or agency reporting the breach of security, and their relationship to the person or agency that experienced the breach of security; (v) the type of person or agency reporting the breach of security; (vi) the person responsible for the breach of security, if known; (vii) the type of personal information compromised, including, but not limited to, Social Security number, driver's license number, financial account number, credit or debit card number, or other data; (viii) whether the person or agency maintains a written information security program; and (ix) any steps the person or agency has taken or plans to take relating to the incident, including updating the written information security program. A person who experienced a breach of security shall file a report with the attorney general and the director of the Office of Consumer Affairs and Business Regulation certifying their credit monitoring services comply with section 3A.

	Massachusetts (Data Breach Requirements)
	(See Other Information). Upon receipt of this notice, the director of consumer affairs and business regulation shall identify any relevant consumer reporting agency or state agency, as deemed appropriate by said director, and forward the names of the identified consumer reporting agencies and state agencies to the notifying person or agency. - - - The person or agency that experienced the breach of security shall provide a sample copy of the notice it sent to consumers to the attorney general and the Office of Consumer Affairs and Business Regulation. - - - As practicable and as not to impede active investigation by the attorney general or other law enforcement agency, the Office of Consumer Affairs and Business Regulation shall: (i) make available electronic copies of the sample notice sent to consumers on its website and post such notice within 1 business day upon receipt from the person that experienced a breach of security; (ii) update the breach of security notification report on its website as soon as practically possible after the information has been verified by said office but not more than 10 business days after receipt unless the information provided is not verifiable; provided, however, that the office shall post said notice as soon as verified; (iii) amend, on a recurring basis, the breach of security notification report to include new information discovered through the investigation process or new subsequent findings from a previously reported breach of security; and (iv) instruct consumers on how they may file a public records request to obtain a copy of the notice provided to the attorney general and said director from the person who experienced a breach of security.
Consumer Reporting Agencies	Such person or agency shall, as soon as practicable and without unreasonable delay, also provide the breach notice to the consumer reporting agencies and state agencies identified by the director of the Office of Consumer Affairs and Business Regulation.
Preemption and Compliance	This law does not relieve a person or agency from the duty to comply with requirements of any applicable general or special law or federal law regarding the protection and privacy of personal information provided, however, a person who maintains procedures for responding to a breach of security pursuant to federal laws, rules, regulations, guidance, or guidelines, is deemed to be in compliance with this chapter. A person is deemed to be in compliance if he or she notifies affected Massachusetts residents in accordance with the maintained or required procedures when a breach occurs and also notifies the attorney general and the director of the Office of Consumer Affairs and Business Regulation of the breach as soon as practicable and without unreasonable delay following the breach. The notice to be provided to the attorney general and the director of the Office of Consumer Affairs and Business Regulation shall consist of, but not be limited to, any steps the person or agency has taken or plans to take relating to the breach pursuant to the applicable federal law, rule, regulation, guidance, or guidelines. If said person or agency does not comply with applicable federal laws, rules, regulations, guidance or guidelines, then he or she shall be subject to the provisions of this chapter.

	Massachusetts (Data Breach Requirements)
Data Processor Obligations	A person or agency that maintains or stores, but does not own or license data that includes personal information about a resident of the commonwealth, shall provide notice, as soon as practicable and without unreasonable delay, when such person or agency (1) knows or has reason to know of a breach of security or (2) when the person or agency knows or has reason to know that the personal information of such resident was acquired or used by an unauthorized person or used for an unauthorized purpose, to the owner or licensor in accordance with this chapter. In addition to providing notice as provided herein, such person or agency shall cooperate with the owner or licensor of such information. Such cooperation shall include, but not be limited to, informing the owner or licensor of the breach of security or unauthorized acquisition or use, the date or approximate date of such incident, and the nature thereof, and any steps the person or agency has taken or plans to take relating to the incident, except that such cooperation shall not be deemed to require the disclosure of confidential business information or trade secrets, or to provide notice to a resident who may have been affected by the breach of security or unauthorized acquisition or use.
Other Information	§ 3A. Breaches of security including Social Security numbers; offer of credit monitoring services required: (a) If a person knows or has reason to know that said person experienced an incident that requires breach notice and such breach of security includes a Social Security number, the person shall contract with a third party to offer to each resident whose Social Security number was disclosed in the breach of security or is reasonably believed to have been disclosed in the breach of security, credit monitoring services at no cost to said resident for a period of not less than 18 months. However, if the person who has experienced a breach of security is a consumer reporting agency, then said agency shall contract with a third party to offer each resident whose Social Security number was disclosed in the breach of security or is reasonably believed to have been disclosed in the breach of security, credit monitoring services at no cost to such resident for a period of not less than 42 months. Said contracts shall not include reciprocal agreements for services in lieu of payment or fees. The person or agency shall provide all information necessary for the resident to enroll in credit monitoring services and shall include information on how the resident may place a security freeze on the resident's consumer credit report. (b) A person that experienced a breach of security shall not require a resident to waive the resident's right to a private right of action as a condition of the offer of credit monitoring services.

MASSACHUSETTS

Data Disposal and Security: M.G.L. ch. 93I, §§ 1-2; ch. 93H, § 2; 201 Mass. Code Regs. 17.01-05.

The numbering and internal citations herein are derived from the applicable state statute. See statute for any applicable exceptions or exemptions.

	Massachusetts (Data Disposal)
Key Terms	The term "personal information" means a resident's first name and last name or first initial and last name in combination with any one or more of the following data elements that relate to the resident: (a) Social Security number; (b) Driver's license number or Massachusetts identification card number; (c) Financial account, credit, or debit card number, with or without any required security code, access code, personal identification number, or password that would permit access to a resident's financial account; or (d) A biometric indicator.
Written policies	See Data Disposal (third party's shall implement and monitor compliance with policies and procedures).
Data Disposal	When disposing of records, each agency or person shall meet the following minimum standards for proper disposal of records containing personal information: (a) Paper documents containing personal information shall be either redacted, burned, pulverized, or shredded so that personal information cannot practicably be read or reconstructed; (b) Electronic media and other non-paper media containing personal information shall be destroyed or erased so that personal information cannot practicably be read or reconstructed. - - - Any agency or person disposing of personal information may contract with a third party to dispose of personal information in accordance with this chapter. Any third party hired to dispose of material containing personal information shall implement and monitor compliance with policies and procedures that prohibit unauthorized access to or acquisition or use of personal information during the collection, transportation, and disposal of personal information.

	Massachusetts (Security Requirements)
Key Terms	The term "personal information" means a Massachusetts resident's first name and last name or first initial and last name in combination with any one or more of the following data elements that relate to such resident: (a) Social Security number; (b) Driver's license number or state-issued identification card number; or (c) Financial account, credit, or debit card number, with or without any required security code, access code, personal identification number, or password, that would permit access to a resident's financial account.

	Massachusetts (Security Requirements)
Security Requirements	Every person that owns or licenses personal information about a resident of the commonwealth shall develop, implement, and maintain a comprehensive information security program that is written in one or more readily accessible parts and contains administrative, technical, and physical safeguards that are appropriate to: (a) The size, scope, and type of business of the person obligated to safeguard the personal information under such comprehensive information security program; (b) The amount of resources available to such person; (c) The amount of stored data; and (d) The need for security and confidentiality of both consumer and employee information. - - - The safeguards contained in such a program must be consistent with the safeguards for protection of personal information and information of a similar character set forth in any state or federal regulations by which the person who owns or licenses such information may be regulated.
Written policies	Every comprehensive information security program shall include: (a) Designating one or more employees to maintain the comprehensive information security program; (b) Identifying and assessing reasonably foreseeable internal and external risks to the security, confidentiality, and/or integrity of any electronic, paper or other records containing personal information, and evaluating and improving, where necessary, the effectiveness of the current safeguards for limiting such risks, including but not limited to: 1. ongoing employee (including temporary and contract employee) training; 2. employee compliance with policies and procedures; and 3. means for detecting and preventing security system failures. (c) Developing security policies for employees relating to the storage, access, and transportation of records containing personal information outside of business premises. (d) Imposing disciplinary measures for violations of the comprehensive information security program rules. (e) Preventing terminated employees from accessing records containing personal information. (f) Oversee service providers, by: 1. Taking reasonable steps to select and retain third-party service providers that are capable of maintaining appropriate security measures to protect such personal information consistent with 201 CMR 17.00 and any applicable federal regulations; and 2. Requiring such third-party service providers by contract to implement and maintain such appropriate security measures for personal information; provided, however, that until March 1, 2012, a contract a person has entered into with a third-party service provider to perform services for said person or functions on said person's behalf satisfies the provisions of 201 CMR 17.03(2)(f)2, even if the contract does not include a requirement that the third-party service provider maintain such appropriate safeguards, as long as said person entered into the contract no later than March 1, 2010. (g) Reasonable restrictions upon physical access to records containing personal information, and storage of such records and data in locked facilities, storage areas or containers. (h) Regular monitoring to ensure that the comprehensive information security program is operating in a manner reasonably calculated to prevent unauthorized access to or unauthorized use of personal information; and upgrading information safeguards as necessary to limit risks.

	Massachusetts (Security Requirements)
	(i) Reviewing the scope of the security measures at least annually or whenever there is a material change in business practices that may reasonably implicate the security or integrity of records containing personal information. (j) Documenting responsive actions taken in connection with any incident involving a breach of security, and mandatory post-incident review of events and actions taken, if any, to make changes in business practices relating to protection of personal information.
Computer System Requirements	Every person that owns or licenses personal information about a resident of the commonwealth and electronically stores or transmits such information shall include in its written, comprehensive information security program the establishment and maintenance of a security system covering its computers, including any wireless system, that, at a minimum, and to the extent technically feasible, shall have the following elements: (1) Secure user authentication protocols including: (a) control of user IDs and other identifiers; (b) a reasonably secure method of assigning and selecting passwords, or use of unique identifier technologies, such as biometrics or token devices; (c) control of data security passwords to ensure that such passwords are kept in a location and/or format that does not compromise the security of the data they protect; (d) restricting access to active users and active user accounts only; and (e) blocking access to user identification after multiple unsuccessful attempts to gain access or the limitation placed on access for the particular system; (2) Secure access control measures that: (a) restrict access to records and files containing personal information to those who need such information to perform their job duties; and (b) assign unique identifications plus passwords, which are not vendor supplied default passwords, to each person with computer access, that are reasonably designed to maintain the integrity of the security of the access controls; (3) Encryption of all transmitted records and files containing personal information that will travel across public networks, and encryption of all data containing personal information to be transmitted wirelessly; (4) Reasonable monitoring of systems for unauthorized use of or access to personal information; (5) Encryption of all personal information stored on laptops or other portable devices; (6) For files containing personal information on a system that is connected to the internet, there must be reasonably up-to-date firewall protection and operating system security patches, reasonably designed to maintain the integrity of the personal information; (7) Reasonably up-to-date versions of system security agent software which must include malware protection and reasonably up-to-date patches and virus definitions, or a version of such software that can still be supported with up-to-date patches and virus definitions, and is set to receive the most current security updates on a regular basis; and (8) Education and training of employees on the proper use of the computer security system and the importance of personal information security.
Other Information	Every person who owns or licenses personal information about a resident of the commonwealth shall be in full compliance with these requirements on or before March 1, 2010.

MICHIGAN

Data Breach Requirements: Mich.C.L.A. § 445.63 and 445.72.

The numbering and internal citations herein are derived from the applicable state statute.

	Michigan (Data Breach Requirements)
Personal Information	The term "personal information" means the first name or first initial and last name linked to 1 or more of the following data elements of a resident of this state: (i) Social Security number. (ii) Driver's license number or state personal identification card number. (iii) Demand deposit or other financial account number, or credit card or debit card number, in combination with any required security code, access code, or password that would permit access to any of the resident's financial accounts.
Security Breach Definition	The term "breach of the security of a database" or "security breach" means the unauthorized access and acquisition of data that compromises the security or confidentiality of personal information maintained by a person or agency as part of a database of personal information regarding multiple individuals.
Good Faith Exception	A "security breach" does not include unauthorized access to data by an employee or other individual if the access meets all of the following: (i) The employee or other individual acted in good faith in accessing the data. (ii) The access was related to the activities of the agency or person. (iii) The employee or other individual did not misuse any personal information or disclose any personal information to an unauthorized person.
Risk of Harm Analysis	A breach notice is not required if a person or agency determines that the security breach has not or is not likely to cause substantial loss or injury to, or result in identity theft with respect to, one or more residents of this state. - - - In determining whether a security breach is not likely to cause substantial loss or injury to, or result in identity theft with respect to, one or more residents of this state, a person or agency shall act with the care an ordinarily prudent person or agency in like position would exercise under similar circumstances.
Notification Timeline	A person or agency shall provide the breach notice without unreasonable delay.
Security and Investigation Exceptions	A person or agency may delay providing a breach notification if either of the following is met: (a) A delay is necessary in order for the person or agency to take any measures necessary to determine the scope of the security breach and restore the reasonable integrity of the database. However, the agency or person shall provide the notice required under this subsection without unreasonable delay after the person or agency completes the measures necessary to determine the scope of the security breach and restore the reasonable integrity of the database. (b) A law enforcement agency determines and advises the agency or person that providing a notice will impede a criminal or civil investigation or jeopardize homeland or national security. However, the agency or person shall provide the notice required under this section without unreasonable delay after the law enforcement agency determines that providing the notice will no longer impede the investigation or jeopardize homeland or national security.

	Michigan (Data Breach Requirements)
Notification Content Requirements	A breach notice shall do all of the following: (a) For a notice provided under subsection (5)(a) or (b) (postal and electronic notice), be written in a clear and conspicuous manner and contain the content required under subdivisions (c) to (g). (b) For a notice provided under subsection (5)(c) (telephone), clearly communicate the content required under subdivisions (c) to (g) to the recipient of the telephone call. (c) Describe the security breach in general terms. (d) Describe the type of personal information that is the subject of the unauthorized access or use. (e) If applicable, generally describe what the agency or person providing the notice has done to protect data from further security breaches. (f) Include a telephone number where a notice recipient may obtain assistance or additional information. (g) Remind notice recipients of the need to remain vigilant for incidents of fraud and identity theft.
Delivery Methods	5) Except as provided in subsection (11) (a public utilities exception), an agency or person shall provide any notice required under this section by providing one or more of the following to the recipient: (a) Written notice sent to the recipient at the recipient's postal address in the records of the agency or person. (b) Written notice sent electronically to the recipient if any of the following are met: (i) The recipient has expressly consented to receive electronic notice. (ii) The person or agency has an existing business relationship with the recipient that includes periodic email communications and, based on those communications, the person or agency reasonably believes that it has the recipient's current email address. (iii) The person or agency conducts its business primarily through internet account transactions or on the internet. (c) If not otherwise prohibited by state or federal law, notice given by telephone by an individual who represents the person or agency if all of the following are met: (i) The notice is not given in whole or in part by use of a recorded message. (ii) The recipient has expressly consented to receive notice by telephone, or if the recipient has not expressly consented to receive notice by telephone, the person or agency also provides notice under subdivision (a) or (b) if the notice by telephone does not result in a live conversation between the individual representing the person or agency and the recipient within three business days after the initial attempt to provide telephonic notice. (d) Substitute notice, if the person or agency demonstrates that the cost of providing notice under subdivision (a), (b), or (c) will exceed $250,000 or that the person or agency has to provide notice to more than 500,000 residents of this state.
Substitute Notice	A person or agency provides substitute notice under this subdivision by doing all of the following: (i) If the person or agency has electronic mail addresses for any of the residents of this state who are entitled to receive the notice, providing electronic notice to those residents. (ii) If the person or agency maintains a website, conspicuously posting the notice on that website. (iii) Notifying major statewide media. A substitute notification shall include a telephone number or a website address that a person may use to obtain additional assistance and information.

	Michigan (Data Breach Requirements)
Notice to Government Agencies	N/A
Consumer Reporting Agencies	Except as provided in this subsection, after a person or agency provides a notice under this section, the person or agency shall notify each consumer reporting agency that compiles and maintains files on consumers on a nationwide basis of the security breach without unreasonable delay. A notification under this subsection shall include the number of notices that the person or agency provided to residents of this state and the timing of those notices. This subsection does not apply if either of the following is met: (a) The person or agency is required under this section to provide notice of a security breach to 1,000 or fewer residents of this state. (b) The person or agency is subject to 15 USC 6801 to 6809 (Gramm-Leach-Bliley Act).
Preemption and Compliance	A financial institution that is subject to, and has notification procedures in place that are subject to examination by the financial institution's appropriate regulator for compliance with, the interagency guidance on response programs for unauthorized access to customer information and customer notice prescribed by the board of governors of the federal reserve system and the other federal bank and thrift regulatory agencies, or similar guidance prescribed and adopted by the national credit union administration, and its affiliates, is considered to be in compliance with this section. - - - A person or agency that is subject to and complies with the Health Insurance Portability and Accountability Act of 1996 (HIPAA) and with regulations promulgated under that act for the prevention of unauthorized access to customer information and customer notice is considered to be in compliance with this section.
Data Processor Obligations	Unless the person or agency determines that the security breach has not or is not likely to cause substantial loss or injury to, or result in identity theft with respect to, one or more residents of this state, a person or agency that maintains a database that includes data that the person or agency does not own or license that discovers a breach of the security of the database shall provide a notice to the owner or licensor of the information of the security breach.
Other Information	A person that provides notice of a security breach when a security breach has not occurred, with the intent to defraud, is guilty of a misdemeanor punishable as follows: (a) Except as otherwise provided under subdivisions (b) and (c), by imprisonment for not more than 93 days or a fine of not more than $250 for each violation, or both. (b) For a second violation, by imprisonment for not more than 93 days or a fine of not more than $500 for each violation, or both. (c) For a third or subsequent violation, by imprisonment for not more than 93 days or a fine of not more than $750 for each violation, or both.

MICHIGAN

Data Disposal and Security: Mich.C.L.A. §§ 445.63 and 445.72a.

The numbering and internal citations herein are derived from the applicable state statute. See statute for any applicable exceptions or exemptions.

	Michigan (Data Disposal and Security)
Key Terms	The term "personal identifying information" means a name, number, or other information that is used for the purpose of identifying a specific person or providing access to a person's financial accounts, including, but not limited to, a person's name, address, telephone number, driver license or state personal identification card number, Social Security number, place of employment, employee identification number, employer or taxpayer identification number, government passport number, health insurance identification number, mother's maiden name, demand deposit account number, savings account number, financial transaction device account number or the person's account password, any other account password in combination with sufficient information to identify and access the account, automated or electronic signature, biometrics, stock or other security certificate or account number, credit card number, vital record, or medical records or information. - - - The term "personal information" means the first name or first initial and last name linked to one or more of the following data elements of a resident of this state: (i) Social Security number. (ii) Driver license number or state personal identification card number. (iii) Demand deposit or other financial account, credit, or debit card number, in combination with any required security code, access code, or password that would permit access to any of the resident's financial accounts. - - - The term "destroy" means to destroy or arrange for the destruction of data by shredding, erasing, or otherwise modifying the data so that they cannot be read, deciphered, or reconstructed through generally available means.
Data Disposal	A person or agency that maintains a database that includes personal information regarding multiple individuals shall destroy any data that contain personal information concerning an individual when that data is removed from the database and the person or agency is not retaining the data elsewhere for another purpose not prohibited by state or federal law.
Other Information	The data disposal requirements shall not prohibit a person or agency from retaining data that contain personal information for purposes of an investigation, audit, or internal review. - - - A person or agency is considered to be in compliance with this section if the person or agency is subject to federal law concerning the disposal of records containing personal identifying information and the person or agency is in compliance with that federal law.

MINNESOTA

Data Breach Requirements: Minn. Stat. § 325E.61.

The numbering and internal citations herein are derived from the applicable state statute.

	Minnesota (Data Breach Requirements)
Personal Information	The term "personal information" means an individual's first name or first initial and last name in combination with any one or more of the following data elements, when the data element is not secured by encryption or another method of technology that makes electronic data unreadable or unusable, or was secured and the encryption key, password, or other means necessary for reading or using the data was also acquired: (1) Social Security number; (2) Driver's license number or Minnesota identification card number; or (3) Account number or credit or debit card number, in combination with any required security code, access code, or password that would permit access to an individual's financial account.
Security Breach Definition	The term "breach of the security of the system" means unauthorized acquisition of computerized data that compromises the security, confidentiality, or integrity of personal information maintained by the person or business.
Good Faith Exception	Good faith acquisition of personal information by an employee or agent of the person or business for the purposes of the person or business is not a breach of the security system, provided that the personal information is not used or subject to further unauthorized disclosure.
Risk of Harm Analysis	N/A
Notification Timeline	The breach notification must be made in the most expedient time possible and without unreasonable delay, consistent with the legitimate needs of law enforcement, or with any measures necessary to determine the scope of the breach, identify the individuals affected, and restore the reasonable integrity of the data system.
Security and Investigation Exceptions	The breach notification may be delayed to a date certain if a law enforcement agency affirmatively determines that the notification will impede a criminal investigation.
Notification Content Requirements	N/A
Delivery Methods	A breach notice may be provided by one of the following methods: (1) written notice to the most recent available address the person or business has in its records; (2) electronic notice, if the person's primary method of communication with the individual is by electronic means, or if the notice provided is consistent with the provisions regarding electronic records and signatures in 15 U.S.C. § 7001 (The Electronic Signatures in Global and National Commerce Act); or (3) substitute notice, if the person or business demonstrates that the cost of providing notice would exceed $250,000, or that the affected class of subject persons to be notified exceeds 500,000, or the person or business does not have sufficient contact information.

	Minnesota (Data Breach Requirements)
Substitute Notice	Substitute notice must consist of all of the following: (i) Email notice when the person or business has an email address for the subject persons; (ii) Conspicuous posting of the notice on the website page of the person or business, if the person or business maintains one; and (iii) Notification to major statewide media.
Notice to Government Agencies	N/A
Consumer Reporting Agencies	If a person discovers circumstances requiring breach notification of more than 500 persons at one time, the person shall also notify, within 48 hours, all consumer reporting agencies of the timing, distribution, and content of the notices.
Preemption and Compliance	This law does not apply to any "financial institution" as defined by United States Code, Title 15, Section 6809(3).
Data Processor Obligations	Any person or business that maintains data that includes personal information that the person or business does not own shall notify the owner or licensee of the information of any breach of the security of the data immediately following discovery, if the personal information was, or is reasonably believed to have been, acquired by an unauthorized person.

MISSISSIPPI

Data Breach Requirements: Miss. Code § 75-24-29 et seq.

The numbering and internal citations herein are derived from the applicable state statute.

	Mississippi (Data Breach Requirements)
Personal Information	The term "personal information" means an individual's first name or first initial and last name in combination with any one or more of the following data elements: (i) Social Security number; (ii) Driver's license number, state identification card number, or tribal identification card number; or (iii) An account number or credit or debit card number in combination with any required security code, access code, or password that would permit access to an individual's financial account.
Security Breach Definition	The term "breach of security" means unauthorized acquisition of electronic files, media, databases, or computerized data containing personal information of any resident of this state when access to the personal information has not been secured by encryption or by any other method or technology that renders the personal information unreadable or unusable.
Good Faith Exception	N/A
Risk of Harm Analysis	A breach notification shall not be required if, after an appropriate investigation, the person reasonably determines that the breach will not likely result in harm to the affected individuals.
Notification Timeline	The breach disclosure shall be made without unreasonable delay, subject to the provisions of subsections (4) (data processor obligations) and (5) (security and investigation exceptions) of this section and the completion of an investigation by the person to determine the nature and scope of the incident, to identify the affected individuals, or to restore the reasonable integrity of the data system.
Security and Investigation Exceptions	A breach notification shall be delayed for a reasonable period of time if a law enforcement agency determines that the notification will impede a criminal investigation or national security and the law enforcement agency has made a request that the notification be delayed. Any such delayed notification shall be made after the law enforcement agency determines that notification will not compromise the criminal investigation or national security and so notifies the person of that determination.
Notification Content Requirements	N/A
Delivery Methods	A breach notice may be provided by one of the following methods: (a) Written notice; (b) Telephone notice; (c) Electronic notice, if the person's primary means of communication with the affected individuals is by electronic means or if the notice is consistent with the provisions regarding electronic records and signatures set forth in 15 U.S.C. § 7001 (The Electronic Signatures in Global and National Commerce Act); or (d) Substitute notice, provided the person demonstrates that the cost of providing notice in accordance with paragraph (a), (b) or (c) of this subsection would exceed $5,000, that the affected class of subject persons to be notified exceeds 5,000 individuals, or the person does not have sufficient contact information.

	Mississippi (Data Breach Requirements)
Substitute Notice	Substitute notice shall consist of the following: email notice when the person has an email address for the affected individuals; conspicuous posting of the notice on the website of the person if the person maintains one; and notification to major statewide media, including newspapers, radio, and television.
Notice to Government Agencies	N/A
Consumer Reporting Agencies	N/A
Preemption and Compliance	Any person that maintains such a security breach procedure pursuant to the rules, regulations, procedures, or guidelines established by the primary or federal functional regulator, as defined in 15 USCS 6809(2), shall be deemed to be in compliance with the security breach notification requirements of this section, provided the person notifies affected individuals in accordance with the policies or the rules, regulations, procedures, or guidelines established by the primary or federal functional regulator in the event of a breach of security of the system.
Data Processor Obligations	Any person who conducts business in this state that maintains computerized data which includes personal information that the person does not own or license shall notify the owner or licensee of the information of any breach of the security of the data as soon as practicable following its discovery, if the personal information was, or is reasonably believed to have been, acquired by an unauthorized person for fraudulent purposes.

MISSOURI

Data Breach Requirements: Mo. Ann. Stat. § 407.1500.

The numbering and internal citations herein are derived from the applicable state statute.

	Missouri (Data Breach Requirements)
Personal Information	The term "personal information" means an individual's first name or first initial and last name in combination with any one or more of the following data elements that relate to the individual if any of the data elements are not encrypted, redacted, or otherwise altered by any method or technology in such a manner that the name or data elements are unreadable or unusable: (a) Social Security number; (b) Driver's license number or other unique identification number created or collected by a government body; (c) Financial account number, credit card number, or debit card number in combination with any required security code, access code, or password that would permit access to an individual's financial account; (d) Unique electronic identifier or routing code, in combination with any required security code, access code, or password that would permit access to an individual's financial account; (e) Medical information; or (f) Health insurance information.
Security Breach Definition	The term "breach of security" or "breach" means the unauthorized access to and unauthorized acquisition of personal information maintained in computerized form by a person that compromises the security, confidentiality, or integrity of the personal information.
Good Faith Exception	Good faith acquisition of personal information by a person or that person's employee or agent for a legitimate purpose of that person is not a breach of security, provided that the personal information is not used in violation of applicable law or in a manner that harms or poses an actual threat to the security, confidentiality, or integrity of the personal information.
Risk of Harm Analysis	A breach notification is not required if, after an appropriate investigation by the person or after consultation with the relevant federal, state, or local agencies responsible for law enforcement, the person determines that a risk of identity theft or other fraud to any consumer is not reasonably likely to occur as a result of the breach. Such a determination shall be documented in writing and the documentation shall be maintained for five years.
Notification Timeline	A breach notification shall be: (a) Made without unreasonable delay; (b) Consistent with the legitimate needs of law enforcement; and (c) Consistent with any measures necessary to determine sufficient contact information and to determine the scope of the breach and restore the reasonable integrity, security, and confidentiality of the data system.
Security and Investigation Exceptions	A breach notice may be delayed if a law enforcement agency informs the person that notification may impede a criminal investigation or jeopardize national or homeland security, provided that such request by law enforcement is made in writing or the person documents such request contemporaneously in writing, including the name of the law enforcement officer making the request and the officer's law enforcement agency engaged in the investigation. The breach notice shall be provided without unreasonable delay after the law enforcement agency communicates to the person its determination that notice will no longer impede the investigation or jeopardize national or homeland security.

	Missouri (Data Breach Requirements)
Notification Content Requirements	A breach notice shall at minimum include a description of the following: (a) The incident in general terms; (b) The type of personal information that was obtained as a result of the breach of security; (c) A telephone number that the affected consumer may call for further information and assistance, if one exists; (d) Contact information for consumer reporting agencies; (e) Advice that directs the affected consumer to remain vigilant by reviewing account statements and monitoring free credit reports.
Delivery Methods	A breach notice may be provided by one of the following methods: (a) Written notice; (b) Electronic notice for those consumers for whom the person has a valid email address and who have agreed to receive communications electronically, if the notice provided is consistent with 15 U.S.C. § 7001 (The Electronic Signatures in Global and National Commerce Act) regarding electronic records and signatures for notices legally required to be in writing; (c) Telephonic notice, if such contact is made directly with the affected consumers; or (d) Substitute notice, if: a. The person demonstrates that the cost of providing notice would exceed $100,000; or b. The class of affected consumers to be notified exceeds 150,000; or c. The person does not have sufficient contact information or consent to satisfy paragraphs (a), (b), or (c) of this subdivision, for only those affected consumers without sufficient contact information or consent; or d. The person is unable to identify particular affected consumers, for only those unidentifiable consumers.
Substitute Notice	(7) Substitute notice shall consist of all the following: (a) Email notice when the person has an electronic mail address for the affected consumer; (b) Conspicuous posting of the notice or a link to the notice on the internet website of the person if the person maintains an internet website; and (c) Notification to major statewide media.
Notice to Government Agencies	In the event a person provides notice to more than 1,000 consumers at one time, the person shall notify, without unreasonable delay, the attorney general's office of the timing, distribution, and content of the notice.
Consumer Reporting Agencies	In the event a person provides notice to more than 1,000 consumers at one time, the person shall notify, without unreasonable delay, all consumer reporting agencies of the timing, distribution, and content of the notice.

	Missouri (Data Breach Requirements)
Preemption and Compliance	A person that is regulated by state or federal law and that maintains procedures for a breach of the security of the system pursuant to the laws, rules, regulations, guidances, or guidelines established by its primary or functional state or federal regulator is deemed to be in compliance with this section if the person notifies affected consumers in accordance with the maintained procedures when a breach occurs. - - - (3) A financial institution that is: (a) Subject to and in compliance with the Federal Interagency Guidance Response Programs for Unauthorized Access to Customer Information and Customer Notice, issued on March 29, 2005, by the board of governors of the Federal Reserve System, the Federal Deposit Insurance Corporation, the Office of the Comptroller of the Currency, and the Office of Thrift Supervision, and any revisions, additions, or substitutions relating to said interagency guidance; or (b) Subject to and in compliance with the National Credit Union Administration regulations in 12 CFR Part 748; or (c) Subject to and in compliance with the provisions of Title V of the Gramm-Leach-Bliley Act; shall be deemed to be in compliance with this section.
Data Processor Obligations	Any person that maintains or possesses records or data containing personal information of residents of Missouri that the person does not own or license, or any person that conducts business in Missouri that maintains or possesses records or data containing personal information of a resident of Missouri that the person does not own or license, shall notify the owner or licensee of the information of any breach of security immediately following discovery of the breach, consistent with the legitimate needs of law enforcement as provided in the law.

MONTANA

Data Breach Requirements: Mont. Code Ann. § 30-14-1702; 1704.

The numbering and internal citations herein are derived from the applicable state statute.

	Montana (Data Breach Requirements)
Personal Information	The term "personal information" means an individual's first name or first initial and last name in combination with any one or more of the following data elements, when either the name or the data elements are not encrypted: (A) Social Security number; (B) Driver's license number, state identification card number, or tribal identification card number; (C) Account number or credit or debit card number, in combination with any required security code, access code, or password that would permit access to an individual's financial account; (D) Medical record information as defined in 33-19-104; (E) Taxpayer identification number; or (F) Identity protection personal identification number issued by the United States Internal Revenue Service.
Security Breach Definition	A "breach of the security of the data system" means unauthorized acquisition of computerized data that materially compromises the security, confidentiality, or integrity of personal information maintained by the person or business and causes or is reasonably believed to cause loss or injury to a Montana resident.
Good Faith Exception	Good faith acquisition of personal information by an employee or agent of the person or business for the purposes of the person or business is not a breach of the security of the data system, provided that the personal information is not used or subject to further unauthorized disclosure.
Risk of Harm Analysis	See Security Breach Definition (loss or injury standard).
Notification Timeline	The breach notification must be made without unreasonable delay, consistent with the legitimate needs of law enforcement, or consistent with any measures necessary to determine the scope of the breach and restore the reasonable integrity of the data system.
Security and Investigation Exceptions	The breach notification may be delayed if a law enforcement agency determines that the notification will impede a criminal investigation and requests a delay in notification. The breach notification must be made after the law enforcement agency determines that it will not compromise the investigation.
Notification Content Requirements	See Other Information.
Delivery Methods	A breach notice may be provided by one of the following methods: (i) Written notice; (ii) Electronic notice, if the notice provided is consistent with the provisions regarding electronic records and signatures set forth in 15 U.S.C. § 7001 (The Electronic Signatures in Global and National Commerce Act); (iii) Telephonic notice; or (iv) Substitute notice, if the person or business demonstrates that: (A) the cost of providing notice would exceed $250,000; (B) the affected class of subject persons to be notified exceeds 500,000; or (C) the person or business does not have sufficient contact information.

	Montana (Data Breach Requirements)
Substitute Notice	Substitute notice must consist of the following: (i) An electronic mail notice when the person or business has an electronic mail address for the subject persons; and (ii) Conspicuous posting of the notice on the website page of the person or business if the person or business maintains one; or (iii) Notification to applicable local or statewide media.
Notice to Government Agencies	Any person or business that is required to issue a breach notification shall simultaneously submit an electronic copy of the notification and a statement providing the date and method of distribution of the notification to the attorney general's Office of Consumer Protection, excluding any information that personally identifies any individual who is entitled to receive notification. If a notification is made to more than one individual, a single copy of the notification must be submitted that indicates the number of individuals in the state who received notification.
Consumer Reporting Agencies	N/A
Preemption and Compliance	No express provision.
Data Processor Obligations	Any person or business that maintains computerized data that includes personal information that the person or business does not own shall notify the owner or licensee of the information of any breach of the security of the data system immediately following discovery if the personal information was or is reasonably believed to have been acquired by an unauthorized person.
Other Information	If a business discloses a security breach to any individual and gives a notice to the individual that suggests, indicates, or implies to the individual that the individual may obtain a copy of the file on the individual from a consumer credit reporting agency, the business shall coordinate with the consumer reporting agency as to the timing, content, and distribution of the notice to the individual. The coordination may not unreasonably delay the notice to the affected individuals.

MONTANA

Data Disposal and Security: Mont. Code Ann. §§ 30-14-1702 and 30-14-1703.

The numbering and internal citations herein are derived from the applicable state statute. See statute for any applicable exceptions or exemptions.

	Montana (Data Disposal and Security)
Key Terms	The term "personal information" means an individual's name, signature, address, or telephone number, in combination with one or more additional pieces of information about the individual, consisting of the individual's passport number, driver's license or state identification number, insurance policy number, bank account number, credit card number, debit card number, passwords or personal identification numbers required to obtain access to the individual's finances, or any other financial information as provided by rule. A Social Security number, in and of itself, constitutes personal information.
Data Disposal	A business shall take all reasonable steps to destroy or arrange for the destruction of a customer's records within its custody or control containing personal information that is no longer necessary to be retained by the business by shredding, erasing, or otherwise modifying the personal information in those records to make it unreadable or undecipherable.

NEBRASKA

Data Breach Requirements: Neb. Rev. Stat. §§ 87-802 and 87-808.

The numbering and internal citations herein are derived from the applicable state statute.

	Nebraska (Data Breach Requirements)
Personal Information	The term "personal information" means either of the following: (a) A Nebraska resident's first name or first initial and last name in combination with any one or more of the following data elements that relate to the resident if either the name or the data elements are not encrypted, redacted, or otherwise altered by any method or technology in such a manner that the name or data elements are unreadable: (i) Social Security number; (ii) Motor vehicle operator's license number or state identification card number; (iii) Account number or credit or debit card number, in combination with any required security code, access code, or password that would permit access to a resident's financial account; (iv) Unique electronic identification number or routing code, in combination with any required security code, access code, or password; or (v) Unique biometric data, such as a fingerprint, voice print, or retina or iris image, or other unique physical representation; or (b) A username or email address, in combination with a password or security question and answer, that would permit access to an online account.
Security Breach Definition	The term "breach of the security of the system" means the unauthorized acquisition of unencrypted computerized data that compromises the security, confidentiality, or integrity of personal information maintained by an individual or a commercial entity.
Good Faith Exception	Good faith acquisition of personal information by an employee or agent of an individual or a commercial entity for the purposes of the individual or the commercial entity is not a breach of the security of the system if the personal information is not used or subject to further unauthorized disclosure.
Risk of Harm Analysis	An individual or a commercial entity that conducts business in Nebraska and that owns or licenses computerized data that includes personal information about a resident of Nebraska shall, when it becomes aware of a breach of the security of the system, conduct in good faith a reasonable and prompt investigation to determine the likelihood that personal information has been or will be used for an unauthorized purpose. If the investigation determines that the use of information about a Nebraska resident for an unauthorized purpose has occurred or is reasonably likely to occur, the individual or commercial entity shall give notice to the affected Nebraska resident.
Notification Timeline	A breach notification shall be made as soon as possible and without unreasonable delay, consistent with the legitimate needs of law enforcement and consistent with any measures necessary to determine the scope of the breach and to restore the reasonable integrity of the computerized data system
Security and Investigation Exceptions	A breach notice may be delayed if a law enforcement agency determines that the notice will impede a criminal investigation. Notice shall be made in good faith, without unreasonable delay, and as soon as possible after the law enforcement agency determines that notification will no longer impede the investigation.
Notification Content Requirements	N/A

	Nebraska (Data Breach Requirements)
Delivery Methods	A breach notice may be provided by one of the following methods: (a) Written notice; (b) Telephonic notice; (c) Electronic notice, if the notice provided is consistent with the provisions regarding electronic records and signatures set forth in 15 U.S.C. § 7001 (The Electronic Signatures in Global and National Commerce Act); (d) Substitute notice, if the individual or commercial entity required to provide notice demonstrates that the cost of providing notice will exceed $75,000, that the affected class of Nebraska residents to be notified exceeds 100,000 residents, or that the individual or commercial entity does not have sufficient contact information to provide notice. Substitute notice under this subdivision requires all of the following: (i) Email notice if the individual or commercial entity has email addresses for the members of the affected class of Nebraska residents; (ii) Conspicuous posting of the notice on the website of the individual or commercial entity if the individual or commercial entity maintains a website; and (iii) Notice to major statewide media outlets; or (e) Substitute notice, if the individual or commercial entity required to provide notice has ten employees or fewer and demonstrates that the cost of providing notice will exceed $10,000. Substitute notice under this subdivision requires all of the following: (i) Email notice if the individual or commercial entity has email addresses for the members of the affected class of Nebraska residents; (ii) Notification by a paid advertisement in a local newspaper that is distributed in the geographic area in which the individual or commercial entity is located, which advertisement shall be of sufficient size that it covers at least one-quarter of a page in the newspaper and shall be published in the newspaper at least once a week for three consecutive weeks; (iii) Conspicuous posting of the notice on the website of the individual or commercial entity if the individual or commercial entity maintains a website; and (iv) Notification to major media outlets in the geographic area in which the individual or commercial entity is located.
Substitute Notice	<u>See</u> Delivery Methods.
Notice to Government Agencies	If a breach notice is required under this law, the individual or commercial entity shall also, not later than the time when notice is provided to the Nebraska resident, provide notice of the breach of security of the system to the attorney general.
Consumer Reporting Agencies	N/A
Preemption and Compliance	An individual or a commercial entity that is regulated by state or federal law and that maintains procedures for a breach of the security of the system pursuant to the laws, rules, regulations, guidances, or guidelines established by its primary or functional state or federal regulator is deemed to be in compliance with Section 87-803 if the individual or commercial entity notifies affected Nebraska residents and the attorney general in accordance with the maintained procedures in the event of a breach of the security of the system.

	Nebraska (Data Breach Requirements)
Data Processor Obligations	An individual or a commercial entity that maintains computerized data that includes personal information that the individual or commercial entity does not own or license shall give notice to and cooperate with the owner or licensee of the information of any breach of the security of the system when it becomes aware of a breach if use of personal information about a Nebraska resident for an unauthorized purpose occurred or is reasonably likely to occur. Cooperation includes, but is not limited to, sharing with the owner or licensee information relevant to the breach, not including information proprietary to the individual or commercial entity.

NEBRASKA

Data Disposal and Security: Neb. Rev. Stat. § 87-808.

The numbering and internal citations herein are derived from the applicable state statute. See statute for any applicable exceptions or exemptions.

	Nebraska (Data Disposal and Security)
Key Terms	The term "personal information" means either of the following: (a) A Nebraska resident's first name or first initial and last name in combination with any one or more of the following data elements that relate to the resident if either the name or the data elements are not encrypted, redacted, or otherwise altered by any method or technology in such a manner that the name or data elements are unreadable: (i) Social Security number; (ii) Motor vehicle operator's license number or state identification card number; (iii) Account, credit, or debit card number, in combination with any required security code, access code, or password that would permit access to a resident's financial account; (iv) Unique electronic identification number or routing code, in combination with any required security code, access code, or password; or (v) Unique biometric data, such as a fingerprint, voice print, or retina or iris image, or other unique physical representation; or (b) A username or email address, in combination with a password or security question and answer, that would permit access to an online account.
Security Requirements	To protect personal information from unauthorized access, acquisition, destruction, use, modification, or disclosure, an individual or a commercial entity that conducts business in Nebraska and owns, licenses, or maintains computerized data that includes personal information about a resident of Nebraska shall implement and maintain reasonable security procedures and practices that are appropriate to the nature and sensitivity of the personal information owned, licensed, or maintained and the nature and size of, and the resources available to, the business and its operations. This includes safeguards that protect the personal information when the individual or commercial entity disposes of the personal information. - - - An individual or commercial entity that discloses computerized data that includes personal information about a Nebraska resident to a nonaffiliated, third-party service provider shall require by contract that the service provider implement and maintain reasonable security procedures and practices that: (i) Are appropriate to the nature of the personal information disclosed to the service provider; and (ii) Are reasonably designed to help protect the personal information from unauthorized access, acquisition, destruction, use, modification, or disclosure. This does not apply to any contract entered into before July 19, 2018. Any such contract renewed on or after July 19, 2018, shall comply with the requirements of this subsection.
Data Disposal	See Security Requirements (safeguards when disposing personal information).

NEVADA

Data Breach Requirements: Nev. R.S. § 603A.010 et seq.

The numbering and internal citations herein are derived from the applicable state statute.

	Nevada (Data Breach Requirements)
Personal Information	The term "personal information" means a natural person's first name or first initial and last name in combination with any one or more of the following data elements, when the name and data elements are not encrypted: (a) Social Security number. (b) Driver's license number, driver authorization card number, or identification card number. (c) Account number, credit card number, or debit card number, in combination with any required security code, access code, or password that would permit access to the person's financial account. (d) A medical identification number or a health insurance identification number. (e) A username, unique identifier, or email address in combination with a password, access code, or security question and answer that would permit access to an online account.
Security Breach Definition	The term "breach of the security of the system data" means unauthorized acquisition of computerized data that materially compromises the security, confidentiality, or integrity of personal information maintained by the data collector.
Good Faith Exception	The term "breach of the security of the system data" does not include the good faith acquisition of personal information by an employee or agent of the data collector for a legitimate purpose of the data collector, so long as the personal information is not used for a purpose unrelated to the data collector or subject to further unauthorized disclosure.
Risk of Harm Analysis	N/A
Notification Timeline	A breach notification must be made in the most expedient time possible and without unreasonable delay, consistent with the legitimate needs of law enforcement or any measures necessary to determine the scope of the breach and restore the reasonable integrity of the system data.
Security and Investigation Exceptions	A breach notification may be delayed if a law enforcement agency determines that the notification will impede a criminal investigation. The breach notification must be made after the law enforcement agency determines that the notification will not compromise the investigation.
Notification Content Requirements	N/A
Delivery Methods	A breach notice may be provided by one of the following methods: (a) Written notification. (b) Electronic notification, if the notification provided is consistent with the provisions in 15 U.S.C. § 7001 (The Electronic Signatures in Global and National Commerce Act). (c) Substitute notification, if the data collector demonstrates that the cost of providing notification would exceed $250,000, the affected class of subject persons to be notified exceeds 500,000, or the data collector does not have sufficient contact information.

	Nevada (Data Breach Requirements)
Substitute Notice	Substitute notification must consist of all the following: (1) Notification by email when the data collector has electronic mail addresses for the subject persons. (2) Conspicuous posting of the notification on the internet website of the data collector, if the data collector maintains an internet website. (3) Notification to major statewide media.
Notice to Government Agencies	N/A
Consumer Reporting Agencies	If a data collector determines that notification is required to be given pursuant to the provisions of this section to more than 1,000 persons at any one time, the data collector shall also notify, without unreasonable delay, any consumer reporting agency that compiles and maintains files on consumers on a nationwide basis, of the time the notification is distributed and the content of the notification.
Preemption and Compliance	A data collector which is subject to and complies with the privacy and security provisions of the Gramm-Leach-Bliley Act shall be deemed to be in compliance with the notification requirements of this section.
Data Processor Obligations	Any data collector that maintains computerized data which includes personal information that the data collector does not own shall notify the owner or licensee of the information of any breach of the security of the system data immediately following discovery if the personal information was, or is reasonably believed to have been, acquired by an unauthorized person.

NEVADA

Data Disposal and Security: Nev. R.S. §§ 603A.040, 603A.100, 603A.200, 603A.210, and 603A.215.

The numbering and internal citations herein are derived from the applicable state statute. See statute for any applicable exceptions or exemptions.

	Nevada (Data Disposal and Security)
Key Terms	The term "personal information" means a natural person's first name or first initial and last name in combination with any one or more of the following data elements, when the name and data elements are not encrypted: (a) Social Security number. (b) Driver's license number, driver authorization card number or identification card number. (c) Account, credit, or debit card number, in combination with any required security code, access code or password that would permit access to the person's financial account. (d) A medical identification number or health insurance identification number. (e) A username, unique identifier or electronic mail address in combination with a password, access code or security question and answer that would permit access to an online account. - - - The term "reasonable measures to ensure the destruction" means any method that modifies the records containing the personal information in such a way as to render the personal information contained in the records unreadable or undecipherable, including, without limitation: (1) Shredding of the record containing the personal information; or (2) Erasing of the personal information from the records.
Security Requirements	A data collector that maintains records which contain personal information of a resident of this state shall implement and maintain reasonable security measures to protect those records from unauthorized access, acquisition, destruction, use, modification, or disclosure. - - - A contract for the disclosure of the personal information of a Nevada resident which is maintained by a data collector must include a provision requiring the person to whom the information is disclosed to implement and maintain reasonable security measures to protect those records from unauthorized access, acquisition, destruction, use, modification, or disclosure.
Data Disposal	A business that maintains records that contain personal information concerning the customers of the business shall take reasonable measures to ensure the destruction of those records when the business decides that it will no longer maintain the records.

	Nevada (Data Disposal and Security)
Other Information	1. If a data collector doing business in Nevada accepts a payment card in connection with a sale of goods or services, the data collector shall comply with the current version of the Payment Card Industry (PCI) Data Security Standard, as adopted by the PCI Security Standards Council or its successor organization, with respect to those transactions, not later than the date for compliance set forth in the PCI Data Security Standard or by the PCI Security Standards Council or its successor organization. - - - 2. A data collector doing business in Nevada to whom subsection 1 does not apply shall not: (a) Transfer any personal information through an electronic, nonvoice transmission other than a facsimile to a person outside of the secure system of the data collector unless the data collector uses encryption to ensure the security of electronic transmission; or (b) Move any data storage device containing personal information beyond the logical or physical controls of the data collector, its data storage contractor or, if the data storage device is used by or is a component of a multifunctional device, a person who assumes the obligation of the data collector to protect personal information, unless the data collector uses encryption to ensure the security of the information.

NEW HAMPSHIRE

Data Breach Requirements: N.H. RSA § 359-C:19 et seq.

The numbering and internal citations herein are derived from the applicable state statute.

	New Hampshire (Data Breach Requirements)
Personal Information	The term "personal information" means an individual's first name or initial and last name in combination with any one or more of the following data elements, when either the name or the data elements are not encrypted: (1) Social Security number. (2) Driver's license number or other government identification number. (3) Account number, credit card number, or debit card number, in combination with any required security code, access code, or password that would permit access to an individual's financial account.
Security Breach Definition	The term "security breach" unauthorized acquisition of computerized data that compromises the security or confidentiality of personal information maintained by a person doing business in this state.
Good Faith Exception	Good faith acquisition of personal information by an employee or agent of a person for the purposes of the person's business shall not be considered a security breach, provided that the personal information is not used or subject to further unauthorized disclosure.
Risk of Harm Analysis	Any person doing business in this state who owns or licenses computerized data that includes personal information shall, when it becomes aware of a security breach, promptly determine the likelihood that the information has been or will be misused. If the determination is that misuse of the information has occurred or is reasonably likely to occur, or if a determination cannot be made, the person shall notify the affected individuals.
Notification Timeline	A breach notification shall be made as soon as possible or as quickly as possible.
Security and Investigation Exceptions	A breach notification may be delayed if a law enforcement agency or national or homeland security agency determines that the notification will impede a criminal investigation or jeopardize national or homeland security.
Notification Content Requirements	A breach notice shall include at a minimum: (a) A description of the incident in general terms. (b) The approximate date of breach. (c) The type of personal information obtained as a result of the security breach. (d) The telephonic contact information of the person subject to this section.
Delivery Methods	A breach notice may be provided by one of the following methods: (a) Written notice. (b) Electronic notice, if the agency or business' primary means of communication with affected individuals is by electronic means. (c) Telephonic notice, provided that a log of each such notification is kept by the person or business who notifies affected persons. (d) Substitute notice, if the person demonstrates that the cost of providing notice would exceed $5,000, that the affected class of subject individuals to be notified exceeds 1,000, or the person does not have sufficient contact information or consent to provide notice pursuant to subparagraphs I(a)-I(c). (e) Notice pursuant to the person's internal notification procedures maintained as part of an information security policy for the treatment of personal information.

	New Hampshire (Data Breach Requirements)
Substitute Notice	Substitute notice shall consist of all of the following: (1) Email notice when the person has an email address for the affected individuals. (2) Conspicuous posting of the notice on the person's business website, if the person maintains one. (3) Notification to major statewide media.
Notice to Government Agencies	Any person engaged in trade or commerce that is subject to RSA 358-A:3, Section I, shall also notify the regulator that has primary regulatory authority over such trade or commerce. All other persons shall notify the New Hampshire attorney general's office. The notice shall include the anticipated date of the notice to the individuals and the approximate number of individuals in this state who will be notified. The person is not required to provide to any regulator or the New Hampshire attorney general's office the names of the individuals entitled to receive the notice or any personal information relating to them.
Consumer Reporting Agencies	If a person is required to notify more than 1,000 consumers of a breach, the person shall also notify, without unreasonable delay, all consumer reporting agencies of the anticipated date of the notification to the consumers, the approximate number of consumers who will be notified, and the content of the notice. Nothing in this paragraph shall be construed to require the person to provide to any consumer reporting agency the names of the consumers entitled to receive the notice or any personal information relating to them. This requirement does not apply to a person who is subject to Title V of the Gramm-Leach-Bliley Act.
Preemption and Compliance	Any person engaged in trade or commerce that is subject to RSA 358-A:3 and who maintains procedures for security breach notification pursuant to the laws, rules, regulations, guidances, or guidelines issued by a state or federal regulator shall be deemed to be in compliance with this subdivision if he or she acts in accordance with such laws, rules, regulations, guidances, or guidelines.
Data Processor Obligations	Any person or business that maintains computerized data that includes personal information that the person or business does not own shall notify and cooperate with the owner or licensee of the information of any breach of the security of the data immediately following discovery if the personal information was acquired by an unauthorized person. Cooperation includes sharing with the owner or licensee information relevant to the breach, except that such cooperation shall not be deemed to require the disclosure of confidential or business information or trade secrets.

NEW JERSEY

<u>Data Breach Requirements</u>: N.J.S.A. §§ 56:8-161, 56:8-163, and 56:8-165.

The numbering and internal citations herein are derived from the applicable state statute.

	New Jersey (Data Breach Requirements)
Personal Information	The term "personal information" means an individual's first name or first initial and last name linked with any one or more of the following data elements: (1) Social Security number; (2) Driver's license number or state identification card number; (3) Account number or credit or debit card number, in combination with any required security code, access code, or password that would permit access to an individual's financial account; or (4) Username, email address, or any other account holder identifying information, in combination with any password or security question and answer that would permit access to an online account. Dissociated data that, if linked, would constitute personal information is personal information if the means to link the dissociated data were accessed in connection with access to the dissociated data.
Security Breach Definition	The term "breach of security" means unauthorized access to electronic files, media, or data containing personal information that compromises the security, confidentiality, or integrity of personal information when access to the personal information has not been secured by encryption or by any other method or technology that renders the personal information unreadable or unusable.
Good Faith Exception	Good faith acquisition of personal information by an employee or agent of the business for a legitimate business purpose is not a breach of security, provided that the personal information is not used for a purpose unrelated to the business or subject to further unauthorized disclosure.
Risk of Harm Analysis	A breach notification shall not be required if the business or public entity establishes that misuse of the information is not reasonably possible. Any determination shall be documented in writing and retained for five (5) years.
Notification Timeline	A breach notification shall be made in the most expedient time possible and without unreasonable delay, consistent with the legitimate needs of law enforcement, or any measures necessary to determine the scope of the breach and restore the reasonable integrity of the data system.
Security and Investigation Exceptions	A breach notification shall be delayed if a law enforcement agency determines that the notification will impede a criminal or civil investigation and that agency has made a request that the notification be delayed. The breach notification shall be made after the law enforcement agency determines that its disclosure will not compromise the investigation and notifies that business or public entity.
Notification Content Requirements	<u>See</u> Other Information.

	New Jersey (Data Breach Requirements)
Delivery Methods	A breach notice may be provided by one of the following methods: (1) Written notice; (2) Electronic notice, if the notice provided is consistent with the provisions regarding electronic records and signatures set forth in 15 U.S.C. § 7001 (The Electronic Signatures in Global and National Commerce Act); or (3) Substitute notice, if the business or public entity demonstrates that the cost of providing notice would exceed $250,000, or that the affected class of subject persons to be notified exceeds 500,000, or the business or public entity does not have sufficient contact information.
Substitute Notice	Substitute notice shall consist of all of the following: (a) Email notice when the business or public entity has an email address; (b) Conspicuous posting of the notice on the internet website page of the business or public entity, if the business or public entity maintains one; and (c) Notification to major statewide media.
Notice to Government Agencies	Any business or public entity required to disclose a breach of security of a customer's personal information shall, in advance of the disclosure to the customer, report the breach of security and any information pertaining to the breach to the Division of State Police in the Department of Law and Public Safety for investigation or handling, which may include dissemination or referral to other appropriate law enforcement entities.
Consumer Reporting Agencies	In addition to any other breach notification required under the law, in the event that a business or public entity discovers circumstances requiring notification of more than 1,000 persons at one time, the business or public entity shall also notify, without unreasonable delay, all consumer reporting agencies that compile or maintain files on consumers on a nationwide basis of the timing, distribution, and content of the notices.
Preemption and Compliance	No express provision.
Data Processor Obligations	Any business or public entity that compiles or maintains computerized records that include personal information on behalf of another business or public entity shall notify that business or public entity, who shall notify its New Jersey customers of any breach of security of the computerized records immediately following discovery, if the personal information was, or is reasonably believed to have been, accessed by an unauthorized person.
Other Information	Notwithstanding subsection d (substitute notice), in the case of a breach of security involving a username or password, in combination with any password or security question and answer that would permit access to an online account, and no other personal information as defined in Section 10 of P.L.2005, c. 226 (C.56:8-161), the business or public entity may provide the notification in electronic or other form that directs the customer whose personal information has been breached to promptly change any password and security question or answer, as applicable, or to take other appropriate steps to protect the online account with the business or public entity and all other online accounts for which the customer uses the same username or email address and password or security question or answer. Any business or public entity that furnishes an email account shall not provide notification to the email account that is subject to a security breach. The business or public entity shall provide notice by another method or by clear and conspicuous notice delivered to the customer online when the customer is connected to the online account from an internet protocol address or online location from which the business or public entity knows the customer customarily accesses the account.

NEW JERSEY

Data Disposal and Security: N.J.S.A. § 56:8-161 and 56:8-162.

The numbering and internal citations herein are derived from the applicable state statute. See statute for any applicable exceptions or exemptions.

	New Jersey (Data Disposal and Security)
Key Terms	The term "personal information" means an individual's first name or first initial and last name linked with any one or more of the following data elements: (1) Social Security number; (2) Driver's license number or State identification card number; (3) Account, credit, or debit card number, in combination with any required security code, access code, or password that would permit access to an individual's financial account; or (4) Username, email address, or any other account holder identifying information, in combination with any password or security question and answer that would permit access to an online account. Dissociated data that, if linked, would constitute personal information is personal information if the means to link the dissociated data were accessed in connection with access to the dissociated data.
Data Disposal	A business or public entity shall destroy, or arrange for the destruction of, a customer's records within its custody or control containing personal information, which is no longer to be retained by the business or public entity, by shredding, erasing, or otherwise modifying the personal information in those records to make it unreadable, undecipherable, or nonreconstructable through generally available means.

NEW MEXICO

Data Breach Requirements: NMSA 1978, § 57-12C-1 et seq.

The numbering and internal citations herein are derived from the applicable state statute.

	New Mexico (Data Breach Requirements)
Personal Information	The term "personal identifying information" means an individual's first name or first initial and last name in combination with one or more of the following data elements that relate to the individual, when the data elements are not protected through encryption or redaction or otherwise rendered unreadable or unusable: (a) Social Security number; (b) Driver's license number; (c) Government-issued identification number; (d) Account number, credit card number, or debit card number in combination with any required security code, access code, or password that would permit access to a person's financial account; or (e) Biometric data.
Security Breach Definition	The term "security breach" means the unauthorized acquisition of unencrypted computerized data, or of encrypted computerized data and the confidential process or key used to decrypt the encrypted computerized data, that compromises the security, confidentiality, or integrity of personal identifying information maintained by a person.
Good Faith Exception	A security breach does not include the good-faith acquisition of personal identifying information by an employee or agent of a person for a legitimate business purpose of the person, provided that the personal identifying information is not subject to further unauthorized disclosure.
Risk of Harm Analysis	A breach notification to affected New Mexico residents is not required if, after an appropriate investigation, the person determines that the security breach does not give rise to a significant risk of identity theft or fraud.
Notification Timeline	A breach notification shall be made in the most expedient time possible, but not later than 45 calendar days following discovery of the security breach.
Security and Investigation Exceptions	The breach notification may be delayed: A. if a law enforcement agency determines that the notification will impede a criminal investigation; or B. as necessary to determine the scope of the security breach and restore the integrity, security, and confidentiality of the data system.
Notification Content Requirements	The breach notification shall contain: A. The name and contact information of the notifying person; B. A list of the types of personal identifying information that are reasonably believed to have been the subject of a security breach, if known; C. The date of the security breach, the estimated date of the breach, or the range of dates within which the security breach occurred, if known; D. A general description of the security breach incident; E. The toll-free telephone numbers and addresses of the major consumer reporting agencies; F. Advice that directs the recipient to review personal account statements and credit reports, as applicable, to detect errors resulting from the security breach; and G. Advice that informs the recipient of the notification of the recipient's rights pursuant to the federal Fair Credit Reporting Act.

	New Mexico (Data Breach Requirements)
Delivery Methods	A breach notice may be provided by one of the following methods: (1) United States mail; (2) Electronic notification, if the person required to make the notification primarily communicates with the New Mexico resident by electronic means or if the notice provided is consistent with the requirements of 15 U.S.C. § 7001 (The Electronic Signatures in Global and National Commerce Act); or (3) A substitute notification, if the person demonstrates that: (a) the cost of providing notification would exceed $100,000; (b) the number of residents to be notified exceeds 50,000; or (c) the person does not have on record a physical address or sufficient contact information for the residents that the person or business is required to notify.
Substitute Notice	Substitute notification shall consist of: (1) Sending electronic notification to the email address of those residents for whom the person has a valid email address; (2) Posting notification of the security breach in a conspicuous location on the website of the person required to provide notification if the person maintains a website; and (3) Sending written notification to the office of the attorney general and major media outlets in New Mexico.
Notice to Government Agencies	A person who is required to issue a breach notification to more than 1,000 New Mexico residents as a result of a single security breach shall notify the Office of the Attorney General in the most expedient time possible, and no later than 45 calendar days, subject to the security and investigation exceptions.
Consumer Reporting Agencies	A person that is required to issue a breach notification to more than 1,000 New Mexico residents as a result of a single security breach shall notify the office of the major consumer reporting agencies in the most expedient time possible, and no later than 45 calendar days, subject to the security and investigation exceptions.
Preemption and Compliance	The breach notification requirements shall not apply to a person subject to the federal Gramm-Leach-Bliley Act or the Health Insurance Portability and Accountability Act of 1996 (HIPAA).
Data Processor Obligations	Any person that is licensed to maintain or possess computerized data containing personal identifying information of a New Mexico resident that the person does not own or license shall notify the owner or licensee of the information of any security breach in the most expedient time possible, but not later than 45 calendar days following discovery of the breach, except as provided in Section 9 of the Data Breach Notification Act, provided that notification to the owner or licensee of the information is not required if, after an appropriate investigation, the person determines that the security breach does not give rise to a significant risk of identity theft or fraud.
Other Information	A person required to notify the attorney general and consumer reporting agencies of a security breach shall notify the attorney general of the number of New Mexico residents that received a breach notification and shall provide a copy of the notification that was sent to affected residents within 45 calendar days following discovery of the security breach, subject to the security and investigation exceptions.

NEW MEXICO

Data Disposal and Security: NMSA 1978, §§ 57-12c-2 - 57-12c-5.

The numbering and internal citations herein are derived from the applicable state statute. See statute for any applicable exceptions or exemptions.

	New Mexico (Data Disposal and Security)
Key Terms	The term "personal identifying information" means an individual's first name or first initial and last name in combination with one or more of the following data elements that relate to the individual, when the data elements are not protected through encryption or redaction or otherwise rendered unreadable or unusable: (a) Social Security number; (b) Driver's license number; (c) Government-issued identification number; (d) Account, credit, or debit card number in combination with any required security code, access code, or password that would permit access to a person's financial account; or (e) Biometric data. - - - The term "proper disposal" means shredding, erasing, or otherwise modifying the personal identifying information contained in the records to make the personal identifying information unreadable or undecipherable. - - - The term "service provider" means any person that receives, stores, maintains, licenses, processes, or otherwise is permitted access to personal identifying information through its provision of services directly to a person that is subject to regulation.
Security Requirements	A person that owns or licenses personal identifying information of a New Mexico resident shall implement and maintain reasonable security procedures and practices appropriate to the nature of the information to protect the personal identifying information from unauthorized access, destruction, use, modification, or disclosure. - - - A person that discloses personal identifying information of a New Mexico resident pursuant to a contract with a service provider shall require by contract that the service provider implement and maintain reasonable security procedures and practices appropriate to the nature of the personal identifying information and to protect it from unauthorized access, destruction, use, modification or disclosure.
Data Disposal	A person that owns or licenses records containing personal identifying information of a New Mexico resident shall arrange for proper disposal of the records when they are no longer reasonably needed for business purposes.

NEW YORK

Data Breach Requirements: NY Gen. Bus. § 899-aa.

The numbering and internal citations herein are derived from the applicable state statute.

	New York (Data Breach Requirements)
Personal Information	(a) The term "personal information" shall mean any information concerning a natural person which, because of name, number, personal mark, or other identifier, can be used to identify such natural person. - - - (b) The term "private information" shall mean either: (i) personal information consisting of any information in combination with any one or more of the following data elements, when either the data element or the combination of personal information plus the data element is not encrypted, or is encrypted with an encryption key that has also been accessed or acquired: (1) Social Security number; (2) Driver's license number or non-driver identification card number; (3) Account number, credit, or debit card number, in combination with any required security code, access code, password, or other information that would permit access to an individual's financial account; (4) Account number, credit, or debit card number, if circumstances exist wherein such number could be used to access an individual's financial account without additional identifying information, security code, access code, or password; or (5) Biometric information, meaning data generated by electronic measurements of an individual's unique physical characteristics, such as a fingerprint, voice print, retina or iris image, or other unique physical representation or digital representation of biometric data that are used to authenticate or ascertain the individual's identity; or (ii) a Username or email address in combination with a password or security question and answer that would permit access to an online account.
Security Breach Definition	The term "breach of the security of the system" means unauthorized access to or acquisition of, or access to or acquisition without valid authorization, of computerized data that compromises the security, confidentiality, or integrity of private information maintained by a business.
Good Faith Exception	Good faith access to, or acquisition of, private information by an employee or agent of the business for the purposes of the business is not a breach of the security of the system, provided that the private information is not used or subject to unauthorized disclosure.
Risk of Harm Analysis	A breach notice to affected persons under this section is not required if the exposure of private information was an inadvertent disclosure by persons authorized to access private information, and the person or business reasonably determines such exposure will not likely result in misuse of such information, or financial harm to the affected persons or emotional harm in the case of unknown disclosure of online credentials. Such a determination must be documented in writing and maintained for at least five years. If the incident affects more than 500 residents of New York, the person or business shall provide the written determination to the state attorney general within ten days after the determination.
Notification Timeline	A breach notification shall be made in the most expedient time possible and without unreasonable delay, consistent with the legitimate needs of law enforcement or any measures necessary to determine the scope of the breach and restore the integrity of the system.

	New York (Data Breach Requirements)
Security and Investigation Exceptions	The breach notification may be delayed if a law enforcement agency determines that such notification impedes a criminal investigation. The notification shall be made after such law enforcement agency determines that such notification does not compromise such investigation.
Notification Content Requirements	Regardless of the method by which notice is provided, such notice shall include contact information for the person or business making the notification, the telephone numbers and websites of the relevant state and federal agencies that provide information regarding security breach response and identity theft prevention and protection information, and a description of the categories of information that were, or are reasonably believed to have been, accessed or acquired by a person without valid authorization, including specification of which of the elements of personal information and private information were, or are reasonably believed to have been, so accessed or acquired.
Delivery Methods	A breach notice may be provided by one of the following methods: (a) Written notice; (b) Electronic notice, provided that the person to whom notice is required has expressly consented to receiving said notice in electronic form and a log of each such notification is kept by the person or business who notifies affected persons in such form. In no case, however, shall any person or business require a person to consent to accepting said notice in said form as a condition of establishing any business relationship or engaging in any transaction; (c) Telephone notification, provided that a log of each such notification is kept by the person or business who notifies affected persons; or (d) Substitute notice, if a business demonstrates to the state attorney general that the cost of providing notice would exceed $250,000, or that the affected class of subject persons to be notified exceeds 500,000, or that such business does not have sufficient contact information.
Substitute Notice	Substitute notice shall consist of all of the following: (1) Email notice when such business has an email address for the subject persons, except if the breached information includes an email address in combination with a password or security question and answer that would permit access to the online account, in which case the person or business shall instead provide clear and conspicuous notice delivered to the consumer online when the consumer is connected to the online account from an internet protocol address or from an online location that the person or business knows the consumer customarily uses to access the online account; (2) Conspicuous posting of the notice on such business's website page, if such business maintains one; and (3) Notification to major statewide media.

	New York (Data Breach Requirements)
Notice to Government Agencies	In the event that any New York residents are to be notified, the person or business shall notify the New York Attorney General, the Department of State, and the Division of State Police as to the timing, content, and distribution of the notices and approximate number of affected persons. They shall also provide a copy of the template of the notice sent to affected persons. Such notice shall be made without delaying notice to affected New York residents. - - - Any covered entity required to provide notification of a breach, including breach of information that is not "private information" to the secretary of Health and Human Services, pursuant to the Health Insurance Portability and Accountability Act of 1996 (HIPAA) or the Health Information Technology for Economic and Clinical Health Act (HITECH), as amended from time to time, shall provide such notification to the state attorney general within five business days of notifying the secretary.
Consumer Reporting Agencies	In the event that more than 5,000 New York residents are to be notified at one time, the person or business shall also notify consumer reporting agencies as to the timing, content, and distribution of the notices and approximate number of affected persons. Such notice shall be made without delaying notice to affected New York residents.
Preemption and Compliance	If the breach notice is made to affected persons pursuant to the breach notification requirements under any of the following laws, nothing shall require any additional notice to those affected persons, but notice still shall be provided to the New York Attorney General, the Department of State, and the relevant division of New York State Police and to consumer reporting agencies: (i) Regulations promulgated pursuant to Title V of the Gramm-Leach-Bliley Act; (ii) Regulations implementing HIPAA and HITECH; (iii) Part 500 of Title 23 of the official Compilation of Rules and Regulations of the State of New York, as amended from time to time; or (iv) Any other data security rules and regulations of, and the statutes administered by, any official department, division, commission, or agency of the federal or New York state government as such rules, regulations, or statutes are interpreted by such department, division, commission, or agency or by the federal or New York state courts.
Data Processor Obligations	Any person or business that maintains computerized data that includes private information that such person or business does not own shall notify the owner or licensee of the information of any breach of the security of the system immediately following discovery, if the private information was, or is reasonably believed to have been, accessed, or acquired by a person without valid authorization.
Other Information	In determining whether information has been accessed, or is reasonably believed to have been accessed, by an unauthorized person or a person without valid authorization, such business may consider, among other factors, indications that the information was viewed, communicated with, used, or altered by a person without valid authorization or by an unauthorized person. In determining whether information has been acquired, or is reasonably believed to have been acquired, by an unauthorized person or a person without valid authorization, such business may consider the following factors, among others: (1) indications that the information is in the physical possession and control of an unauthorized person, such as a lost or stolen computer or other device containing information; or (2) indications that the information has been downloaded or copied; or (3) indications that the information was used by an unauthorized person, such as fraudulent accounts opened or instances of identity theft reported.

NEW YORK

Data Disposal and Security: NY Gen. Bus. §§ 399-h, 899-aa(1)(b), and § 899-bb.

The numbering and internal citations herein are derived from the applicable state statute. See statute for any applicable exceptions or exemptions.

	New York (Data Disposal)
Key Terms	The term "dispose" means to throw out or away or to get rid of and shall not include a sale of a record or the transfer of a record for value. - - - The term "personal information" means any information concerning a natural person which, because of name, number, personal mark, or other identifier, can be used to identify such natural person. - - - The term "personal identifying information" means personal information consisting of any information in combination with any one or more of the following data elements, when either the personal information or the data element is not encrypted, or encrypted with an encryption key that is included in the same record as the encrypted personal information or data element: (i) Social Security number; (ii) Driver's license number or non-driver identification card number; or (iii) Mother's maiden name, financial services account number or code, savings account number or code, checking account number or code, debit card number or code, automated teller machine number or code, electronic serial number, or personal identification number; - - - The term "personal identification number" means any number or code that may be used alone or in conjunction with any other information to assume the identity of another person or access financial resources or credit of another person.
Data Disposal	No person, business, firm, partnership, association, or corporation, not including the state or its political subdivisions, shall dispose of a record containing personal identifying information unless the person, business, firm, partnership, association, or corporation, or other person under contract with the business, firm, partnership, association, or corporation does any of the following: a. Shreds the record before the disposal of the record; b. Destroys the personal identifying information contained in the record; c. Modifies the record to make the personal identifying information unreadable; or d. Takes actions consistent with commonly accepted industry practices that it reasonably believes will ensure that no unauthorized person will have access to the personal identifying information contained in the record.
Other Information	An individual person shall not be required to comply with this subdivision unless he or she is conducting business for profit.

	New York (Security Requirements)
Key Terms	The term "personal information" means any information concerning a natural person which, because of name, number, personal mark, or other identifier, can be used to identify such natural person. - - - The term "private information" means either: (i) personal information consisting of any information in combination with any one or more of the following data elements, when either the data element or the combination of personal information plus the data element is not encrypted, or is encrypted with an encryption key that has also been accessed or acquired: (1) Social Security number; (2) Driver's license number or non-driver identification card number; (3) Account, credit, or debit card number, in combination with any required security code, access code, password, or other information that would permit access to an individual's financial account; (4) Account, credit, or debit card number, if circumstances exist wherein such number could be used to access an individual's financial account without additional identifying information, security code, access code, or password; or (5) Biometric information, meaning data generated by electronic measurements of an individual's unique physical characteristics, such as a fingerprint, voice print, retina or iris image, or other unique physical representation, or digital representation of biometric data that are used to authenticate or ascertain the individual's identity; or (ii) Username or email address in combination with a password or security question and answer that would permit access to an online account. - - - The term "compliant regulated entity" shall mean any person or business that is subject to, and in compliance with, any of the following data security requirements: (i) Regulations promulgated pursuant to Title V of the federal Gramm-Leach-Bliley Act; (ii) Regulations implementing the Health Insurance Portability and Accountability Act of 1996, and the Health Information Technology for Economic and Clinical Health Act (HITECH), as amended from time to time; (iii) Part 500 of title 23 of the official compilation of codes, rules and regulations of the state of New York, as amended from time to time; or (iv) Any other data security rules and regulations of, and the statutes administered by, any official department, division, commission or agency of the federal or New York state government as such rules, regulations, or statutes are interpreted by such department, division, commission, or agency or by the federal or New York state courts. - - - The term "small business" means any person or business with (i) fewer than 50 employees; (ii) less than $3,000,000 in gross annual revenue in each of the last three fiscal years; or (iii) less than $5,000,000 in year-end total assets, calculated in accordance with generally accepted accounting principles.

	New York (Security Requirements)
Security Requirements	(a) Any person or business that owns or licenses computerized data which includes private information of a resident of New York shall develop, implement, and maintain reasonable safeguards to protect the security, confidentiality, and integrity of the private information including, but not limited to, disposal of data. - - - (b) A person or business shall be deemed to be in compliance with paragraph (a) of this subdivision if it either: (i) is a compliant-regulated entity as defined in subdivision one of this section; or (ii) implements a data security program that includes the following: (A) Reasonable administrative safeguards such as the following, in which the person or business: (1) Designates one or more employees to coordinate the security program; (2) Identifies reasonably foreseeable internal and external risks; (3) Assesses the sufficiency of safeguards in place to control the identified risks; (4) Trains and manages employees in the security program practices and procedures; (5) Selects service providers capable of maintaining appropriate safeguards, and requires those safeguards by contract; and (6) Adjusts the security program in light of business changes or new circumstances; and (B) Reasonable technical safeguards such as the following, in which the person or business: (1) Assesses risks in network and software design; (2) Assesses risks in information processing, transmission, and storage; (3) Detects, prevents, and responds to attacks or system failures; and (4) Regularly tests and monitors the effectiveness of key controls, systems, and procedures; and (C) Reasonable physical safeguards such as the following, in which the person or business: (1) Assesses risks of information storage and disposal; (2) Detects, prevents and responds to intrusions; (3) Protects against unauthorized access to or use of private information during or after the collection, transportation, and destruction or disposal of the information; and (4) Disposes of private information within a reasonable amount of time after it is no longer needed for business purposes by erasing electronic media so that the information cannot be read or reconstructed.
Other Information	A small business complies with these requirements if the small business's security program contains reasonable administrative, technical, and physical safeguards that are appropriate for the size and complexity of the small business, the nature and scope of the small business's activities, and the sensitivity of the personal information the small business collects from or about consumers.

NORTH CAROLINA

Data Breach Requirements: N.C.G.S. §§ 75-61, 75-65.

The numbering and internal citations herein are derived from the applicable state statute.

	North Carolina (Data Breach Requirements)
Personal Information	The term "personal information" means a person's first name or first initial and last name in combination with identifying information as defined in G.S. 14-113.20(b). - - - G.S. 14-113.20(b): (b) The term "identifying information" includes the following: (1) Social Security or employer taxpayer identification numbers. (2) Driver's license, state identification card, or passport numbers. (3) Checking account numbers. (4) Savings account numbers. (5) Credit card numbers. (6) Debit card numbers. (7) Personal Identification (PIN) Code as defined in G.S. 14-113.8(6). (8) Electronic identification numbers, electronic mail names or addresses, internet account numbers, or internet identification names. (9) Digital signatures. (10) Any other numbers or information that can be used to access a person's financial resources. (11) Biometric data. (12) Fingerprints. (13) Passwords. (14) Parent's legal surname prior to marriage. - - - However, personal information shall not include electronic identification numbers, electronic mail names or addresses, internet account numbers, internet identification names, parent's legal surname prior to marriage, or a password unless this information would permit access to a person's financial account or resources.
Security Breach Definition	The term "security breach" means an incident of unauthorized access to and acquisition of unencrypted and unredacted records or data containing personal information where illegal use of the personal information has occurred or is reasonably likely to occur or that creates a material risk of harm to a consumer. Any incident of unauthorized access to and acquisition of encrypted records or data containing personal information along with the confidential process or key shall constitute a security breach.
Good Faith Exception	Good faith acquisition of personal information by an employee or agent of the business for a legitimate purpose is not a security breach, provided that the personal information is not used for a purpose other than a lawful purpose of the business and is not subject to further unauthorized disclosure.
Risk of Harm Analysis	See Security Breach Definition (illegal use and material risk of harm standard).
Notification Timeline	The breach notification shall be made without unreasonable delay, consistent with the legitimate needs of law enforcement, and consistent with any measures necessary to determine sufficient contact information, determine the scope of the breach, and restore the reasonable integrity, security, and confidentiality of the data system.

	North Carolina (Data Breach Requirements)
Security and Investigation Exceptions	The breach notification shall be delayed if a law enforcement agency informs the business that notification may impede a criminal investigation or jeopardize national or homeland security, provided that such request is made in writing or the business documents such request contemporaneously in writing, including the name of the law enforcement officer making the request and the officer's law enforcement agency engaged in the investigation. The breach notice shall be provided without unreasonable delay after the law enforcement agency communicates to the business its determination that notice will no longer impede the investigation or jeopardize national or homeland security.
Notification Content Requirements	The breach notice shall be clear and conspicuous and include all of the following: (1) A description of the incident in general terms. (2) A description of the type of personal information that was subject to the unauthorized access and acquisition. (3) A description of the general acts of the business to protect the personal information from further unauthorized access. (4) A telephone number for the business that the person may call for further information and assistance, if one exists. (5) Advice that directs the person to remain vigilant by reviewing account statements and monitoring free credit reports. (6) The toll-free numbers and addresses for the major consumer reporting agencies. (7) The toll-free numbers, addresses, and website addresses for the Federal Trade Commission and the North Carolina Attorney General's Office, along with a statement that the individual can obtain information from these sources about preventing identity theft.
Delivery Methods	A breach notice may be provided by one of the following methods: (1) Written notice. (2) Electronic notice, for those persons for whom it has a valid email address and who have agreed to receive communications electronically if the notice provided is consistent with the provisions regarding electronic records and signatures for notices legally required to be in writing, set forth in 15 U.S.C. § 7001 (The Electronic Signatures in Global and National Commerce Act). (3) Telephonic notice provided that contact is made directly with the affected persons. (4) Substitute notice, if the business demonstrates that the cost of providing notice would exceed $250,000, or that the affected class of subject persons to be notified exceeds 500,000, or if the business does not have sufficient contact information or consent to satisfy subdivisions (1), (2), or (3) of this subsection, for only those affected persons without sufficient contact information or consent, or if the business is unable to identify particular affected persons, for only those unidentifiable affected persons.
Substitute Notice	Substitute notice shall consist of all the following: a. Email notice when the business has an electronic mail address for the subject persons. b. Conspicuous posting of the notice on the website page of the business, if one is maintained. c. Notification to major statewide media.

	North Carolina (Data Breach Requirements)
Notice to Government Agencies	In the event a business provides notice to an affected person of a breach, the business shall notify without unreasonable delay the Consumer Protection Division of the Attorney General's Office of the nature of the breach, the number of consumers affected by the breach, steps taken to investigate the breach, steps taken to prevent a similar breach in the future, and information regarding the timing, distribution, and content of the notice.
Consumer Reporting Agencies	In the event a business provides notice to more than 1,000 persons at one time of a breach, the business shall notify, without unreasonable delay, the Consumer Protection Division of the Attorney General's Office and all consumer reporting agencies of the timing, distribution, and content of the notice.
Preemption and Compliance	A financial institution that is subject to and in compliance with the Federal Interagency Guidance Response Programs for Unauthorized Access to Consumer Information and Customer Notice or a credit union that is subject to and in compliance with the Final Guidance on Response Programs for Unauthorized Access to Member Information and Member Notice shall be deemed to be in compliance with this law.
Data Processor Obligations	Any business that maintains or possesses records or data containing personal information of residents of North Carolina that the business does not own or license, or any business that conducts business in North Carolina that maintains or possesses records or data containing personal information that the business does not own or license, shall notify the owner or licensee of the information of any security breach immediately following discovery of the breach, consistent with the legitimate needs of law enforcement.

NORTH CAROLINA

Data Disposal and Security: N.C.G.S. § 75-61, and 75-64.

The numbering and internal citations herein are derived from the applicable state statute. See statute for any applicable exceptions or exemptions.

	North Carolina (Data Disposal and Security)
Key Terms	The term "disposal" includes the following: a. The discarding or abandonment of records containing personal information. b. The sale, donation, discarding, or transfer of any medium, including computer equipment or computer media, containing records of personal information, or other non-paper media upon which records of personal information are stored, or other equipment for non-paper storage of information. - - - The term "personal information" means a person's first name or first initial and last name in combination with identifying information as defined in G.S. 14-113.20(b). Personal information does not include publicly available directories containing information an individual has voluntarily consented to have publicly disseminated or listed, including name, address, and telephone number, and does not include information made lawfully available to the general public from federal, state, or local government records. - - - G.S. 14-113.20(b): (b) The term "identifying information" includes the following: (1) Social Security or employer taxpayer identification numbers. (2) Driver's license, state identification card, or passport numbers. (3) Checking account numbers. (4) Savings account numbers. (5) Credit card numbers. (6) Debit card numbers. (7) Personal Identification (PIN) Code as defined in G.S. 14-113.8(6). (8) Electronic identification numbers, electronic mail names or addresses, internet account numbers, or internet identification names. (9) Digital signatures. (10) Any other numbers or information that can be used to access a person's financial resources. (11) Biometric data. (12) Fingerprints. (13) Passwords. (14) Parent's legal surname prior to marriage. - - - However, personal information shall *not* include electronic identification numbers, email names or addresses, internet account numbers, internet identification names, parent's legal surname prior to marriage, or a password *unless* this information would permit access to a person's financial account or resources. - - - The term "personal information" does not include publicly available directories containing information an individual has voluntarily consented to have publicly disseminated or listed, including name, address, and telephone number, and does not include information made lawfully available to the general public from federal, state, or local government records.

	North Carolina (Data Disposal and Security)
Written Policy	See Data Disposal (implementing and monitoring compliance with policies and procedures).
Data Disposal	Any business that conducts business in North Carolina and any business that maintains or otherwise possesses personal information of a resident of North Carolina must take reasonable measures to protect against unauthorized access to or use of the information in connection with or after its disposal. The reasonable measures must include: (1) Implementing and monitoring compliance with policies and procedures that require the burning, pulverizing, or shredding of papers containing personal information so that information cannot be practicably read or reconstructed. (2) Implementing and monitoring compliance with policies and procedures that require the destruction or erasure of electronic media and other non-paper media containing personal information so that the information cannot practicably be read or reconstructed. (3) Describing procedures relating to the adequate destruction or proper disposal of personal records as official policy in the writings of the business entity. - - - A business may, after due diligence, enter into a written contract with, and monitor compliance by, another party engaged in the business of record destruction to destroy personal information in a manner consistent with this section. Due diligence should ordinarily include one or more of the following: (1) Reviewing an independent audit of the disposal business's operations or its compliance with this statute or its equivalent. (2) Obtaining information about the disposal business from several references or other reliable sources and requiring that the disposal business be certified by a recognized trade association or similar third party with a reputation for high standards of quality review. (3) Reviewing and evaluating the disposal business's information security policies or procedures or taking other appropriate measures to determine the competency and integrity of the disposal business.
Other Information	A disposal business that conducts business in North Carolina or disposes of personal information of residents of North Carolina must take all reasonable measures to dispose of records containing personal information by implementing and monitoring compliance with policies and procedures that protect against unauthorized access to or use of personal information during or after the collection and transportation and disposing of such information.

NORTH DAKOTA

Data Breach Requirements: N.D.C.C. § 51-30-01 et seq.

The numbering and internal citations herein are derived from the applicable state statute.

	North Dakota (Data Breach Requirements)
Personal Information	The term "personal information" means an individual's first name or first initial and last name in combination with any of the following data elements, when the name and the data elements are not encrypted: (1) The individual's Social Security number; (2) The operator's license number assigned to an individual by the department of transportation under Section 39-06-14; (3) A nondriver color photo identification card number assigned to the individual by the Department of Transportation under Section 39-06-03.1; (4) The individual's financial institution account number, credit card number, or debit card number in combination with any required security code, access code, or password that would permit access to an individual's financial accounts; (5) The individual's date of birth; (6) The maiden name of the individual's mother; (7) Medical information; (8) Health insurance information; (9) An identification number assigned to the individual by the individual's employer in combination with any required security code, access code, or password; or (10) The individual's digitized or other electronic signature.
Security Breach Definition	The term "breach of the security system" means unauthorized acquisition of computerized data when access to personal information has not been secured by encryption or by any other method or technology that renders the electronic files, media, or databases unreadable or unusable.
Good Faith Exception	Good-faith acquisition of personal information by an employee or agent of the person is not a breach of the security of the system, if the personal information is not used or subject to further unauthorized disclosure.
Risk of Harm Analysis	N/A
Notification Timeline	The breach notification must be made in the most expedient time possible and without unreasonable delay, consistent with the legitimate needs of law enforcement, or any measures necessary to determine the scope of the breach and to restore the integrity of the data system.
Security and Investigation Exceptions	The breach notification may be delayed if a law enforcement agency determines that the notification will impede a criminal investigation. The breach notification must be made after the law enforcement agency determines that the notification will not compromise the investigation.
Notification Content Requirements	N/A

	North Dakota (Data Breach Requirements)
Delivery Methods	A breach notice may be provided by one of the following methods: 1. Written notice; 2. Electronic notice, if the notice provided is consistent with the provisions regarding electronic records and signatures set forth in 15 U.S.C. § 7001 (The Electronic Signatures in Global and National Commerce Act); or 3. Substitute notice, if the person demonstrates that the cost of providing notice would exceed $250,000, or that the affected class of subject persons to be notified exceeds 500,000, or the person does not have sufficient contact information.
Substitute Notice	Substitute notice consists of the following: a. Email notice when the person has an email address for the subject persons; b. Conspicuous posting of the notice on the person's website page, if the person maintains one; and c. Notification to major statewide media.
Notice to Government Agencies	Any person that experiences a breach of the security system shall disclose to the attorney general by mail or email any breach which exceeds 250 individuals.
Consumer Reporting Agencies	N/A
Preemption and Compliance	A financial institution, trust company, or credit union that is subject to, examined for, and in compliance with the federal interagency guidance on response programs for unauthorized access to customer information and customer notice is in compliance with this chapter. A covered entity, business associate, or subcontractor subject to breach notification requirements under Title 45, Code of Federal Regulations, Subpart D, Part 164 (HIPAA), is considered to be in compliance with this chapter.
Data Processor Obligations	Any person that maintains computerized data that includes personal information that the person does not own shall notify the owner or licensee of the information of the breach of the security of the data immediately following the discovery, if the personal information was, or is reasonably believed to have been, acquired by an unauthorized person.

OHIO

Data Breach Requirements: Ohio R.C. § 1349.19.

The numbering and internal citations herein are derived from the applicable state statute.

	Ohio (Data Breach Requirements)
Personal Information	The term "personal information" means an individual's name, consisting of the individual's first name or first initial and last name, in combination with and linked to any one or more of the following data elements, when the data elements are not encrypted, redacted, or altered by any method or technology in such a manner that the data elements are unreadable: (i) Social Security number; (ii) Driver's license number or state identification card number; (iii) Account number or credit or debit card number, in combination with and linked to any required security code, access code, or password that would permit access to an individual's financial account.
Security Breach Definition	The term "breach of the security of the system" means unauthorized access to and acquisition of computerized data that compromises the security or confidentiality of personal information owned or licensed by a person and that causes, reasonably is believed to have caused, or reasonably is believed will cause a material risk of identity theft or other fraud to the person or property of an Ohio resident.
Good Faith Exception	Good faith acquisition of personal information by an employee or agent of the person for the purposes of the person is not a breach of the security of the system, provided that the personal information is not used for an unlawful purpose or subject to further unauthorized disclosure.
Risk of Harm Analysis	Any person that owns or licenses computerized data that includes personal information shall disclose any breach of the security of the system, following its discovery or notification of the breach of the security of the system, to any resident of this state whose personal information was, or reasonably is believed to have been, accessed and acquired by an unauthorized person if the access and acquisition by the unauthorized person causes or reasonably is believed will cause a material risk of identity theft or other fraud to the resident.
Notification Timeline	The breach notification shall be made in the most expedient time possible, but not later than 45 days following its discovery or notification of the breach in the security of the system, subject to the legitimate needs of law enforcement activities and consistent with any measures necessary to determine the scope of the breach, including which residents' personal information was accessed and acquired, and to restore the reasonable integrity of the data system.
Security and Investigation Exceptions	The breach notification may be delayed if a law enforcement agency determines that the disclosure or notification will impede a criminal investigation or jeopardize homeland or national security, in which case the person shall make the disclosure or notification after the law enforcement agency determines that disclosure or notification will not compromise the investigation or jeopardize homeland or national security.
Notification Content Requirements	N/A

	Ohio (Data Breach Requirements)
Delivery Methods	A breach notice may be provided by one of the following methods: (1) Written notice; (2) Electronic notice, if the person's primary method of communication with the resident to whom the disclosure must be made is by electronic means; (3) Telephone notice; (4) Substitute notice in accordance with this division, if the person required to disclose demonstrates that the person does not have sufficient contact information to provide notice in a manner described in division (E)(1), (2), or (3) of this section, or that the cost of providing disclosure or notice to residents to whom disclosure or notification is required would exceed $250,000, or that the affected class of subject residents to whom disclosure or notification is required exceeds 500,000 persons. Substitute notice under this division shall consist of all of the following: (a) Email notice if the person has an email address for the resident to whom the disclosure must be made; (b) Conspicuous posting of the disclosure or notice on the person's website, if the person maintains one; (c) Notification to major media outlets, to the extent that the cumulative total of the readership, viewing audience, or listening audience of all of the outlets so notified equals or exceeds 75 percent of the population of this state. (5) Substitute notice in accordance with this division, if the person required to disclose demonstrates that the person is a business entity with ten employees or fewer and that the cost of providing the disclosures or notices to residents to whom disclosure or notification is required will exceed $10,000. Substitute notice under this division shall consist of all of the following: (a) Notification by a paid advertisement in a local newspaper that is distributed in the geographic area in which the business entity is located, which advertisement shall be of sufficient size that it covers at least one-quarter of a page in the newspaper and shall be published in the newspaper at least once a week for three consecutive weeks; (b) Conspicuous posting of the disclosure or notice on the business entity's website, if the entity maintains one; (c) Notification to major media outlets in the geographic area in which the business entity is located.
Substitute Notice	See Delivery Methods.
Notice to Government Agencies	N/A
Consumer Reporting Agencies	If a person discovers circumstances that require disclosure under this section to more than 1,000 residents of this state involved in a single occurrence of a breach of the security of the system, the person shall notify, without unreasonable delay, all consumer reporting agencies of the timing, distribution, and content of the disclosure given by the person to the residents of this state.
Preemption and Compliance	A financial institution, trust company, or credit union or any affiliate of a financial institution, trust company, or credit union that is required by federal law, including, but not limited to, any federal statute, regulation, regulatory guidance, or other regulatory action, to notify its customers of an information security breach with respect to information about those customers and that is subject to examination by its functional government regulatory agency for compliance with the applicable federal law, is exempt from the requirements of this section. - - - This law does not apply to any person or entity that is a covered entity as defined in 45 C.F.R. 160.103, as amended.

	Ohio (Data Breach Requirements)
Data Processor Obligations	Any person that, on behalf of or at the direction of another person or on behalf of or at the direction of any governmental entity, is the custodian of or stores computerized data that includes personal information, shall notify that other person or governmental entity of any breach of the security of the system in an expeditious manner, if the personal information was, or reasonably is believed to have been, accessed and acquired by an unauthorized person and if the access and acquisition by the unauthorized person causes or reasonably is believed will cause a material risk of identity theft or other fraud to a resident of this state.
Other Information	The data breach notification may be made pursuant to any provision of a contract entered into by the person with another person prior to the date the breach of the security of the system occurred if that contract does not conflict with any provision of this law and does not waive any provision of this law.

OKLAHOMA

Data Breach Requirements: Okla. Stat. tit. 24, § 162 et seq.

The numbering and internal citations herein are derived from the applicable state statute.

	Oklahoma (Data Breach Requirements)
Personal Information	The term "personal information" means the first name or first initial and last name in combination with and linked to any one or more of the following data elements that relate to a resident of this state, when the data elements are neither encrypted nor redacted: a. Social Security number; b. Driver's license number or state identification card number issued in lieu of a driver's license; or c. Financial account number, credit card or debit card number, in combination with any required security code, access code, or password that would permit access to the financial accounts of a resident.
Security Breach Definition	The term "breach of the security of a system" means the unauthorized access and acquisition of unencrypted and unredacted computerized data that compromises the security or confidentiality of personal information maintained by an individual or entity as part of a database of personal information regarding multiple individuals and that causes, or the individual or entity reasonably believes has caused or will cause, identity theft or other fraud to any resident of this state.
Good Faith Exception	Good faith acquisition of personal information by an employee or agent of an individual or entity for the purposes of the individual or the entity is not a breach of the security of the system, provided that the personal information is not used for a purpose other than a lawful purpose of the individual or entity or subject to further unauthorized disclosure.
Risk of Harm Analysis	An individual or entity must disclose the breach of the security of the system if encrypted information is accessed and acquired in an unencrypted form or if the security breach involves a person with access to the encryption key and the individual or entity reasonably believes that such breach has caused or will cause identity theft or other fraud to any resident of this state.
Notification Timeline	Except as provided in subsection D (security and investigation exceptions) or in order to take any measures necessary to determine the scope of the breach and to restore the reasonable integrity of the system, the disclosure shall be made without unreasonable delay.
Security and Investigation Exceptions	A breach notification may be delayed if a law enforcement agency determines and advises the individual or entity that the notice will impede a criminal or civil investigation or homeland or national security. Notice must be made without unreasonable delay after the law enforcement agency determines that notification will no longer impede the investigation or jeopardize national or homeland security.
Notification Content Requirements	N/A

	Oklahoma (Data Breach Requirements)
Delivery Methods	A breach notice may be provided by one of the following methods: a. Written notice to the postal address in the records of the individual or entity; b. Telephone notice; c. Electronic notice; or d. Substitute notice, if the individual or the entity required to provide notice demonstrates that the cost of providing notice will exceed $50,000.00, or that the affected class of residents to be notified exceeds 100,000 persons, or that the individual or the entity does not have sufficient contact information or consent to provide notice as described in subparagraph a, b or c of this paragraph.
Substitute Notice	Substitute notice consists of any two of the following: (1) Email notice if the individual or the entity has email addresses for the members of the affected class of residents; (2) Conspicuous posting of the notice on the Internet website of the individual or the entity if the individual or the entity maintains a public Internet website; or (3) Notice to major statewide media.
Notice to Government Agencies	N/A (other state sector laws may apply).
Consumer Reporting Agencies	N/A
Preemption and Compliance	A financial institution that complies with the notification requirements prescribed by the Federal Interagency Guidance on Response Programs for Unauthorized Access to Customer Information and Customer Notice is deemed to be in compliance with the provisions of this act. An entity that complies with the notification requirements or procedures pursuant to the rules, regulation, procedures, or guidelines established by the primary or functional federal regulator of the entity shall be deemed to be in compliance with the provisions of this act.
Data Processor Obligations	An individual or entity that maintains computerized data that includes personal information that the individual or entity does not own or license shall notify the owner or licensee of the information of any breach of the security of the system. This should be done as soon as practicable following discovery, if the personal information was or if the entity reasonably believes was accessed and acquired by an unauthorized person.

OREGON

Data Breach Requirements: Or. Rev. Stat. § 646A.600 et seq.

The numbering and internal citations herein are derived from the applicable state statute.

	Oregon (Data Breach Requirements)
Personal Information	The term "personal information" means: (A) A consumer's first name or first initial and last name in combination with any one or more of the following data elements, if encryption, redaction or other methods have not rendered the data elements unusable or if the data elements are encrypted and the encryption key has been acquired: (i) A consumer's Social Security number; (ii) A consumer's driver's license number or state identification card number issued by the Department of Transportation; (iii) A consumer's passport number or other identification number issued by the United States; (iv) A consumer's financial account number, credit card number or debit card number, in combination with any required security code, access code or password that would permit access to a consumer's financial account, or any other information or combination of information that a person reasonably knows or should know would permit access to the consumer's financial account; (v) Data from automatic measurements of a consumer's physical characteristics, such as an image of a fingerprint, retina or iris, that are used to authenticate the consumer's identity in the course of a financial transaction or other transaction; (vi) A consumer's health insurance policy number or health insurance subscriber identification number in combination with any other unique identifier that a health insurer uses to identify the consumer; or (vii) Any information about a consumer's medical history or mental or physical condition or about a health care professional's medical diagnosis or treatment of the consumer. (B) A username or other means of identifying a consumer for the purpose of permitting access to the consumer's account, together with any other method necessary to authenticate the username or means of identification. (C) Any of the data elements or any combination of the data elements described in subparagraph (A) or (B) of this paragraph without the consumer's username, or the consumer's first name or first initial and last name, if: (i) Encryption, redaction or other methods have not rendered the data element or combination of data elements unusable; and (ii) The data element or combination of data elements would enable a person to commit identity theft against a consumer.
Security Breach Definition	The term "breach of security" means an unauthorized acquisition of computerized data that materially compromises the security, confidentiality or integrity of personal information that a person maintains or possesses.
Good Faith Exception	A "breach of security" does not include an inadvertent acquisition of personal information by a person or the person's employee or agent if the personal information is not used in violation of applicable law or in a manner that harms or poses an actual threat to the security, confidentiality or integrity of the personal information.

	Oregon (Data Breach Requirements)
Risk of Harm Analysis	A covered entity does not need to notify consumers of a breach of security if, after an appropriate investigation or after consultation with relevant federal, state or local law enforcement agencies, the covered entity reasonably determines that the consumers whose personal information was subject to the breach of security are unlikely to suffer harm. The covered entity must document the determination in writing and maintain the documentation for at least five years.
Notification Timeline	A covered entity shall give notice of a breach of security in the most expeditious manner possible, without unreasonable delay, but not later than 45 days after discovering or receiving notification of the breach of security.
Security and Investigation Exceptions	A covered entity may delay giving the breach notice only if a law enforcement agency determines that a notification will impede a criminal investigation and if the law enforcement agency requests in writing that the covered entity delay the notification.
Notification Content Requirements	A data breach notice must include, at a minimum: (a) A description of the breach of security in general terms; (b) The approximate date of the breach of security; (c) The type of personal information that was subject to the breach of security; (d) Contact information for the covered entity; (e) Contact information for national consumer reporting agencies; and (f) Advice to the consumer to report suspected identity theft to law enforcement, including the attorney general and the Federal Trade Commission.
Delivery Methods	A breach notice may be provided by one of the following methods: (a) In writing; (b) Electronically, if the covered entity customarily communicates with the consumer electronically or if the notice is consistent with the provisions regarding electronic records and signatures set forth in 15 U.S.C. § 7001 (The Electronic Signatures in Global and National Commerce Act); (c) By telephone, if the covered entity contacts the affected consumer directly; or (d) With substitute notice, if the covered entity demonstrates that the cost of notification otherwise would exceed $250,000 or that the affected class of consumers exceeds 350,000, or if the covered entity does not have sufficient contact information to notify affected consumers.
Substitute Notice	Substitute notice means: (A) Posting the notice or a link to the notice conspicuously on the covered entity's website if the covered entity maintains a website; and (B) Notifying major statewide television and newspaper media.
Notice to Government Agencies	A breach notification shall be provided to the attorney general, either in writing or electronically, if the number of consumers to whom the covered entity must send the notice exceeds 250.
Consumer Reporting Agencies	If a covered entity discovers or receives notice of a breach of security that affects more than 1,000 consumers, the covered entity shall notify, without unreasonable delay, all consumer reporting agencies that compile and maintain reports on consumers on a nationwide basis of the timing, distribution and content of the notice the covered entity gave to affected consumers. It shall include any police report number assigned to the breach of security. A covered entity may not delay notifying affected consumers of a breach of security in order to notify consumer reporting agencies.

	Oregon (Data Breach Requirements)
Preemption and Compliance	The law does not apply to: (a) Personal information that is subject to, and a person that complies with, notification requirements or procedures for a breach of security that the person's primary or functional federal regulator adopts, promulgates or issues in rules, regulations, procedures, guidelines or guidance, if the personal information and the person would otherwise be subject to ORS 646A.600 to 646A.628. (b) Personal information that is subject to, and a person that complies with, a state or federal law that provides greater protection to personal information and disclosure requirements at least as thorough as the protections and disclosure requirements provided under this section. (c) A covered entity or vendor that complies with regulations promulgated under Title V of the Gramm-Leach-Bliley Act, as that Act existed on January 1, 2020, if personal information that is subject to ORS 646A.600 to 646A.628 is also subject to that Act. (d) A covered entity or vendor that complies with regulations promulgated under the Health Insurance Portability and Accountability Act of 1996 and the Health Information Technology for Economic and Clinical Health Act (HITECH), as those acts existed on January 1, 2020, if personal information that is subject to ORS 646A.600 to 646A.628 is also subject to those acts. Notwithstanding these exemptions, a person, a covered entity or a vendor shall provide to the attorney general within a reasonable time at least one copy of any notice the person, the covered entity or the vendor sends to consumers or to the person's, the covered entity's or the vendor's primary or functional regulator in compliance with this section or with other state or federal laws or regulations that apply to the person, the covered entity or the vendor as a consequence of a breach of security, if the breach of security affects more than 250 consumers.
Data Processor Obligations	(a) A vendor that discovers a breach of security or has reason to believe that a breach has occurred shall notify a covered entity with which the vendor has a contract as soon as is practicable but not later than ten days after discovering the breach or having a reason to believe that the breach occurred. (b) If a vendor has a contract with another vendor that, in turn, has a contract with a covered entity, the vendor shall notify the other vendor of a breach of security as provided in paragraph (a) of this subsection. (c) A vendor shall notify the attorney general in writing or electronically if the vendor was subject to a breach of security that involved the personal information of more than 250 consumers or a number of consumers that the vendor could not determine. The stipulations in this paragraph do not apply to the vendor if the covered entity described in paragraph (a) or (b) of this subsection has notified the attorney general in accordance with the requirements of this section.

	Oregon (Data Breach Requirements)
Other Information	Before providing the breach notice, a covered entity shall undertake reasonable measures that are necessary to: (A) Determine sufficient contact information for the intended recipient of the notice; (B) Determine the scope of the breach of security; and (C) Restore the reasonable integrity, security and confidentiality of the personal information. - - - (a) If a covered entity must notify a consumer of a breach of security under this section, and in connection with the notification the covered entity or an agent or affiliate of the covered entity offers to provide credit monitoring services or identity theft prevention and mitigation services without charge to the consumer, the covered entity, the agent or the affiliate may not condition the provision of the services on the consumer's providing the covered entity, the agent or the affiliate with a credit or debit card number or on the consumer's acceptance of any other service the covered entity offers to provide for a fee. (b) If a covered entity or an agent or affiliate of the covered entity offers additional credit monitoring services or identity theft prevention and mitigation services for a fee to a consumer under the circumstances described in paragraph (a) of this subsection, the covered entity, the agent or the affiliate must separately, distinctly, clearly and conspicuously disclose in the offer for the additional credit monitoring services or identity theft prevention and mitigation services that the covered entity, the agent or the affiliate will charge the consumer a fee. (c) The terms and conditions of any contract under which one person offers or provides credit monitoring services or identity theft prevention and mitigation services on behalf of another person under the circumstances described in paragraph (a) of this subsection must require compliance with the requirements of paragraphs (a) and (b) of this subsection.

OREGON

Data Disposal and Security: Or. Rev. Stat. §§ 646A.602, 646A.622 and 285B.123.

The numbering and internal citations herein are derived from the applicable state statute. See statute for any applicable exceptions or exemptions.

	Oregon (Data Disposal and Security)
Key Terms	The term "personal information" means: (A) A consumer's first name or first initial and last name in combination with any one or more of the following data elements, if encryption, redaction or other methods have not rendered the data elements unusable or if the data elements are encrypted and the encryption key has been acquired. A consumer's: (i) Social Security number; (ii) Driver license number or state identification card number issued by the Department of Transportation; (iii) Passport number or other identification number issued by the United States; (iv) Financial account, credit, or debit card number, in combination with any required security code, access code or password that would permit access to a consumer's financial account, or any other information or combination of information that a person reasonably knows or should know would permit access to the consumer's financial account; (v) Data from automatic measurements of a consumer's physical characteristics, such as an image of a fingerprint, retina or iris, that are used to authenticate the consumer's identity in the course of a financial transaction or other transaction; (vi) Health insurance policy number or health insurance subscriber identification number in combination with any other unique identifier that a health insurer uses to identify the consumer; or (vii) Any information about a consumer's medical history or mental or physical condition or about a health care professional's medical diagnosis or treatment of the consumer. (B) Username or other means of identifying a consumer for the purpose of permitting access to the consumer's account, together with any other method necessary to authenticate the username or means of identification. (C) Any of the data elements or any combination of the data elements described in subparagraph (A) or (B) of this paragraph without the consumer's username, or the consumer's first name or first initial and last name, if: (i) Encryption, redaction or other methods have not rendered the data element or combination of data elements unusable; and (ii) The data element or combination of data elements would enable a person to commit identity theft against a consumer. - - - The term "small business" means a business having 100 or fewer employees. - - - The term "vendor" means a person with which a covered entity contracts to maintain, store, manage, process, or otherwise access personal information for the purpose of, or in connection with, providing services to or on behalf of the covered entity.

	Oregon (Data Disposal and Security)
Security Requirements	(1) A covered entity and a vendor shall develop, implement, and maintain reasonable safeguards to protect the security, confidentiality, and integrity of personal information, including safeguards that protect the personal information when the covered entity or vendor disposes of the personal information. - - - (2) A covered entity or vendor complies with subsection (1) of this section if the covered entity or vendor: (a) Complies with a state or federal law that provides greater protection to personal information than the protections that this section provides. (b) Complies with regulations promulgated under Title V of the Gramm-Leach-Bliley Act, if personal information that is subject to ORS 646A.600 to 646A.628 is also subject to the Act. (c) Complies with regulations that implement the Health Insurance Portability and Accountability Act of 1996 (HIPAA) and the Health Information Technology for Economic and Clinical Health Act (HITECH), as those acts were in effect on January 1, 2020, if personal information that is subject to ORS 646A.600 to 646A.628 is also subject to those acts. (d) Implements an information security program that includes: (A) Administrative safeguards such as: (i) Designating one or more employees to coordinate the security program; (ii) Identifying reasonably foreseeable internal and external risks with reasonable regularity; (iii) Assessing whether existing safeguards adequately control the identified risks; (iv) Training and managing employees in security program practices and procedures with reasonable regularity; (v) Selecting service providers that are capable of maintaining appropriate safeguards and practices, and requiring the service providers by contract to maintain the safeguards and practices; (vi) Adjusting the security program in light of business changes, potential threats or new circumstances; and (vii) Reviewing user access privileges with reasonable regularity; (B) Technical safeguards such as: (i) Assessing risks and vulnerabilities in network and software design and taking reasonably timely action to address the risks and vulnerabilities; (ii) Applying security updates and a reasonable security patch management program to software that might reasonably be at risk of or vulnerable to a breach of security; (iii) Monitoring, detecting, preventing, and responding to attacks or system failures; and (iv) Regularly testing, monitoring, and taking action to address the effectiveness of key controls, systems, and procedures; and

	Oregon (Data Disposal and Security)
	(C) Physical safeguards such as: (i) Assessing, in light of current technology, risks of information collection, storage, usage, retention, access, and disposal and implementing reasonable methods to remedy or mitigate identified risks; (ii) Monitoring, detecting, preventing, isolating and responding to intrusions timely and with reasonable regularity; (iii) Protecting against unauthorized access to or use of personal information during or after collecting, using, storing, transporting, retaining, destroying or disposing of the personal information; and (iv) Disposing of personal information, whether the covered entity or vendor disposes of the personal information on or off the covered entity's or vendor's premises or property, after the covered entity or vendor no longer needs the personal information for business purposes or as required by local, state or federal law by burning, pulverizing, shredding, or modifying a physical record and by destroying or erasing electronic media so that the information cannot be read or reconstructed.
Written Policy	<u>See</u> Security Requirements.
Data Disposal	<u>See</u> Security Requirements. A covered entity or vendor complies with the data disposal requirements in subsection (2)(d)(C)(iv) if the covered entity or vendor contracts with another person engaged in the business of record destruction to dispose of personal information in a manner that is consistent with the same requirements.
Other Information	A person that is an owner of a small business complies with the obligation to implement and maintain reasonable safeguards if the person's information security and disposal program contains administrative, technical and physical safeguards and disposal measures that are appropriate for the size and complexity of the small business, the nature and scope of the small business's activities, and the sensitivity of the personal information the small business collects from or about consumers

PENNSYLVANIA

Data Breach Requirements: PA St. 73 P.S. § 2302 et seq.

The numbering and internal citations herein are derived from the applicable state statute.

	Pennsylvania (Data Breach Requirements)
Personal Information	The term "personal information" means: (1) An individual's first name or first initial and last name in combination with and linked to any one or more of the following data elements when the data elements are not encrypted or redacted: (i) Social Security number. (ii) Driver's license number or a state identification card number issued in lieu of a driver's license. (iii) Financial account number, credit or debit card number, in combination with any required security code, access code or password that would permit access to an individual's financial account. (iv) Medical information. (v) Health insurance information. (vi) A user name or e-mail address, in combination with a password or security question and answer that would permit access to an online account.
Security Breach Definition	The term "breach of the security of the system" means the unauthorized access and acquisition of computerized data that materially compromises the security or confidentiality of personal information maintained by the entity as part of a database of personal information regarding multiple individuals and that causes or the entity reasonably believes has caused or will cause loss or injury to any resident of this commonwealth.
Good Faith Exception	Good faith acquisition of personal information by an employee or agent of the entity for the purposes of the entity is not a breach of the security of the system if the personal information is not used for a purpose other than the lawful purpose of the entity and is not subject to further unauthorized disclosure.
Risk of Harm Analysis	N/A
Notification Timeline	Except for the law enforcement exception (see Security and Investigations Exceptions) or in order to take any measures necessary to determine the scope of the breach and to restore the reasonable integrity of the data system, the breach notice shall be made without unreasonable delay.
Security and Investigation Exceptions	A breach notification may be delayed if a law enforcement agency determines and advises the entity in writing specifically referencing this breach notification law that the notification will impede a criminal or civil investigation. The notification required by this act shall be made after the law enforcement agency determines that it will not compromise the investigation or national or homeland security.
Notification Content Requirements	See Delivery Methods (content requirements for telephonic notices).

	Pennsylvania (Data Breach Requirements)
Delivery Methods	A breach notice may be provided by one of the following methods: (1) Written notice to the last known home address for the individual. (2) Telephonic notice, if the individual can be reasonably expected to receive the notice and it is given in a clear and conspicuous manner, describes the incident in general terms and verifies personal information but does not require the individual to provide personal information, and the individual is provided with a telephone number to call or Internet website to visit for further information or assistance. (3) Email notice, if a prior business relationship exists and the person or entity has a valid email address for the individual. (3) (i) Electronic notice, if the notice directs the person whose personal information has been materially compromised by a breach of the security of the system to promptly change the person's password and security question or answer, as applicable, or to take other steps appropriate to protect the person's online account to the extent the entity has sufficient contact information for the person (4)(i) Substitute notice, if the entity demonstrates one of the following: (A) The cost of providing notice would exceed $100,000. (B) The affected class of subject persons to be notified exceeds 175,000. (C) The entity does not have sufficient contact information.
Substitute Notice	Substitute notice shall consist of all of the following: (A) Email notice when the entity has an email address for the subject persons. (B) Conspicuous posting of the notice on the entity's Internet website if the entity maintains one. (C) Notification to major Statewide media.
Notice to Government Agencies	N/A
Consumer Reporting Agencies	When an entity provides notification under this act to more than 1,000 persons at one time, the entity shall also notify, without unreasonable delay, all consumer reporting agencies of the timing, distribution, and number of notices.
Preemption and Compliance	A financial institution that complies with the notification requirements prescribed by the Federal Interagency Guidance on Response Programs for Unauthorized Access to Customer Information and Customer Notice is deemed to be in compliance with this act. - - - An entity that complies with the notification requirements or procedures pursuant to the rules, regulations, procedures, or guidelines established by the entity's primary or functional federal regulator shall be in compliance with this act.
Data Processor Obligations	A vendor that maintains, stores, or manages computerized data on behalf of another entity shall provide notice of any breach of the security system following discovery by the vendor to the entity on whose behalf the vendor maintains, stores, or manages the data. The entity shall be responsible for making the determinations and discharging any remaining duties under this law.

	Pennsylvania (Data Breach Requirements)
Other Information	An entity must provide notice of the breach if encrypted information is accessed and acquired in an unencrypted form, if the security breach is linked to a breach of the security of the encryption or if the security breach involves a person with access to the encryption key. Electronic notification: In the case of a breach of the security of the system involving personal information for a user name or e-mail address in combination with a password or security question and answer that would permit access to an online account, the entity, to the extent that it has sufficient contact information for the person, may comply with this section by providing the breach of the security of the system notification in electronic or other form that directs the person whose personal information has been materially compromised by the breach of the security of the system to promptly change the person's password and security question or answer, as applicable or to take other steps appropriate to protect the online account with the entity and other online accounts for which the person whose personal information has been materially compromised by the breach of the security of the system uses the same user name or e-mail address and password or security question or answer.

RHODE ISLAND

Data Breach Requirements: R.I. Gen. Laws § 11-49.3-1 et seq.

The numbering and internal citations herein are derived from the applicable state statute.

	Rhode Island (Data Breach Requirements)
Personal Information	The term "personal information" means an individual's first name or first initial and last name in combination with any one or more of the following data elements, when the name and the data elements are not encrypted or are in hard copy, paper format: (i) Social Security number; (ii) Driver's license number, Rhode Island identification card number, or tribal identification number; (iii) Account number, credit, or debit card number, in combination with any required security code, access code, password, or personal identification number, that would permit access to an individual's financial account; (iv) Medical or health insurance information; or (v) Email address with any required security code, access code, or password that would permit access to an individual's personal, medical, insurance, or financial account.
Security Breach Definition	The term "breach of the security of the system" means unauthorized access or acquisition of unencrypted, computerized data information that compromises the security, confidentiality, or integrity of personal information maintained by the person.
Good Faith Exception	The good faith acquisition of personal information by an employee or agent of the agency for the purposes of the agency is not a breach of the security of the system; provided that the personal information is not used or subject to further unauthorized disclosure.
Risk of Harm Analysis	A covered entity shall provide notification of any disclosure of personal information, or any breach of the security of the system, that poses a significant risk of identity theft to any resident of Rhode Island whose personal information was, or is reasonably believed to have been, acquired by an unauthorized person or entity.
Notification Timeline	The breach notification shall be made in the most expedient time possible, but no later than 45 calendar days after confirmation of the breach and the ability to ascertain the information required to fulfill the notice requirements, and shall be consistent with the legitimate needs of law enforcement.
Security and Investigation Exceptions	The breach notification may be delayed if a federal, state, or local law enforcement agency determines that the notification will impede a criminal investigation. The federal, state, or local law enforcement agency must notify the person of the request to delay notification without unreasonable delay. If notice is delayed due to such determination, then, as soon as the federal, state, or local law enforcement agency determines and informs the person that notification no longer poses a risk of impeding an investigation, notice shall be provided as soon as practicable. The person shall cooperate with federal, state, or local law enforcement in its investigation of any breach of security or unauthorized acquisition or use, which shall include the sharing of information relevant to the incident; provided however, that such disclosure shall not require the disclosure of confidential business information or trade secrets.

	Rhode Island (Data Breach Requirements)
Notification Content Requirements	(d) The notification to individuals must include the following information to the extent known: (1) A general and brief description of the incident, including how the security breach occurred and the number of affected individuals; (2) The type of information that was subject to the breach; (3) Date of breach, estimated date of breach, or the date range within which the breach occurred; (4) Date that the breach was discovered; (5) A clear and concise description of any remediation services offered to affected individuals including toll free numbers and websites to contact: (i) The credit reporting agencies; (ii) Remediation service providers; (iii) The attorney general; and (6) A clear and concise description of the consumer's ability to file or obtain a police report; how a consumer requests a security freeze and the necessary information to be provided when requesting the security freeze; and that fees may be required to be paid to the consumer reporting agencies.
Delivery Methods	A breach notice may be provided by one of the following methods: (i) Written notice; (ii) Electronic notice, if the notice provided is consistent with the provisions regarding electronic records and signatures set forth in 15 U.S.C. § 7001 (The Electronic Signatures in Global and National Commerce Act); or (iii) Substitute notice, if the person demonstrates that the cost of providing notice would exceed $25,000, or that the affected class of subject persons to be notified exceeds 50,000, or the person does not have sufficient contact information.
Substitute Notice	Substitute notice shall consist of all of the following: (A) Email notice when the person has an email address for the subject persons; (B) Conspicuous posting of the notice on the municipal agency, state agency, or person's website page, if the person maintains one; and (C) Notification to major statewide media.
Notice to Government Agencies	In the event that more than 500 Rhode Island residents are to be notified, the covered entity shall notify the attorney general as to the timing, content, and distribution of the notices and the approximate number of affected individuals.
Consumer Reporting Agencies	In the event that more than 500 Rhode Island residents are to be notified, the covered entity shall notify the major credit reporting agencies as to the timing, content, and distribution of the notices and the approximate number of affected individuals.

	Rhode Island (Data Breach Requirements)
Preemption and Compliance	A covered entity shall be deemed to be in compliance with the security breach notification requirements of § 11-49.3-4 if the person maintains a security breach procedure pursuant to the rules, regulations, procedures, or guidelines established by the primary or functional regulator, as defined in 15 U.S.C. § 6809(2), and notifies subject persons in accordance with the policies or the rules, regulations, procedures, or guidelines established by the primary or functional regulator in the event of a breach of security of the system. - - - A financial institution, trust company, credit union, or its affiliates that is subject to and examined for, and found in compliance with, the Federal Interagency Guidelines on Response Programs for Unauthorized Access to Customer Information and Customer Notice shall be deemed in compliance with this chapter. - - - A provider of health care, health care service plan, health insurer, or a covered entity governed by the medical privacy and security rules issued pursuant to the Health Insurance Portability and Accountability Act of 1996 (HIPAA) shall be deemed in compliance with this chapter.
Data Processor Obligations	N/A (See State Specific Information Security Requirements and third-party contracting obligations)
Other Information	A "remediation service provider" means any person who, in the usual course of business, provides services pertaining to a consumer credit report including, but not limited to, credit report monitoring and alerts, that are intended to mitigate the potential for identity theft. - - - Notification to the attorney general and the major credit reporting agencies by a covered entity shall be made without delaying notice to affected Rhode Island residents.

RHODE ISLAND

Data Disposal and Security: R.I. Gen. Laws §§ 11-49.3-2 and 11-49.3-3.

The numbering and internal citations herein are derived from the applicable state statute. See statute for any applicable exceptions or exemptions.

	Rhode Island (Data Disposal and Security)
Key Terms	The term "personal information" means an individual's first name or first initial and last name in combination with any one or more of the following data elements, when the name and the data elements are not encrypted or are in hard copy, paper format: (i) Social Security number; (ii) Driver's license number, Rhode Island identification card number, or tribal identification number; (iii) Account, credit, or debit card number, in combination with any required security code, access code, password, or personal identification number, that would permit access to an individual's financial account; (iv) Medical or health insurance information; or (v) Email address with any required security code, access code, or password that would permit access to an individual's personal, medical, insurance, or financial account.
Security Requirements	A person who or that stores, collects, processes, maintains, acquires, uses, owns, or licenses personal information about a Rhode Island resident shall implement and maintain a risk-based information security program that contains reasonable security procedures and practices appropriate to the size and scope of the organization; the nature of the information; and the purpose for which the information was collected in order to protect the personal information from unauthorized access, use, modification, destruction, or disclosure and to preserve the confidentiality, integrity, and availability of such information. - - - A person shall not retain personal information for a period longer than is reasonably required to provide the services requested; to meet the purpose for which it was collected; or in accordance with a written retention policy or as may be required by law. - - - A person who discloses personal information about a Rhode Island resident to a nonaffiliated third party shall require by written contract that the third party implement and maintain reasonable security procedures and practices appropriate to the size and scope of the organization; the nature of the information; and the purpose for which the information was collected in order to protect the personal information from unauthorized access, use, modification, destruction, or disclosure.
Written Policy	<u>See</u> Security Requirements (written retention policy).
Data Disposal	A person shall destroy all personal information, regardless of the medium that such information is in, in a secure manner, including, but not limited to, shredding, pulverization, incineration, or erasure.

SOUTH CAROLINA

Data Breach Requirements: S.C. Code Ann. § 39-1-90.

The numbering and internal citations herein are derived from the applicable state statute.

	South Carolina (Data Breach Requirements)
Personal Information	The term "personal identifying information" means the first name or first initial and last name in combination with and linked to any one or more of the following data elements that relate to a resident of this State, when the data elements are neither encrypted nor redacted: (a) Social Security number; (b) Driver's license number or state identification card number issued instead of a driver's license; (c) Financial account number, or credit card or debit card number in combination with any required security code, access code, or password that would permit access to a resident's financial account; or (d) Other numbers or information which may be used to access a person's financial accounts or numbers or information issued by a governmental or regulatory entity that uniquely will identify an individual.
Security Breach Definition	The term "breach of the security of the system" means unauthorized access to and acquisition of computerized data that was not rendered unusable through encryption, redaction, or other methods that compromises the security, confidentiality, or integrity of personal identifying information maintained by the person, when illegal use of the information has occurred or is reasonably likely to occur or use of the information creates a material risk of harm to a resident.
Good Faith Exception	Good faith acquisition of personal identifying information by an employee or agent of the person for the purposes of its business is not a breach of the security of the system if the personal identifying information is not used or subject to further unauthorized disclosure.
Risk of Harm Analysis	A covered entity shall disclose a breach of the security of the system following discovery or notification of the breach of the data to a resident of this state whose personal identifying information that was not rendered unusable through encryption, redaction, or other methods was, or is reasonably believed to have been, acquired by an unauthorized person when the illegal use of the information has occurred or is reasonably likely to occur or use of the information creates a material risk of harm to the resident.
Notification Timeline	The breach notification must be made in the most expedient time possible and without unreasonable delay, consistent with the legitimate needs of law enforcement or with measures necessary to determine the scope of the breach and restore the reasonable integrity of the data system.
Security and Investigation Exceptions	The breach notification may be delayed if a law enforcement agency determines that the notification impedes a criminal investigation. The notification must be made after the law enforcement agency determines that it no longer compromises the investigation.
Notification Content Requirements	N/A

	South Carolina (Data Breach Requirements)
Delivery Methods	A breach notice may be provided by one of the following methods: (1) Written notice; (2) Electronic notice, if the person's primary method of communication with the individual is by electronic means or is consistent with the provisions regarding electronic records and signatures in 15 U.S.C. § 7001 (The Electronic Signatures in Global and National Commerce Act); (3) Telephonic notice; or (4) Substitute notice, if the person demonstrates that the cost of providing notice exceeds $250.000 or that the affected class of subject persons to be notified exceeds 500,000 or the person has insufficient contact information.
Substitute Notice	Substitute notice consists of: (a) Email notice when the person has an email address for the subject persons; (b) Conspicuous posting of the notice on the website page of the person, if the person maintains one; or (c) Notification to major statewide media.
Notice to Government Agencies	If a business provides breach notices to more than 1,000 persons at one time, the business shall notify, without unreasonable delay, the Consumer Protection Division of the Department of Consumer Affairs of the timing, distribution, and content of the notice.
Consumer Reporting Agencies	If a business provides breach notices to more than 1,000 persons at one time, the business shall notify, without unreasonable delay, all consumer reporting agencies that compile and maintain files on a nationwide basis of the timing, distribution, and content of the notice.
Preemption and Compliance	This law does not apply to a bank or financial institution that is subject to and in compliance with the privacy and security provision of the Gramm-Leach-Bliley Act. - - - A financial institution that is subject to and in compliance with the federal Interagency Guidance Response Programs for Unauthorized Access to Consumer Information and Customer Notice is considered to be in compliance with this section.
Data Processor Obligations	A person conducting business in this state and maintaining computerized data, or other data that includes personal identifying information that the person does not own, shall notify the owner or licensee of the information of a breach of the security of the data immediately following discovery, if the personal identifying information was, or is reasonably believed to have been, acquired by an unauthorized person.

SOUTH CAROLINA

Data Disposal and Security: S.C. Code Ann. §§ 37-20-110 and 37-20-190.

The numbering and internal citations herein are derived from the applicable state statute. See statute for any applicable exceptions or exemptions.

	South Carolina (Data Disposal and Security)
Key Terms	The term "personal identifying information" means personal identifying information as defined in Section 16-13-510(D). It does not mean information about vehicular accidents, driving violations, and driver's status. - - - Section 16-13-510(D): The term "personal identifying information" includes, but is not limited to: (1) Social Security numbers; (2) Driver's license numbers or state identification card numbers issued instead of a driver's license; (3) Checking account numbers; (4) Savings account numbers; (5) Credit card numbers; (6) Debit card numbers; (7) Personal identification (PIN) numbers; (8) Electronic identification numbers; (9) Digital signatures; (10) Dates of birth; (11) Current or former names, including first and last names, middle and last names, or first, middle, and last names, but only when the names are used in combination with, and linked to, other identifying information provided in this section; (12) Current or former addresses, but only when the addresses are used in combination with, and linked to, other identifying information provided in this section; or (13) Other numbers, passwords, or information which may be used to access a person's financial resources, numbers, or information issued by a governmental or regulatory entity that uniquely will identify an individual or an individual's financial resources. - - - The term "disposal" means the (a) discarding or abandonment of records containing personal identifying information; or (b) sale, donation, discarding, or transfer of any medium, including computer equipment or computer media, containing records of personal identifying information, other non-paper media upon which records of personal identifying information are stored, or other equipment for non-paper storage of information.
Data Disposal	When a business disposes of a business record that contains personal identifying information of a customer of a business, the business shall modify, by shredding, erasing, or other means, the personal identifying information to make it unreadable or undecipherable. - - - A business is considered to comply with this law if it contracts with a person engaged in the business of disposing of records for the modification of personal identifying information on behalf of the business in accordance with this law.

SOUTH DAKOTA

Data Breach Requirements: South Dakota CL § 22-40-19 et seq.

The numbering and internal citations herein are derived from the applicable state statute.

	South Dakota (Data Breach Requirements)
Personal Information	The term "personal information" means a person's first name or first initial and last name, in combination with any one or more of the following data elements: (a) Social Security number; (b) Driver's license number or other unique identification number created or collected by a government body; (c) Account, credit card, or debit card number, in combination with any required security code, access code, password, routing number, PIN, or any additional information that would permit access to a person's financial account; (d) Health information as defined in 45 CFR 160.103; or (e) An identification number assigned to a person by the person's employer in combination with any required security code, access code, password, or biometric data generated from measurements or analysis of human body characteristics for authentication purposes. - - - The term "protected information" includes: (a) A username or email address, in combination with a password, security question answer, or other information that permits access to an online account; and (b) Account number or credit or debit card number, in combination with any required security code, access code, or password that permits access to a person's financial account;
Security Breach Definition	The term "breach of system security" means the unauthorized acquisition of unencrypted computerized data or encrypted computerized data and the encryption key by any person that materially compromises the security, confidentiality, or integrity of personal or protected information maintained by the information holder.
Good Faith Exception	A "breach of system security" does not include the good faith acquisition of personal or protected information by an employee or agent of the information holder for the purposes of the information holder if the personal or protected information is not used or subject to further unauthorized disclosure.
Risk of Harm Analysis	An information holder is not required to make a data breach notification if, following an appropriate investigation and notice to the attorney general, the information holder reasonably determines that the breach will not likely result in harm to the affected person. The information holder shall document the determination under this section in writing and maintain the documentation for not less than three years.
Notification Timeline	The breach notification shall be made not later than 60 days from the discovery or notification of the breach of system security, unless a longer period of time is required due to the legitimate needs of law enforcement.
Security and Investigation Exceptions	A breach notification may be delayed if a law enforcement agency determines that the notification will impede a criminal investigation. If the notification is delayed, the notification shall be made not later than 30 days after the law enforcement agency determines that notification will not compromise the criminal investigation.
Notification Content Requirements	N/A

	South Dakota (Data Breach Requirements)
Delivery Methods	A breach notice may be provided by one of the following methods: (1) Written notice; (2) Electronic notice, if the electronic notice is consistent with the provisions regarding electronic records and signatures set forth in 15 U.S.C. § 7001 (The Electronic Signatures in Global and National Commerce Act) in effect as of January 1, 2018, or if the information holder's primary method of communication with the resident of this state has been by electronic means; or (3) Substitute notice, if the information holder demonstrates that the cost of providing notice would exceed $250,000, that the affected class of persons to be notified exceeds 500,000 persons, or that the information holder does not have sufficient contact information and the notice consists of each of the following: (a) Email notice, if the information holder has an email address for the subject persons; (b) Conspicuous posting of the notice on the information holder's website, if the information holder maintains a website page; and (c) Notification to statewide media.
Substitute Notice	<u>See</u> Delivery Methods.
Notice to Government Agencies	Any information holder that experiences a breach of system security shall disclose to the attorney general by mail or electronic mail any breach that exceeds 250 state residents.
Consumer Reporting Agencies	If an information holder discovers circumstances that require a breach notification, the information holder shall also notify, without unreasonable delay, all consumer reporting agencies and any other credit bureau or agency that compiles and maintains files on consumers on a nationwide basis, of the timing, distribution, and content of the notice.
Preemption and Compliance	Any information holder that is regulated by federal law or regulation, including the Health Insurance Portability and Accountability Act of 1996 or the Gramm-Leach-Bliley Act and that maintains procedures for a breach of system security pursuant to the laws, rules, regulations, guidance, or guidelines established by its primary or functional federal regulator is deemed to be in compliance with this law if the information holder notifies affected South Dakota residents in accordance with the provisions of the applicable federal law or regulation.
Data Processor Obligations	N/A
Other Information	"Unauthorized person," any person not authorized to acquire or disclose personal information, or any person authorized by the information holder to access personal information who has acquired or disclosed the personal information outside the guidelines for access of disclosure established by the information holder.

TENNESSEE

Data Breach Requirements: Tenn.C.A. § 47-18-2107 et seq.

The numbering and internal citations herein are derived from the applicable state statute.

	Tennessee (Data Breach Requirements)
Personal Information	Personal information (A) Means an individual's first name or first initial and last name, in combination with any one (1) or more of the following data elements: (i) Social Security number; (ii) Driver's license number; or (iii) Account, credit card, or debit card number, in combination with any required security code, access code, or password that would permit access to an individual's financial account.
Security Breach Definition	The term "breach of system security" means the acquisition of unencrypted computerized data; or encrypted computerized data and the encryption key by an unauthorized person that materially compromises the security, confidentiality, or integrity of personal information maintained by the information holder.
Good Faith Exception	A "breach of system security" does not include the good faith acquisition of personal information by an employee or agent of the information holder for the purposes of the information holder if the personal information is not used or subject to further unauthorized disclosure.
Risk of Harm Analysis	N/A
Notification Timeline	The breach notification must be made no later than 45 days from the discovery or notification of the breach of system security, unless a longer period of time is required due to the legitimate needs of law enforcement.
Security and Investigation Exceptions	The breach notification may be delayed if a law enforcement agency determines that the notification will impede a criminal investigation. If the notification is delayed, it must be made no later than 45 days after the law enforcement agency determines that notification will not compromise the investigation.
Notification Content Requirements	N/A
Delivery Methods	A breach notice may be provided by one of the following methods: (1) Written notice; (2) Electronic notice, if the notice provided is consistent with the provisions regarding electronic records and signatures set forth in 15 U.S.C. § 7001 (The Electronic Signatures in Global and National Commerce Act) or if the information holder's primary method of communication with the resident of this state has been by electronic means; or (3) Substitute notice, if the information holder demonstrates that the cost of providing notice would exceed $250,000, that the affected class of subject persons to be notified exceeds 500,000 persons, or the information holder does not have sufficient contact information and the notice consists of all of the following: (A) Email notice, when the information holder has an email address for the subject persons; (B) Conspicuous posting of the notice on the information holder's website, if the information holder maintains a website page; and (C) Notification to major statewide media.

	Tennessee (Data Breach Requirements)
Substitute Notice	See Delivery Methods.
Notice to Government Agencies	N/A
Consumer Reporting Agencies	If an information holder discovers circumstances requiring breach notification to more than 1,000 persons at one time, the information holder must also notify, without unreasonable delay, all consumer reporting agencies and credit bureaus that compile and maintain files on consumers on a nationwide basis, of the timing, distribution, and content of the notices.
Preemption and Compliance	This law does not apply to any information holder that is subject to: (1) Title V of the Gramm-Leach-Bliley Act; or (2) The Health Insurance Portability and Accountability Act of 1996, as amended.
Data Processor Obligations	Any information holder that maintains computerized data that includes personal information that the information holder does not own shall notify the owner or licensee of the information of any breach of system security if the personal information was, or is reasonably believed to have been, acquired by an unauthorized person. The disclosure must be made no later than 45 days from the discovery or notification of the breach of system security, unless a longer period of time is required due to the legitimate needs of law enforcement.
Other Information	"Unauthorized person" includes an employee of the information holder who is discovered by the information holder to have obtained personal information with the intent to use it for an unlawful purpose.

TENNESSEE

Data Disposal and Security: Tenn.C.A. § 39-14-150.

The numbering and internal citations herein are derived from the applicable state statute. See statute for any applicable exceptions or exemptions.

	Tennessee (Data Disposal and Security)
Key Terms	The term "personal identifying information" means a customer's: (A) Social Security number; (B) Driver license identification number; (C) Savings account number; (D) Checking account number; (E) PIN (personal identification number) or password; (F) Complete credit or debit card number; (G) Demand deposit account number; (H) Health insurance identification number; or (I) Unique biometric data.
Data Disposal	If a private entity or business maintains a record that contains any personal identifying information concerning one of its customers, and the entity, by law, practice, or policy discards such records after a specified period of time, any record containing the personal identifying information shall not be discarded unless the business: (A) Shreds or burns the customer's record before discarding the record; (B) Erases the personal identifying information contained in the customer's record before discarding the record; (C) Modifies the customer's record to make the personal identifying information unreadable before discarding the record; or (D) Takes action to destroy the customer's personal identifying information in a manner that it reasonably believes will ensure that no unauthorized persons have access to the personal identifying information contained in the customer's record for the period of time between the record's disposal and the record's destruction.
Other Information	The methods of destroying the personal identifying information set forth herein shall be considered the minimum standards. If a private entity or business by law, practice or policy currently is required to have or otherwise has in place more stringent methods and procedures for destroying the personal identifying information in a customer's record, the private entity or business may continue to destroy the identifying information in the more stringent manner.

TEXAS

Data Breach Requirements: Texas Bus. & Com. Code §§ 521.002, 521.053, 521.151.

The numbering and internal citations herein are derived from the applicable state statute.

	Texas (Data Breach Requirements)
Personal Information	The term "sensitive personal information" means (A) An individual's first name or first initial and last name in combination with any one or more of the following items, if the name and the items are not encrypted: (i) Social Security number; (ii) Driver's license number or government-issued identification number; or (iii) Account, credit, or debit card number in combination with any required security code, access code, or password that would permit access to an individual's financial account; or (B) Information that identifies an individual and relates to: (i) The physical or mental health or condition of the individual; (ii) The provision of health care to the individual; or (iii) Payment for the provision of health care to the individual.
Security Breach Definition	The term "breach of system security" means unauthorized acquisition of computerized data that compromises the security, confidentiality, or integrity of sensitive personal information maintained by a person, including data that is encrypted if the person accessing the data has the key required to decrypt the data.
Good Faith Exception	Good faith acquisition of sensitive personal information by an employee or agent of the person for the purposes of the person is not a breach of system security unless the person uses or discloses the sensitive personal information in an unauthorized manner.
Risk of Harm Analysis	N/A
Notification Timeline	The breach notification shall be made without unreasonable delay and in each case not later than the 60th day after the date on which the person determines that the breach occurred, except as provided by subsection (d) (law enforcement exception) or as necessary to determine the scope of the breach and restore the reasonable integrity of the data system.
Security and Investigation Exceptions	A person may delay providing a breach notice at the request of a law enforcement agency that determines that the notification will impede a criminal investigation. The notification shall be made as soon as the law enforcement agency determines that the notification will not compromise the investigation.
Notification Content Requirements	See Notice to Government Agencies.
Delivery Methods	A breach notice may be provided by one of the following methods: (1) Written notice at the last known address of the individual; (2) Electronic notice, if the notice is provided in accordance with 15 U.S.C. § 7001 (The Electronic Signatures in Global and National Commerce Act); or (3) Substitute notice if the person required to give notice demonstrates that the cost of providing notice would exceed $250,000, the number of affected persons exceeds 500,000, or the person does not have sufficient contact information,

	Texas (Data Breach Requirements)
Substitute Notice	Substitute notice shall consist of the following: (1) Electronic mail, if the person has electronic mail addresses for the affected persons; (2) Conspicuous posting of the notice on the person's website; or (3) Notice published in or broadcast on major statewide media.
Notice to Government Agencies	A person who is required to disclose or provide notification of a breach of system security shall notify the attorney general of that breach not later than the 60th day after the date on which the person determines that the breach occurred if it involves at least 250 residents of this state. The notification must include: (1) A detailed description of the nature and circumstances of the breach or the use of sensitive personal information acquired as a result of the breach; (2) The number of residents of this state affected by the breach at the time of notification; (3) The number of affected residents that have been sent a disclosure of the breach by mail or other direct method of communication at the time of notification; (4) The measures taken by the person regarding the breach; (5) Any measures the person intends to take regarding the breach after the notification under this subsection; and (6) Information regarding whether law enforcement is engaged in investigating the breach.
Consumer Reporting Agencies	If a person is required to notify, at one time, more than 10,000 persons of a breach, the person shall also notify each consumer reporting agency that maintains files on consumers on a nationwide basis, of the timing, distribution, and content of the notices. The person shall provide the notice required by this subsection without unreasonable delay.
Preemption and Compliance	N/A
Data Processor Obligations	Any person who maintains computerized data that includes sensitive personal information not owned by the person shall notify the owner or license holder of the information of any breach of system security immediately after discovering the breach, if the sensitive personal information was, or is reasonably believed to have been, acquired by an unauthorized person.
Other Information	If the individual whose sensitive personal information was, or is reasonably believed to have been, acquired by an unauthorized person is a resident of a state that requires an organization to provide a breach notice, the notice under Texas law may be provided under that state's law or under Texas law. - - - The attorney general shall post on its publicly accessible Internet website a listing of the notifications it received pursuant to this law, excluding any sensitive personal information, any information that may compromise a data system's security, and any other information reported to the attorney general that is made confidential by law. The attorney general shall: (1) Update the listing not later than the 30th day after the date the attorney general receives notification of a new breach of system security; (2) Remove a notification from the listing not later than the first anniversary of the date the attorney general added the notification to the listing if the person who provided the notification has not notified the attorney general of any additional breaches; and (3) Maintain only the most recently updated listing on the attorney general's website.

TEXAS

Data Disposal and Security: Texas Bus. & Com. Code. §§ 521.002, 521.052.

The numbering and internal citations herein are derived from the applicable state statute. See statute for any applicable exceptions or exemptions.

	Texas (Data Disposal and Security)
Key Terms	The term "personal identifying information" means information that alone or in conjunction with other information identifies an individual, including an individual's: (A) Name, social security number, date of birth, or government-issued identification number; (B) Mother's maiden name; (C) Unique biometric data, including the individual's fingerprint, voice print, and retina or iris image; (D) Unique electronic identification number, address, or routing code; and (E) Telecommunication access device as defined by Section 32.51, Penal Code. - - - The term "sensitive personal information" means an individual's first name or first initial and last name in combination with any one or more of the following items, if the name and the items are not encrypted: (i) Social Security number; (ii) Driver's license number or government-issued identification number; or (iii) Account, credit, or debit card number in combination with any required security code, access code, or password that would permit access to an individual's financial account; or (B) Information that identifies an individual and relates to: (i) The physical or mental health or condition of the individual; (ii) The provision of health care to the individual; or (iii) Payment for the provision of health care to the individual. - - - The term "sensitive personal information" does not include publicly available information that is lawfully made available to the public from the federal government or a state or local government.
Security Requirements	A business shall implement and maintain reasonable procedures, including taking any appropriate corrective action, to protect from unlawful use or disclosure any sensitive personal information collected or maintained by the business in the regular course of business.
Data Disposal	A business shall destroy or arrange for the destruction of customer records containing sensitive personal information within the business's custody or control that are not to be retained by the business by: (1) Shredding; (2) Erasing; or (3) Otherwise modifying the sensitive personal information in the records to make the information unreadable or indecipherable through any means.

UTAH

Data Breach Requirements: Utah Code § 13-44-102 et seq.

The numbering and internal citations herein are derived from the applicable state statute.

	Utah (Data Breach Requirements)
Personal Information	The term "personal information" means a person's first name or first initial and last name, combined with any one or more of the following data elements relating to that person when either the name or date element is unencrypted or not protected by another method that renders the data unreadable or unusable: (i) Social Security number; (ii)(A) financial account number, or credit or debit card number, and (B) any required security code, access code, or password that would permit access to the person's account; or (iii) Driver's license number or state identification card number.
Security Breach Definition	The term "breach of system security" means an unauthorized acquisition of computerized data maintained by a person that compromises the security, confidentiality, or integrity of personal information.
Good Faith Exception	A "breach of system security" does not include the acquisition of personal information by an employee or agent of the person possessing unencrypted computerized data unless the personal information is used for an unlawful purpose or disclosed in an unauthorized manner.
Risk of Harm Analysis	A person who owns or licenses computerized data that includes personal information concerning a Utah resident shall, when the person becomes aware of a breach of system security, conduct in good faith a reasonable and prompt investigation to determine the likelihood that personal information has been or will be misused for identity theft or fraud purposes. If such an investigation reveals that the misuse of personal information for identity theft or fraud purposes has occurred, or is reasonably likely to occur, the person shall provide notification to each affected Utah resident.
Notification Timeline	The breach notification shall be provided in the most expedient time possible without unreasonable delay: considering legitimate investigative needs of law enforcement, after determining the scope of the breach of system security, and after restoring the reasonable integrity of the system.
Security and Investigation Exceptions	A person may delay providing the breach notification at the request of a law enforcement agency that determines that notification may impede a criminal investigation. A person who delays providing notification under subsection (4) (a) shall provide notification in good faith without unreasonable delay in the most expedient time possible after the law enforcement agency informs the person that notification will no longer impede the criminal investigation.
Notification Content Requirements	N/A

	Utah (Data Breach Requirements)
Delivery Methods	5(a) A breach notice may be provided by one of the following methods: (i) in writing by first-class mail to the most recent address the person has for the resident; (ii) electronically, if the person's primary method of communication with the resident is by electronic means, or if provided in accordance with the consumer disclosure provisions of 15 U.S.C. § 7001 (The Electronic Signatures in Global and National Commerce Act); (iii) by telephone, including through the use of automatic dialing technology not prohibited by other law; or (iv) for residents of the state for whom notification in a manner described in subsections (5)(a)(i) through (iii) is not feasible, by publishing notice of the breach of system security: (A) in a newspaper of general circulation; and (B) as required in Section 45-1-101 (see Other Information).
Substitute Notice	See Delivery Methods.
Notice to Government Agencies	N/A
Consumer Reporting Agencies	N/A
Preemption and Compliance	The data breach notification law does not apply to a financial institution or an affiliate, as defined in 15 U.S.C. Sec. 6809, of a financial institution. - - - A person who is regulated by state or federal law and maintains procedures for a breach of system security under applicable law established by the primary state or federal regulator is considered to be in compliance with this part if the person notifies each affected Utah resident in accordance with the other applicable law in the event of a breach.
Data Processor Obligations	A person who maintains computerized data that includes personal information that the person does not own or license shall notify and cooperate with the owner or licensee of the information of any breach of system security immediately following the person's discovery of the breach if misuse of the personal information occurs or is reasonably likely to occur. Cooperation includes sharing information relevant to the breach with the owner or licensee of the information.
Other Information	§ 45-1-101. Legal notice publication requirements: (1) As used in this section: (a) "Average advertisement rate" means: (i) in determining a rate for publication on the public legal notice website or in a newspaper that primarily distributes publications in a county of the third, fourth, fifth, or sixth class, a newspaper's gross advertising revenue for the preceding calendar quarter divided by the gross column-inch space used in the newspaper for advertising for the previous calendar quarter; or

	Utah (Data Breach Requirements)
	(ii) in determining a rate for publication in a newspaper that primarily distributes publications in a county of the first or second class, a newspaper's average rate for all qualifying advertising segments for the preceding calendar quarter for an advertisement: (A) published in the same section of the newspaper as the legal notice; and (B) of the same column-inch space as the legal notice. (b) "Column-inch space" means a unit of space that is one standard column wide by one inch high. (c) "Gross advertising revenue" means the total revenue obtained by a newspaper from all of its qualifying advertising segments. (d)(i) "Legal notice" means: (A) a communication required to be made public by a state statute or state agency rule; or (B) a notice required for judicial proceedings or by judicial decision. (ii) "Legal notice" does not include: (A) a public notice published by a public body in accordance with the provisions of Sections 52-4-202 and 63A-16-601; or (B) a notice of delinquency in the payment of property taxes described in Section 59-2-1332.5. (e) "Local district" is as defined in Section 17B-1-102. (f) "Public legal notice website" means the website described in Subsection (2)(b) for the purpose of publishing a legal notice online. (g)(i) "Qualifying advertising segment" means, except as provided in Subsection (1)(g)(ii), a category of print advertising sold by a newspaper, including classified advertising, line advertising, and display advertising. (ii) "Qualifying advertising segment" does not include legal notice advertising. (h) "Special service district" is as defined in Section 17D-1-102. (2) Except as provided in Subsections (8) and (9), notwithstanding any other legal notice provision established by law, a person required by law to publish legal notice shall publish the notice: (a)(i) as required by the statute establishing the legal notice requirement; or (ii) by serving legal notice, by certified mail or in person, directly on all parties for whom the statute establishing the legal notice requirement requires legal notice, if: (A) the direct service of legal notice does not replace publication in a newspaper that primarily distributes publications in a county of the third, fourth, fifth, or sixth class; (B) the statute clearly identifies the parties; (C) the person can prove that the person has identified all parties for whom notice is required; and (D) the person keeps a record of the service for at least two years; and (b) on a public legal notice website established by the combined efforts of Utah's newspapers that collectively distribute newspapers to the majority of newspaper subscribers in the state. (3) The public legal notice website shall: (a) be available for viewing and searching by the general public, free of charge; and (b) accept legal notice posting from any newspaper in the state.

	Utah (Data Breach Requirements)
	(4) A person that publishes legal notice as required under Subsection (2) is not relieved from complying with an otherwise applicable requirement under Title 52, Chapter 4, Open and Public Meetings Act. (5) If legal notice is required by law and one option for complying with the requirement is publication in a newspaper, or if a local district or a special service district publishes legal notice in a newspaper, the newspaper: (a) may not charge more for publication than the newspaper's average advertisement rate; and (b) shall publish the legal notice on the public legal notice website at no additional cost. (6) If legal notice is not required by law, or if legal notice is required by law and the person providing legal notice, in accordance with the requirements of law, chooses not to publish the legal notice in a newspaper, or if a local district or a special service district with an annual operating budget of less than $250,000 chooses to publish a legal notice on the public notice website without publishing the complete notice in the newspaper, a newspaper: (a) may not charge more than an amount equal to 15% of the newspaper's average advertisement rate for publishing five column lines in the newspaper to publish legal notice on the public legal notice website; (b) may not require that the legal notice be published in the newspaper; and (c) at the request of the person publishing on the legal notice website, shall publish in the newspaper up to five column lines, at no additional charge, that briefly describe the legal notice and provide the web address where the full public legal notice can be found. (7) If a newspaper offers to publish the type of legal notice described in Subsection (5), it may not refuse to publish the type of legal notice described in Subsection (6). (8) Notwithstanding the requirements of a statute that requires the publication of legal notice, if legal notice is required by law to be published by a local district or a special service district with an annual operating budget of $250,000 or more, the local district or special service district shall satisfy its legal notice publishing requirements by: (a) mailing a written notice, postage prepaid: (i) to each voter in the local district or special service district; and (ii) that contains the information required by the statute that requires the publication of legal notice; or (b) publishing the legal notice in a newspaper and on the legal public notice website as described in Subsection (5). (9) Notwithstanding the requirements of a statute that requires the publication of legal notice, if legal notice is required by law to be published by a local district or a special service district with an annual operating budget of less than $250,000, the local district or special service district shall satisfy its legal notice publishing requirements by: (a) mailing a written notice, postage prepaid: (i) to each voter in the local district or special service district; and (ii) that contains the information required by the statute that requires the publication of legal notice; or (b) publishing the legal notice in a newspaper and on the public legal notice website as described in Subsection (5); or (c) publishing the legal notice on the public legal notice website as described in Subsection (6).

UTAH

Data Disposal and Security: Utah Code § 13-44-201.

The numbering and internal citations herein are derived from the applicable state statute. See statute for any applicable exceptions or exemptions.

	Utah (Data Disposal and Security)
Key Terms	The term "personal information" means a person's first name or first initial and last name, combined with any one or more of the following data elements relating to that person when either the name or date element is unencrypted or not protected by another method that renders the data unreadable or unusable: (i) Social Security number; (ii)(A) Financial account, credit, or debit card number; and (B) Any required security code, access code, or password that would permit access to the person's account; or (iii) Driver's license number or state identification card number.
Security Requirements	Any person who conducts business in the state and maintains personal information shall implement and maintain reasonable procedures to prevent unlawful use or disclosure of personal information collected or maintained in the regular course of business.
Data Disposal	Any person who conducts business in the state and maintains personal information shall implement and maintain reasonable procedures to destroy, or arrange for the destruction of, records containing personal information that are not to be retained by the person. The destruction of records shall be by: (a) Shredding; (b) Erasing; or (c) Otherwise modifying the personal information to make the information indecipherable.

VERMONT

Data Breach Requirements: 9 V.S.A. § 2430 et seq.

The numbering and internal citations herein are derived from the applicable state statute.

	Vermont (Data Breach Requirements)
Personal Information	The term "personally identifiable information" means a consumer's first name or first initial and last name in combination with one or more of the following digital data elements, when the data elements are not encrypted, redacted, or protected by another method that renders them unreadable or unusable by unauthorized persons: (i) A Social Security number; (ii) A driver's license or nondriver state identification card number, individual taxpayer identification number, passport number, military identification card number, or other identification number that originates from a government identification document that is commonly used to verify identity for a commercial transaction; (iii) A financial account number or credit or debit card number, if the number could be used without additional identifying information, access codes, or passwords; (iv) A password, personal identification number, or other access code for a financial account; (v) Unique biometric data generated from measurements or technical analysis of human body characteristics used by the owner or licensee of the data to identify or authenticate the consumer, such as a fingerprint, retina or iris image, or other unique physical representation or digital representation of biometric data; (vi) Genetic information; and (vii)(I) Health records or records of a wellness program or similar program of health promotion or disease prevention; (II) a health care professional's medical diagnosis or treatment of the consumer; or (III) a health insurance policy number. - - - "Login credentials" means a consumer's username or email address, in combination with a password or an answer to a security question, that together permit access to an online account.
Security Breach Definition	The term "security breach" means unauthorized acquisition of electronic data, or a reasonable belief of an unauthorized acquisition of electronic data, that compromises the security, confidentiality, or integrity of a consumer's personally identifiable information or login credentials maintained by a data collector.
Good Faith Exception	A "security breach" does not include good faith but unauthorized acquisition of personally identifiable information or login credentials by an employee or agent of the data collector for a legitimate purpose of the data collector, provided that the personally identifiable information or login credentials are not used for a purpose unrelated to the data collector's business or subject to further unauthorized disclosure.

	Vermont (Data Breach Requirements)
Risk of Harm Analysis	Notice of a security breach is not required if the data collector establishes that misuse of personally identifiable information or login credentials is not reasonably possible and the data collector provides notice of the determination that the misuse of the personally identifiable information or login credentials is not reasonably possible as follows. If the data collector establishes that misuse of the personally identifiable information or login credentials is not reasonably possible, the data collector shall provide notice of its determination that misuse of the personally identifiable information or login credentials is not reasonably possible and a detailed explanation for said determination to the Vermont Attorney General or to the Department of Financial Regulation in the event that the data collector is a person or entity licensed or registered with the Department under Title 8 or this title. The data collector may designate its notice and detailed explanation to the Vermont Attorney General or the Department of Financial Regulation as "trade secret" if the notice and detailed explanation meet the definition of trade secret contained in 1 V.S.A. § 317(c)(9). - - - If a data collector established that misuse of personally identifiable information or login credentials was not reasonably possible and subsequently obtains facts indicating that misuse of the personally identifiable information or login credentials has occurred or is occurring, the data collector shall provide notice of the security breach.
Notification Timeline	A breach notification shall be made in the most expedient time possible and without unreasonable delay, but not later than 45 days after the discovery or notification, consistent with the legitimate needs of the law enforcement agency, or with any measures necessary to determine the scope of the security breach and restore the reasonable integrity, security, and confidentiality of the data system.
Security and Investigation Exceptions	The breach notice to a consumer shall be delayed upon request of a law enforcement agency. A law enforcement agency may request the delay if it believes that notification may impede a law enforcement investigation, or a national or Homeland Security investigation, or jeopardize public safety or national or Homeland Security interests. In the event law enforcement makes the request for a delay in a manner other than in writing, the data collector shall document such request contemporaneously in writing, including the name of the law enforcement officer making the request and the officer's law enforcement agency engaged in the investigation. A law enforcement agency shall promptly notify the data collector in writing when the law enforcement agency no longer believes that notification may impede a law enforcement investigation or a national or Homeland Security investigation or jeopardize public safety or national or Homeland Security interests. The data collector shall provide notice without unreasonable delay upon receipt of a written communication, which includes facsimile or electronic communication, from the law enforcement agency withdrawing its request for delay.

	Vermont (Data Breach Requirements)
Notification Content Requirements	The breach notice shall be clear and conspicuous. A notice to a consumer of a security breach involving personally identifiable information shall include a description of each of the following, if known to the data collector: (A) the incident in general terms; (B) the type of personally identifiable information that was subject to the security breach; (C) the general acts of the data collector to protect the personally identifiable information from further security breach; (D) a telephone number, toll-free if available, that the consumer may call for further information and assistance; (E) advice that directs the consumer to remain vigilant by reviewing account statements and monitoring free credit reports; and (F) the approximate date of the security breach. - - - If a security breach is limited to an unauthorized acquisition of login credentials for an online account other than an email account, the data collector shall provide notice of the security breach to the consumer electronically or through one or more of the methods authorized (<u>See</u> Delivery Methods) and shall advise the consumer to take steps necessary to protect the online account, including to change his or her login credentials for the account and for any other account for which the consumer uses the same login credentials.
Delivery Methods	A breach notice may be provided by one of the following methods: (A)(i) written notice mailed to the consumer's residence; (ii) electronic notice, for those consumers for whom the data collector has a valid email address, if: (I) the data collector's primary method of communication with the consumer is by electronic means, the electronic notice does not request or contain a hypertext link to a request that the consumer provide personal information, and the electronic notice conspicuously warns consumers not to provide personal information in response to electronic communications regarding security breaches; or (II) the notice is consistent with the provisions regarding electronic records and signatures for notices in 15 U.S.C. § 7001 (The Electronic Signatures in Global and National Commerce Act); or (iii) telephonic notice, provided that telephonic contact is made directly with each affected consumer and not through a prerecorded message. (B)(i) Substitute notice, if: (I) the data collector demonstrates that the lowest cost of providing notice to affected consumers pursuant to subdivision (6)(A) of this subsection among written, email, or telephonic notice would exceed $10,000; or (II) the data collector does not have sufficient contact information. (ii) A data collector shall provide substitute notice by: (I) conspicuously posting the notice on the data collector's website if the data collector maintains one; and (II) notifying major statewide and regional media. - - -

	Vermont (Data Breach Requirements)
	If a security breach is limited to an unauthorized acquisition of login credentials for an email account: (A) the data collector shall not provide notice of the security breach through the email account; and (B) the data collector shall provide notice of the security breach through one or more of authorized methods (see Delivery Methods) or by clear and conspicuous notice delivered to the consumer online when the consumer is connected to the online account from an internet protocol address or online location from which the data collector knows the consumer customarily accesses the account.
Substitute Notice	See Delivery Methods.
Notice to Government Agencies	(3) A data collector or other entity subject to this subchapter shall provide notice of a breach to the Office of the Attorney General or to the Department of Financial Regulation, as applicable, as follows: (A) A data collector or other entity regulated by the Department of Financial Regulation under Title 8 or this title shall provide notice of a breach to the department. All other data collectors or other entities subject to this subchapter shall provide notice of a breach to the attorney general. (B)(i) The data collector shall notify the attorney general or the department, as applicable, of the date of the security breach and the date of discovery of the breach and shall provide a preliminary description of the breach within 14 business days, consistent with the legitimate needs of the law enforcement agency of the data collector's discovery of the security breach, or when the data collector provides notice to consumers, whichever is sooner. (ii) Notwithstanding subdivision (B)(i), a data collector who, prior to the date of the breach, on a form and in a manner prescribed by the attorney general, had sworn in writing to the attorney general that it maintains written policies and procedures to maintain the security of personally identifiable information or login credentials and respond to a breach in a manner consistent with Vermont law shall notify the attorney general of the date of the security breach and the date of discovery of the breach and shall provide a description of the breach prior to providing notice of the breach to consumers. (iii) If the date of the breach is unknown at the time notice is sent to the attorney general or to the department, the data collector shall send the attorney general or the department the date of the breach as soon as it is known. (iv) Unless otherwise ordered by a court of this state for good cause shown, a notice provided under this subdivision (3)(B) shall not be disclosed to any person other than the department, the authorized agent, or representative of the attorney general, a state's attorney, or another law enforcement officer engaged in legitimate law enforcement activities without the consent of the data collector. (C)(i) When the data collector provides notice of the breach pursuant to subdivision (1) of this subsection (b), the data collector shall notify the attorney general or the department, as applicable, of the number of Vermont consumers affected, if known to the data collector, and shall provide a copy of the notice provided to consumers. (ii) The data collector may send to the attorney general or the department, as applicable, a second copy of the consumer notice, from which is redacted the type of personally identifiable information or login credentials that was subject to the breach, and which the attorney general or the department shall use for any public disclosure of the breach. (D) If a security breach is limited to an unauthorized acquisition of login credentials, a data collector is only required to provide notice of the security breach to the Office of the Attorney General or Department of Financial Regulation, as applicable, if the login credentials were acquired directly from the data collector or its agent.

	Vermont (Data Breach Requirements)
Consumer Reporting Agencies	In the event a data collector provides a breach notice to more than 1,000 consumers at one time, the data collector shall notify, without unreasonable delay, all consumer reporting agencies of the timing, distribution, and content of the notice. This subsection shall not apply to a person who is licensed or registered under Title 8 by the Department of Financial Regulation.
Preemption and Compliance	A data collector that is subject to the privacy, security, and breach notification rules adopted in pursuant to the Health Insurance Portability and Accountability Act of 1996 (HIPAA) is deemed to be in compliance with this subchapter if: (1) the data collector experiences a security breach that is limited to personally identifiable information specified in 2430(10)(A)(vii); and (2) the data collector provides notice to affected consumers pursuant to the requirements of the breach notification rule in HIPAA. - - - Except as provided in subdivision (3) of this subsection, a financial institution that is subject to the following guidances, and to any revisions, additions, or substitutions relating to an interagency guidance, shall be exempt from this section: (1) The Federal Interagency Guidance Response Programs for Unauthorized Access to Consumer Information and Customer Notice. (2) Final Guidance on Response Programs for Unauthorized Access to Member Information and Member Notice, issued on April 14, 2005, by the National Credit Union Administration. (3) A financial institution regulated by the Department of Financial Regulation that is subject to subdivision (1) or (2) of this subsection shall notify the department as soon as possible after it becomes aware of an incident involving unauthorized access to or use of personally identifiable information.
Data Processor Obligations	Any data collector that maintains or possesses computerized data containing personally identifiable information or login credentials that the data collector does not own or license or any data collector that acts or conducts business in Vermont that maintains or possesses records or data containing personally identifiable information or login credentials that the data collector does not own or license shall notify the owner or licensee of the information of any security breach immediately following discovery of the breach, consistent with the legitimate needs of law enforcement.

	Vermont (Data Breach Requirements)
Other Information	The term "Data collector" means a person who, for any purpose, whether by automated collection or otherwise, handles, collects, disseminates, or otherwise deals with personally identifiable information, and includes the State, State agencies, political subdivisions of the State, public and private universities, privately and publicly held corporations, limited liability companies, financial institutions, and retail operators. - - - In determining whether personally identifiable information or login credentials have been acquired or are reasonably believed to have been acquired by a person without valid authorization, a data collector may consider the following factors, among others: (i) indications that the information is in the physical possession and control of a person without valid authorization, such as a lost or stolen computer or other device containing information; (ii) indications that the information has been downloaded or copied; (iii) indications that the information was used by an unauthorized person, such as fraudulent accounts opened or instances of identity theft reported; or (iv) that the information has been made public. - - - (B) A Vermont law enforcement agency with a reasonable belief that a security breach has or may have occurred at a specific business shall notify the business in writing of its belief. The agency shall also notify the business that additional information on the security breach may need to be furnished to the Office of the Attorney General or the Department of Financial Regulation and shall include the website and telephone number for the office and the department in the notice.

VERMONT

Data Disposal and Security: 9 V.S.A. § 2445.

The numbering and internal citations herein are derived from the applicable state statute. See statute for any applicable exceptions or exemptions.

	Vermont (Data Disposal and Security)
Key Terms	The term "personal information" means the following information that identifies, relates to, describes, or is capable of being associated with a particular individual: his or her signature, Social Security number, physical characteristics or description, passport number, driver's license or State identification card number, insurance policy number, bank account number, credit card number, debit card number, or any other financial information.
Written Policy	See Other Information (implementing and monitoring compliance with policies and procedures).
Data Disposal	A business shall take all reasonable steps to destroy or arrange for the destruction of a customer's records within its custody or control containing personal information that is no longer to be retained by the business by shredding, erasing, or otherwise modifying the personal information in those records to make it unreadable or indecipherable through any means for the purpose of: (1) Ensuring the security and confidentiality of customer personal information; (2) Protecting against any anticipated threats or hazards to the security or integrity of customer personal information; and (3) Protecting against unauthorized access to or use of customer personal information that could result in substantial harm or inconvenience to any customer.
Other Information	An entity that is in the business of disposing of personal financial information that conducts business in Vermont or disposes of personal information of residents of Vermont must take all reasonable measures to dispose of records containing personal information by implementing and monitoring compliance with policies and procedures that protect against unauthorized access to or use of personal information during or after the collection and transportation and disposing of such information.

VIRGINIA

Data Breach Requirements: Va. Code Ann. § 18.2-186.6.

The numbering and internal citations herein are derived from the applicable state statute.

	Virginia (Data Breach Requirements)
Personal Information	The term "personal information" means the first name or first initial and last name in combination with and linked to any one or more of the following data elements that relate to a Virginia resident, when the data elements are neither encrypted nor redacted: 1. Social Security number; 2. Driver's license number or state identification card number issued in lieu of a driver's license number; 3. Financial account number, or credit card or debit card number, in combination with any required security code, access code, or password that would permit access to a resident's financial accounts; 4. Passport number; or 5. Military identification number.
Security Breach Definition	The term "breach of the security of the system" means the unauthorized access and acquisition of unencrypted and unredacted computerized data that compromises the security or confidentiality of personal information maintained by an individual or entity as part of a database of personal information regarding multiple individuals and that causes, or the individual or entity reasonably believes has caused, or will cause, identity theft or other fraud to any Virginia resident.
Good Faith Exception	Good faith acquisition of personal information by an employee or agent of an individual or entity for the purposes of the individual or entity is not a breach of the security of the system, provided that the personal information is not used for a purpose other than a lawful purpose of the individual or entity or subject to further unauthorized disclosure.
Risk of Harm Analysis	If unencrypted or unredacted personal information was or is reasonably believed to have been accessed and acquired by an unauthorized person and causes, or the individual or entity reasonably believes has caused or will cause, identity theft or another fraud to any Virginia resident, an individual or entity that owns or licenses computerized data that includes personal information shall disclose the breach. - - - An individual or entity shall disclose the breach of the security of the system if encrypted information is accessed and acquired in an unencrypted form, or if the security breach involves a person with access to the encryption key and the individual or entity reasonably believes that such a breach has caused or will cause identity theft or other fraud to any Virginia resident.
Notification Timeline	The breach notification shall be provided without unreasonable delay, provided a notification may be reasonably delayed to allow the individual or entity to determine the scope of the breach of the security of the system and restore the reasonable integrity of the system.
Security and Investigation Exceptions	The breach notification may be delayed if, after the individual or entity notifies a law-enforcement agency, the law-enforcement agency determines and advises the individual or entity that the notice will impede a criminal or civil investigation, or homeland or national security. Notice shall be made without unreasonable delay after the law-enforcement agency determines that the notification will no longer impede the investigation or jeopardize national or homeland security.

	Virginia (Data Breach Requirements)
Notification Content Requirements	A breach notification shall include a description of the following: (1) The incident in general terms; (2) The type of personal information that was subject to the unauthorized access and acquisition; (3) The general acts of the individual or entity to protect the personal information from further unauthorized access; (4) A telephone number that the person may call for further information and assistance, if one exists; and (5) Advice that directs the person to remain vigilant by reviewing account statements and monitoring free credit reports.
Delivery Methods	A breach notice may be provided by one of the following methods: 1. Written notice to the last known postal address in the records of the individual or entity; 2. Telephone notice; 3. Electronic notice; or 4. Substitute notice, if the individual or the entity required to provide notice demonstrates that the cost of providing notice will exceed $50,000, the affected class of Virginia residents to be notified exceeds 100,000 residents, or the individual or the entity does not have sufficient contact information or consent to provide notice as described in subdivisions 1, 2, or 3 of this definition.
Substitute Notice	Substitute notice consists of all of the following: a. Email notice if the individual or the entity has email addresses for the members of the affected class of residents; b. Conspicuous posting of the notice on the website of the individual or the entity if the individual or the entity maintains a website; and c. Notice to major statewide media.
Notice to Government Agencies	A breach notification shall be provided to the Office of the Attorney General and any affected resident of the commonwealth without unreasonable delay. - - - In the event an individual or entity provides notice to more than 1,000 persons at one time, the individual or entity shall notify, without unreasonable delay, the Office of the Attorney General of the timing, distribution, and content of the notice.
Consumer Reporting Agencies	In the event an individual or entity provides notice to more than 1,000 persons at one time, the individual or entity shall notify, without unreasonable delay, the Office of the Attorney General and all consumer reporting agencies of the timing, distribution, and content of the notice.
Preemption and Compliance	An entity that is subject to Title V of the Gramm-Leach-Bliley Act and maintains procedures for notification of a breach of the security of the system in accordance with the provision of that act and any rules, regulations, or guidelines promulgated thereto shall be deemed to be in compliance with this law. - - - An entity that complies with the notification requirements or procedures pursuant to the rules, regulations, procedures, or guidelines established by the entity's primary or functional state or federal regulator shall be in compliance with this law.

	Virginia (Data Breach Requirements)
Data Processor Obligations	An individual or entity that maintains computerized data that includes personal information that the individual or entity does not own or license shall notify the owner or licensee of the information of any breach of the security of the system without unreasonable delay following discovery of the breach of the security of the system, if the personal information was accessed and acquired by an unauthorized person or the individual or entity reasonably believes the personal information was accessed and acquired by an unauthorized person.
Other Information	Nothing in this law shall apply to an individual or entity regulated by the State Corporation Commission's Bureau of Insurance. - - - The provisions of this section shall not apply to criminal intelligence systems subject to the restrictions of 28 C.F.R. Part 23 that are maintained by law enforcement agencies of the commonwealth and the organized Criminal Gang File of the Virginia Criminal Information Network (VCIN), established pursuant to Chapter 2 (§ 52-12 et seq.) of Title 52. - - - Notwithstanding any other provision of this section, any employer or payroll service provider that owns or licenses computerized data relating to income tax withheld pursuant to Article 16 (§ 58.1-460 et seq.) of Chapter 3 of Title 58.1 shall notify the Office of the Attorney General without unreasonable delay after the discovery or notification of unauthorized access and acquisition of unencrypted and unredacted computerized data containing a taxpayer identification number in combination with the income tax withheld for that taxpayer that compromises the confidentiality of such data and that creates a reasonable belief that an unencrypted and unredacted version of such information was accessed and acquired by an unauthorized person, and causes, or the employer or payroll provider reasonably believes has caused or will cause, identity theft or other fraud. With respect to employers, this subsection applies only to information regarding the employer's employees, and does not apply to information regarding the employer's customers or other non-employees. Such employer or payroll service provider shall provide the Office of the Attorney General with the name and federal employer identification number of the employer as defined in § 58.1-460 that may be affected by the compromise in confidentiality. Upon receipt of such notice, the Office of the Attorney General shall notify the Department of Taxation of the compromise in confidentiality. The notification required under this subsection that does not otherwise require notification under this section shall not be subject to any other notification, requirement, exemption, or penalty contained in this section.

* * * * *

VIRGINIA

Data Disposal and Security: See the Virginia Consumer Data Protection Act (Appendix 5).

WASHINGTON

Data Breach Requirements: RCW § 19.255.005 et seq.

The numbering and internal citations herein are derived from the applicable state statute.

	Washington (Data Breach Requirements)
Personal Information	(2)(a) The term "personal information" means: (i) An individual's first name or first initial and last name in combination with any one or more of the following data elements: (A) Social Security number; (B) Driver's license number or Washington identification card number; (C) Account number or credit or debit card number, in combination with any required security code, access code, or password that would permit access to an individual's financial account, or any other numbers or information that can be used to access a person's financial account; (D) Full date of birth; (E) Private key that is unique to an individual and that is used to authenticate or sign an electronic record; (F) Student, military, or passport identification number; (G) Health insurance policy number or health insurance identification number; (H) Any information about a consumer's medical history or mental or physical condition or about a health care professional's medical diagnosis or treatment of the consumer; or (I) Biometric data generated by automatic measurements of an individual's biological characteristics such as a fingerprint, voiceprint, eye retinas, irises, or other unique biological patterns or characteristics that are used to identify a specific individual; (ii) Username or email address in combination with a password or security questions and answers that would permit access to an online account; and (iii) Any of the data elements or any combination of the data elements described in (a)(i) of this subsection without the consumer's first name or first initial and last name if: (A) Encryption, redaction, or other methods have not rendered the data element or combination of data elements unusable; and (B) The data element or combination of data elements would enable a person to commit identity theft against a consumer.
Security Breach Definition	The term "breach of the security of the system" means unauthorized acquisition of data that compromises the security, confidentiality, or integrity of personal information maintained by the person or business.
Good Faith Exception	Good faith acquisition of personal information by an employee or agent of the person or business for the purposes of the person or business is not a breach of the security of the system when the personal information is not used or subject to further unauthorized disclosure.
Risk of Harm Analysis	A breach notice is not required if the breach of the security of the system is not reasonably likely to subject consumers to a risk of harm. The breach of secured personal information must be disclosed if the information acquired and accessed is not secured during a security breach or if the confidential process, encryption key, or other means to decipher the secured information was acquired by an unauthorized person.

	Washington (Data Breach Requirements)
Notification Timeline	The breach notification to affected consumers must be made in the most expedient time possible, without unreasonable delay, and no more than 30 calendar days after the breach was discovered, unless the delay is at the request of law enforcement, or the delay is due to any measures necessary to determine the scope of the breach and restore the reasonable integrity of the data system.
Security and Investigation Exceptions	The breach notification may be delayed if the data owner or licensee contacts a law enforcement agency after discovery of a breach of the security of the system and a law enforcement agency determines that the notification will impede a criminal investigation. The notification shall be made after the law enforcement agency determines that it will not compromise the investigation.
Notification Content Requirements	Any person or business that is required to issue a breach notification shall meet all of the following requirements: (a) The notification must be written in plain language; and (b) The notification must include, at a minimum, the following information: (i) The name and contact information of the reporting person or business subject to this section; (ii) A list of the types of personal information that were or are reasonably believed to have been the subject of a breach; (iii) A time frame of exposure, if known, including the date of the breach and the date of the discovery of the breach; and (iv) The toll-free telephone numbers and addresses of the major credit reporting agencies if the breach exposed personal information.
Delivery Methods	A breach notice may be provided by one of the following methods: (a) Written notice; (b) Electronic notice, if the notice provided is consistent with the provisions regarding electronic records and signatures set forth in 15 U.S.C. § 7001 (The Electronic Signatures in Global and National Commerce Act); (c) Substitute notice, if the person or business demonstrates that the cost of providing notice would exceed $250,000, or that the affected class of subject persons to be notified exceeds 500,000, or the person or business does not have sufficient contact information; or (d)(i) If the breach of the security of the system involves personal information including a username or password, notice may be provided electronically or by email. The notice must also inform the person whose personal information has been breached to promptly change his or her password and security question or answer, as applicable, or to take other appropriate steps to protect the online account with the person or business and all other online accounts for which the person whose personal information has been breached uses the same username or email address and password or security question or answer; (ii) However, when the breach of the security of the system involves login credentials of an email account furnished by the person or business, the person or business may not provide the notification to that email address, but must provide notice using another method described in this subsection (4). The notice must also inform the person whose personal information has been breached to promptly change his or her password and security question or answer, as applicable, or to take other appropriate steps to protect the online account with the person or business and all other online accounts for which the person whose personal information has been breached uses the same username or email address and password or security question or answer.

	Washington (Data Breach Requirements)
Substitute Notice	Substitute notice shall consist of all of the following: (i) Email notice when the person or business has an email address for the subject persons; (ii) Conspicuous posting of the notice on the website page of the person or business, if the person or business maintains one; and (iii) Notification to major statewide media.
Notice to Government Agencies	(a) Any person or business that is required to issue a breach notification to more than 500 Washington residents as a result of a single breach shall notify the attorney general of the breach no more than 30 days after the breach was discovered. The notice to the attorney general shall include the following information: (i) The number of Washington consumers affected by the breach, or an estimate if the exact number is not known; (ii) A list of the types of personal information that were or are reasonably believed to have been the subject of a breach; (iii) A time frame of exposure, if known, including the date of the breach and the date of the discovery of the breach; (iii) A time frame of exposure, if known, including the date of the breach and the date of the discovery of the breach; (iv) A summary of steps taken to contain the breach; and (v) A single sample copy of the security breach notification, excluding any personally identifiable information. (b) The notice to the attorney general must be updated if any of the information identified herein is unknown at the time notice is due.
Consumer Reporting Agencies	N/A

	Washington (Data Breach Requirements)
Preemption and Compliance	(1) A covered entity under the federal health insurance portability and accountability act of 1996, 42 U.S.C. Sec. 1320d et seq., is deemed to have complied with the requirements of this chapter with respect to protected health information if it has complied with section 13402 of the federal health information technology for economic and clinical health act, P.L. 111-5 as it existed on July 24, 2015. Covered entities shall notify the attorney general pursuant to RCW 19.255.010(7) in compliance with the timeliness of notification requirements of section 13402 of the federal health information technology for economic and clinical health act, P.L. 111-5 as it existed on July 24, 2015, notwithstanding the timeline in RCW 19.255.010(7). (2) A financial institution under the authority of the Office of the Comptroller of the Currency, the Federal Deposit Insurance Corporation, the National Credit Union Administration, or the Federal Reserve System is deemed to have complied with the requirements of this chapter with respect to "sensitive customer information" as defined in the interagency guidelines establishing information security standards, 12 C.F.R. Part 30, Appendix B, 12 C.F.R. Part 208, Appendix D-2, 12 C.F.R. Part 225, Appendix F, and 12 C.F.R. Part 364, Appendix B, and 12 C.F.R. Part 748, Appendices A and B, as they existed on July 24, 2015, if the financial institution provides notice to affected consumers pursuant to the interagency guidelines and the notice complies with the customer notice provisions of the interagency guidelines establishing information security standards and the interagency guidance on response programs for unauthorized access to customer information and customer notice under 12 C.F.R. Part 364 as it existed on July 24, 2015. The entity shall notify the attorney general pursuant to RCW 19.255.010 in addition to providing notice to its primary federal regulator.
Data Processor Obligations	Any person or business that maintains or possesses data that may include personal information that the person or business does not own or license shall notify the owner or licensee of the information of any breach of the security of the data immediately following discovery, if the personal information was, or is reasonably believed to have been, acquired by an unauthorized person.

WASHINGTON

Data Disposal and Security: RCW § 19.215.010 et seq..

The numbering and internal citations herein are derived from the applicable state statute. See statute for any applicable exceptions or exemptions.

	Washington (Data Disposal and Security)
Key Terms	The term "destroy personal information" means shredding, erasing, or otherwise modifying personal information in records to make the personal information unreadable or undecipherable through any reasonable means. - - - The term "personal financial" and "health information" mean information that is identifiable to an individual and that is commonly used for financial or health care purposes, including account numbers, access codes or passwords, information gathered for account security purposes, credit card numbers, information held for the purpose of account access or transaction initiation, or information that relates to medical history or status. - - - The term "personal identification number issued by a government entity" means a taxpayer identification number, Social Security number, driver's license or permit number, state identification card number issued by the department of licensing, or any other number or code issued by a government entity for the purpose of personal identification that is protected and is not available to the public under any circumstances. - - - The term "record" includes any material, regardless of the physical form, on which information is recorded or preserved by any means, including in written or spoken words, graphically depicted, printed, or electromagnetically transmitted.
Data Disposal	An entity must take all reasonable steps to destroy, or arrange for the destruction of, personal financial and health information and personal identification numbers issued by government entities in an individual's records within its custody or control when the entity is disposing of records that it will no longer retain. This requirement does not apply to the disposal of records by a transfer of the records, not otherwise prohibited by law, to another entity, including a transfer to archive or otherwise preserve public records as required by law.
Other Information	An entity is not liable under these requirements for records it has relinquished to the custody and control of the individual to whom the records pertain.

WEST VIRGINIA

Data Breach Requirements: W. Va. Code § 46A-2A-101 et seq.

The numbering and internal citations herein are derived from the applicable state statute.

	West Virginia (Data Breach Requirements)
Personal Information	The term "personal information" means the first name or first initial and last name linked to any one or more of the following data elements that relate to a resident of this state, when the data elements are neither encrypted nor redacted: (A) Social Security number; (B) Driver's license number or state identification card number issued in lieu of a driver's license; or (C) Financial account number, or credit card, or debit card number in combination with any required security code, access code, or password that would permit access to a resident's financial accounts.
Security Breach Definition	The term "breach of the security of a system" means the unauthorized access and acquisition of unencrypted and unredacted computerized data that compromises the security or confidentiality of personal information maintained by an individual or entity as part of a database of personal information regarding multiple individuals and that causes the individual or entity to reasonably believe that the breach of security has caused or will cause identity theft or other fraud to any resident of this state.
Good Faith Exception	Good faith acquisition of personal information by an employee or agent of an individual or entity for the purposes of the individual or the entity is not a breach of the security of the system, provided that the personal information is not used for a purpose other than a lawful purpose of the individual or entity or subject to further unauthorized disclosure.
Risk of Harm Analysis	An individual or entity that owns or licenses computerized data that includes personal information shall give notice of any breach of the security of the system following discovery or notification of the breach of the security of the system to any resident of this state whose unencrypted and unredacted personal information was or is reasonably believed to have been accessed and acquired by an unauthorized person and that causes, or the individual or entity reasonably believes has caused or will cause, identity theft or other fraud to any resident of this state. - - - An individual or entity must give notice of the breach of the security of the system if encrypted information is accessed and acquired in an unencrypted form or if the security breach involves a person with access to the encryption key and the individual or entity reasonably believes that such breach has caused or will cause identity theft or other fraud to any resident of this state.
Notification Timeline	Except as provided in subsection (e) (law enforcement exception) or in order to take any measures necessary to determine the scope of the breach and to restore the reasonable integrity of the system, the notice shall be made without unreasonable delay.
Security and Investigation Exceptions	A breach notice may be delayed if a law-enforcement agency determines and advises the individual or entity that the notice will impede a criminal or civil investigation or homeland or national security. Notice must be made without unreasonable delay after the law enforcement agency determines that notification will no longer impede the investigation or jeopardize national or homeland security.

	West Virginia (Data Breach Requirements)
Notification Content Requirements	The breach notice shall include: (1) To the extent possible, a description of the categories of information that were reasonably believed to have been accessed or acquired by an unauthorized person, including Social Security numbers, driver's licenses, or state identification numbers and financial data; (2) A telephone number or website address that the individual may use to contact the entity or the agent of the entity and from whom the individual may learn: (A) What types of information the entity maintained about that individual or about individuals in general; and (B) Whether or not the entity maintained information about that individual. (3) The toll-free contact telephone numbers and addresses for the major credit reporting agencies and information on how to place a fraud alert or security freeze.
Delivery Methods	A breach notice may be provided by one of the following methods: (A) Written notice to the postal address in the records of the individual or entity; (B) Telephonic notice; (C) Electronic notice, if the notice provided is consistent with the provisions regarding electronic records and signatures, set forth in 15 U.S.C. § 7001 (The Electronic Signatures in Global and National Commerce Act). (D) Substitute notice, if the individual or the entity required to provide notice demonstrates that the cost of providing notice will exceed $50,000 or that the affected class of residents to be notified exceeds 100,000 persons, or that the individual or the entity does not have sufficient contact information or to provide notice as described in paragraph (A), (B) or (C).
Substitute Notice	Substitute notice consists of any two of the following: (i) Email notice if the individual or the entity has email addresses for the members of the affected class of residents; (ii) Conspicuous posting of the notice on the website of the individual or the entity if the individual or the entity maintains a website; or (iii) Notice to major statewide media.
Notice to Government Agencies	N/A
Consumer Reporting Agencies	If an entity is required to notify more than 1,000 persons of a breach, the entity shall also notify, without unreasonable delay, all consumer reporting agencies that compile and maintain files on a nationwide basis of the timing, distribution and content of the notices. Nothing in this subsection shall be construed to require the entity to provide to the consumer reporting agency the names or other personal identifying information of breach notice recipients. This subsection shall not apply to an entity who is subject to Title V of the Gramm-Leach-Bliley Act.
Preemption and Compliance	<u>See</u> Consumer Reporting Agencies (GLBA exception). - - - A financial institution that responds in accordance with the notification guidelines prescribed by the Federal Interagency Guidance on Response Programs for Unauthorized Access to Customer Information and Customer Notice is deemed to be in compliance with this article. - - - An entity that complies with the notification requirements or procedures pursuant to the rules, regulations, procedures, or guidelines established by the entity's primary or functional regulator shall be in compliance with this article.

	West Virginia (Data Breach Requirements)
Data Processor Obligations	An individual or entity that maintains computerized data that includes personal information that the individual or entity does not own or license shall give notice to the owner or licensee of the information of any breach of the security of the system as soon as practicable following discovery, if the personal information was or the entity reasonably believes was accessed and acquired by an unauthorized person.

WISCONSIN

Data Breach Requirements: Wis. Stat. § 134.98.

The numbering and internal citations herein are derived from the applicable state statute.

	Wisconsin (Data Breach Requirements)
Personal Information	(b) The term "personal information" means an individual's last name and the individual's first name or first initial, in combination with and linked to any of the following elements, if the element is not publicly available information and is not encrypted, redacted, or altered in a manner that renders the element unreadable: 1. The individual's Social Security number. 2. The individual's driver's license number or state identification number. 3. The individual's financial account number, including a credit or debit card account number, or any security code, access code, or password that would permit access to the individual's financial account. 4. The individual's deoxyribonucleic acid (DNA) profile, as defined in s. 939.74(2d)(a). 5. The individual's unique biometric data, including fingerprint, voice print, retina or iris image, or any other unique physical representation.
Security Breach Definition	If an entity whose principal place of business is located in this state or an entity that maintains or licenses personal information in this state knows that personal information in the entity's possession has been acquired by a person whom the entity has not authorized to acquire the personal information, the entity shall make reasonable efforts to notify each subject of the personal information.
Good Faith Exception	An entity is not required to provide a breach notice if the personal information was acquired in good faith by an employee or agent of the entity, if the personal information is used for a lawful purpose of the entity.
Risk of Harm Analysis	An entity is not required to provide a breach notice if the acquisition of personal information does not create a material risk of identity theft or fraud to the subject of the personal information.
Notification Timeline	The breach notice shall be provided within a reasonable time, not to exceed 45 days after the entity learns of the acquisition of personal information. A determination as to reasonableness herein shall include consideration of the number of notices that an entity must provide and the methods of communication available to the entity.
Security and Investigation Exceptions	A law enforcement agency may, in order to protect an investigation or homeland security, ask an entity not to provide a breach notice that is otherwise required for any period of time, and the notification process shall begin at the end of that time period. Notwithstanding, if an entity receives such a request, the entity may not provide notice of or publicize an unauthorized acquisition of personal information, except as authorized by the law enforcement agency that made the request.
Notification Content Requirements	The breach notice shall indicate that the entity knows of the unauthorized acquisition of personal information pertaining to the subject of the personal information. - - - Upon written request by a person who has received a breach notice, the entity that provided the notice shall identify the personal information that was acquired.

	Wisconsin (Data Breach Requirements)
Delivery Methods	An entity shall provide the breach notice by mail or by a method the entity has previously employed to communicate with the subject of the personal information. If an entity cannot with reasonable diligence determine the mailing address of the subject of the personal information, and if the entity has not previously communicated with the subject of the personal information, the entity shall provide notice by a method reasonably calculated to provide actual notice to the subject of the personal information.
Substitute Notice	See Delivery Methods (reasonably calculated standard).
Notice to Government Agencies	N/A
Consumer Reporting Agencies	If, as the result of a single incident, an entity is required to notify 1,000 or more individuals that personal information pertaining to the individuals has been acquired, the entity shall without unreasonable delay notify all consumer reporting agencies of the timing, distribution, and content of the notices sent to the individuals.
Preemption and Compliance	The law does not apply to any of the following: (a) An entity that is subject to, and in compliance with, the privacy and security requirements of 15 USC 6801 to 6827, or a person that has a contractual obligation to such an entity, if the entity or person has in effect a policy concerning breaches of information security. (b) An entity that is described in 45 CFR 164.104(a), if the entity complies with the requirements of 45 CFR part 164.
Data Processor Obligations	If a person, other than an individual, who stores personal information pertaining to a resident of this state, but does not own or license the personal information, knows that the personal information has been acquired by a person whom the person storing the personal information has not authorized to acquire the personal information, and the person storing the personal information has not entered into a contract with the person that owns or licenses the personal information, the person storing the personal information shall notify the person that owns or licenses the personal information of the acquisition as soon as practicable.
Other Information	(b) If an entity whose principal place of business is not located in this state knows that personal information pertaining to a resident of this state has been acquired by a person whom the entity has not authorized to acquire the personal information, the entity shall make reasonable efforts to notify each resident of this state who is the subject of the personal information. The notice shall indicate that the entity knows of the unauthorized acquisition of personal information pertaining to the resident of this state who is the subject of the personal information.

WISCONSIN

Data Disposal and Security: Wis. Stat. § 134.97.

The numbering and internal citations herein are derived from the applicable state statute. See statute for any applicable exceptions or exemptions.

	Wisconsin (Data Disposal and Security)
Key Terms	The term "dispose" does not include a sale of a record or the transfer of a record for value. - - - The term "personal information" means any of the following: 1. Personally identifiable data about an individual's medical condition, if the data are not generally considered to be public knowledge. 2. Personally identifiable data that contain an individual's account or customer number, account balance, balance owing, credit balance, or credit limit, if the data relate to an individual's account or transaction with a financial institution. 3. Personally identifiable data provided by an individual to a financial institution upon opening an account or applying for a loan or credit. 4. Personally identifiable data about an individual's federal, state, or local tax returns. - - - The term "personally identifiable" means capable of being associated with a particular individual through one or more identifiers or other information or circumstances.
Data Disposal	A financial institution, medical business, or tax preparation business may not dispose of a record containing personal information unless the financial institution, medical business, tax preparation business, or other person under contract with the financial institution, medical business, or tax preparation business does any of the following: (a) Shreds the record before the disposal of the record. (b) Erases the personal information contained in the record before the disposal of the record. (c) Modifies the record to make the personal information unreadable before the disposal of the record. (d) Takes actions that it reasonably believes will ensure that no unauthorized person will have access to the personal information contained in the record for the period between the record's disposal and the record's destruction.

WYOMING

Data Breach Requirements: Wyo. Stat. Ann. §§ 40-12-501 - 502, and 6-3-901(b)(iii) to (xiv).

The numbering and internal citations herein are derived from the applicable state statute.

	Wyoming (Data Breach Requirements)
Personal Information	The term "personal identifying information" means the first name or first initial and last name of a person in combination with one (1) or more of the data elements specified in W.S. 6-3-901(b)(iii) through (xiv), when the data elements are not redacted. - - - W.S. 6-3-901(b): (iii) Social Security number; (iv) Driver's license number; (v) Account, credit card, or debit card number in combination with any security code, access code or password that would allow access to a financial account of the person; (vi) Tribal identification card; (vii) Federal or state government issued identification card; (viii) Shared secrets or security tokens that are known to be used for databased authentication; (ix) A username or email address, in combination with a password or security question and answer that would permit access to an online account; (x) A birth or marriage certificate; (xi) Medical information, meaning a person's medical history, mental or physical condition, or medical treatment or diagnosis by a health care professional; (xii) Health insurance information, meaning a person's health insurance policy number or subscriber identification number, any unique identifier used by a health insurer to identify the person or information related to a person's application and claims history; (xiii) Unique biometric data, meaning data generated from measurements or analysis of human body characteristics for authentication purposes; or (xiv) An individual taxpayer identification number.
Security Breach Definition	The term "breach of the security of the data system" means unauthorized acquisition of computerized data that materially compromises the security, confidentiality, or integrity of personal identifying information maintained by a person or business and causes or is reasonably believed to cause loss or injury to a resident of this state.
Good Faith Exception	Good faith acquisition of personal identifying information by an employee or agent of a person or business for the purposes of the person or business is not a breach of the security of the data system, provided that the personal identifying information is not used or subject to further unauthorized disclosure.
Risk of Harm Analysis	An individual who or commercial entity that conducts business in Wyoming and owns or licenses computerized data that includes personal identifying information about a resident of Wyoming shall, when it becomes aware of a breach of the security of the system, conduct in good faith a reasonable and prompt investigation to determine the likelihood that personal identifying information has been or will be misused. If the investigation determines that the misuse of personal identifying information about a Wyoming resident has occurred or is reasonably likely to occur, the individual or the commercial entity shall give the breach notice.

	Wyoming (Data Breach Requirements)
Notification Timeline	A breach notice shall be made in the most expedient time possible and without unreasonable delay, consistent with the legitimate needs of law enforcement and consistent with any measures necessary to determine the scope of the breach and to restore the reasonable integrity of the computerized data system.
Security and Investigation Exceptions	The breach notification may be delayed if a law enforcement agency determines in writing that the notification may seriously impede a criminal investigation.
Notification Content Requirements	The breach notification shall include, at a minimum: (i) A toll-free number: (A) That the individual may use to contact the person collecting the data, or his agent; and (B) From which the individual may learn the toll-free contact telephone numbers and addresses for the major credit reporting agencies. (ii) The types of personal identifying information that were or are reasonably believed to have been the subject of the breach; (iii) A general description of the breach incident; (iv) The approximate date of the breach of security, if that information is reasonably possible to determine at the time notice is provided; (v) In general terms, the actions taken by the individual or commercial entity to protect the system containing the personal identifying information from further breaches; (vi) Advice that directs the person to remain vigilant by reviewing account statements and monitoring credit reports; (vii) Whether notification was delayed as a result of a law enforcement investigation, if that information is reasonably possible to determine at the time the notice is provided.
Delivery Methods	A breach notice may be provided by one of the following methods: (i) Written notice; (ii) Electronic mail notice; (iii) Substitute notice, if the person demonstrates: (A) That the cost of providing notice would exceed $10,000 for Wyoming-based persons or businesses, and $250,000 for all other businesses operating but not based in Wyoming; (B) That the affected class of subject persons to be notified exceeds 10,000 for Wyoming-based persons or businesses and 500,000 for all other businesses operating but not based in Wyoming; or (C) The person does not have sufficient contact information.
Substitute Notice	"Substitute notice" means: (A) An email notice when the person or business has an email address for the subject persons; (B) Conspicuous posting of the notice on the website page of the person or business if the person or business maintains one; and (C) Publication in applicable local or statewide media. - - - Substitute notice shall consist of all of the following: (A) Conspicuous posting of the notice on the internet, the world wide web or a similar proprietary or common carrier electronic system site of the person collecting the data, if the person maintains any of those public online outlets; and (B) Notification to major statewide media. The notice to media shall include a toll-free phone number where an individual can learn whether that individual's personal information is included in the security breach.

	Wyoming (Data Breach Requirements)
Notice to Government Agencies	N/A
Consumer Reporting Agencies	N/A
Preemption and Compliance	Any financial institution as defined in 15 U.S.C. 6809 or federal credit union as defined by 12 U.S.C. 1752 that maintains notification procedures subject to the requirements of 15 U.S.C. 6801(b)(3) and 12 C.F.R. Part 364 Appendix B or Part 748 Appendix B, is deemed to be in compliance with this section if the financial institution notifies affected Wyoming customers in compliance with the requirements of 15 U.S.C. 6801 through 6809 and 12 C.F.R. Part 364 Appendix B or Part 748 Appendix B. - - - A covered entity or business associate that is subject to and complies with the Health Insurance Portability and Accountability Act of 1996 (HIPAA), and the regulations promulgated under that act, is deemed to be in compliance with this section if the covered entity or business associate notifies affected Wyoming customers or entities in compliance with the requirements of HIPAA.
Data Processor Obligations	Any person who maintains computerized data that includes personal identifying information on behalf of another business entity shall disclose to the business entity for which the information is maintained any breach of the security of the system as soon as practicable following the determination that personal identifying information was, or is reasonably believed to have been, acquired by an unauthorized person. The person who maintains the data on behalf of another business entity and the business entity on whose behalf the data is maintained may agree which person or entity will provide any required breach notice, provided only a single notice for each breach shall be required. If agreement regarding notification cannot be reached, the person who has the direct business relationship with the resident of this state shall provide the breach notice.

THE HEALTH INSURANCE PORTABILITY AND ACCOUNTABILITY ACT (HIPAA) BREACH RULES

Data Breach Requirements: 45 C.F.R. §§ 160.103, 164.400 et seq.

The numbering and internal citations herein are derived from the applicable state statute.

	HIPAA (Data Breach Requirements)
Protected Health Information	The term "protected health information" means individually identifiable health information, including demographic data, that relates to: (i) an individual's past, present or future physical or mental health or condition, (ii) the provision of health care to the individual, or (iii) the past, present, or future payment for the provision of health care to the individual, and that identifies the individual or for which there is a reasonable basis to believe it can be used to identify the individual. - - - The term "unsecured protected health information" means protected health information that is not rendered unusable, unreadable, or indecipherable to unauthorized persons through the use of a technology or methodology specified by the Office of the Secretary of Health and Human Services (HHS).
Security Breach Definition	A "breach" means the acquisition, access, use, or disclosure of protected health information in a manner not permitted under the HIPAA Privacy Rule, which compromises the security or privacy of the protected health information.
Good Faith and Other Exclusions	A breach does not include: (i) Any unintentional acquisition, access, or use of protected health information by a workforce member or person acting under the authority of a covered entity or a business associate, if such acquisition, access, or use was made in good faith and within the scope of authority and does not result in further use or disclosure in a manner not permitted under the HIPAA Privacy Rule. (ii) Any inadvertent disclosure by a person who is authorized to access protected health information at a covered entity or business associate to another person authorized to access protected health information at the same covered entity or business associate, or organized health care arrangement in which the covered entity participates, and the information received as a result of such disclosure is not further used or disclosed in a manner not permitted under the HIPAA Privacy Rule. (iii) A disclosure of protected health information where a covered entity or business associate has a good faith belief that an unauthorized person to whom the disclosure was made would not reasonably have been able to retain such information.
Low Probability Analysis	An acquisition, access, use, or disclosure of protected health information in a manner not permitted under the HIPAA Privacy Rule is presumed to be a breach, unless the covered entity or business associate, as applicable, demonstrates that there is a low probability that the protected health information has been compromised based on a risk assessment of at least the following factors: (i) The nature and extent of the protected health information involved, including the types of identifiers and the likelihood of re-identification; (ii) The unauthorized person who used the protected health information or to whom the disclosure was made; (iii) Whether the protected health information was actually acquired or viewed; and (iv) The extent to which the risk to the protected health information has been mitigated.
Notification Timeline	A covered entity shall provide the breach notification without unreasonable delay and in no case later than 60 calendar days after discovery of a breach.

	HIPAA (Data Breach Requirements)
Security and Investigation Exceptions	If a law enforcement official states to a covered entity or business associate that a breach notification would impede a criminal investigation or cause damage to national security, a covered entity or business associate shall: (a) If the statement is in writing and specifies the time for which a delay is required, delay such notification, notice, or posting for the time period specified by the official; or (b) If the statement is made orally, document the statement, including the identity of the official making the statement, and delay the notification, notice, or posting temporarily and no longer than 30 days from the date of the oral statement, unless a written statement as described in paragraph (a) of this section is submitted during that time.
Notification Content Requirements	The breach notification shall include, to the extent possible: (A) A brief description of what happened, including the date of the breach and the date of the discovery of the breach, if known; (B) A description of the types of unsecured protected health information that were involved in the breach (such as whether full name, Social Security number, date of birth, home address, account number, diagnosis, disability code, or other types of information were involved); (C) Any steps individuals should take to protect themselves from potential harm resulting from the breach; (D) A brief description of what the covered entity involved is doing to investigate the breach, to mitigate harm to individuals, and to protect against any further breaches; and (E) Contact procedures for individuals to ask questions or learn additional information, which shall include a toll-free telephone number, an email address, website, or postal address. - - - The breach notification shall be written in plain language.
Delivery Methods	A breach notice may be provided by one of the following methods: (1) Written notice; (i) Written notification by first-class mail to the individual at the last known address of the individual or, if the individual agrees to electronic notice and such agreement has not been withdrawn, by email. The notification may be provided in one or more mailings as information is available; or (ii) If the covered entity knows the individual is deceased and has the address of the next of kin or personal representative of the individual (as specified under § 164.502(g)(4) of subpart E), written notification by first-class mail to either the next of kin or personal representative of the individual. The notification may be provided in one or more mailings as information is available. (2) Substitute notice. In the case in which there is insufficient or out-of-date contact information that precludes written notification, a substitute form of notice reasonably calculated to reach the individual shall be provided. Substitute notice need not be provided in the case in which there is insufficient or out-of-date contact information that precludes written notification to the next of kin or personal representative of the individual. (i) In the case in which there is insufficient or out-of-date contact information for fewer than ten individuals, then such substitute notice may be provided by an alternative form of written notice, telephone, or other means.

	HIPAA (Data Breach Requirements)
	(ii) In the case in which there is insufficient or out-of-date contact information for ten or more individuals, then such substitute notice shall: (A) Be in the form of either a conspicuous posting for a period of 90 days on the home page of the website of the covered entity involved, or conspicuous notice in major print or broadcast media in geographic areas where the individuals affected by the breach likely reside; and (B) Include a toll-free phone number that remains active for at least 90 days where an individual can learn whether the individual's unsecured protected health information may be included in the breach. (3) In any case deemed by the covered entity to require urgency because of possible imminent misuse of unsecured protected health information, the covered entity may provide information to individuals by telephone or other means, as appropriate, in addition to notice provided hereunder.
Substitute Notice	See Delivery Methods.
Notice to Government Agencies	A covered entity shall, following the discovery of a breach of unsecured protected health information, notify the HHS secretary as follows: (1) For breaches involving 500 or more individuals, a covered entity shall, except as provided in § 164.412 (law enforcement exception), provide a breach notification to the HHS secretary contemporaneously with the notice furnished to individuals and in the manner specified on the HHS website. (2) For breaches involving fewer than 500 individuals, a covered entity shall maintain a log or other documentation of such breaches and, not later than 60 days after the end of each calendar year, provide a breach notification to the HHS secretary in the manner specified on the HHS website.
Notice to the Media	For a breach of unsecured protected health information involving more than 500 residents of a state or jurisdiction, a covered entity shall, notify prominent media outlets serving the state or jurisdiction, without unreasonable delay and in no case later than 60 calendar days after discovery of a breach. The notification shall include the content requirements above (see Notification Content Requirements).
Preemption and Compliance	N/A
Data Processor Obligations	Except as provided in § 164.412 (law enforcement exception), a business associate shall, following the discovery of a breach of unsecured protected health information, notify the covered entity of such breach without unreasonable delay and in no case later than 60 calendar days after discovery of a breach. The breach notification shall include, to the extent possible, the identification of each individual whose unsecured protected health information has been, or is reasonably believed by the business associate to have been, accessed, acquired, used, or disclosed during the breach. - - - A business associate shall provide the covered entity with any other available information that the covered entity is required to include in notification to the individual.

	HIPAA (Data Breach Requirements)
Other Information	The covered entity or business associate, as applicable, shall have the burden of demonstrating that all breach notifications were made as required or that the use or disclosure of protected health information did not constitute a breach. - - - A breach shall be treated as discovered by a covered entity as of the first day on which such breach is known to the covered entity, or, by exercising reasonable diligence would have been known to the covered entity. A covered entity shall be deemed to have knowledge of a breach if such breach is known, or by exercising reasonable diligence would have been known, to any person, other than the person committing the breach, who is a workforce member or agent of the covered entity (determined in accordance with the federal common law of agency). - - - For more information on reporting a breach to HHS, see https://ocrportal.hhs.gov/ocr/breach/wizard_breach.jsf?faces-redirect=true.

DEFENSE FEDERAL ACQUISITION REGULATION SUPPLEMENT

Data Breach Requirements: 48 CFR § 252.204-7012. Safeguarding covered defense information and cyber incident reporting.

The numbering and internal citations herein are derived from the applicable state statute.

	DFARS / CDI & Cyber Incident Reporting (Data Breach Requirements)
Key Terms	The term "covered contractor information system" means an unclassified information system that is owned, or operated by or for, a contractor and that processes, stores, or transmits covered defense information. - - - The term "covered defense information" means unclassified controlled technical information or other information, as described in the Controlled Unclassified Information (CUI) Registry at http://www.archives.gov/cui/registry/category-list.html. This requires safeguarding or dissemination controls pursuant to and consistent with law, regulations, and governmentwide policies, and is (1) Marked or otherwise identified in the contract, task order, or delivery order and provided to the contractor by or on behalf of DoD in support of the performance of the contract; or (2) Collected, developed, received, transmitted, used, or stored by or on behalf of the contractor in support of the performance of the contract. - - - The term "controlled technical information" means technical information with military or space application that is subject to controls on the access, use, reproduction, modification, performance, display, release, disclosure, or dissemination. Controlled technical information would meet the criteria, if disseminated, for distribution statements B through F using the criteria set forth in DoD Instruction 5230.24, Distribution Statements on Technical Documents. The term does not include information that is lawfully publicly available without restrictions. - - - The term "technical information" means technical data or computer software, as those terms are defined in the clause at DFARS 252.227-7013, Rights in Technical Data - Noncommercial Items, regardless of whether or not the clause is incorporated in this solicitation or contract. Examples of technical information include research and engineering data, engineering drawings, and associated lists, specifications, standards, process sheets, manuals, technical reports, technical orders, catalog-item identifications, data sets, studies and analyses and related information, and computer software executable code and source code.
Security Breach Definition	The term "cyber incident" means actions taken through the use of computer networks that result in a compromise or an actual or potentially adverse effect on an information system and/or the information residing therein. - - - Compromise means disclosure of information to unauthorized persons, or a violation of the security policy of a system, in which unauthorized intentional or unintentional disclosure, modification, destruction, or loss of an object, or the copying of information to unauthorized media may have occurred.
Notification Timeline	The breach notification must be provided to the Defense Department within 72 hours of discovery of any cyber incident. See https://dibnet.dod.mil.
Notification Content Requirements	The cyber incident report shall be treated as information created by or for DoD and shall include, at a minimum, the required elements at https://dibnet.dod.mil.

CYBER INCIDENT REPORTING FOR CRITICAL INFRASTRUCTURE ACT OF 2022 (CIRCIA)

Data Breach Requirements: 6 U.S.C. § 681 et seq.

At the time of publication, the CIRCIA regulations have not been finalized.
Please see page 253 for more information.

	DFARS / CDI & Cyber Incident Reporting (Data Breach Requirements)
Delivery Methods	A data breach report shall be submitted via https://dibnet.dod.mil. - - - In order to report cyber incidents, the Contractor or subcontractor shall have or acquire a DoD-approved medium assurance certificate to report cyber incidents. For information on obtaining a DoD-approved medium assurance certificate, see https://public.cyber.mil/eca/.
Data Processor Obligations	The Contractor shall - (1) Include this clause in subcontracts, or similar contractual instruments, for operationally critical support, or for which subcontract performance will involve covered defense information, including subcontracts for commercial items, without alteration, except to identify the parties. The Contractor shall determine if the information required for subcontractor performance retains its identity as covered defense information and will require protection under this clause, and, if necessary, consult with the Contracting Officer; and (2) Require subcontractors to (i) Notify the prime Contractor (or next higher-tier subcontractor) when submitting a request to vary from a NIST SP 800-171 security requirement to the Contracting Officer; and (ii) Provide the incident report number, automatically assigned by DoD, to the prime Contractor (or next higher-tier subcontractor) as soon as practicable, when reporting a cyber incident to DoD.
Malicious Code	When the Contractor or subcontractors discover and isolate malicious software in connection with a reported cyber incident, submit the malicious software to DoD Cyber Crime Center (DC3) in accordance with instructions provided by DC3 or the Contracting Officer. Do not send the malicious software to the Contracting Officer.
Media Preservation	When a Contractor discovers a cyber incident has occurred, the Contractor shall preserve and protect images of all known affected information systems identified and all relevant monitoring/packet capture data for at least 90 days from the submission of the cyber incident report to allow DoD to request the media or decline interest.
Other Information	When the Contractor discovers a cyber incident that affects a covered contractor information system or the covered defense information residing therein, or that affects the contractor's ability to perform the requirements of the contract that are designated as operationally critical support and identified in the contract, the Contractor shall conduct a review for evidence of compromise of covered defense information, including, but not limited to, identifying compromised computers, servers, specific data, and user accounts. This review shall also include analyzing covered contractor information system(s) that were part of the cyber incident, as well as other information systems on the Contractor's network(s), that may have been accessed as a result of the incident in order to identify compromised covered defense information, or that affect the Contractor's ability to provide operationally critical support. - - - If DoD elects to conduct a damage assessment, the Contracting Officer will request that the Contractor provide all of the damage assessment information gathered in accordance with paragraph (e), media preservation and protection of this clause. - - - Upon request by DoD, the Contractor shall provide DoD with access to additional information or equipment that is necessary to conduct a forensic analysis.

U.S. STATE AND LOCAL BIOMETRIC PROTECTION LAWS

ILLINOIS

Citation: 740 ILCS 14/1 et seq.

The numbering and internal citations herein are derived from the applicable state statute.

	Illinois (Biometric Requirements)
Biometric Information	The term "biometric identifier" means a retina or iris scan, fingerprint, voiceprint, or scan of hand or face geometry. The term "biometric identifier" does not include: (1) Writing samples or written signatures, (2) Photographs, (3) Human biological samples used for valid scientific testing or screening, (4) Demographic data, (5) Tattoo descriptions, or physical descriptions such as height, weight, hair color, or eye color, (6) Donated organs, tissues, or parts as defined in the Illinois Anatomical Gift Act or blood or serum stored on behalf of recipients or potential recipients of living or cadaveric transplants and obtained or stored by a federally designated organ procurement agency, (7) Biological materials regulated under the Genetic Information Privacy Act, (8) Information captured from a patient in a health care setting or information collected, used, or stored for health care treatment, payment, or operations under the Health Insurance Portability and Accountability Act of 1996 (HIPAA), (9) X-ray, roentgen process, computed tomography, MRI, PET scan, mammography, or other image or film of the human anatomy used to diagnose, prognose, or treat an illness or other medical condition or to further validate scientific testing or screening. - - - The term "biometric information" means any information, regardless of how it is captured, converted, stored, or shared, based on an individual's biometric identifier used to identify an individual. Biometric information does not include information derived from items or procedures excluded under the definition of biometric identifiers.
Written Policy Requirement	A private entity in possession of biometric identifiers or biometric information must develop a written policy, made available to the public, establishing (i) a retention schedule and (ii) guidelines for permanently destroying biometric identifiers and biometric information when required by law (see Data Retention Limits).
Key Collection Obligations	No private entity may collect, capture, purchase, receive through trade, or otherwise obtain a person's or a customer's biometric identifier or biometric information, unless it first: (1) Informs the subject or the subject's legally authorized representative in writing that a biometric identifier or biometric information is being collected or stored; (2) Informs the subject or the subject's legally authorized representative in writing of the specific purpose and length of term for which a biometric identifier or biometric information is being collected, stored, and used; and (3) Receives a written release executed by the subject of the biometric identifier or biometric information or the subject's legally authorized representative.

	Illinois (Biometric Requirements)
Disclosure Limitations	No private entity in possession of a biometric identifier or biometric information may disclose, redisclose, or otherwise disseminate a person's or a customer's biometric identifier or biometric information unless: (1) The subject of the biometric identifier or biometric information or the subject's legally authorized representative consents to the disclosure or redisclosure; (2) The disclosure or redisclosure completes a financial transaction requested or authorized by the subject of the biometric identifier or the biometric information or the subject's legally authorized representative; (3) The disclosure or redisclosure is required by state or federal law or municipal ordinance; or (4) The disclosure is required pursuant to a valid warrant or subpoena issued by a court of competent jurisdiction.
Data Retention Limitations	A private entity must destroy biometric identifiers and biometric information when the initial purpose for collecting or obtaining such identifiers or information has been satisfied or within three years of the individual's last interaction with the private entity, whichever occurs first.
Sale Prohibitions	No private entity in possession of a biometric identifier or biometric information may sell, lease, trade, or otherwise profit from a person's or a customer's biometric identifier or biometric information.
Consent Required	Yes (see Key Obligations; Disclosure Limits).
Security Measures	A private entity in possession of a biometric identifier or biometric information shall: (1) Store, transmit, and protect from disclosure all biometric identifiers and biometric information using the reasonable standard of care within the private entity's industry; and (2) Store, transmit, and protect from disclosure all biometric identifiers and biometric information in a manner that is the same as or more protective than the manner in which the private entity stores, transmits, and protects other confidential and sensitive information.
Private Right of Action	Yes
Preemption and Compliance	The law shall not be construed to: (a) Impact the admission or discovery of biometric identifiers and biometric information in any action of any kind in any court, or before any tribunal, board, agency, or person. (b) Conflict with the X-Ray Retention Act, the Health Insurance Portability and Accountability Act of 1996 (HIPAA), and the rules promulgated under either act. (c) Apply in any manner to a financial institution or an affiliate of a financial institution that is subject to Title V of the Gramm-Leach-Bliley Act and the rules promulgated thereunder. (d) Conflict with the Private Detective, Private Alarm, Private Security, Fingerprint Vendor, and Locksmith Act of 2004 and the rules promulgated thereunder. (e) Apply to a contractor, subcontractor, or agent of a state agency or local unit of government when working for that state agency or local unit of government.
Data Processor Obligations	N/A
Exceptions	Absent a valid warrant or subpoena issued by a court of competent jurisdiction, a private entity in possession of biometric identifiers or biometric information must comply with its established retention schedule and destruction guidelines.

	Illinois (Biometric Requirements)
Other Information	The term "confidential and sensitive information" means personal information that can be used to uniquely identify an individual or an individual's account or property. Examples of confidential and sensitive information include, but are not limited to, a genetic marker, genetic testing information, a unique identifier number to locate an account or property, an account number, a PIN number, a pass code, a driver's license number, or a Social Security number. - - - The term "written release" means informed written consent or, in the context of employment, a release executed by an employee as a condition of employment.

NEW YORK CITY, NEW YORK

Citation: New York City, N.Y., Municipal Code § 22-1201 et seq.

The numbering and internal citations herein are derived from the applicable state statute.

	New York City (Biometric Requirements)
Biometric Information	The term "biometric identifier information" means a physiological or biological characteristic that is used by or on behalf of a commercial establishment, singly or in combination, to identify, or assist in identifying, an individual, including, but not limited to: (i) a retina or iris scan, (ii) a fingerprint or voiceprint, (iii) a scan of hand or face geometry, or any other identifying characteristic.
Written Policy Requirement	N/A
Key Collection Obligations	Any commercial establishment that collects, retains, converts, stores, or shares biometric identifier information of customers must disclose such collection, retention, conversion, storage, or sharing, as applicable, by placing a clear and conspicuous sign near all of the commercial establishment's customer entrances notifying customers in plain, simple language that customers' biometric identifier information is being collected, retained, converted, stored or shared, as applicable.
Disclosure Limitations	See Key Obligations.
Data Retention Limitations	N/A
Sale Prohibitions	It shall be unlawful to sell, lease, trade, or share in exchange for anything of value or otherwise profit from the transaction of biometric identifier information.
Consent Required	N/A
Security Measures	N/A (see N.Y. Gen. Bus. Law § 899-bb(2)).
Private Right of Action	Yes, with partial cure period available.
Preemption and Compliance	The biometric disclosure requirements shall not apply to financial institutions. The term "financial institution" means a bank, trust company, national bank, savings bank, federal mutual savings bank, savings and loan association, federal savings and loan association, federal mutual savings and loan association, credit union, federal credit union, branch of a foreign banking corporation, public pension fund, retirement system, securities broker, securities dealer, or securities firm, but does not include a commercial establishment whose primary business is the retail sale of goods and services to customers and provides limited financial services such as the issuance of credit cards or in-store financing to customers.
Data Processor Obligations	N/A (see N.Y. Gen. Bus. Law § 899-bb(2)).
Exceptions	The law does not apply to the collection, storage, sharing, or use of biometric identifier information by government agencies, employees, or agents. The law does not apply to biometric identifier information collected through photographs or video recordings, if: (i) the images or videos collected are not analyzed by software or applications that identify, or that assist with the identification of, individuals based on physiological or biological characteristics, and (ii) the images or video are not shared with, sold, or leased to third-parties other than law enforcement agencies.

	New York City (Biometric Requirements)
Other Information	The term "commercial establishment" means a place of entertainment, a retail store, or a food and drink establishment. - - - The term "customer" means a purchaser or lessee, or a prospective purchaser or lessee, of goods or services from a commercial establishment.

PORTLAND, OREGON

Citation: Title 34, Portland City Code, § 34.10.010 et seq.

The numbering and internal citations herein are derived from the applicable state statute.

	Portland (Biometric Requirements)
Facial Recognition	The term "face recognition" means the automated searching for a reference image in an image repository by comparing the facial features of a probe image with the features of images contained in an image repository (one-to-many search). A face recognition search will typically result in one or more most likely candidates—or candidate images—ranked by computer-evaluated similarity or will return a negative result. - - - The term "face recognition technologies" means automated or semi-automated processes using face recognition that assist in identifying, verifying, detecting, or characterizing facial features of an individual or capturing information about an individual based on an individual's face.
Written Policy Requirement	N/A
Key Collection Obligations	Except as provided in the Exceptions section below (see Exceptions), a private entity shall not use face recognition technologies in places of public accommodation within the boundaries of the City of Portland.
Disclosure Limitations	See Key Collection Obligations.
Data Retention Limitations	See Key Collection Obligations.
Sale Prohibitions	See Key Collection Obligations.
Consent Required	See Key Collection Obligations.
Security Measures	N/A (See Or. Rev. Stat. § 646A.622).
Private Right of Action	Yes
Data Processor Obligations	N/A (See Or. Rev. Stat. § 646A.622).
Exceptions	The prohibition on facial recognition does not apply to use of face recognition technologies: A. To the extent necessary for a private entity to comply with federal, state, or local laws; B. For user verification purposes by an individual to access the individual's own personal or employer-issued communication and electronic devices; or C. In automatic face detection services in social media applications.
Other Information	The term "places of public accommodation" means any place or service offering to the public accommodations advantages, facilities, or privileges, whether in the nature of goods, services, lodgings, amusements, transportation, or otherwise. It does not include: an institution, bona fide club, private residence, or place of accommodation that is in its nature distinctly private.

TEXAS

Citation: Texas Bus. & Com. Code § 503.001.

The numbering and internal citations herein are derived from the applicable state statute.

	Texas (Biometric Requirements)
Biometric Information	The term "biometric identifier" means a retina or iris scan, fingerprint, voiceprint, or record of hand or face geometry.
Written Policy Requirement	N/A
Key Collection Obligations	A person may not capture a biometric identifier of an individual for a commercial purpose unless the person: (1) Informs the individual before capturing the biometric identifier; and (2) Receives the individual's consent to capture the biometric identifier.
Disclosure Limitations	A person who possesses a biometric identifier of an individual that is captured for a commercial purpose may not sell, lease, or otherwise disclose the biometric identifier to another person unless: (A) The individual consents to the disclosure for identification purposes in the event of the individual's disappearance or death; (B) The disclosure completes a financial transaction that the individual requested or authorized; (C) The disclosure is required or permitted by a federal statute or by a state statute other than Chapter 552, Government Code; or (D) The disclosure is made by or to a law enforcement agency for a law enforcement purpose in response to a warrant.
Data Retention Limitations	A person who possesses a biometric identifier of an individual that is captured for a commercial purpose shall destroy the biometric identifier within a reasonable time, but not later than the first anniversary of the date the purpose for collecting the identifier expires. Notwithstanding, if a biometric identifier is used in connection with an instrument or document that is required by another law to be maintained for a longer period, the person who possesses the biometric identifier shall destroy the biometric identifier within a reasonable time, but not later than the first anniversary of the date the instrument or document is no longer required to be maintained by law. - - - If a biometric identifier captured for a commercial purpose has been collected for security purposes by an employer, the purpose for collecting the identifier is presumed to expire on termination of the employment relationship.
Sale Prohibitions	See Disclosure Limitations.
Consent Required	Yes
Security Measures	A person who possesses a biometric identifier of an individual that is captured for a commercial purpose shall store, transmit, and protect from disclosure the biometric identifier using reasonable care and in a manner that is the same as or more protective than the manner in which the person stores, transmits, and protects any other confidential information the person possesses.
Private Right of Action	No

	Texas (Biometric Requirements)
Preemption and Compliance	This section does not apply to voiceprint data retained by a financial institution or an affiliate of a financial institution, as those terms are defined by 15 U.S.C. Section 6809.

WASHINGTON

Citation: RCW § 19.375.010 et seq.

The numbering and internal citations herein are derived from the applicable state statute.

	Washington (Biometric Requirements)
Biometric Information	The term "biometric identifier" means data generated by automatic measurements of an individual's biological characteristics, such as a fingerprint, voiceprint, eye retinas, irises, or other unique biological patterns or characteristics that are used to identify a specific individual. - - - The term "biometric identifier" does not include a physical or digital photograph, video or audio recording or data generated therefrom, or information collected, used, or stored for health care treatment, payment, or operations under the Health Insurance Portability and Accountability Act of 1996 (HIPAA). - - - The term "biometric identifier" means an automated identification system capable of capturing, processing, and storing a biometric identifier, comparing the biometric identifier to one or more references, and matching the biometric identifier to a specific individual.
Written Policy Requirement	N/A
Key Collection Obligations	A person may not enroll a biometric identifier in a database for a commercial purpose, without first providing notice, obtaining consent, or providing a mechanism to prevent the subsequent use of a biometric identifier for a commercial purpose. - - - Notice is a disclosure, that is not considered affirmative consent, that is given through a procedure reasonably designed to be readily available to affected individuals. The exact notice and type of consent required to achieve compliance is context-dependent.
Disclosure Limitations	(3) Unless consent has been obtained from the individual, a person who has enrolled an individual's biometric identifier may not sell, lease, or otherwise disclose the biometric identifier to another person for a commercial purpose unless the disclosure: (a) Is consistent with other sections of this law; (b) Is necessary to provide a product or service subscribed to, requested, or expressly authorized by the individual; (c) Is necessary to effect, administer, enforce, or complete a financial transaction that the individual requested, initiated, or authorized, and the third party to whom the biometric identifier is disclosed maintains confidentiality of the biometric identifier and does not further disclose the biometric identifier except as otherwise permitted under the law; (d) Is required or expressly authorized by a federal or state statute, or court order; (e) Is made to a third party that contractually promises that the biometric identifier will not be further disclosed and will not be enrolled in a database for a commercial purpose inconsistent with the notice and consent described in this law; or (f) Is made to prepare for litigation or to respond to or participate in judicial process.

	Washington (Biometric Requirements)
Data Retention Limitations	A person who knowingly possesses a biometric identifier of an individual that has been enrolled for a commercial purpose may retain the biometric identifier no longer than is reasonably necessary to (i) comply with a court order, statute, or public records retention schedule specified under federal, state, or local law; (ii) protect against or prevent actual or potential fraud, criminal activity, claims, security threats, or liability; and (iii) provide the services for which the biometric identifier was enrolled.
Sale Prohibitions	See Disclosure Limitations.
Consent Required	Partial
Security Measures	A person who knowingly possesses a biometric identifier of an individual that has been enrolled for a commercial purpose must take reasonable care to guard against unauthorized access to and acquisition of biometric identifiers that are in the possession or under the control of the person.
Private Right of Action	No
Preemption and Compliance	Nothing in this law applies (i) in any manner to a financial institution or an affiliate of a financial institution that is subject to Title V of the Gramm-Leach-Bliley Act and the rules promulgated thereunder, (ii) to activities subject to the Health Insurance Privacy and Portability Act of 1996 (HIPAA) and the rules promulgated thereunder.
Exceptions	Nothing in this section requires an entity to provide notice and obtain consent to collect, capture, or enroll a biometric identifier and store it in a biometric system, or otherwise, in furtherance of a security purpose. - - - The limitations on disclosure and retention of biometric identifiers do not apply to disclosure or retention of biometric identifiers that have been unenrolled. The term “enroll” means to capture a biometric identifier of an individual, convert it into a reference template that cannot be reconstructed into the original output image, and store it in a database that matches the biometric identifier to a specific individual.
Other Information	A person who enrolls a biometric identifier of an individual for a commercial purpose or obtains a biometric identifier of an individual from a third party for a commercial purpose may not use or disclose it in a manner that is materially inconsistent with the terms under which the biometric identifier was originally provided without obtaining consent for the new terms of use or disclosure. - - - The term “security purpose” means the purpose of preventing shoplifting, fraud, or any other misappropriation or theft of a thing of value, including tangible and intangible goods, services, and other purposes in furtherance of protecting the security or integrity of software, accounts, applications, online services, or any person.

EXECUTIVE ORDERS AND FEDERAL GUIDANCE

EXEC. ORDER 13636, IMPROVING CRITICAL INFRASTRUCTURE CYBERSECURITY

By the authority vested in me as President by the Constitution and the laws of the United States of America, it is hereby ordered as follows:

Section 1. Policy.

Repeated cyber intrusions into critical infrastructure demonstrate the need for improved cybersecurity. The cyber threat to critical infrastructure continues to grow and represents one of the most serious national security challenges we must confront. The national and economic security of the United States depends on the reliable functioning of the Nation's critical infrastructure in the face of such threats. It is the policy of the United States to enhance the security and resilience of the Nation's critical infrastructure and to maintain a cyber environment that encourages efficiency, innovation, and economic prosperity while promoting safety, security, business confidentiality, privacy, and civil liberties. We can achieve these goals through a partnership with the owners and operators of critical infrastructure to improve cybersecurity information sharing and collaboratively develop and implement risk-based standards.

Sec. 2. Critical Infrastructure.

As used in this order, the term critical infrastructure means systems and assets, whether physical or virtual, so vital to the United States that the incapacity or destruction of such systems and assets would have a debilitating impact on security, national economic security, national public health or safety, or any combination of those matters.

Sec. 3. Policy Coordination.

Policy coordination, guidance, dispute resolution, and periodic in-progress reviews for the functions and programs described and assigned herein shall be provided through the interagency process established in Presidential Policy Directive-1 of February 13, 2009 (Organization of the National Security Council System), or any successor.

Sec. 4. Cybersecurity Information Sharing.

(a) It is the policy of the United States Government to increase the volume, timeliness, and quality of cyber threat information shared with U.S. private sector entities so that these entities may better protect and defend themselves against cyber threats. Within 120 days of the date of this order, the Attorney General, the Secretary of Homeland Security (the "Secretary"), and the Director of National Intelligence shall each issue instructions consistent with their authorities and with the requirements of section 12(c) of this order to ensure the timely production of unclassified reports of cyber threats to the U.S. homeland that identify a specific targeted entity. The instructions shall address the need to protect intelligence and law enforcement sources, methods, operations, and investigations.

(b) The Secretary and the Attorney General, in coordination with the Director of National Intelligence, shall establish a process that rapidly disseminates the reports produced pursuant to section 4(a) of this order to the targeted entity. Such process shall also, consistent with the need to protect national security information, include the dissemination of classified reports to critical infrastructure entities authorized to receive them. The Secretary and the Attorney General, in coordination with the Director of National Intelligence, shall establish a system for tracking the production, dissemination, and disposition of these reports.

(c) To assist the owners and operators of critical infrastructure in protecting their systems from unauthorized access, exploitation, or harm, the Secretary, consistent with 6 U.S.C. 143 and in collaboration with the Secretary of Defense, shall, within 120 days of the date of this order, establish procedures to expand the Enhanced Cybersecurity Services program to all critical infrastructure sectors. This voluntary information sharing program will provide classified cyber threat and technical information from the Government to eligible critical infrastructure companies or commercial service providers that offer security services to critical infrastructure.

(d) The Secretary, as the Executive Agent for the Classified National Security Information Program created under Executive Order 13549 of August 18, 2010 (Classified National Security Information Program for State, Local, Tribal, and Private Sector Entities), shall expedite the processing of security clearances to appropriate personnel employed by critical infrastructure owners and operators, prioritizing the critical infrastructure identified in section 9 of this order.

(e) In order to maximize the utility of cyber threat information sharing with the private sector, the Secretary shall expand the use of programs that bring private sector subject-matter experts into Federal service on a temporary basis. These subject matter experts should provide advice regarding the content, structure, and types of information most useful to critical infrastructure owners and operators in reducing and mitigating cyber risks.

Sec. 5. Privacy and Civil Liberties Protections.

(a) Agencies shall coordinate their activities under this order with their senior agency officials for privacy and civil liberties and ensure that privacy and civil liberties protections are incorporated into such activities. Such protections shall be based upon the Fair Information Practice Principles and other privacy and civil liberties policies, principles, and frameworks as they apply to each agency's activities.

(b) The Chief Privacy Officer and the Officer for Civil Rights and Civil Liberties of the Department of Homeland Security (DHS) shall assess the privacy and civil liberties risks of the functions and programs undertaken by DHS as called for in this order and shall recommend to the Secretary ways to minimize or mitigate such risks, in a publicly available report, to be released within 1 year of the date of this order. Senior agency privacy and civil liberties officials for other agencies engaged in activities under this order shall conduct assessments of their agency activities and provide those assessments to DHS for consideration and inclusion in the report. The report shall be reviewed on an annual basis and revised as necessary. The report may contain a classified annex if necessary. Assessments shall include evaluation of activities against the Fair Information Practice Principles and other applicable privacy and civil liberties policies, principles, and frameworks. Agencies shall consider the assessments and recommendations of the report in implementing privacy and civil liberties protections for agency activities.

(c) In producing the report required under subsection (b) of this section, the Chief Privacy Officer and the Officer for Civil Rights and Civil Liberties of DHS shall consult with the Privacy and Civil Liberties Oversight Board and coordinate with the Office of Management and Budget (OMB).

(d) Information submitted voluntarily in accordance with 6 U.S.C. 133 by private entities under this order shall be protected from disclosure to the fullest extent permitted by law.

Sec. 6. Consultative Process.

The Secretary shall establish a consultative process to coordinate improvements to the cybersecurity of critical infrastructure. As part of the consultative process, the Secretary shall engage and consider the advice, on matters set forth in this order, of the Critical Infrastructure Partnership Advisory Council; Sector Coordinating Councils; critical infrastructure owners and operators; Sector-Specific Agencies; other relevant agencies; independent regulatory agencies; State, local, territorial, and tribal governments; universities; and outside experts.

Sec. 7. Baseline Framework to Reduce Cyber Risk to Critical Infrastructure.

(a) The Secretary of Commerce shall direct the Director of the National Institute of Standards and Technology (the "Director") to lead the development of a framework to reduce cyber risks to critical infrastructure (the "Cybersecurity Framework"). The Cybersecurity Framework shall include a set of standards, methodologies, procedures, and processes that align policy, business, and technological approaches to address cyber risks. The Cybersecurity Framework shall incorporate voluntary consensus standards and industry best practices to the fullest extent possible. The Cybersecurity Framework shall be consistent with voluntary international standards when such international standards will advance the objectives of this order, and shall meet the requirements of the National Institute of Standards and Technology Act, as amended (15 U.S.C. 271 et seq.), the National Technology Transfer and Advancement Act of 1995 (Public Law 104-113), and OMB Circular A-119, as revised.

(b) The Cybersecurity Framework shall provide a prioritized, flexible, repeatable, performance-based, and cost-effective approach, including information security measures and controls, to help owners and operators of critical infrastructure identify, assess, and manage cyber risk. The Cybersecurity Framework shall focus on identifying cross-sector security standards and guidelines applicable to critical infrastructure. The Cybersecurity Framework will also identify areas for improvement that should be addressed through future collaboration with particular sectors and standards-developing organizations. To enable technical innovation and account for organizational differences, the Cybersecurity Framework will provide guidance that is technology neutral and that enables critical infrastructure sectors to benefit from a competitive market for products and services that meet the standards, methodologies, procedures, and processes developed to address cyber risks. The Cybersecurity Framework shall include guidance for measuring the performance of an entity in implementing the Cybersecurity Framework.

(c) The Cybersecurity Framework shall include methodologies to identify and mitigate impacts of the Cybersecurity Framework and associated information security measures or controls on business confidentiality, and to protect individual privacy and civil liberties.

(d) In developing the Cybersecurity Framework, the Director shall engage in an open public review and comment process. The Director shall also consult with the Secretary, the National Security Agency, Sector-Specific Agencies and other interested agencies including OMB, owners and operators of critical infrastructure, and other stakeholders through the consultative process established in section 6 of this order. The Secretary, the Director of National Intelligence, and the heads of other relevant agencies shall provide threat and vulnerability information and technical expertise to inform the development of the Cybersecurity Framework. The Secretary shall provide performance goals for the Cybersecurity Framework informed by work under section 9 of this order.

(e) Within 240 days of the date of this order, the Director shall publish a preliminary version of the Cybersecurity Framework (the "preliminary Framework"). Within 1 year of the date of this order, and after coordination with the Secretary to ensure suitability under section 8 of this order, the Director shall publish a final version of the Cybersecurity Framework (the "final Framework").

(f) Consistent with statutory responsibilities, the Director will ensure the Cybersecurity Framework and related guidance is reviewed and updated as necessary, taking into consideration technological changes, changes in cyber risks, operational feedback from owners and operators of critical infrastructure, experience from the implementation of section 8 of this order, and any other relevant factors.

Sec. 8. Voluntary Critical Infrastructure Cybersecurity Program.

(a) The Secretary, in coordination with Sector-Specific Agencies, shall establish a voluntary program to support the adoption of the Cybersecurity Framework by owners and operators of critical infrastructure and any other interested entities (the "Program").

(b) Sector-Specific Agencies, in consultation with the Secretary and other interested agencies, shall coordinate with the Sector Coordinating Councils to review the Cybersecurity Framework and, if necessary, develop implementation guidance or supplemental materials to address sector-specific risks and operating environments.

(c) Sector-Specific Agencies shall report annually to the President, through the Secretary, on the extent to which owners and operators notified under section 9 of this order are participating in the Program.

(d) The Secretary shall coordinate establishment of a set of incentives designed to promote participation in the Program. Within 120 days of the date of this order, the Secretary and the Secretaries of the Treasury and Commerce each shall make recommendations separately to the President, through the Assistant to the President for Homeland Security and Counterterrorism and the Assistant to the President for Economic Affairs, that shall include analysis of the benefits and relative effectiveness of such incentives, and whether the incentives would require legislation or can be provided under existing law and authorities to participants in the Program.

(e) Within 120 days of the date of this order, the Secretary of Defense and the Administrator of General Services, in consultation with the Secretary and the Federal Acquisition Regulatory Council, shall make recommendations to the President, through the Assistant to the President for Homeland Security and Counterterrorism and the Assistant to the President for Economic Affairs, on the feasibility, security benefits, and relative merits of incorporating security standards into acquisition planning and contract administration. The report shall address what steps can be taken to harmonize and make consistent existing procurement requirements related to cybersecurity.

Sec. 9. Identification of Critical Infrastructure at Greatest Risk.

(a) Within 150 days of the date of this order, the Secretary shall use a risk-based approach to identify critical infrastructure where a cybersecurity incident could reasonably result in catastrophic regional or national effects on public health or safety, economic security, or national security. In identifying critical infrastructure for this purpose, the Secretary shall use the consultative process established in section 6 of this order and draw upon the expertise of Sector-Specific Agencies. The Secretary shall apply consistent, objective criteria in identifying such critical infrastructure. The Secretary shall not identify any commercial information technology products or consumer information technology services under this section. The Secretary shall review and update the list of identified critical infrastructure under this section on an annual basis, and provide such list to the President, through the Assistant to the President for Homeland Security and Counterterrorism and the Assistant to the President for Economic Affairs.

(b) Heads of Sector-Specific Agencies and other relevant agencies shall provide the Secretary with information necessary to carry out the responsibilities under this section. The Secretary shall develop a process for other relevant stakeholders to submit information to assist in making the identifications required in subsection (a) of this section.

(c) The Secretary, in coordination with Sector-Specific Agencies, shall confidentially notify owners and operators of critical infrastructure identified under subsection (a) of this section that they have been so identified, and ensure identified owners and operators are provided the basis for the determination. The Secretary shall establish a process through which owners and operators of critical infrastructure may submit relevant information and request reconsideration of identifications under subsection (a) of this section.

Sec. 10. Adoption of Framework.

(a) Agencies with responsibility for regulating the security of critical infrastructure shall engage in a consultative process with DHS, OMB, and the National Security Staff to review the preliminary Cybersecurity Framework and determine if current cybersecurity regulatory requirements are sufficient given current and projected risks. In making such determination, these agencies shall consider the identification of critical infrastructure required under section 9 of this order. Within 90 days of the publication of the preliminary Framework, these agencies shall submit a report to the President, through the Assistant to the President for Homeland Security and Counterterrorism, the Director of OMB, and the Assistant to the President for Economic Affairs, that states whether or not the agency has clear authority to establish requirements based upon the Cybersecurity Framework to sufficiently address current and projected cyber risks to critical infrastructure, the existing authorities identified, and any additional authority required.

(b) If current regulatory requirements are deemed to be insufficient, within 90 days of publication of the final Framework, agencies identified in subsection (a) of this section shall propose prioritized, risk-based, efficient, and coordinated actions, consistent with Executive Order 12866 of September 30, 1993 (Regulatory Planning and Review), Executive Order 13563 of January 18, 2011 (Improving Regulation and Regulatory Review), and Executive Order 13609 of May 1, 2012 (Promoting International Regulatory Cooperation), to mitigate cyber risk.

(c) Within 2 years after publication of the final Framework, consistent with Executive Order 13563 and Executive Order 13610 of May 10, 2012 (Identifying and Reducing Regulatory Burdens), agencies identified in subsection (a) of this section shall, in consultation with owners and operators of critical infrastructure, report to OMB on any critical infrastructure subject to ineffective, conflicting, or excessively burdensome cybersecurity requirements. This report shall describe efforts made by agencies, and make recommendations for further actions, to minimize or eliminate such requirements.

(d) The Secretary shall coordinate the provision of technical assistance to agencies identified in subsection (a) of this section on the development of their cybersecurity workforce and programs.

(e) Independent regulatory agencies with responsibility for regulating the security of critical infrastructure are encouraged to engage in a consultative process with the Secretary, relevant Sector-Specific Agencies, and other affected parties to consider prioritized actions to mitigate cyber risks for critical infrastructure consistent with their authorities.

Sec. 11. Definitions.

(a) “Agency” means any authority of the United States that is an “agency” under 44 U.S.C. 3502(1), other than those considered to be independent regulatory agencies, as defined in 44 U.S.C. 3502(5).

(b) “Critical Infrastructure Partnership Advisory Council” means the council established by DHS under 6 U.S.C. 451 to facilitate effective interaction and coordination of critical infrastructure protection activities among the Federal Government; the private sector; and State, local, territorial, and tribal governments.

(c) “Fair Information Practice Principles” means the eight principles set forth in Appendix A of the National Strategy for Trusted Identities in Cyberspace.

(d) “Independent regulatory agency” has the meaning given the term in 44 U.S.C. 3502(5).

(e) “Sector Coordinating Council” means a private sector coordinating council composed of representatives of owners and operators within a particular sector of critical infrastructure established by the National Infrastructure Protection Plan or any successor.

(f) “Sector-Specific Agency” has the meaning given the term in Presidential Policy Directive-21 of February 12, 2013 (Critical Infrastructure Security and Resilience), or any successor.

Sec. 12. General Provisions.

(a) This order shall be implemented consistent with applicable law and subject to the availability of appropriations. Nothing in this order shall be construed to provide an agency with authority for regulating the security of critical infrastructure in addition to or to a greater extent than the authority the agency has under existing law. Nothing in this order shall be construed to alter or limit any authority or responsibility of an agency under existing law.

(b) Nothing in this order shall be construed to impair or otherwise affect the functions of the Director of OMB relating to budgetary, administrative, or legislative proposals.

(c) All actions taken pursuant to this order shall be consistent with requirements and authorities to protect intelligence and law enforcement sources and methods. Nothing in this order shall be interpreted to supersede measures established under authority of law to protect the security and integrity of specific activities and associations that are in direct support of intelligence and law enforcement operations.

(d) This order shall be implemented consistent with U.S. international obligations.

(e) This order is not intended to, and does not, create any right or benefit, substantive or procedural, enforceable at law or in equity by any party against the United States, its departments, agencies, or entities, its officers, employees, or agents, or any other person.

EXEC. ORDER 13800, STRENGTHENING THE CYBERSECURITY OF FEDERAL NETWORKS AND CRITICAL INFRASTRUCTURE

By the authority vested in me as President by the Constitution and the laws of the United States of America, and to protect American innovation and values, it is hereby ordered as follows:

Section 1. Cybersecurity of Federal Networks.

(a) Policy.

The executive branch operates its information technology (IT) on behalf of the American people. Its IT and data should be secured responsibly using all United States Government capabilities. The President will hold heads of executive departments and agencies (agency heads) accountable for managing cybersecurity risk to their enterprises. In addition, because risk management decisions made by agency heads can affect the risk to the executive branch as a whole, and to national security, it is also the policy of the United States to manage cybersecurity risk as an executive branch enterprise.

(b) Findings.

(i) Cybersecurity risk management comprises the full range of activities undertaken to protect IT and data from unauthorized access and other cyber threats, to maintain awareness of cyber threats, to detect anomalies and incidents adversely affecting IT and data, and to mitigate the impact of, respond to, and recover from incidents. Information sharing facilitates and supports all of these activities.

(ii) The executive branch has for too long accepted antiquated and difficult-to-defend IT.

(iii) Effective risk management involves more than just protecting IT and data currently in place. It also requires planning so that maintenance, improvements, and modernization occur in a coordinated way and with appropriate regularity.

(iv) Known but unmitigated vulnerabilities are among the highest cybersecurity risks faced by executive departments and agencies (agencies). Known vulnerabilities include using operating systems or hardware beyond the vendor's support lifecycle, declining to implement a vendor's security patch, or failing to execute security-specific configuration guidance.

(v) Effective risk management requires agency heads to lead integrated teams of senior executives with expertise in IT, security, budgeting, acquisition, law, privacy, and human resources.

(c) Risk Management.

(i) Agency heads will be held accountable by the President for implementing risk management measures commensurate with the risk and magnitude of the harm that would result from unauthorized access, use, disclosure, disruption, modification, or destruction of IT and data. They will also be held accountable by the President for ensuring that cybersecurity risk management processes are aligned with strategic, operational, and budgetary planning processes, in accordance with chapter 35, subchapter II of title 44, United States Code.

(ii) Effective immediately, each agency head shall use The Framework for Improving Critical Infrastructure Cybersecurity (the Framework) developed by the National Institute of Standards and Technology, or any successor document, to manage the agency's cybersecurity risk. Each agency head shall provide a risk management report to the Secretary of Homeland Security and the Director of the Office of Management and Budget (OMB) within 90 days of the date of this order. The risk management report shall:

(A) document the risk mitigation and acceptance choices made by each agency head as of the date of this order, including: (1) the strategic, operational, and budgetary considerations that informed those choices; and (2) any accepted risk, including from unmitigated vulnerabilities; and

(B) describe the agency's action plan to implement the Framework.

(iii) The Secretary of Homeland Security and the Director of OMB, consistent with chapter 35, subchapter II of title 44, United States Code, shall jointly assess each agency's risk management report to determine whether the risk mitigation and acceptance choices set forth in the reports are appropriate and sufficient to manage the cybersecurity risk to the executive branch enterprise in the aggregate (the determination).

(iv) The Director of OMB, in coordination with the Secretary of Homeland Security, with appropriate support from the Secretary of Commerce and the Administrator of General Services, and within 60 days of receipt of the agency risk management reports outlined in subsection (c)(ii) of this section, shall submit to the President, through the Assistant to the President for Homeland Security and Counterterrorism, the following:

(A) the determination; and (B) a plan to: (1) adequately protect the executive branch enterprise, should the determination identify insufficiencies; (2) address immediate unmet budgetary needs necessary to manage risk to the executive branch enterprise; (3) establish a regular process for reassessing and, if appropriate, reissuing the determination, and addressing future, recurring unmet budgetary needs necessary to manage risk to the executive branch enterprise; (4) clarify, reconcile, and reissue, as necessary and to the extent permitted by law, all policies, standards, and guidelines issued by any agency in furtherance of chapter 35, subchapter II of title 44, United States Code, and, as necessary and to the extent permitted by law, issue policies, standards, and guidelines in furtherance of this order; and (5) align these policies, standards, and guidelines with the Framework.

(v) The agency risk management reports described in subsection (c)(ii) of this section and the determination and plan described in subsections (c)(iii) and (iv) of this section may be classified in full or in part, as appropriate.

(vi) Effective immediately, it is the policy of the executive branch to build and maintain a modern, secure, and more resilient executive branch IT architecture. (A) Agency heads shall show preference in their procurement for shared IT services, to the extent permitted by law, including email, cloud, and cybersecurity services. (B) The Director of the American Technology Council shall coordinate a report to the President from the Secretary of Homeland Security, the Director of OMB, and the Administrator of General Services, in consultation with the Secretary of Commerce, as appropriate, regarding modernization of Federal IT. The report shall: (1) be completed within 90 days of the date of this order; and (2) describe the legal, policy, and budgetary considerations relevant to, as well as the technical feasibility and cost effectiveness, including timelines and milestones, of, transitioning all agencies, or a subset of agencies, to: (aa) one or more consolidated network architectures; and (bb) shared IT services, including email, cloud, and cybersecurity services. (C) The report described in subsection (c)(vi)(B) of this section shall assess the effects of transitioning all agencies, or a subset of agencies, to shared IT services with respect to cybersecurity, including by making recommendations to ensure consistency with section 227 of the Homeland Security Act (6 U.S.C. 148) and compliance with policies and practices issued in accordance with section 3553 of title 44, United States Code. All agency heads shall supply such information concerning their current IT architectures and plans as is necessary to complete this report on time.

(vii) For any National Security System, as defined in section 3552(b)(6) of title 44, United States Code, the Secretary of Defense and the Director of National Intelligence, rather than the Secretary of Homeland Security and the Director of OMB, shall implement this order to the maximum extent feasible and appropriate. The Secretary of Defense and the Director of National Intelligence shall provide a report to the Assistant to the President for National Security Affairs and the Assistant to the President for Homeland Security and Counterterrorism describing their implementation of subsection (c) of this section within 150 days of the date of this order. The report described in this subsection shall include a justification for any deviation from the requirements of subsection (c), and may be classified in full or in part, as appropriate.

Sec. 2. Cybersecurity of Critical Infrastructure.

(a) Policy.

It is the policy of the executive branch to use its authorities and capabilities to support the cybersecurity risk management efforts of the owners and operators of the Nation's critical infrastructure (as defined in section 5195c(e) of title 42, United States Code) (critical infrastructure entities), as appropriate.

(b) Support to Critical Infrastructure at Greatest Risk.

The Secretary of Homeland Security, in coordination with the Secretary of Defense, the Attorney General, the Director of National Intelligence, the Director of the Federal Bureau of Investigation, the heads of appropriate sector-specific agencies, as defined in Presidential Policy Directive 21 of February 12, 2013 (Critical Infrastructure Security and Resilience) (sector-specific agencies), and all other appropriate agency heads, as identified by the Secretary of Homeland Security, shall:

(i) identify authorities and capabilities that agencies could employ to support the cybersecurity efforts of critical infrastructure entities identified pursuant to section 9 of Executive Order 13636 of February 12, 2013 (Improving Critical Infrastructure Cybersecurity), to be at greatest risk of attacks that could reasonably result in catastrophic regional or national effects on public health or safety, economic security, or national security (section 9 entities);

(ii) engage section 9 entities and solicit input as appropriate to evaluate whether and how the authorities and capabilities identified pursuant to subsection (b)(i) of this section might be employed to support cybersecurity risk management efforts and any obstacles to doing so;

(iii) provide a report to the President, which may be classified in full or in part, as appropriate, through the Assistant to the President for Homeland Security and Counterterrorism, within 180 days of the date of this order, that includes the following: (A) the authorities and capabilities identified pursuant to subsection (b)(i) of this section; (B) the results of the engagement and determination required pursuant to subsection (b)(ii) of this section; and (C) findings and recommendations for better supporting the cybersecurity risk management efforts of section 9 entities; and

(iv) provide an updated report to the President on an annual basis thereafter.

(c) Supporting Transparency in the Marketplace.

The Secretary of Homeland Security, in coordination with the Secretary of Commerce, shall provide a report to the President, through the Assistant to the President for Homeland Security and Counterterrorism, that examines the sufficiency of existing Federal policies and practices to promote appropriate market transparency of cybersecurity risk management practices by critical infrastructure entities, with a focus on publicly traded critical infrastructure entities, within 90 days of the date of this order.

(d) Resilience Against Botnets and Other Automated, Distributed Threats.

The Secretary of Commerce and the Secretary of Homeland Security shall jointly lead an open and transparent process to identify and promote action by appropriate stakeholders to improve the resilience of the internet and communications ecosystem and to encourage collaboration with the goal of dramatically reducing threats perpetrated by automated and distributed attacks (e.g., botnets). The Secretary of Commerce and the Secretary of Homeland Security shall consult with the Secretary of Defense, the Attorney General, the Director of the Federal Bureau of Investigation, the heads of sector-specific agencies, the Chairs of the

Federal Communications Commission and Federal Trade Commission, other interested agency heads, and appropriate stakeholders in carrying out this subsection. Within 240 days of the date of this order, the Secretary of Commerce and the Secretary of Homeland Security shall make publicly available a preliminary report on this effort. Within 1 year of the date of this order, the Secretaries shall submit a final version of this report to the President.

(e) Assessment of Electricity Disruption Incident Response Capabilities.

The Secretary of Energy and the Secretary of Homeland Security, in consultation with the Director of National Intelligence, with State, local, tribal, and territorial governments, and with others as appropriate, shall jointly assess:

(i) the potential scope and duration of a prolonged power outage associated with a significant cyber incident, as defined in Presidential Policy Directive 41 of July 26, 2016 (United States Cyber Incident Coordination), against the United States electric subsector;

(ii) the readiness of the United States to manage the consequences of such an incident; and

(iii) any gaps or shortcomings in assets or capabilities required to mitigate the consequences of such an incident.

The assessment shall be provided to the President, through the Assistant to the President for Homeland Security and Counterterrorism, within 90 days of the date of this order, and may be classified in full or in part, as appropriate.

(f) Department of Defense Warfighting Capabilities and Industrial Base.

Within 90 days of the date of this order, the Secretary of Defense, the Secretary of Homeland Security, and the Director of the Federal Bureau of Investigation, in coordination with the Director of National Intelligence, shall provide a report to the President, through the Assistant to the President for National Security Affairs and the Assistant to the President for Homeland Security and Counterterrorism, on cybersecurity risks facing the defense industrial base, including its supply chain, and United States military platforms, systems, networks, and capabilities, and recommendations for mitigating these risks. The report may be classified in full or in part, as appropriate.

Sec. 3. Cybersecurity for the Nation.

(a) Policy.

To ensure that the internet remains valuable for future generations, it is the policy of the executive branch to promote an open, interoperable, reliable, and secure internet that fosters efficiency, innovation, communication, and economic prosperity, while respecting privacy and guarding against disruption, fraud, and theft. Further, the United States seeks to support the growth and sustainment of a workforce that is skilled in cybersecurity and related fields as the foundation for achieving our objectives in cyberspace.

(b) Deterrence and Protection.

Within 90 days of the date of this order, the Secretary of State, the Secretary of the Treasury, the Secretary of Defense, the Attorney General, the Secretary of Commerce, the Secretary of Homeland Security, and the United States Trade Representative, in coordination with the Director of National Intelligence, shall jointly submit a report to the President, through the Assistant to the President for National Security Affairs and the Assistant to the President for Homeland Security and Counterterrorism, on the Nation's strategic options for deterring adversaries and better protecting the American people from cyber threats.

(c) International Cooperation.

As a highly connected nation, the United States is especially dependent on a globally secure and resilient internet and must work with allies and other partners toward maintaining the policy set forth in this section. Within 45 days of the date of this order, the Secretary of State, the Secretary of the Treasury, the Secretary of Defense, the Secretary of Commerce, and the Secretary of Homeland Security, in coordination with the Attorney General and the Director of the Federal Bureau of Investigation, shall submit reports to the President on their international cybersecurity priorities, including those concerning investigation, attribution, cyber threat information sharing, response, capacity building, and cooperation. Within 90 days of the submission of the reports, and in coordination with the agency heads listed in this subsection, and any other agency heads as appropriate, the Secretary of State shall provide a report to the President, through the Assistant to the President for Homeland Security and Counterterrorism, documenting an engagement strategy for international cooperation in cybersecurity.

(d) Workforce Development.

In order to ensure that the United States maintains a long-term cybersecurity advantage:

(i) The Secretary of Commerce and the Secretary of Homeland Security, in consultation with the Secretary of Defense, the Secretary of Labor, the Secretary of Education, the Director of the Office of Personnel Management, and other agencies identified jointly by the Secretary of Commerce and the Secretary of Homeland Security, shall: (A) jointly assess the scope and sufficiency of efforts to educate and train the American cybersecurity workforce of the future, including cybersecurity-related education curricula, training, and apprenticeship programs, from primary through higher education; and (B) within 120 days of the date of this order, provide a report to the President, through the Assistant to the President for Homeland Security and Counterterrorism, with findings and recommendations regarding how to support the growth and sustainment of the Nation's cybersecurity workforce in both the public and private sectors.

(ii) The Director of National Intelligence, in consultation with the heads of other agencies identified by the Director of National Intelligence, shall: (A) review the workforce development efforts of potential foreign cyber peers in order to help identify foreign workforce development practices likely to affect long-term United States cybersecurity competitiveness; and (B) within 60 days of the date of this order, provide a report to the President through the Assistant to the President for Homeland Security and Counterterrorism on the findings of the review carried out pursuant to subsection (d)(ii)(A) of this section.

(iii) The Secretary of Defense, in coordination with the Secretary of Commerce, the Secretary of Homeland Security, and the Director of National Intelligence, shall: (A) assess the scope and sufficiency of United States efforts to ensure that the United States maintains or increases its advantage in national-security-related cyber capabilities; and (B) within 150 days of the date of this order, provide a report to the President, through the Assistant to the President for Homeland Security and Counterterrorism, with findings and recommendations on the assessment carried out pursuant to subsection (d)(iii)(A) of this section.

(iv) The reports described in this subsection may be classified in full or in part, as appropriate.

Sec. 4. Definitions.

For the purposes of this order:

(a) The term "appropriate stakeholders" means any non-executive-branch person or entity that elects to participate in an open and transparent process established by the Secretary of Commerce and the Secretary of Homeland Security under section 2(d) of this order.

(b) The term "information technology" (IT) has the meaning given to that term in section 11101(6) of title 40,

United States Code, and further includes hardware and software systems of agencies that monitor and control physical equipment and processes.

(c) The term "IT architecture" refers to the integration and implementation of IT within an agency.

(d) The term "network architecture" refers to the elements of IT architecture that enable or facilitate communications between two or more IT assets.

Sec. 5. General Provisions.

(a) Nothing in this order shall be construed to impair or otherwise affect: (i) the authority granted by law to an executive department or agency, or the head thereof; or (ii) the functions of the Director of OMB relating to budgetary, administrative, or legislative proposals.

(b) This order shall be implemented consistent with applicable law and subject to the availability of appropriations.

(c) All actions taken pursuant to this order shall be consistent with requirements and authorities to protect intelligence and law enforcement sources and methods. Nothing in this order shall be construed to supersede measures established under authority of law to protect the security and integrity of specific activities and associations that are in direct support of intelligence or law enforcement operations.

(d) This order is not intended to, and does not, create any right or benefit, substantive or procedural, enforceable at law or in equity by any party against the United States, its departments, agencies, or entities, its officers, employees, or agents, or any other person.

EXEC. ORDER 14028, IMPROVING THE NATION'S CYBERSECURITY

By the authority vested in me as President by the Constitution and the laws of the United States of America, it is hereby ordered as follows:

Section 1. Policy.

The United States faces persistent and increasingly sophisticated malicious cyber campaigns that threaten the public sector, the private sector, and ultimately the American people's security and privacy. The Federal Government must improve its efforts to identify, deter, protect against, detect, and respond to these actions and actors. The Federal Government must also carefully examine what occurred during any major cyber incident and apply lessons learned. But cybersecurity requires more than government action. Protecting our Nation from malicious cyber actors requires the Federal Government to partner with the private sector. The private sector must adapt to the continuously changing threat environment, ensure its products are built and operate securely, and partner with the Federal Government to foster a more secure cyberspace. In the end, the trust we place in our digital infrastructure should be proportional to how trustworthy and transparent that infrastructure is, and to the consequences we will incur if that trust is misplaced.

Incremental improvements will not give us the security we need; instead, the Federal Government needs to make bold changes and significant investments in order to defend the vital institutions that underpin the American way of life. The Federal Government must bring to bear the full scope of its authorities and resources to protect and secure its computer systems, whether they are cloud-based, on-premises, or hybrid. The scope of protection and security must include systems that process data (information technology (IT)) and those that run the vital machinery that ensures our safety (operational technology (OT)).

It is the policy of my Administration that the prevention, detection, assessment, and remediation of cyber incidents is a top priority and essential to national and economic security. The Federal Government must lead by example. All Federal Information Systems should meet or exceed the standards and requirements for cybersecurity set forth in and issued pursuant to this order.

Sec. 2. Removing Barriers to Sharing Threat Information.

(a) The Federal Government contracts with IT and OT service providers to conduct an array of day-to-day functions on Federal Information Systems. These service providers, including cloud service providers, have unique access to and insight into cyber threat and incident information on Federal Information Systems. At the same time, current contract terms or restrictions may limit the sharing of such threat or incident information with executive departments and agencies (agencies) that are responsible for investigating or remediating cyber incidents, such as the Cybersecurity and Infrastructure Security Agency (CISA), the Federal Bureau of Investigation (FBI), and other elements of the Intelligence Community (IC). Removing these contractual barriers and increasing the sharing of information about such threats, incidents, and risks are necessary steps to accelerating incident deterrence, prevention, and response efforts and to enabling more effective defense of agencies' systems and of information collected, processed, and maintained by or for the Federal Government.

(b) Within 60 days of the date of this order, the Director of the Office of Management and Budget (OMB), in consultation with the Secretary of Defense, the Attorney General, the Secretary of Homeland Security, and the Director of National Intelligence, shall review the Federal Acquisition Regulation (FAR) and the Defense Federal Acquisition Regulation Supplement contract requirements and language for contracting with IT and OT service providers and recommend updates to such requirements and language to the FAR Council and other appropriate agencies. The recommendations shall include descriptions of contractors to be covered by the proposed contract language.

(c) The recommended contract language and requirements described in subsection (b) of this section shall be designed to ensure that:

(i) service providers collect and preserve data, information, and reporting relevant to cybersecurity event prevention, detection, response, and investigation on all information systems over which they have control, including systems operated on behalf of agencies, consistent with agencies' requirements;

(ii) service providers share such data, information, and reporting, as they relate to cyber incidents or potential incidents relevant to any agency with which they have contracted, directly with such agency and any other agency that the Director of OMB, in consultation with the Secretary of Defense, the Attorney General, the Secretary of Homeland Security, and the Director of National Intelligence, deems appropriate, consistent with applicable privacy laws, regulations, and policies;

(iii) service providers collaborate with Federal cybersecurity or investigative agencies in their investigations of and responses to incidents or potential incidents on Federal Information Systems, including by implementing technical capabilities, such as monitoring networks for threats in collaboration with agencies they support, as needed; and

(iv) service providers share cyber threat and incident information with agencies, doing so, where possible, in industry-recognized formats for incident response and remediation.

(d) Within 90 days of receipt of the recommendations described in subsection (b) of this section, the FAR Council shall review the proposed contract language and conditions and, as appropriate, shall publish for public comment proposed updates to the FAR.

(e) Within 120 days of the date of this order, the Secretary of Homeland Security and the Director of OMB shall take appropriate steps to ensure to the greatest extent possible that service providers share data with agencies, CISA, and the FBI as may be necessary for the Federal Government to respond to cyber threats, incidents, and risks.

(f) It is the policy of the Federal Government that:

(i) information and communications technology (ICT) service providers entering into contracts with agencies must promptly report to such agencies when they discover a cyber incident involving a software product or service provided to such agencies or involving a support system for a software product or service provided to such agencies;

(ii) ICT service providers must also directly report to CISA whenever they report under subsection (f)(i) of this section to Federal Civilian Executive Branch (FCEB) Agencies, and CISA must centrally collect and manage such information; and

(iii) reports pertaining to National Security Systems, as defined in section 10(h) of this order, must be received and managed by the appropriate agency as to be determined under subsection (g)(i)(E) of this section.

(g) To implement the policy set forth in subsection (f) of this section:

(i) Within 45 days of the date of this order, the Secretary of Homeland Security, in consultation with the Secretary of Defense acting through the Director of the National Security Agency (NSA), the Attorney General, and the Director of OMB, shall recommend to the FAR Council contract language that identifies:

(A) the nature of cyber incidents that require reporting; (B) the types of information regarding cyber incidents that require reporting to facilitate effective cyber incident response and remediation; (C) appropriate and effective protections for privacy and civil liberties; (D) the time periods within which contractors must report cyber incidents based on a graduated scale of severity, with reporting on the most severe cyber incidents not to exceed 3 days after initial detection; (E) National Security Systems reporting requirements; and (F) the type of contractors and associated service providers to be covered by the proposed contract language.

(ii) Within 90 days of receipt of the recommendations described in subsection (g)(i) of this section, the FAR Council shall review the recommendations and publish for public comment proposed updates to the FAR.

(iii) Within 90 days of the date of this order, the Secretary of Defense acting through the Director of the NSA, the Attorney General, the Secretary of Homeland Security, and the Director of National Intelligence shall jointly develop procedures for ensuring that cyber incident reports are promptly and appropriately shared among agencies.

(h) Current cybersecurity requirements for unclassified system contracts are largely implemented through agency-specific policies and regulations, including cloud-service cybersecurity requirements. Standardizing common cybersecurity contractual requirements across agencies will streamline and improve compliance for vendors and the Federal Government.

(i) Within 60 days of the date of this order, the Secretary of Homeland Security acting through the Director of CISA, in consultation with the Secretary of Defense acting through the Director of the NSA, the Director of OMB, and the Administrator of General Services, shall review agency-specific cybersecurity requirements that currently exist as a matter of law, policy, or contract and recommend to the FAR Council standardized contract language for appropriate cybersecurity requirements. Such recommendations shall include consideration of the scope of contractors and associated service providers to be covered by the proposed contract language.

(j) Within 60 days of receiving the recommended contract language developed pursuant to subsection (i) of this section, the FAR Council shall review the recommended contract language and publish for public comment proposed updates to the FAR.

(k) Following any updates to the FAR made by the FAR Council after the public comment period described in subsection (j) of this section, agencies shall update their agency-specific cybersecurity requirements to remove any requirements that are duplicative of such FAR updates.

(l) The Director of OMB shall incorporate into the annual budget process a cost analysis of all recommendations developed under this section.

Sec. 3. Modernizing Federal Government Cybersecurity.

(a) To keep pace with today's dynamic and increasingly sophisticated cyber threat environment, the Federal Government must take decisive steps to modernize its approach to cybersecurity, including by increasing the Federal Government's visibility into threats, while protecting privacy and civil liberties. The Federal Government must adopt security best practices; advance toward Zero Trust Architecture; accelerate movement to secure cloud services, including Software as a Service (SaaS), Infrastructure as a Service (IaaS), and Platform as a Service (PaaS); centralize and streamline access to cybersecurity data to drive analytics for identifying and managing cybersecurity risks; and invest in both technology and personnel to match these modernization goals.

(b) Within 60 days of the date of this order, the head of each agency shall:

(i) update existing agency plans to prioritize resources for the adoption and use of cloud technology as outlined in relevant OMB guidance;

(ii) develop a plan to implement Zero Trust Architecture, which shall incorporate, as appropriate, the migration steps that the National Institute of Standards and Technology (NIST) within the Department of Commerce has outlined in standards and guidance, describe any such steps that have already been completed, identify activities that will have the most immediate security impact, and include a schedule to implement them; and

(iii) provide a report to the Director of OMB and the Assistant to the President and National Security Advisor (APNSA) discussing the plans required pursuant to subsection (b)(i) and (ii) of this section.

(c) As agencies continue to use cloud technology, they shall do so in a coordinated, deliberate way that allows the Federal Government to prevent, detect, assess, and remediate cyber incidents. To facilitate this approach, the migration to cloud technology shall adopt Zero Trust Architecture, as practicable. The CISA shall modernize its current cybersecurity programs, services, and capabilities to be fully functional with cloud-computing environments with Zero Trust Architecture. The Secretary of Homeland Security acting through the Director of CISA, in consultation with the Administrator of General Services acting through the Federal Risk and Authorization Management Program (FedRAMP) within the General Services Administration, shall develop security principles governing Cloud Service Providers (CSPs) for incorporation into agency modernization efforts. To facilitate this work:

(i) Within 90 days of the date of this order, the Director of OMB, in consultation with the Secretary of Homeland Security acting through the Director of CISA, and the Administrator of General Services acting through FedRAMP, shall develop a Federal cloud-security strategy and provide guidance to agencies accordingly. Such guidance shall seek to ensure that risks to the FCEB from using cloud-based services are broadly understood and effectively addressed, and that FCEB Agencies move closer to Zero Trust Architecture.

(ii) Within 90 days of the date of this order, the Secretary of Homeland Security acting through the Director of CISA, in consultation with the Director of OMB and the Administrator of General Services acting through FedRAMP, shall develop and issue, for the FCEB, cloud-security technical reference architecture documentation that illustrates recommended approaches to cloud migration and data protection for agency data collection and reporting.

(iii) Within 60 days of the date of this order, the Secretary of Homeland Security acting through the Director of CISA shall develop and issue, for FCEB Agencies, a cloud-service governance framework. That framework shall identify a range of services and protections available to agencies based on incident severity. That framework shall also identify data and processing activities associated with those services and protections.

(iv) Within 90 days of the date of this order, the heads of FCEB Agencies, in consultation with the Secretary of Homeland Security acting through the Director of CISA, shall evaluate the types and sensitivity of their respective agency's unclassified data, and shall provide to the Secretary of Homeland Security through the Director of CISA and to the Director of OMB a report based on such evaluation. The evaluation shall prioritize identification of the unclassified data considered by the agency to be the most sensitive and under the greatest threat, and appropriate processing and storage solutions for those data.

(d) Within 180 days of the date of this order, agencies shall adopt multi-factor authentication and encryption for data at rest and in transit, to the maximum extent consistent with Federal records laws and other applicable laws. To that end:

(i) Heads of FCEB Agencies shall provide reports to the Secretary of Homeland Security through the Director of CISA, the Director of OMB, and the APNSA on their respective agency's progress in adopting multifactor authentication and encryption of data at rest and in transit. Such agencies shall provide such reports every 60 days after the date of this order until the agency has fully adopted, agency-wide, multi-factor authentication and data encryption.

(ii) Based on identified gaps in agency implementation, CISA shall take all appropriate steps to maximize adoption by FCEB Agencies of technologies and processes to implement multifactor authentication and encryption for data at rest and in transit.

(iii) Heads of FCEB Agencies that are unable to fully adopt multi-factor authentication and data encryption within 180 days of the date of this order shall, at the end of the 180-day period, provide a written rationale to the Secretary of Homeland Security through the Director of CISA, the Director of OMB, and the APNSA.

(e) Within 90 days of the date of this order, the Secretary of Homeland Security acting through the Director of CISA, in consultation with the Attorney General, the Director of the FBI, and the Administrator of General Services acting through the Director of FedRAMP, shall establish a framework to collaborate on cybersecurity and incident response activities related to FCEB cloud technology, in order to ensure effective information sharing among agencies and between agencies and CSPs.

(f) Within 60 days of the date of this order, the Administrator of General Services, in consultation with the Director of OMB and the heads of other agencies as the Administrator of General Services deems appropriate, shall begin modernizing FedRAMP by:

(i) establishing a training program to ensure agencies are effectively trained and equipped to manage FedRAMP requests, and providing access to training materials, including videos-on-demand;

(ii) improving communication with CSPs through automation and standardization of messages at each stage of authorization. These communications may include status updates, requirements to complete a vendor's current stage, next steps, and points of contact for questions;

(iii) incorporating automation throughout the lifecycle of FedRAMP, including assessment, authorization, continuous monitoring, and compliance;

(iv) digitizing and streamlining documentation that vendors are required to complete, including through online accessibility and pre-populated forms; and

(v) identifying relevant compliance frameworks, mapping those frameworks onto requirements in the FedRAMP authorization process, and allowing those frameworks to be used as a substitute for the relevant portion of the authorization process, as appropriate.

Sec. 4. Enhancing Software Supply Chain Security.

(a) The security of software used by the Federal Government is vital to the Federal Government's ability to perform its critical functions. The development of commercial software often lacks transparency, sufficient focus on the ability of the software to resist attack, and adequate controls to prevent tampering by malicious actors. There is a pressing need to implement more rigorous and predictable mechanisms for ensuring that products function securely, and as intended. The security and integrity of "critical software"—software that performs functions critical to trust (such as affording or requiring elevated system privileges or direct access to networking and computing resources)—is a particular concern. Accordingly, the Federal Government must take action to rapidly improve the security and integrity of the software supply chain, with a priority on addressing critical software.

(b) Within 30 days of the date of this order, the Secretary of Commerce acting through the Director of NIST shall solicit input from the Federal Government, private sector, academia, and other appropriate actors to identify existing or develop new standards, tools, and best practices for complying with the standards, procedures, or criteria in subsection (e) of this section. The guidelines shall include criteria that can be used to evaluate software security, include criteria to evaluate the security practices of the developers and suppliers themselves, and identify innovative tools or methods to demonstrate conformance with secure practices.

(c) Within 180 days of the date of this order, the Director of NIST shall publish preliminary guidelines, based on the consultations described in subsection (b) of this section and drawing on existing documents as practicable, for enhancing software supply chain security and meeting the requirements of this section.

(d) Within 360 days of the date of this order, the Director of NIST shall publish additional guidelines that include procedures for periodic review and updating of the guidelines described in subsection (c) of this section.

(e) Within 90 days of publication of the preliminary guidelines pursuant to subsection (c) of this section, the Secretary of Commerce acting through the Director of NIST, in consultation with the heads of such agencies as the Director of NIST deems appropriate, shall issue guidance identifying practices that enhance the security of the software supply chain. Such guidance may incorporate the guidelines published pursuant to subsections (c) and (i) of this section. Such guidance shall include standards, procedures, or criteria regarding:

(i) secure software development environments, including such actions as: (A) using administratively separate build environments; (B) auditing trust relationships; (C) establishing multi-factor, risk-based authentication and conditional access across the enterprise; (D) documenting and minimizing dependencies on enterprise products that are part of the environments used to develop, build, and edit software; (E) employing encryption for data; and (F) monitoring operations and alerts and responding to attempted and actual cyber incidents;

(ii) generating and, when requested by a purchaser, providing artifacts that demonstrate conformance to the processes set forth in subsection (e)(i) of this section;

(iii) employing automated tools, or comparable processes, to maintain trusted source code supply chains, thereby ensuring the integrity of the code;

(iv) employing automated tools, or comparable processes, that check for known and potential vulnerabilities and remediate them, which shall operate regularly, or at a minimum prior to product, version, or update release;

(v) providing, when requested by a purchaser, artifacts of the execution of the tools and processes described in subsection (e)(iii) and (iv) of this section, and making publicly available summary information on completion of these actions, to include a summary description of the risks assessed and mitigated;

(vi) maintaining accurate and up-to-date data, provenance (*i.e.*, origin) of software code or components, and controls on internal and third-party software components, tools, and services present in software development processes, and performing audits and enforcement of these controls on a recurring basis;

(vii) providing a purchaser a Software Bill of Materials (SBOM) for each product directly or by publishing it on a public website;

(viii) participating in a vulnerability disclosure program that includes a reporting and disclosure process;

(ix) attesting to conformity with secure software development practices; and

(x) ensuring and attesting, to the extent practicable, to the integrity and provenance of open source software used within any portion of a product.

(f) Within 60 days of the date of this order, the Secretary of Commerce, in coordination with the Assistant Secretary for Communications and Information and the Administrator of the National Telecommunications and Information Administration, shall publish minimum elements for an SBOM.

(g) Within 45 days of the date of this order, the Secretary of Commerce, acting through the Director of NIST, in consultation with the Secretary of Defense acting through the Director of the NSA, the Secretary of Homeland Security acting through the Director of CISA, the Director of OMB, and the Director of National Intelligence, shall publish a definition of the term “critical software” for inclusion in the guidance issued pursuant to subsection (e) of this section. That definition shall reflect the level of privilege or access required to function, integration and dependencies with other software, direct access to networking and computing resources, performance of a function critical to trust, and potential for harm if compromised.

(h) Within 30 days of the publication of the definition required by subsection (g) of this section, the Secretary of Homeland Security acting through the Director of CISA, in consultation with the Secretary of Commerce acting through the Director of NIST, shall identify and make available to agencies a list of categories of software and software products in use or in the acquisition process meeting the definition of critical software issued pursuant to subsection (g) of this section.

(i) Within 60 days of the date of this order, the Secretary of Commerce acting through the Director of NIST, in consultation with the Secretary of Homeland Security acting through the Director of CISA and with the Director of OMB, shall publish guidance outlining security measures for critical software as defined in subsection (g) of this section, including applying practices of least privilege, network segmentation, and proper configuration.

(j) Within 30 days of the issuance of the guidance described in subsection (i) of this section, the Director of OMB acting through the Administrator of the Office of Electronic Government within OMB shall take appropriate steps to require that agencies comply with such guidance.

(k) Within 30 days of issuance of the guidance described in subsection (e) of this section, the Director of OMB acting through the Administrator of the Office of Electronic Government within OMB shall take appropriate steps to require that agencies comply with such guidelines with respect to software procured after the date of this order.

(l) Agencies may request an extension for complying with any requirements issued pursuant to subsection (k) of this section. Any such request shall be considered by the Director of OMB on a case-by-case basis, and only if accompanied by a plan for meeting the underlying requirements. The Director of OMB shall on a quarterly basis provide a report to the APNSA identifying and explaining all extensions granted.

(m) Agencies may request a waiver as to any requirements issued pursuant to subsection (k) of this section. Waivers shall be considered by the Director of OMB, in consultation with the APNSA, on a case-by-case basis, and shall be granted only in exceptional circumstances and for limited duration, and only if there is an accompanying plan for mitigating any potential risks.

(n) Within 1 year of the date of this order, the Secretary of Homeland Security, in consultation with the Secretary of Defense, the Attorney General, the Director of OMB, and the Administrator of the Office of Electronic Government within OMB, shall recommend to the FAR Council contract language requiring suppliers of software available for purchase by agencies to comply with, and attest to complying with, any requirements issued pursuant to subsections (g) through (k) of this section.

(o) After receiving the recommendations described in subsection (n) of this section, the FAR Council shall review the recommendations and, as appropriate and consistent with applicable law, amend the FAR.

(p) Following the issuance of any final rule amending the FAR as described in subsection (o) of this section, agencies shall, as appropriate and consistent with applicable law, remove software products that do not meet the requirements of the amended FAR from all indefinite delivery indefinite quantity contracts; Federal Supply Schedules; Federal Government-wide Acquisition Contracts; Blanket Purchase Agreements; and Multiple Award Contracts.

(q) The Director of OMB, acting through the Administrator of the Office of Electronic Government within OMB, shall require agencies employing software developed and procured prior to the date of this order (legacy software) either to comply with any requirements issued pursuant to subsection (k) of this section or to provide a plan outlining actions to remediate or meet those requirements, and shall further require agencies seeking renewals of software contracts, including legacy software, to comply with any requirements issued pursuant to subsection (k) of this section, unless an extension or waiver is granted in accordance with subsection (l) or (m) of this section.

(r) Within 60 days of the date of this order, the Secretary of Commerce acting through the Director of NIST, in consultation with the Secretary of Defense acting through the Director of the NSA, shall publish guidelines recommending minimum standards for vendors' testing of their software source code, including identifying recommended types of manual or automated testing (such as code review tools, static and dynamic analysis, software composition tools, and penetration testing).

(s) The Secretary of Commerce acting through the Director of NIST, in coordination with representatives of other agencies as the Director of NIST deems appropriate, shall initiate pilot programs informed by existing consumer product labeling programs to educate the public on the security capabilities of internet-of-Things (IoT) devices and software development practices, and shall consider ways to incentivize manufacturers and developers to participate in these programs.

(t) Within 270 days of the date of this order, the Secretary of Commerce acting through the Director of NIST, in coordination with the Chair of the Federal Trade Commission (FTC) and representatives of other agencies as the Director of NIST deems appropriate, shall identify IoT cybersecurity criteria for a consumer labeling program, and shall consider whether such a consumer labeling program may be operated in conjunction with or modeled after any similar existing government programs consistent with applicable law. The criteria shall reflect increasingly comprehensive levels of testing and assessment that a product may have undergone, and shall use or be compatible with existing labeling schemes that manufacturers use to inform consumers about the security of their products. The Director of NIST shall examine all relevant information, labeling, and incentive programs and employ best practices. This review shall focus on ease of use for consumers and a determination of what measures can be taken to maximize manufacturer participation.

(u) Within 270 days of the date of this order, the Secretary of Commerce acting through the Director of NIST, in coordination with the Chair of the FTC and representatives from other agencies as the Director of NIST deems appropriate, shall identify secure software development practices or criteria for a consumer software labeling program, and shall consider whether such a consumer software labeling program may be operated in conjunction with or modeled after any similar existing government programs, consistent with applicable law. The criteria shall reflect a baseline level of secure practices, and if practicable, shall reflect increasingly comprehensive levels of testing and assessment that a product may have undergone. The Director of NIST shall examine all relevant information, labeling, and incentive programs, employ best practices, and identify, modify, or develop a recommended label or, if practicable, a tiered software security rating system. This review shall focus on ease of use for consumers and a determination of what measures can be taken to maximize participation.

(v) These pilot programs shall be conducted in a manner consistent with OMB Circular A-119 and NIST Special Publication 2000-02 (Conformity Assessment Considerations for Federal Agencies).

(w) Within 1 year of the date of this order, the Director of NIST shall conduct a review of the pilot programs, consult with the private sector and relevant agencies to assess the effectiveness of the programs, determine what improvements can be made going forward, and submit a summary report to the APNSA.

(x) Within 1 year of the date of this order, the Secretary of Commerce, in consultation with the heads of other agencies as the Secretary of Commerce deems appropriate, shall provide to the President, through the APNSA, a report that reviews the progress made under this section and outlines additional steps needed to secure the software supply chain.

Sec. 5. Establishing a Cyber Safety Review Board.

(a) The Secretary of Homeland Security, in consultation with the Attorney General, shall establish the Cyber Safety Review Board (Board), pursuant to section 871 of the Homeland Security Act of 2002 (6 U.S.C. 451).

(b) The Board shall review and assess, with respect to significant cyber incidents (as defined under

Presidential Policy Directive 41 of July 26, 2016 (United States Cyber Incident Coordination) (PPD-41)) affecting FCEB Information Systems or non-Federal systems, threat activity, vulnerabilities, mitigation activities, and agency responses.

(c) The Secretary of Homeland Security shall convene the Board following a significant cyber incident triggering the establishment of a Cyber Unified Coordination Group (UCG) as provided by section V(B)(2) of PPD-41; at any time as directed by the President acting through the APNSA; or at any time the Secretary of Homeland Security deems necessary.

(d) The Board's initial review shall relate to the cyber activities that prompted the establishment of a UCG in December 2020, and the Board shall, within 90 days of the Board's establishment, provide recommendations to the Secretary of Homeland Security for improving cybersecurity and incident response practices, as outlined in subsection (i) of this section.

(e) The Board's membership shall include Federal officials and representatives from private-sector entities. The Board shall comprise representatives of the Department of Defense, the Department of Justice, CISA, the NSA, and the FBI, as well as representatives from appropriate private-sector cybersecurity or software suppliers as determined by the Secretary of Homeland Security. A representative from OMB shall participate in Board activities when an incident under review involves FCEB Information Systems, as determined by the Secretary of Homeland Security. The Secretary of Homeland Security may invite the participation of others on a case-by-case basis depending on the nature of the incident under review.

(f) The Secretary of Homeland Security shall biennially designate a Chair and Deputy Chair of the Board from among the members of the Board, to include one Federal and one private-sector member.

(g) The Board shall protect sensitive law enforcement, operational, business, and other confidential information that has been shared with it, consistent with applicable law.

(h) The Secretary of Homeland Security shall provide to the President through the APNSA any advice, information, or recommendations of the Board for improving cybersecurity and incident response practices and policy upon completion of its review of an applicable incident.

(i) Within 30 days of completion of the initial review described in subsection (d) of this section, the Secretary of Homeland Security shall provide to the President through the APNSA the recommendations of the Board based on the initial review. These recommendations shall describe:

(i) identified gaps in, and options for, the Board's composition or authorities;

(ii) the Board's proposed mission, scope, and responsibilities;

(iii) membership eligibility criteria for private-sector representatives;

(iv) Board governance structure including interaction with the executive branch and the Executive Office of the President;

(v) thresholds and criteria for the types of cyber incidents to be evaluated;

(vi) sources of information that should be made available to the Board, consistent with applicable law and policy;

(vii) an approach for protecting the information provided to the Board and securing the cooperation of affected United States individuals and entities for the purpose of the Board's review of incidents; and (viii) administrative and budgetary considerations required for operation of the Board.

(j) The Secretary of Homeland Security, in consultation with the Attorney General and the APNSA, shall review the recommendations provided to the President through the APNSA pursuant to subsection (i) of this section and take steps to implement them as appropriate.

(k) Unless otherwise directed by the President, the Secretary of Homeland Security shall extend the life of the Board every 2 years as the Secretary of Homeland Security deems appropriate, pursuant to section 871 of the Homeland Security Act of 2002.

Sec. 6. Standardizing the Federal Government's Playbook for Responding to Cybersecurity Vulnerabilities and Incidents.

(a) The cybersecurity vulnerability and incident response procedures currently used to identify, remediate, and recover from vulnerabilities and incidents affecting their systems vary across agencies, hindering the ability of lead agencies to analyze vulnerabilities and incidents more comprehensively across agencies. Standardized response processes ensure a more coordinated and centralized cataloging of incidents and tracking of agencies' progress toward successful responses.

(b) Within 120 days of the date of this order, the Secretary of Homeland Security acting through the Director of CISA, in consultation with the Director of OMB, the Federal Chief Information Officers Council, and the Federal Chief Information Security Council, and in coordination with the Secretary of Defense acting through the Director of the NSA, the Attorney General, and the Director of National Intelligence, shall develop a standard set of operational procedures (playbook) to be used in planning and conducting a cybersecurity vulnerability and incident response activity respecting FCEB Information Systems. The playbook shall:

(i) incorporate all appropriate NIST standards;

(ii) be used by FCEB Agencies; and

(iii) articulate progress and completion through all phases of an incident response, while allowing flexibility so it may be used in support of various response activities.

(c) The Director of OMB shall issue guidance on agency use of the playbook.

(d) Agencies with cybersecurity vulnerability or incident response procedures that deviate from the playbook may use such procedures only after consulting with the Director of OMB and the APNSA and demonstrating that these procedures meet or exceed the standards proposed in the playbook.

(e) The Director of CISA, in consultation with the Director of the NSA, shall review and update the playbook annually, and provide information to the Director of OMB for incorporation in guidance updates.

(f) To ensure comprehensiveness of incident response activities and build confidence that unauthorized cyber actors no longer have access to FCEB Information Systems, the playbook shall establish, consistent with applicable law, a requirement that the Director of CISA review and validate FCEB Agencies' incident response and remediation results upon an agency's completion of its incident response. The Director of CISA may recommend use of another agency or a third-party incident response team as appropriate.

(g) To ensure a common understanding of cyber incidents and the cybersecurity status of an agency, the playbook shall define key terms and use such terms consistently with any statutory definitions of those terms, to the extent practicable, thereby providing a shared lexicon among agencies using the playbook.

Sec. 7. Improving Detection of Cybersecurity Vulnerabilities and Incidents on Federal Government Networks.

(a) The Federal Government shall employ all appropriate resources and authorities to maximize the early detection of cybersecurity vulnerabilities and incidents on its networks. This approach shall include increasing the Federal Government's visibility into and detection of cybersecurity vulnerabilities and threats to agency networks in order to bolster the Federal Government's cybersecurity efforts.

(b) FCEB Agencies shall deploy an Endpoint Detection and Response (EDR) initiative to support proactive detection of cybersecurity incidents within Federal Government infrastructure, active cyber hunting, containment and remediation, and incident response.

(c) Within 30 days of the date of this order, the Secretary of Homeland Security acting through the Director of CISA shall provide to the Director of OMB recommendations on options for implementing an EDR initiative, centrally located to support host-level visibility, attribution, and response regarding FCEB Information Systems.

(d) Within 90 days of receiving the recommendations described in subsection (c) of this section, the Director of OMB, in consultation with Secretary of Homeland Security, shall issue requirements for FCEB Agencies to adopt Federal Government-wide EDR approaches. Those requirements shall support a capability of the Secretary of Homeland Secretary, acting through the Director of CISA, to engage in cyber hunt, detection, and response activities.

(e) The Director of OMB shall work with the Secretary of Homeland Security and agency heads to ensure that agencies have adequate resources to comply with the requirements issued pursuant to subsection (d) of this section.

(f) Defending FCEB Information Systems requires that the Secretary of Homeland Security acting through the Director of CISA have access to agency data that are relevant to a threat and vulnerability analysis, as well as for assessment and threat-hunting purposes. Within 75 days of the date of this order, agencies shall establish or update Memoranda of Agreement (MOA) with CISA for the Continuous Diagnostics and Mitigation Program to ensure object level data, as defined in the MOA, are available and accessible to CISA, consistent with applicable law.

(g) Within 45 days of the date of this order, the Director of the NSA as the National Manager for National Security Systems (National Manager) shall recommend to the Secretary of Defense, the Director of National Intelligence, and the Committee on National Security Systems (CNSS) appropriate actions for improving detection of cyber incidents affecting National Security Systems, to the extent permitted by applicable law, including recommendations concerning EDR approaches and whether such measures should be operated by agencies or through a centralized service of common concern provided by the National Manager.

(h) Within 90 days of the date of this order, the Secretary of Defense, the Director of National Intelligence, and the CNSS shall review the recommendations submitted under subsection (g) of this section and, as appropriate, establish policies that effectuate those recommendations, consistent with applicable law.

(i) Within 90 days of the date of this order, the Director of CISA shall provide to the Director of OMB and the APNSA a report describing how authorities granted under section 1705 of Public Law 116-283, to conduct threat-hunting activities on FCEB networks without prior authorization from agencies, are being implemented. This report shall also recommend procedures to ensure that mission-critical systems are not disrupted, procedures for notifying system owners of vulnerable government systems, and the range of techniques that can be used during testing of FCEB Information Systems. The Director of CISA shall provide quarterly reports to the APNSA and the Director of OMB regarding actions taken under section 1705 of Public Law 116-283.

(j) To ensure alignment between Department of Defense Information Network (DODIN) directives and FCEB Information Systems directives, the Secretary of Defense and the Secretary of Homeland Security, in consultation with the Director of OMB, shall:

(i) within 60 days of the date of this order, establish procedures for the Department of Defense and the

Department of Homeland Security to immediately share with each other Department of Defense Incident Response Orders or Department of Homeland Security Emergency Directives and Binding Operational Directives applying to their respective information networks;

(ii) evaluate whether to adopt any guidance contained in an Order or Directive issued by the other Department, consistent with regulations concerning sharing of classified information; and

(iii) within 7 days of receiving notice of an Order or Directive issued pursuant to the procedures established under subsection (j)(i) of this section, notify the APNSA and Administrator of the Office of Electronic Government within OMB of the evaluation described in subsection (j)(ii) of this section, including a determination whether to adopt guidance issued by the other Department, the rationale for that determination, and a timeline for application of the directive, if applicable.

Sec. 8. Improving the Federal Government's Investigative and Remediation Capabilities.

(a) Information from network and system logs on Federal Information Systems (for both on-premises systems and connections hosted by third parties, such as CSPs) is invaluable for both investigation and remediation purposes. It is essential that agencies and their IT service providers collect and maintain such data and, when necessary to address a cyber incident on FCEB Information Systems, provide them upon request to the Secretary of Homeland Security through the Director of CISA and to the FBI, consistent with applicable law.

(b) Within 14 days of the date of this order, the Secretary of Homeland Security, in consultation with the Attorney General and the Administrator of the Office of Electronic Government within OMB, shall provide to the Director of OMB recommendations on requirements for logging events and retaining other relevant data within an agency's systems and networks. Such recommendations shall include the types of logs to be maintained, the time periods to retain the logs and other relevant data, the time periods for agencies to enable recommended logging and security requirements, and how to protect logs. Logs shall be protected by cryptographic methods to ensure integrity once collected and periodically verified against the hashes throughout their retention. Data shall be retained in a manner consistent with all applicable privacy laws and regulations. Such recommendations shall also be considered by the FAR Council when promulgating rules pursuant to section 2 of this order.

(c) Within 90 days of receiving the recommendations described in subsection (b) of this section, the Director of OMB, in consultation with the Secretary of Commerce and the Secretary of Homeland Security, shall formulate policies for agencies to establish requirements for logging, log retention, and log management, which shall ensure centralized access and visibility for the highest level security operations center of each agency.

(d) The Director of OMB shall work with agency heads to ensure that agencies have adequate resources to comply with the requirements identified in subsection (c) of this section.

(e) To address cyber risks or incidents, including potential cyber risks or incidents, the proposed recommendations issued pursuant to subsection (b) of this section shall include requirements to ensure that, upon request, agencies provide logs to the Secretary of Homeland Security through the Director of CISA and to the FBI, consistent with applicable law. These requirements should be designed to permit agencies to share log information, as needed and appropriate, with other Federal agencies for cyber risks or incidents.

Sec. 9. National Security Systems.

(a) Within 60 days of the date of this order, the Secretary of Defense acting through the National Manager, in coordination with the Director of National Intelligence and the CNSS, and in consultation with the APNSA, shall adopt National Security Systems requirements that are equivalent to or exceed the cybersecurity requirements set forth in this order that are otherwise not applicable to National Security Systems. Such requirements may provide for exceptions in circumstances necessitated by unique mission needs. Such requirements shall be codified in a National Security Memorandum (NSM). Until such time as that NSM is issued, programs, standards, or requirements established pursuant to this order shall not apply with respect to National Security Systems.

(b) Nothing in this order shall alter the authority of the National Manager with respect to National Security Systems as defined in National Security Directive 42 of July 5, 1990 (National Policy for the Security of National Security Telecommunications and Information Systems) (NSD-42). The FCEB network shall continue to be within the authority of the Secretary of Homeland Security acting through the Director of CISA.

Sec. 10. Definitions.

For purposes of this order:

(a) the term “agency” has the meaning ascribed to it under 44 U.S.C. 3502.

(b) the term “auditing trust relationship” means an agreed-upon relationship between two or more system elements that is governed by criteria for secure interaction, behavior, and outcomes relative to the protection of assets.

(c) the term “cyber incident” has the meaning ascribed to an “incident” under 44 U.S.C. 3552(b)(2).

(d) the term “Federal Civilian Executive Branch Agencies” or “FCEB Agencies” includes all agencies except for the Department of Defense and agencies in the Intelligence Community.

(e) the term “Federal Civilian Executive Branch Information Systems” or “FCEB Information Systems” means those information systems operated by Federal Civilian Executive Branch Agencies, but excludes National Security Systems.

(f) the term “Federal Information Systems” means an information system used or operated by an agency or by a contractor of an agency or by another organization on behalf of an agency, including FCEB Information Systems and National Security Systems.

(g) the term “Intelligence Community” or “IC” has the meaning ascribed to it under 50 U.S.C. 3003(4).

(h) the term “National Security Systems” means information systems as defined in 44 U.S.C. 3552(b)(6), 3553(e)(2), and 3553(e)(3).

(i) the term “logs” means records of the events occurring within an organization’s systems and networks. Logs are composed of log entries, and each entry contains information related to a specific event that has occurred within a system or network.

(j) the term “Software Bill of Materials” or “SBOM” means a formal record containing the details and supply chain relationships of various components used in building software. Software developers and vendors often create products by assembling existing open source and commercial software components. The SBOM enumerates these components in a product. It is analogous to a list of ingredients on food packaging. An SBOM is useful to those who develop or manufacture software, those who select or purchase software, and those who operate software. Developers often use available open source and third-party software components to create a product; an SBOM allows the builder to make sure those components are up to date and to respond quickly to new vulnerabilities. Buyers can use an SBOM to perform vulnerability or license analysis, both of which can be used to evaluate risk in a product. Those who operate software can use SBOMs to quickly and easily determine whether they are at potential risk of a newly discovered vulnerability. A widely used, machine-readable SBOM format allows for greater benefits through automation and tool integration. The SBOMs gain greater value when collectively stored in a repository that can be easily queried by other applications and systems. Understanding the supply chain of software, obtaining an SBOM, and using it to analyze known vulnerabilities are crucial in managing risk.

(k) the term "Zero Trust Architecture" means a security model, a set of system design principles, and a coordinated cybersecurity and system management strategy based on an acknowledgement that threats exist both inside and outside traditional network boundaries. The Zero Trust security model eliminates implicit trust in any one element, node, or service and instead requires continuous verification of the operational picture via real-time information from multiple sources to determine access and other system responses. In essence, a Zero Trust Architecture allows users full access but only to the bare minimum they need to perform their jobs. If a device is compromised, zero trust can ensure that the damage is contained. The Zero Trust Architecture security model assumes that a breach is inevitable or has likely already occurred, so it constantly limits access to only what is needed and looks for anomalous or malicious activity. Zero Trust Architecture embeds comprehensive security monitoring; granular risk-based access controls; and system security automation in a coordinated manner throughout all aspects of the infrastructure in order to focus on protecting data in real-time within a dynamic threat environment. This data-centric security model allows the concept of least-privileged access to be applied for every access decision, where the answers to the questions of who, what, when, where, and how are critical for appropriately allowing or denying access to resources based on the combination of sever.

Sec. 11. General Provisions.

(a) Upon the appointment of the National Cyber Director (NCD) and the establishment of the related Office within the Executive Office of the President, pursuant to section 1752 of Public Law 116-283, portions of this order may be modified to enable the NCD to fully execute its duties and responsibilities.

(b) Nothing in this order shall be construed to impair or otherwise affect: (i) the authority granted by law to an executive department or agency, or the head thereof; or (ii) the functions of the Director of the Office of Management and Budget relating to budgetary, administrative, or legislative proposals.

(c) This order shall be implemented in a manner consistent with applicable law and subject to the availability of appropriations.

(d) This order is not intended to, and does not, create any right or benefit, substantive or procedural, enforceable at law or in equity by any party against the United States, its departments, agencies, or entities, its officers, employees, or agents, or any other person.

(e) Nothing in this order confers authority to interfere with or to direct a criminal or national security investigation, arrest, search, seizure, or disruption operation or to alter a legal restriction that requires an agency to protect information learned in the course of a criminal or national security investigation.

U.S. DEPARTMENT OF THE TREASURY: UPDATED ADVISORY ON POTENTIAL SANCTIONS RISKS FOR FACILITATING RANSOMWARE PAYMENTS

Date: September 21, 2021[1]

The U.S. Department of the Treasury's Office of Foreign Assets Control (OFAC) is issuing this updated advisory to highlight the sanctions risks associated with ransomware payments in connection with malicious cyber-enabled activities and the proactive steps companies can take to mitigate such risks, including actions that OFAC would consider to be "mitigating factors" in any related enforcement action.[2]

Demand for ransomware payments has increased during the COVID-19 pandemic as cyber actors target online systems that U.S. persons rely on to continue conducting business. Companies that facilitate ransomware payments to cyber actors on behalf of victims, including financial institutions, cyber insurance firms, and companies involved in digital forensics and incident response, not only encourage future ransomware payment demands but also may risk violating OFAC regulations. The U.S. government strongly discourages all private companies and citizens from paying ransom or extortion demands and recommends focusing on strengthening defensive and resilience measures to prevent and protect against ransomware attacks.

This advisory describes the potential sanctions risks associated with making and facilitating ransomware payments and provides information for contacting relevant U.S. government agencies, including OFAC if there is any reason to suspect the cyber actor demanding ransomware payment may be sanctioned or otherwise have a sanctions nexus.[3]

Background on Ransomware Attacks

Ransomware is a form of malicious software ("malware") designed to block access to a computer system or data, often by encrypting data or programs on information technology systems to extort ransom payments from victims in exchange for decrypting the information and restoring victims' access to their systems or data. In some cases, in addition to the attack, cyber actors threaten to publicly disclose victims' sensitive files. The cyber actors then demand a ransomware payment, usually through virtual currency, in exchange for a key to decrypt the files and restore victims' access to systems or data.

In recent years, ransomware attacks have become more focused, sophisticated, costly, and numerous. According to the Federal Bureau of Investigation (FBI), there was a nearly 21 percent increase in reported ransomware cases and a 225 percent increase in associated losses from 2019 to 2020.[4] Ransomware attacks are carried out against private and governmental entities of all sizes and in all sectors, including organizations operating critical infrastructure, such as hospitals. Often attacks also take place against vulnerable entities such as school districts and smaller businesses, in part due to the attacker's assumption that such victims may have fewer resources to invest in cyber protection and will make quick payment to restore services.

---

1 This advisory is explanatory only and does not have the force of law. It does not modify statutory authorities, Executive Orders, or regulations. It is not intended to be, nor should it be interpreted as, comprehensive, or as imposing requirements under U.S. law, or otherwise addressing any requirements under applicable law. Please see the legally binding provisions cited for relevant legal authorities.

2 This advisory updates and supersedes OFAC's *Advisory on Potential Sanctions Risks for Facilitating Ransomware Payments* of October 1, 2020.

3 This advisory is limited to sanctions risks related to ransomware and is not intended to address issues related to information security practitioners' cyber threat intelligence-gathering efforts more broadly. For guidance related to those activities, see guidance from the U.S. Department of Justice, *Legal Considerations when Gathering Online Cyber Threat Intelligence and Purchasing Data from Illicit Sources* (February 2020), available at https://www.justice.gov/criminal-ccips/page/file/1252341/download.

4 *Compare* Federal Bureau of Investigation, Internet Crime Complaint Center, *2019 Internet Crime Report*, available at https://pdf.ic3.gov/2019_IC3Report.pdf, *with* Federal Bureau of Investigation, Internet Crime Complaint Center, *2020 Internet Crime Report*, available at https://www.ic3.gov/Media/PDF/AnnualReport/2020_IC3Report.pdf.

OFAC Designations of Malicious Cyber Actors

OFAC has designated numerous malicious cyber actors under its cyber-related sanctions program and other sanctions programs, including perpetrators of ransomware attacks and those who facilitate ransomware transactions. For example, starting in 2013, a ransomware variant known as Cryptolocker was used to infect more than 234,000 computers, approximately half of which were in the United States.[5] OFAC designated the developer of Cryptolocker, Evgeniy Mikhailovich Bogachev, in December 2016.[6]

Starting in late 2015 and lasting approximately 34 months, SamSam ransomware was used to target mostly U.S. government institutions and companies, including the City of Atlanta, the Colorado Department of Transportation, and a large healthcare company. In November 2018, OFAC designated two Iranians for providing material support to a malicious cyber activity and identified two virtual currency addresses used to funnel SamSam ransomware proceeds.[7]

In May 2017, a ransomware known as WannaCry 2.0 infected approximately 300,000 computers in at least 150 countries. This attack was linked to the Lazarus Group, a cybercriminal organization sponsored by North Korea. OFAC designated the Lazarus Group and two subgroups, Bluenoroff and Andariel, in September 2019.[8]

Beginning in 2015, Evil Corp, a Russia-based cybercriminal organization, used the Dridex malware to infect computers and harvest login credentials from hundreds of banks and financial institutions in over 40 countries, causing more than $100 million in theft. In December 2019, OFAC designated Evil Corp and its leader, Maksim Yakubets, for their development and distribution of the Dridex malware.[9]

In September 2021, OFAC designated SUEX OTC, S.R.O. ("SUEX"), a virtual currency exchange, for its part in facilitating financial transactions for ransomware actors, involving illicit proceeds from at least eight ransomware variants. Analysis of known SUEX transactions showed that over 40% of SUEX's known transaction history was associated with illicit actors.[10]

OFAC has imposed, and will continue to impose, sanctions on these actors and others who materially assist, sponsor, or provide financial, material, or technological support for these activities.[11]

Ransomware Payments with a Sanctions Nexus Threaten U.S. National Security Interests

Facilitating a ransomware payment that is demanded as a result of malicious cyber activities may enable criminals and adversaries with a sanctions nexus to profit and advance their illicit aims. For example, ransomware payments made to sanctioned persons or to comprehensively sanctioned jurisdictions could be used to fund activities adverse to the national security and foreign policy objectives of the United States. Such payments not only encourage and enrich malicious actors, but also perpetuate and incentivize additional

5 Press Release, U.S. Dept. of Justice, U.S. Leads Multi-National Action Against "Gameover Zeus" Botnet and "Cryptolocker" Ransomware, Charges Botnet Administrator (June 2, 2014), available at https://www.justice.gov/opa/pr/us-leads-multi-national-action-against-gameover-zeus-botnet-and-cryptolocker-ransomware.

6 Press Release, U.S. Dept. of the Treasury, Treasury Sanctions Two Individuals for Malicious Cyber-Enabled Activities (Dec. 29, 2016), available at https://www.treasury.gov/press-center/press-releases/Pages/jl0693.aspx.

7 Press Release, U.S. Dept. of the Treasury, Treasury Designates Iran-Based Financial Facilitators of Malicious Cyber Activity and for the First Time Identifies Associated Digital Currency Addresses (Nov. 28, 2018), available at https://home.treasury.gov/news/press-releases/sm556.

8 Press Release, U.S. Dept. of the Treasury, Treasury Sanctions North Korean State-Sponsored Malicious Cyber Groups (Sept. 13, 2019), available at https://home.treasury.gov/news/press-releases/sm774.

9 Press Release, U.S. Dept. of the Treasury, Treasury Sanctions Evil Corp, the Russia-Based Cybercriminal Group Behind Dridex Malware (Dec. 5, 2019), available at https://home.treasury.gov/news/press-releases/sm845.

10 Press Release, U.S. Dept. of the Treasury, Treasury Takes Robust Actions to Counter Ransomware (Sept. 21, 2021), available at https://home.treasury.gov/news/press-releases/jy0364.

11 Federal charges have also been brought in connection with each of the aforementioned ransomware schemes. See, e.g., Press Release, U.S. Dept. of Justice, Russian National Charged with Decade-Long Series of Hacking and Bank Fraud Offenses Resulting in Tens of Millions in Losses and Second Russian National Charged with Involvement in Deployment of "Bugat" Malware (Dec. 5, 2019), available at https://www.justice.gov/opa/pr/russian-national-charged-decade-long-series-hacking-and-bank-fraud-offenses-resulting-tens; and Press Release U.S. Dept. of Justice, Three North Korean Military Hackers Indicted in Wide-Ranging Scheme to Commit Cyberattacks and Financial Crimes Across the Globe (Feb. 17, 2021), available at https://www.justice.gov/opa/pr/three-north-korean-military-hackers-indicted-wide-ranging-scheme-commit-cyberattacks-and#:~:text=A%20federal%20indictment%20unsealed%20today,and%20companies%2C%20to%20create%20.

attacks. Moreover, there is no guarantee that companies will regain access to their data or be free from further attacks themselves. For these reasons, the U.S. government strongly discourages the payment of cyber ransom or extortion demands.

Facilitating Ransomware Payments on Behalf of a Victim May Violate OFAC Regulations

Under the authority of the International Emergency Economic Powers Act (IEEPA) or the Trading with the Enemy Act (TWEA),[12] U.S. persons are generally prohibited from engaging in transactions, directly or indirectly, with individuals or entities ("persons") on OFAC's Specially Designated Nationals and Blocked Persons List (SDN List), other blocked persons, and those covered by comprehensive country or region embargoes (e.g., Cuba, the Crimea region of Ukraine, Iran, North Korea, and Syria). Additionally, any transaction that causes a violation under IEEPA, including a transaction by a non-U.S. person that causes a U.S. person to violate any IEEPA-based sanctions prohibitions, is also prohibited. U.S. persons, wherever located, are also generally prohibited from facilitating actions of non-U.S. persons that could not be directly performed by U.S. persons due to U.S. sanctions regulations.

OFAC may impose civil penalties for sanctions violations based on strict liability, meaning that a person subject to U.S. jurisdiction may be held civilly liable even if such person did not know or have reason to know that it was engaging in a transaction that was prohibited under sanctions laws and regulations administered by OFAC. OFAC's Economic Sanctions Enforcement Guidelines (Enforcement Guidelines)[13] provide more information regarding OFAC's enforcement of U.S. economic sanctions, including the factors that OFAC generally considers when determining an appropriate response to an apparent violation. Enforcement responses range from non-public responses, including issuing a No Action Letter or a Cautionary Letter, to public responses, such as civil monetary penalties.

Sanctions Compliance Program and Defensive/Resilience Measures

Under OFAC's Enforcement Guidelines, the existence, nature, and adequacy of a sanctions compliance program is a factor that OFAC may consider when determining an appropriate enforcement response to an apparent violation of U.S. sanctions laws or regulations.

As a general matter, OFAC encourages financial institutions and other companies to implement a risk-based compliance program to mitigate exposure to sanctions-related violations.[14] This also applies to companies that engage with victims of ransomware attacks, such as those involved in providing cyber insurance, digital forensics and incident response, and financial services that may involve processing ransom payments (including depository institutions and money services businesses). In particular, the sanctions compliance programs of these companies should account for the risk that a ransomware payment may involve an SDN or blocked person, or a comprehensively embargoed jurisdiction. Companies involved in facilitating ransomware payments on behalf of victims should also consider whether they have regulatory obligations under Financial Crimes Enforcement Network (FinCEN) regulations.[15]

Meaningful steps taken to reduce the risk of extortion by a sanctioned actor through adopting or improving cybersecurity practices, such as those highlighted in the Cybersecurity and Infrastructure Security Agency's (CISA) September 2020 Ransomware Guide,[16] will be considered a significant mitigating factor in any OFAC enforcement response.[17] Such steps could include maintaining offline backups of data, developing

12 50 U.S.C. §§ 4301–41; 50 U.S.C. §§ 1701–06.

13 31 C.F.R. part 501, appx. A.

14 To assist the public in developing an effective sanctions compliance program, in 2019, OFAC published *A Framework for OFAC Compliance Commitments*, intended to provide organizations with a framework for the five essential components of a risk-based sanctions compliance program. The *Framework* is available at https://home.treasury.gov/system/files/126/framework_ofac_cc.pdf.

15 *See* FinCEN Guidance, FIN-2020-A006, *Advisory on Ransomware and the Use of the Financial System to Facilitate Ransom Payments*, October 1, 2020, for applicable anti-money laundering obligations related to financial institutions in the ransomware context.

16 *See* Cybersecurity and Infrastructure Security Agency Guidance, *Ransomware Guide*, September 2020, https://www.cisa.gov/sites/default/files/publications/CISA_MS-ISAC_Ransomware%20Guide_S508C.pdf.

17 *See* the U.S. government's website, https://www.cisa.gov/stopransomware, for additional guidance.

incident response plans, instituting cybersecurity training, regularly updating antivirus and anti-malware software, and employing authentication protocols, among others.

Cooperation with OFAC and Law Enforcement

Another factor that OFAC will consider under the Enforcement Guidelines is the reporting of ransomware attacks to appropriate U.S. government agencies and the nature and extent of a subject person's cooperation with OFAC, law enforcement, and other relevant agencies, including whether an apparent violation of U.S. sanctions is voluntarily self-disclosed. In the case of ransomware payments that may have a sanctions nexus, OFAC will consider a company's self-initiated and complete report of a ransomware attack to law enforcement or other relevant U.S. government agencies, such as CISA or the U.S. Department of the Treasury's Office of Cybersecurity and Critical Infrastructure Protection (OCCIP), made as soon as possible after discovery of an attack, to be a voluntary self-disclosure and a significant mitigating factor in determining an appropriate enforcement response. OFAC will also consider a company's full and ongoing cooperation with law enforcement both during and after a ransomware attack — e.g., providing all relevant information such as technical details, ransom payment demand, and ransom payment instructions as soon as possible — to be a significant mitigating factor.

While the resolution of each potential enforcement matter depends on the specific facts and circumstances, OFAC would be more likely to resolve apparent violations involving ransomware attacks with a non-public response (i.e., a No Action Letter or a Cautionary Letter) when the affected party took the mitigating steps described above, particularly reporting the ransomware attack to law enforcement as soon as possible and providing ongoing cooperation.

OFAC Licensing Policy

Ransomware payments benefit illicit actors and can undermine the national security and foreign policy objectives of the United States. For this reason, license applications involving ransomware payments demanded as a result of malicious cyber-enabled activities will continue to be reviewed by OFAC on a case-by-case basis with a presumption of denial.

Victims of Ransomware Attacks Should Contact Relevant Government Agencies

OFAC strongly encourages all victims and those involved with addressing ransomware attacks to report the incident to CISA, their local FBI field office, the FBI Internet Crime Complaint Center, or their local U.S. Secret Service office as soon as possible. Victims should also report ransomware attacks and payments to Treasury's OCCIP and contact OFAC if there is any reason to suspect a potential sanctions nexus with regard to a ransomware payment. As noted, in doing so victims can receive significant mitigation from OFAC when determining an appropriate enforcement response in the event a sanctions nexus is found in connection with a ransomware payment.

By reporting ransomware attacks as soon as possible, victims may also increase the likelihood of recovering access to their data through other means, such as alternative decryption tools, and in some circumstances may be able to recover some of the ransomware payment. Additionally, reporting ransomware attacks and payments provides critical information needed to track cyber actors, hold them accountable, and prevent or disrupt future attacks.

Contact Information for U.S. Department of Treasury Agencies:

- **U.S. Department of the Treasury's Office of Foreign Assets Control**
  - Sanctions Compliance and Evaluation Division: ofac_feedback@treasury.gov; (202) 622-2490 / (800) 540-6322
  - Licensing Division: https://licensing.ofac.treas.gov/; (202) 622-2480

- **U.S. Department of the Treasury's Office of Cybersecurity and Critical Infrastructure Protection (OCCIP)**
  - OCCIP-Coord@treasury.gov; (202) 622-3000

- **U.S. Department of the Treasury's Financial Crimes Enforcement Network (FinCEN)**
  - FinCEN Regulatory Support Section: frc@fincen.gov

Contact Information for Other Relevant U.S. Government Agencies:

- **Federal Bureau of Investigation Cyber Task Force**
  - https://www.ic3.gov/default.aspx; www.fbi.gov/contact-us/field

- **U.S. Secret Service Cyber Fraud Task Force**
  - https://secretservice.gov/contact/field-offices

- **Cybersecurity and Infrastructure Security Agency**
  - https://us-cert.cisa.gov/forms/report

- **Homeland Security Investigations Field Office**
  - https://www.ice.gov/contact/hsi

Ransomware Prevention Resources:

- **U.S. Government StopRansomWare.gov Website**
  - https://www.cisa.gov/stopransomware

- **CISA Ransomware Guide**
  - https://www.cisa.gov/stopransomware/ransomware-guide

If you have any questions regarding the scope of any sanctions requirements described in this advisory, please contact OFAC's Sanctions Compliance and Evaluation Division at (800) 540-6322 or (202) 622-2490.

THE WHITE HOUSE, OPEN LETTER ON PROTECTING AGAINST RANSOMWARE

TO: Corporate Executives and Business Leaders

FROM: Anne Neuberger, Deputy Assistant to the President and Deputy National Security Advisor for Cyber and Emerging Technology

SUBJECT: What We Urge You To Do To Protect Against The Threat of Ransomware

DATE: June 2, 2021

The number and size of ransomware incidents have increased significantly, and strengthening our nation's resilience from cyberattacks – both private and public sector – is a top priority of the President's.

Under President Biden's leadership, the Federal Government is stepping up to do its part, working with like-minded partners around the world to disrupt and deter ransomware actors. These efforts include disrupting ransomware networks, working with international partners to hold countries that harbor ransomware actors accountable, developing cohesive and consistent policies towards ransom payments and enabling rapid tracing and interdiction of virtual currency proceeds.

The private sector also has a critical responsibility to protect against these threats. All organizations must recognize that no company is safe from being targeted by ransomware, regardless of size or location. But there are immediate steps you can take to protect yourself, as well as your customers and the broader economy. Much as our homes have locks and alarm systems and our office buildings have guards and security to meet the threat of theft, we urge you to take ransomware crime seriously and ensure your corporate cyber defenses match the threat.

The most important takeaway from the recent spate of ransomware attacks on U.S., Irish, German and other organizations around the world is that companies that view ransomware as a threat to their core business operations rather than a simple risk of data theft will react and recover more effectively. To understand your risk, business executives should immediately convene their leadership teams to discuss the ransomware threat and review corporate security posture and business continuity plans to ensure you have the ability to continue or quickly restore operations.

Below you will find the U.S. Government's recommended best practices – we've selected a small number of highly impactful steps to help you focus and make rapid progress on driving down risk.

What We Urge You To Do Now

Implement the five best practices from the President's Executive Order: President Biden's Improving the Nation's Cybersecurity Executive Order is being implemented with speed and urgency across the Federal Government. We're leading by example because these five best practices are high impact: multifactor authentication (because passwords alone are routinely compromised), endpoint detection & response (to hunt for malicious activity on a network and block it), encryption (so if data is stolen, it is unusable) and a skilled, empowered security team (to patch rapidly, and share and incorporate threat information in your defenses). These practices will significantly reduce the risk of a successful cyberattack.

Backup your data, system images, and configurations, regularly test them, and keep the backups offline: Ensure that backups are regularly tested and that they are not connected to the business network, as many ransomware variants try to find and encrypt or delete accessible backups. Maintaining current backups offline is critical because if your network data is encrypted with ransomware, your organization can restore systems.

Update and patch systems promptly: This includes maintaining the security of operating systems, applications, and firmware, in a timely manner. Consider using a centralized patch management system; use a risk-based assessment strategy to drive your patch management program.

Test your incident response plan: There's nothing that shows the gaps in plans more than testing them. Run through some core questions and use those to build an incident response plan: Are you able to sustain business operations without access to certain systems? For how long? Would you turn off your manufacturing operations if business systems such as billing were offline?

Check Your Security Team's Work: Use a 3rd party pen tester to test the security of your systems and your ability to defend against a sophisticated attack. Many ransomware criminals are aggressive and sophisticated and will find the equivalent of unlocked doors.

Segment your networks: There's been a recent shift in ransomware attacks – from stealing data to disrupting operations. It's critically important that your corporate business functions and manufacturing/production operations are separated and that you carefully filter and limit internet access to operational networks, identify links between these networks and develop workarounds or manual controls to ensure ICS networks can be isolated and continue operating if your corporate network is compromised. Regularly test contingency plans such as manual controls so that safety critical functions can be maintained during a cyber incident.

Ransomware attacks have disrupted organizations around the world, from hospitals across Ireland, Germany and France, to pipelines in the United States and banks in the U.K. The threats are serious and they are increasing. We urge you to take these critical steps to protect your organizations and the American public. The U.S. Government is working with countries around the world to hold ransomware actors and the countries who harbor them accountable, but we cannot fight the threat posed by ransomware alone. The private sector has a distinct and key responsibility. The federal government stands ready to help you implement these best practices.

Additional Resources

FACT SHEET: President Signs Executive Order Charting New Course to Improve the Nation's Cybersecurity and Protect Federal Government Networks

CISA - RANSOMWARE GUIDANCE AND RESOURCES

CYBER INCIDENT REPORTING FOR CRITICAL INFRASTRUCTURE ACT OF 2022

SEC. 101. SHORT TITLE.

This division may be cited as the "Cyber Incident Reporting for Critical Infrastructure Act of 2022".

SEC. 102. DEFINITIONS.

In this division:

(1) COVERED CYBER INCIDENT; COVERED ENTITY; CYBER INCIDENT; INFORMATION SYSTEM;

RANSOM PAYMENT; RANSOMWARE ATTACK; SECURITY VULNERABILITY.—The terms "covered cyber incident", "covered entity", "cyber incident", "information system", "ransom payment", "ransomware attack", and "security vulnerability" have the meanings given those terms in section 2240 of the Homeland Security Act of 2002, as added by section 103 of this division.

(2) DIRECTOR.—The term "Director" means the Director of the Cybersecurity and Infrastructure Security Agency.

SEC. 103. CYBER INCIDENT REPORTING.

(a) CYBER INCIDENT REPORTING.—Title XXII of the Homeland Security Act of 2002 (6 U.S.C. 651 et seq.) is amended—

(1) in section 2209(c) (6 U.S.C. 659(c))—

(A) in paragraph (11), by striking "; and" and inserting a semicolon;

(B) in paragraph (12), by striking the period at the end and inserting "; and"; and

(C) by adding at the end the following:

(13) receiving, aggregating, and analyzing reports related to covered cyber incidents (as defined in section 2240) submitted by covered entities (as defined in section 2240) and reports related to ransom payments (as defined in section 2240) submitted by covered entities (as defined in section 2240) in furtherance of the activities specified in sections 2202(e), 2203, and 2241, this subsection, and any other authorized activity of the Director, to enhance the situational awareness of cybersecurity threats across critical infrastructure sectors."; and

(2) by adding at the end the following:

Subtitle D—Cyber Incident Reporting

SEC. 2240. DEFINITIONS.

In this subtitle:

(1) CENTER.—The term 'Center' means the center established under section 2209.

(2) CLOUD SERVICE PROVIDER.—The term 'cloud service provider' means an entity offering products or services related to cloud computing, as defined by the National Institute of Standards and Technology in NIST Special Publication 800–145 and any amendatory or superseding document relating thereto.

(3) COUNCIL.—The term 'Council' means the Cyber Incident Reporting Council described in section 2246.

(4) COVERED CYBER INCIDENT.—The term 'covered cyber incident' means a substantial cyber incident experienced by a covered entity that satisfies the definition and criteria established by the Director in the final rule issued pursuant to section 2242(b).

(5) COVERED ENTITY.—The term 'covered entity' means an entity in a critical infrastructure sector, as defined in Presidential Policy Directive 21, that satisfies the definition established by the Director in the final rule issued pursuant to section 2242(b).

(6) CYBER INCIDENT.—The term 'cyber incident'—(A) has the meaning given the term 'incident' in section 2209; and (B) does not include an occurrence that imminently, but not actually, jeopardizes—(i) information on information systems; or (ii) information systems.

(7) CYBER THREAT.—The term 'cyber threat' has the meaning given the term 'cybersecurity threat' in section 2201.

(8) CYBER THREAT INDICATOR; CYBERSECURITY PURPOSE; DEFENSIVE MEASURE; FEDERAL ENTITY; SECURITY VULNERABILITY.—The terms 'cyber threat indicator', 'cybersecurity purpose', 'defensive measure', 'Federal entity', and 'security vulnerability' have the meanings given those terms in section 102 of the Cybersecurity Act of 2015 (6 U.S.C. 1501).

(9) INCIDENT; SHARING.—The terms 'incident' and 'sharing' have the meanings given those terms in section 2209.

(10) INFORMATION SHARING AND ANALYSIS ORGANIZATION.—The term 'Information Sharing and Analysis Organization' has the meaning given the term in section 2222.

(11) INFORMATION SYSTEM.—The term 'information system'—(A) has the meaning given the term in section 3502 of title 44, United States Code; and (B) includes industrial control systems, such as supervisory control and data acquisition systems, distributed control systems, and programmable logic controllers.

(12) MANAGED SERVICE PROVIDER.—The term 'managed service provider' means an entity that delivers services, such as network, application, infrastructure, or security services, via ongoing and regular support and active administration on the premises of a customer, in the data center of the entity (such as hosting), or in a third party data center.

(13) RANSOM PAYMENT.—The term 'ransom payment' means the transmission of any money or other property or asset, including virtual currency, or any portion thereof, which has at any time been delivered as ransom in connection with a ransomware attack.

(14) RANSOMWARE ATTACK.—The term 'ransomware attack'—(A) means an incident that includes the use or threat of use of unauthorized or malicious code on an information system, or the use or threat of use of another digital mechanism such as a denial of service attack, to interrupt or disrupt the operations of an information system or compromise the confidentiality, availability, or integrity of electronic data stored on, processed by, or transiting an information system to extort a demand for a ransom payment; and (B) does not include any such event where the demand for payment is—(i) not genuine; or (ii) made in good faith by an entity in response to a specific request by the owner or operator of the information system.

(15) SECTOR RISK MANAGEMENT AGENCY.—The term 'Sector Risk Management Agency' has the meaning given the term in section 2201.

(16) SIGNIFICANT CYBER INCIDENT.—The term 'significant cyber incident' means a cyber incident, or a group of related cyber incidents, that the Secretary determines is likely to result in demonstrable harm to the national security interests, foreign relations, or economy of the United States or to the public confidence, civil liberties, or public health and safety of the people of the United States.

(17) SUPPLY CHAIN COMPROMISE.—The term 'supply chain compromise' means an incident within the supply chain of an information system that an adversary can leverage or does leverage to jeopardize the confidentiality, integrity, or availability of the information system or the information the system processes, stores, or transmits, and can occur at any point during the life cycle.

(18) VIRTUAL CURRENCY.—The term 'virtual currency' means the digital representation of value that functions as a medium of exchange, a unit of account, or a store of value.

(19) VIRTUAL CURRENCY ADDRESS.—The term 'virtual currency address' means a unique public cryptographic key identifying the location to which a virtual currency payment can be made.

SEC. 2241. CYBER INCIDENT REVIEW.

(a) ACTIVITIES.—The Center shall—

(1) receive, aggregate, analyze, and secure, using processes consistent with the processes developed pursuant to the Cybersecurity Information Sharing Act of 2015 (6 U.S.C. 1501 et seq.) reports from covered entities related to a covered cyber incident to assess the effectiveness of security controls, identify tactics, techniques, and procedures adversaries use to overcome those controls and other cybersecurity purposes, including to assess potential impact of cyber incidents on public health and safety and to enhance situational awareness of cyber threats across critical infrastructure sectors;

(2) coordinate and share information with appropriate Federal departments and agencies to identify and track ransom payments, including those utilizing virtual currencies;

(3) leverage information gathered about cyber incidents to—

(A) enhance the quality and effectiveness of information sharing and coordination efforts with appropriate entities, including agencies, sector coordinating councils, Information Sharing and Analysis Organizations, State, local, Tribal, and territorial governments, technology providers, critical infrastructure owners and operators, cybersecurity and cyber incident response firms, and security researchers; and

(B) provide appropriate entities, including sector coordinating councils, Information Sharing and Analysis Organizations, State, local, Tribal, and territorial governments, technology providers, cybersecurity and cyber incident response firms, and security researchers, with timely, actionable, and anonymized reports of cyber incident campaigns and trends, including, to the maximum extent practicable, related contextual information, cyber threat indicators, and defensive measures, pursuant to section 2245;

(4) establish mechanisms to receive feedback from stakeholders on how the Agency can most effectively receive covered cyber incident reports, ransom payment reports, and other voluntarily provided information, and how the Agency can most effectively support private sector cybersecurity;

(5) facilitate the timely sharing, on a voluntary basis, between relevant critical infrastructure owners and operators of information relating to covered cyber incidents and ransom payments, particularly with respect to ongoing cyber threats or security vulnerabilities and identify and disseminate ways to prevent or mitigate similar cyber incidents in the future;

(6) for a covered cyber incident, including a ransomware attack, that also satisfies the definition of a significant cyber incident, or is part of a group of related cyber incidents that together satisfy such definition, conduct a review of the details surrounding the covered cyber incident or group of those incidents and identify and disseminate ways to prevent or mitigate similar incidents in the future;

(7) with respect to covered cyber incident reports under section 2242(a) and 2243 involving an ongoing cyber threat or security vulnerability, immediately review those reports for cyber threat indicators that can be anonymized and disseminated, with defensive measures, to appropriate stakeholders, in coordination with other divisions within the Agency, as appropriate;

(8) publish quarterly unclassified, public reports that describe aggregated, anonymized observations, findings, and recommendations based on covered cyber incident reports, which may be based on the unclassified information contained in the briefings required under subsection (c);

(9) proactively identify opportunities, consistent with the protections in section 2245, to leverage and utilize data on cyber incidents in a manner that enables and strengthens cybersecurity research carried out by academic institutions and other private sector organizations, to the greatest extent practicable; and

(10) in accordance with section 2245 and subsection (b) of this section, as soon as possible but not later than 24 hours after receiving a covered cyber incident report, ransom payment report, voluntarily submitted information pursuant to section 2243, or information received pursuant to a request for information or subpoena under section 2244, make available the information to appropriate Sector Risk Management Agencies and other appropriate Federal agencies.

(b) INTERAGENCY SHARING.—The President or a designee of the President—

(1) may establish a specific time requirement for sharing information under subsection (a)(10); and

(2) shall determine the appropriate Federal agencies under subsection (a)(10).

(c) PERIODIC BRIEFING.—Not later than 60 days after the effective date of the final rule required under section 2242(b), and on the first day of each month thereafter, the Director, in consultation with the National Cyber Director, the Attorney General, and the Director of National Intelligence, shall provide to the majority leader of the Senate, the minority leader of the Senate, the Speaker of the House of Representatives, the minority leader of the House of Representatives, the Committee on Homeland Security and Governmental Affairs of the Senate, and the Committee on Homeland Security of the House of Representatives a briefing that characterizes the national cyber threat landscape, including the threat facing Federal agencies and covered entities, and applicable intelligence and law enforcement information, covered cyber incidents, and ransomware attacks, as of the date of the briefing, which shall—

(1) include the total number of reports submitted under sections 2242 and 2243 during the preceding month, including a breakdown of required and voluntary reports;

(2) include any identified trends in covered cyber incidents and ransomware attacks over the course of the preceding month and as compared to previous reports, including any trends related to the information collected in the reports submitted under sections 2242 and 2243, including—(A) the infrastructure, tactics, and techniques malicious cyber actors commonly use; and (B) intelligence gaps that have impeded, or currently are impeding, the ability to counter covered cyber incidents and ransomware threats;

(3) include a summary of the known uses of the information in reports submitted under sections 2242 and 2243; and

(4) include an unclassified portion, but may include a classified component.

SEC. 2242. REQUIRED REPORTING OF CERTAIN CYBER INCIDENTS.

(a) IN GENERAL.—

(1) COVERED CYBER INCIDENT REPORTS.—

(A) IN GENERAL.—A covered entity that experiences a covered cyber incident shall report the covered cyber incident to the Agency not later than 72 hours after the covered entity reasonably believes that the covered cyber incident has occurred.

(B) LIMITATION.—The Director may not require reporting under subparagraph (A) any earlier than 72 hours after the covered entity reasonably believes that a covered cyber incident has occurred.

(2) RANSOM PAYMENT REPORTS.—

(A) IN GENERAL.—A covered entity that makes a ransom payment as the result of a ransomware attack against the covered entity shall report the payment to the Agency not later than 24 hours after the ransom payment has been made.

(B) APPLICATION.—The requirements under subparagraph (A) shall apply even if the ransomware attack is not a covered cyber incident subject to the reporting requirements under paragraph (1).

(3) SUPPLEMENTAL REPORTS.—A covered entity shall promptly submit to the Agency an update or supplement to a previously submitted covered cyber incident report if substantial new or different information becomes available or if the covered entity makes a ransom payment after submitting a covered cyber incident report required under paragraph (1), until such date that such covered entity notifies the Agency that the covered cyber incident at issue has concluded and has been fully mitigated and resolved.

(4) PRESERVATION OF INFORMATION.—Any covered entity subject to requirements of paragraph (1), (2), or (3) shall preserve data relevant to the covered cyber incident or ransom payment in accordance with procedures established in the final rule issued pursuant to subsection (b).

(5) EXCEPTIONS.—

(A) REPORTING OF COVERED CYBER INCIDENT WITH RANSOM PAYMENT.—If a covered entity is the victim of a covered cyber incident and makes a ransom payment prior to the 72 hour requirement under paragraph (1), such that the reporting requirements under paragraphs (1) and (2) both apply, the covered entity may submit a single report to satisfy the requirements of both paragraphs in accordance with procedures established in the final rule issued pursuant to subsection (b).

(B) SUBSTANTIALLY SIMILAR REPORTED INFORMATION.—

(i) IN GENERAL.—Subject to the limitation described in clause (ii), where the Agency has an agreement in place that satisfies the requirements of section 104(a) of the Cyber Incident Reporting for Critical Infrastructure Act of 2022, the requirements under paragraphs (1), (2), and (3) shall not apply to a covered entity required by law, regulation, or contract to report substantially similar information to another Federal agency within a substantially similar timeframe.

(ii) LIMITATION.—The exemption in clause (i) shall take effect with respect to a covered entity once an agency agreement and sharing mechanism is in place between the Agency and the respective Federal agency, pursuant to section 104(a) of the Cyber Incident Reporting for Critical Infrastructure Act of 2022.

(iii) RULES OF CONSTRUCTION.—Nothing in this paragraph shall be construed to— (I) exempt a covered entity from the reporting requirements under paragraph (3) unless the supplemental report also meets the requirements of clauses (i) and (ii) of this paragraph; (II) prevent the Agency from contacting an entity submitting information to another Federal agency that is provided to the Agency pursuant to section 104 of the Cyber Incident Reporting for Critical Infrastructure Act of 2022; or (III) prevent an entity from communicating with the Agency.

(C) DOMAIN NAME SYSTEM.—The requirements under paragraphs (1), (2) and (3) shall not apply to a covered entity or the functions of a covered entity that the Director determines constitute critical infrastructure owned, operated, or governed by multi-stakeholder organizations that develop, implement, and enforce policies concerning the Domain Name System, such as the Internet Corporation for Assigned Names and Numbers or the Internet Assigned Numbers Authority.

(6) MANNER, TIMING, AND FORM OF REPORTS.—Reports made under paragraphs (1), (2),

and (3) shall be made in the manner and form, and within the time period in the case of reports made under paragraph (3), prescribed in the final rule issued pursuant to subsection (b).

(7) EFFECTIVE DATE.—Paragraphs (1) through (4) shall take effect on the dates prescribed in the final rule issued pursuant to subsection (b).

(b) RULEMAKING.—

(1) NOTICE OF PROPOSED RULEMAKING.—Not later than 24 months after the date of enactment of this section, the Director, in consultation with Sector Risk Management Agencies, the Department of Justice, and other Federal agencies, shall publish in the Federal Register a notice of proposed rulemaking to implement subsection (a).

(2) FINAL RULE.—Not later than 18 months after publication of the notice of proposed rulemaking under paragraph (1), the Director shall issue a final rule to implement subsection (a).

(3) SUBSEQUENT RULEMAKINGS.—

(A) IN GENERAL.—The Director is authorized to issue regulations to amend or revise the final rule issued pursuant to paragraph (2).

(B) PROCEDURES.—Any subsequent rules issued under subparagraph (A) shall comply with the requirements under chapter 5 of title 5, United States Code, including the issuance of a notice of proposed rulemaking under section 553 of such title.

(c) ELEMENTS.—The final rule issued pursuant to subsection (b) shall be composed of the following elements:

(1) A clear description of the types of entities that constitute covered entities, based on—

(A) the consequences that disruption to or compromise of such an entity could cause to national security, economic security, or public health and safety;

(B) the likelihood that such an entity may be targeted by a malicious cyber actor, including a foreign country; and

(C) the extent to which damage, disruption, or unauthorized access to such an entity, including the accessing of sensitive cybersecurity vulnerability information or penetration testing tools or techniques, will likely enable the disruption of the reliable operation of critical infrastructure.

(2) A clear description of the types of substantial cyber incidents that constitute covered cyber incidents, which shall—

(A) at a minimum, require the occurrence of—

(i) a cyber incident that leads to substantial loss of confidentiality, integrity, or availability of such information system or network, or a serious impact on the safety and resiliency of operational systems and processes;

(ii) a disruption of business or industrial operations, including due to a denial of service attack, ransomware attack, or exploitation of a zero day vulnerability, against (I) an information system or network; or (II) an operational technology system or process; or

(iii) unauthorized access or disruption of business or industrial operations due to loss of service facilitated through, or caused by, a compromise of a cloud service provider, managed service provider, or other third-party data hosting provider or by a supply chain compromise;

(B) consider—

(i) the sophistication or novelty of the tactics used to perpetrate such a cyber incident, as well as the type, volume, and sensitivity of the data at issue;

(ii) the number of individuals directly or indirectly affected or potentially affected by such a cyber incident; and

(iii) potential impacts on industrial control systems, such as supervisory control and data acquisition systems, distributed control systems, and programmable logic controllers; and

(C) exclude—

(i) any event where the cyber incident is perpetrated in good faith by an entity in response to a specific request by the owner or operator of the information system; and

(ii) the threat of disruption as extortion, as described in section 2240(14)(A).

(3) A requirement that, if a covered cyber incident or a ransom payment occurs following an exempted threat described in paragraph (2)(C)(ii), the covered entity shall comply with the requirements in this subtitle in reporting the covered cyber incident or ransom payment.

(4) A clear description of the specific required contents of a report pursuant to subsection (a)(1), which shall include the following information, to the extent applicable and available, with respect to a covered cyber incident:

(A) A description of the covered cyber incident, including—

(i) identification and a description of the function of the affected information systems, networks, or devices that were, or are reasonably believed to have been, affected by such cyber incident;

(ii) a description of the unauthorized access with substantial loss of confidentiality, integrity, or availability of the affected information system or network or disruption of business or industrial operations;

(iii) the estimated date range of such incident; and

(iv) the impact to the operations of the covered entity.

(B) Where applicable, a description of the vulnerabilities exploited and the security defenses that were in place, as well as the tactics, techniques, and procedures used to perpetrate the covered cyber incident.

(C) Where applicable, any identifying or contact information related to each actor reasonably believed to be responsible for such cyber incident.

(D) Where applicable, identification of the category or categories of information that were, or are reasonably believed to have been, accessed or acquired by an unauthorized person.

(E) The name and other information that clearly identifies the covered entity impacted by the covered cyber incident, including, as applicable, the State of incorporation or formation of the covered entity, trade names, legal names, or other identifiers.

(F) Contact information, such as telephone number or electronic mail address, that the Agency may use to contact the covered entity or an authorized agent of such covered entity, or, where applicable, the service provider of such covered entity acting with the express permission of, and at the direction of, the covered entity to assist with compliance with the requirements of this subtitle.

(5) A clear description of the specific required contents of a report pursuant to subsection (a)(2), which shall be the following information, to the extent applicable and available, with respect to a ransom payment:

(A) A description of the ransomware attack, including the estimated date range of the attack.

(B) Where applicable, a description of the vulnerabilities, tactics, techniques, and procedures used to perpetrate the ransomware attack.

(C) Where applicable, any identifying or contact information related to the actor or actors reasonably believed to be responsible for the ransomware attack.

(D) The name and other information that clearly identifies the covered entity that made the ransom payment or on whose behalf the payment was made.

(E) Contact information, such as telephone number or electronic mail address, that the Agency may use to contact the covered entity that made the ransom payment or an authorized agent of such covered entity, or, where applicable, the service provider of such covered entity acting with the express permission of, and at the direction of, that covered entity to assist with compliance with the requirements of this subtitle.

(F) The date of the ransom payment.

(G) The ransom payment demand, including the type of virtual currency or other commodity requested, if applicable.

(H) The ransom payment instructions, including information regarding where to send the payment, such as the virtual currency address or physical address the funds were requested to be sent to, if applicable.

(I) The amount of the ransom payment.

(6) A clear description of the types of data required to be preserved pursuant to subsection (a)(4), the period of time for which the data is required to be preserved, and allowable uses, processes, and procedures.

(7) Deadlines and criteria for submitting supplemental reports to the Agency required under subsection (a)(3), which shall—

(A) be established by the Director in consultation with the Council;

(B) consider any existing regulatory reporting requirements similar in scope, purpose, and timing to the reporting requirements to which such a covered entity may also be subject, and make efforts to harmonize the timing and contents of any such reports to the maximum extent practicable;

(C) balance the need for situational awareness with the ability of the covered entity to conduct cyber incident response and investigations; and

(D) provide a clear description of what constitutes substantial new or different information.

(8) Procedures for—

(A) entities, including third parties pursuant to subsection (d)(1), to submit reports required by paragraphs (1), (2), and (3) of subsection (a), including the manner and form thereof, which shall include, at a minimum, a concise, user-friendly web-based form;

(B) the Agency to carry out—

(i) the enforcement provisions of section 2244, including with respect to the issuance, service, withdrawal, referral process, and enforcement of subpoenas, appeals and due process procedures;

(ii) other available enforcement mechanisms including acquisition, suspension and debarment procedures; and

(iii) other aspects of noncompliance;

(C) implementing the exceptions provided in subsection (a)(5); and

(D) protecting privacy and civil liberties consistent with processes adopted pursuant to section 105(b) of the Cybersecurity Act of 2015 (6 U.S.C. 1504(b)) and anonymizing and safeguarding, or no longer retaining, information received and disclosed through covered cyber incident reports and ransom payment reports that is known to be personal information of a specific individual or information that identifies a specific individual that is not directly related to a cybersecurity threat.

(9) Other procedural measures directly necessary to implement subsection (a).

(d) THIRD PARTY REPORT SUBMISSION AND RANSOM PAYMENT.—

(1) REPORT SUBMISSION.—A covered entity that is required to submit a covered cyber incident report or a ransom payment report may use a third party, such as an incident response company, insurance provider, service provider, Information Sharing and Analysis Organization, or law firm, to submit the required report under subsection (a).

(2) RANSOM PAYMENT.—If a covered entity impacted by a ransomware attack uses a third party to make a ransom payment, the third party shall not be required to submit a ransom payment report for itself under subsection (a)(2).

(3) DUTY TO REPORT.—Third-party reporting under this subparagraph does not relieve a covered entity from the duty to comply with the requirements for covered cyber incident report or ransom payment report submission.

(4) RESPONSIBILITY TO ADVISE.—Any third party used by a covered entity that knowingly makes a ransom payment on behalf of a covered entity impacted by a ransomware attack shall advise the impacted covered entity of the responsibilities of the impacted covered entity regarding reporting ransom payments under this section.

(e) OUTREACH TO COVERED ENTITIES.—

(1) IN GENERAL.—The Agency shall conduct an outreach and education campaign to inform likely covered entities, entities that offer or advertise as a service to customers to make or facilitate ransom payments on behalf of covered entities impacted by ransomware attacks and other appropriate entities of the requirements of paragraphs (1), (2), and (3) of subsection (a).

(2) ELEMENTS.—The outreach and education campaign under paragraph (1) shall include the following:

(A) An overview of the final rule issued pursuant to subsection (b).

(B) An overview of mechanisms to submit to the Agency covered cyber incident reports, ransom payment reports, and information relating to the disclosure, retention, and use of covered cyber incident reports and ransom payment reports under this section.

(C) An overview of the protections afforded to covered entities for complying with the requirements under paragraphs (1), (2), and (3) of subsection (a).

(D) An overview of the steps taken under section 2244 when a covered entity is not in compliance with the reporting requirements under subsection (a).

(E) Specific outreach to cybersecurity vendors, cyber incident response providers, cybersecurity insurance entities, and other entities that may support covered entities.

(F) An overview of the privacy and civil liberties requirements in this subtitle.

(3) COORDINATION.—In conducting the outreach and education campaign required under paragraph (1), the Agency may coordinate with—

(A) the Critical Infrastructure Partnership Advisory Council established under section 871;

(B) Information Sharing and Analysis Organizations;

(C) trade associations;

(D) information sharing and analysis centers;

(E) sector coordinating councils; and

(F) any other entity as determined appropriate by the Director.

(f) EXEMPTION.—Sections 3506(c), 3507, 3508, and 3509 of title 44, United States Code, shall not apply to any action to carry out this section.

(g) RULE OF CONSTRUCTION.—Nothing in this section shall affect the authorities of the Federal Government to implement the requirements of Executive Order 14028 (86 Fed. Reg. 26633; relating to improving the nation's cybersecurity), including changes to the Federal Acquisition Regulations and remedies to include suspension and debarment.

(h) SAVINGS PROVISION.—Nothing in this section shall be construed to supersede or to abrogate, modify, or otherwise limit the authority that is vested in any officer or any agency of the United States Government to regulate or take action with respect to the cybersecurity of an entity.

SEC. 2243. VOLUNTARY REPORTING OF OTHER CYBER INCIDENTS.

(a) IN GENERAL.—Entities may voluntarily report cyber incidents or ransom payments to the Agency that are not required under paragraph (1), (2), or (3) of section 2242(a), but may enhance the situational awareness of cyber threats.

(b) VOLUNTARY PROVISION OF ADDITIONAL INFORMATION IN REQUIRED REPORTS.—Covered entities may voluntarily include in reports required under paragraph (1), (2), or (3) of section 2242(a) information that is not required to be included, but may enhance the situational awareness of cyber threats.

(c) APPLICATION OF PROTECTIONS.—The protections under section 2245 applicable to reports made under section 2242 shall apply in the same manner and to the same extent to reports and information submitted under subsections (a) and (b).

SEC. 2244. NONCOMPLIANCE WITH REQUIRED REPORTING.

(a) PURPOSE.—In the event that a covered entity that is required to submit a report under section 2242(a) fails to comply with the requirement to report, the Director may obtain information about the cyber incident or ransom payment by engaging the covered entity directly to request information about the cyber incident or ransom payment, and if the Director is unable to obtain information through such engagement, by issuing a subpoena to the covered entity, pursuant to subsection (c), to gather information sufficient to determine whether a covered cyber incident or ransom payment has occurred.

(b) INITIAL REQUEST FOR INFORMATION.—

(1) IN GENERAL.—If the Director has reason to believe, whether through public reporting or other information in the possession of the Federal Government, including through analysis performed pursuant to paragraph (1) or (2) of section 2241(a), that a covered entity has experienced a covered cyber incident or made a ransom payment but failed to report such cyber incident or payment to the Agency in accordance with section 2242(a), the Director may request additional information from the covered entity to confirm whether or not a covered cyber incident or ransom payment has occurred.

(2) TREATMENT.—Information provided to the Agency in response to a request under paragraph (1) shall be treated as if it was submitted through the reporting procedures established in section 2242.

(c) ENFORCEMENT.—

(1) IN GENERAL.—If, after the date that is 72 hours from the date on which the Director made the request for information in subsection (b), the Director has received no response from the covered entity from which such information was requested, or received an inadequate response, the Director may issue to such covered entity a subpoena to compel disclosure of information the Director deems necessary to determine whether a covered cyber incident or ransom payment has occurred and obtain the information required to be reported pursuant to section 2242 and any implementing regulations, and assess potential impacts to national security, economic security, or public health and safety.

(2) CIVIL ACTION.—

(A) IN GENERAL.—If a covered entity fails to comply with a subpoena, the Director may refer the matter to the Attorney General to bring a civil action in a district court of the United States to enforce such subpoena.

(B) VENUE.—An action under this paragraph may be brought in the judicial district in which the covered entity against which the action is brought resides, is found, or does business.

(C) CONTEMPT OF COURT.—A court may punish a failure to comply with a subpoena issued under this subsection as contempt of court.

(3) NON-DELEGATION.—The authority of the Director to issue a subpoena under this subsection may not be delegated.

(4) AUTHENTICATION.—

(A) IN GENERAL.—Any subpoena issued electronically pursuant to this subsection shall be authenticated with a cryptographic digital signature of an authorized representative of the Agency, or other comparable successor technology, that allows the Agency to demonstrate that such subpoena was issued by the Agency and has not been altered or modified since such issuance.

(B) INVALID IF NOT AUTHENTICATED.—Any subpoena issued electronically pursuant to this subsection that is not authenticated in accordance with subparagraph (A) shall not be considered to be valid by the recipient of such subpoena.

(d) PROVISION OF CERTAIN INFORMATION TO ATTORNEY GENERAL.—

(1) IN GENERAL.—Notwithstanding section 2245(a)(5) and paragraph (b)(2) of this section, if the Director determines, based on the information provided in response to a subpoena issued pursuant to subsection (c), that the facts relating to the cyber incident or ransom payment at issue may constitute grounds for a regulatory enforcement action or criminal prosecution, the Director may provide such information to the Attorney General or the head of the appropriate Federal regulatory agency, who may use such information for a regulatory enforcement action or criminal prosecution.

(2) CONSULTATION.—The Director may consult with the Attorney General or the head of the appropriate Federal regulatory agency when making the determination under paragraph (1).

(e) CONSIDERATIONS.—When determining whether to exercise the authorities provided under this section, the Director shall take into consideration—

(1) the complexity in determining if a covered cyber incident has occurred; and

(2) prior interaction with the Agency or awareness of the covered entity of the policies and procedures of the Agency for reporting covered cyber incidents and ransom payments.

(f) EXCLUSIONS.—This section shall not apply to a State, local, Tribal, or territorial government entity.

(g) REPORT TO CONGRESS.—The Director shall submit to Congress an annual report on the number of times the Director—

(1) issued an initial request for information pursuant to subsection (b);

(2) issued a subpoena pursuant to subsection (c); or

(3) referred a matter to the Attorney General for a civil action pursuant to subsection (c)(2).

(h) PUBLICATION OF THE ANNUAL REPORT.—The Director shall publish a version of the annual report required under subsection (g) on the website of the Agency, which shall include, at a minimum, the number of times the Director—

(1) issued an initial request for information pursuant to subsection (b); or

(2) issued a subpoena pursuant to subsection (c).

(i) ANONYMIZATION OF REPORTS.—The Director shall ensure any victim information contained in a report required to be published under subsection (h) be anonymized before the report is published.

SEC. 2245. INFORMATION SHARED WITH OR PROVIDED TO THE FEDERAL GOVERNMENT.

(a) DISCLOSURE, RETENTION, AND USE.—

(1) AUTHORIZED ACTIVITIES.—Information provided to the Agency pursuant to section 2242 or 2243 may be disclosed to, retained by, and used by, consistent with otherwise applicable provisions of Federal law, any Federal agency or department, component, officer, employee, or agent of the Federal Government solely for—

(A) a cybersecurity purpose;

(B) the purpose of identifying—(i) a cyber threat, including the source of the cyber threat; or (ii) a security vulnerability;

(C) the purpose of responding to, or otherwise preventing or mitigating, a specific threat of death, a specific threat of serious bodily harm, or a specific threat of serious economic harm, including a terrorist act or use of a weapon of mass destruction;

(D) the purpose of responding to, investigating, prosecuting, or otherwise preventing or mitigating, a serious threat to a minor, including sexual exploitation and threats to physical safety; or

(E) the purpose of preventing, investigating, disrupting, or prosecuting an offense arising out of a cyber incident reported pursuant to section 2242 or 2243 or any of the offenses listed in section 105(d)(5)(A)(v) of the Cybersecurity Act of 2015 (6 U.S.C. 1504(d)(5)(A)(v)).

(2) AGENCY ACTIONS AFTER RECEIPT.—

(A) RAPID, CONFIDENTIAL SHARING OF CYBER THREAT INDICATORS.—Upon receiving a covered cyber incident or ransom payment report submitted pursuant to this section, the Agency shall immediately review the report to determine whether the cyber incident that is the subject of the report is connected to an ongoing cyber threat or security vulnerability and where applicable, use such report to identify, develop, and rapidly disseminate to appropriate stakeholders actionable, anonymized cyber threat indicators and defensive measures.

(B) PRINCIPLES FOR SHARING SECURITY VULNERABILITIES.—With respect to information in a covered cyber incident or ransom payment report regarding a security vulnerability referred to in paragraph (1)(B)(ii), the Director shall develop principles that govern the timing and manner in which information relating to security vulnerabilities may be shared, consistent with common industry best practices and United States and international standards.

(3) PRIVACY AND CIVIL LIBERTIES.—Information contained in covered cyber incident and ransom payment reports submitted to the Agency pursuant to section 2242 shall be retained, used, and disseminated, where permissible and appropriate, by the Federal Government in accordance with processes to be developed for the protection of personal information consistent with processes adopted pursuant to section 105 of the Cybersecurity Act of 2015 (6 U.S.C. 1504) and in a manner that protects personal information from unauthorized use or unauthorized disclosure.

(4) DIGITAL SECURITY.—The Agency shall ensure that reports submitted to the Agency pursuant to section 2242, and any information contained in those reports, are collected, stored, and protected at a minimum in accordance with the requirements for moderate impact Federal information systems, as described in Federal Information Processing Standards Publication 199, or any successor document.

(5) PROHIBITION ON USE OF INFORMATION IN REGULATORY ACTIONS.—

(A) IN GENERAL.—A Federal, State, local, or Tribal government shall not use information about a covered cyber incident or ransom payment obtained solely through reporting directly to the Agency in accordance with this subtitle to regulate, including through an enforcement action, the activities of the covered entity or entity that made a ransom payment, unless the government entity expressly allows entities to submit reports to the Agency to meet regulatory reporting obligations of the entity.

(B) CLARIFICATION.—A report submitted to the Agency pursuant to section 2242 or 2243 may, consistent with Federal or State regulatory authority specifically relating to the prevention and mitigation of cybersecurity threats to information systems, inform the development or implementation of regulations relating to such systems.

(b) PROTECTIONS FOR REPORTING ENTITIES AND INFORMATION.—Reports describing covered cyber incidents or ransom payments submitted to the Agency by entities in accordance with section 2242, as well as voluntarily-submitted cyber incident reports submitted to the Agency pursuant to section 2243, shall—

(1) be considered the commercial, financial, and proprietary information of the covered entity when so designated by the covered entity;

(2) be exempt from disclosure under section 552(b)(3) of title 5, United States Code (commonly known as the 'Freedom of Information Act'), as well as any provision of State, Tribal, or local freedom of information law, open government law, open meetings law, open records law, sunshine law, or similar law requiring disclosure of information or records;

(3) be considered not to constitute a waiver of any applicable privilege or protection provided by law, including trade secret protection; and

(4) not be subject to a rule of any Federal agency or department or any judicial doctrine

regarding ex parte communications with a decision-making official.

(c) LIABILITY PROTECTIONS.—

(1) IN GENERAL.—No cause of action shall lie or be maintained in any court by any person or entity and any such action shall be promptly dismissed for the submission of a report pursuant to section 2242(a) that is submitted in conformance with this subtitle and the rule promulgated under section 2242(b), except that this subsection shall not apply with regard to an action by the Federal Government pursuant to section 2244(c)(2).

(2) SCOPE.—The liability protections provided in this subsection shall only apply to or affect litigation that is solely based on the submission of a covered cyber incident report or ransom payment report to the Agency.

(3) RESTRICTIONS.—Notwithstanding paragraph (2), no report submitted to the Agency pursuant to this subtitle or any communication, document, material, or other record, created for the sole purpose of preparing, drafting, or submitting such report, may be received in evidence, subject to discovery, or otherwise used in any trial, hearing, or other proceeding in or before any court, regulatory body, or other authority of the United States, a State, or a political subdivision thereof, provided that nothing in this subtitle shall create a defense to discovery or otherwise affect the discovery of any communication, document, material, or other record not created for the sole purpose of preparing, drafting, or submitting such report.

(d) SHARING WITH NON-FEDERAL ENTITIES.—The Agency shall anonymize the victim who reported the information when making information provided in reports received under section 2242 available to critical infrastructure owners and operators and the general public.

(e) STORED COMMUNICATIONS ACT.—Nothing in this subtitle shall be construed to permit or require disclosure by a provider of a remote computing service or a provider of an electronic communication service to the public of information not otherwise permitted or required to be disclosed under chapter 121 of title 18, United States Code (commonly known as the 'Stored Communications Act').

SEC. 2246. CYBER INCIDENT REPORTING COUNCIL.

(a) RESPONSIBILITY OF THE SECRETARY.—The Secretary shall lead an intergovernmental Cyber Incident Reporting Council, in consultation with the Director of the Office of Management and Budget, the Attorney General, the National Cyber Director, Sector Risk Management Agencies, and other appropriate Federal agencies, to coordinate, deconflict, and harmonize Federal incident reporting requirements, including those issued through regulations.

(b) RULE OF CONSTRUCTION.—Nothing in subsection (a) shall be construed to provide any additional regulatory authority to any Federal entity.

(b) TECHNICAL AND CONFORMING AMENDMENT.—The table of contents in section 1(b) of the Homeland Security Act of 2002 (Public Law 107–296; 116 Stat. 2135) is amended by inserting after the items relating to subtitle C of title XXII the following:

Subtitle D—Cyber Incident Reporting

Sec. 2240. Definitions.

Sec. 2241. Cyber Incident Review.

Sec. 2242. Required reporting of certain cyber incidents.

Sec. 2243. Voluntary reporting of other cyber incidents.

Sec. 2244. Noncompliance with required reporting.

Sec. 2245. Information shared with or provided to the Federal Government.

Sec. 2246. Cyber Incident Reporting Council.

SEC. 104. FEDERAL SHARING OF INCIDENT REPORTS.

(a) CYBER INCIDENT REPORTING SHARING.—

(1) IN GENERAL.—Notwithstanding any other provision of law or regulation, any Federal agency, including any independent establishment (as defined in section 104 of title 5, United States Code), that receives a report from an entity of a cyber incident, including a ransomware attack, shall provide the report to the Agency as soon as possible, but not later than 24 hours after receiving the report, unless a shorter period is required by an agreement made between the Department of Homeland Security (including the Cybersecurity and Infrastructure Security Agency) and the recipient Federal agency. The Director shall share and coordinate each report pursuant to section 2241(b) of the Homeland Security Act of 2002, as added by section 103 of this division.

(2) RULE OF CONSTRUCTION.—The requirements described in paragraph (1) and section 2245(d) of the Homeland Security Act of 2002, as added by section 103 of this division, may not be construed to be a violation of any provision of law or policy that would otherwise prohibit disclosure or provision of information within the executive branch.

(3) PROTECTION OF INFORMATION.—The Director shall comply with any obligations of the recipient Federal agency described in paragraph (1) to protect information, including with respect to privacy, confidentiality, or information security, if those obligations would impose greater protection requirements than this division or the amendments made by this division.

(4) EFFECTIVE DATE.—This subsection shall take effect on the effective date of the final rule issued pursuant to section 2242(b) of the Homeland Security Act of 2002, as added by section 103 of this division.

(5) AGENCY AGREEMENTS.—

(A) IN GENERAL.—The Agency and any Federal agency, including any independent establishment (as defined in section 104 of title 5, United States Code), that receives incident reports from entities, including due to ransomware attacks, shall, as appropriate, enter into a documented agreement to establish policies, processes, procedures, and mechanisms to ensure reports are shared with the Agency pursuant to paragraph (1).

(B) AVAILABILITY.—To the maximum extent practicable, each documented agreement required under subparagraph (A) shall be made publicly available.

(C) REQUIREMENT.—The documented agreements required by subparagraph (A) shall require reports be shared from Federal agencies with the Agency in such time as to meet the overall timeline for covered entity reporting of covered cyber incidents and ransom payments established in section 2242 of the Homeland Security Act of 2002, as added by section 103 of this division.

(b) HARMONIZING REPORTING REQUIREMENTS.—The Secretary of Homeland Security, acting through the Director, shall, in consultation with the Cyber Incident Reporting Council described in section 2246 of the Homeland Security Act of 2002, as added by section 103 of this division, to the maximum extent practicable—

(1) periodically review existing regulatory requirements, including the information required in such reports, to report incidents and ensure that any such reporting requirements and procedures avoid conflicting, duplicative, or burdensome requirements; and

(2) coordinate with appropriate Federal partners and regulatory authorities that receive reports relating to incidents to identify opportunities to streamline reporting processes, and where feasible, facilitate interagency agreements between such authorities to permit the sharing of such reports, consistent with applicable law and policy, without impacting the ability of the Agency to gain timely situational awareness of a covered cyber incident or ransom payment.

SEC. 105. RANSOMWARE VULNERABILITY WARNING PILOT PROGRAM.

(a) PROGRAM.—Not later than 1 year after the date of enactment of this Act, the Director shall establish a ransomware vulnerability warning pilot program to leverage existing authorities and technology to specifically develop processes and procedures for, and to dedicate resources to, identifying information systems that contain security vulnerabilities associated with common ransomware attacks, and to notify the owners of those vulnerable systems of their security vulnerability.

(b) IDENTIFICATION OF VULNERABLE SYSTEMS.—The pilot program established under subsection (a) shall—

(1) identify the most common security vulnerabilities utilized in ransomware attacks and mitigation techniques; and

(2) utilize existing authorities to identify information systems that contain the security vulnerabilities identified in paragraph (1).

(c) ENTITY NOTIFICATION.—

(1) IDENTIFICATION.—If the Director is able to identify the entity at risk that owns or operates a vulnerable information system identified in subsection (b), the Director may notify the owner of the information system.

(2) NO IDENTIFICATION.—If the Director is not able to identify the entity at risk that owns or operates a vulnerable information system identified in subsection (b), the Director may utilize the subpoena authority pursuant to section 2209 of the Homeland Security Act of 2002 (6 U.S.C. 659) to identify and notify the entity at risk pursuant to the procedures under that section.

(3) REQUIRED INFORMATION.—A notification made under paragraph (1) shall include information on the identified security vulnerability and mitigation techniques.

(d) PRIORITIZATION OF NOTIFICATIONS.—To the extent practicable, the Director shall prioritize covered entities for identification and notification activities under the pilot program established under this section.

(e) LIMITATION ON PROCEDURES.—No procedure, notification, or other authorities utilized in the execution of the pilot program established under subsection (a) shall require an owner or operator of a vulnerable information system to take any action as a result of a notice of a security vulnerability made pursuant to subsection (c).

(f) RULE OF CONSTRUCTION.—Nothing in this section shall be construed to provide additional authorities to the Director to identify vulnerabilities or vulnerable systems.

(g) TERMINATION.—The pilot program established under subsection (a) shall terminate on the date that is 4 years after the date of enactment of this Act.

SEC. 106. RANSOMWARE THREAT MITIGATION ACTIVITIES.

(a) JOINT RANSOMWARE TASK FORCE.—

(1) IN GENERAL.—Not later than 180 days after the date of enactment of this Act, the Director, in consultation with the National Cyber Director, the Attorney General, and the Director of the Federal Bureau of Investigation, shall establish and chair the Joint Ransomware Task Force to coordinate an ongoing nationwide campaign against ransomware attacks, and identify and pursue opportunities for international cooperation.

(2) COMPOSITION.—The Joint Ransomware Task Force shall consist of participants from Federal agencies, as determined appropriate by the National Cyber Director in consultation with the Secretary of Homeland Security.

(3) RESPONSIBILITIES.—The Joint Ransomware Task Force, utilizing only existing authorities of each participating Federal agency, shall coordinate across the Federal Government the following activities:

(A) Prioritization of intelligence-driven operations to disrupt specific ransomware actors.

(B) Consult with relevant private sector, State, local, Tribal, and territorial governments and international stakeholders to identify needs and establish mechanisms for providing input into the Joint Ransomware Task Force.

(C) Identifying, in consultation with relevant entities, a list of highest threat ransomware entities updated on an ongoing basis, in order to facilitate— (i) prioritization for Federal action by appropriate Federal agencies; and (ii) identify metrics for success of said actions.

(D) Disrupting ransomware criminal actors, associated infrastructure, and their finances.

(E) Facilitating coordination and collaboration between Federal entities and relevant entities, including the private sector, to improve Federal actions against ransomware threats.

(F) Collection, sharing, and analysis of ransomware trends to inform Federal actions.

(G) Creation of after-action reports and other lessons learned from Federal actions that identify successes and failures to improve subsequent actions.

(H) Any other activities determined appropriate by the Joint Ransomware Task Force to mitigate the threat of ransomware attacks.

(b) RULE OF CONSTRUCTION.—Nothing in this section shall be construed to provide any additional authority to any Federal agency.

SEC. 107. CONGRESSIONAL REPORTING.

(a) REPORT ON STAKEHOLDER ENGAGEMENT.—Not later than 30 days after the date on which the Director issues the final rule under section 2242(b) of the Homeland Security Act of 2002, as added by section 103 of this division, the Director shall submit to the Committee on Homeland Security and Governmental Affairs of the Senate and the Committee on Homeland Security of the House of Representatives a report that describes how the Director engaged stakeholders in the development of the final rule.

(b) REPORT ON OPPORTUNITIES TO STRENGTHEN SECURITY RESEARCH.—Not later than 1 year after the date of enactment of this Act, the Director shall submit to the Committee on Homeland Security and Governmental Affairs of the Senate and the Committee on Homeland Security of the House of Representatives a report describing how the National Cybersecurity and Communications Integration Center established under section 2209 of the Homeland Security Act of 2002 (6 U.S.C. 659) has carried out activities under section 2241(a)(9) of the Homeland Security Act of 2002, as added by section 103 of this division, by proactively identifying opportunities to use cyber incident data to inform and enable cybersecurity research within the academic and private sector.

(c) REPORT ON RANSOMWARE VULNERABILITY WARNING PILOT PROGRAM.—Not later than 1 year after the date of enactment of this Act, and annually thereafter for the duration of the pilot program established under section 105, the Director shall submit to the Committee on Homeland Security and Governmental Affairs of the Senate and the Committee on Homeland Security of the House of Representatives a report, which may include a classified annex, on the effectiveness of the pilot program, which shall include a discussion of the following:

(1) The effectiveness of the notifications under section 105(c) in mitigating security vulnerabilities and the threat of ransomware.

(2) Identification of the most common vulnerabilities utilized in ransomware.

(3) The number of notifications issued during the preceding year.

(4) To the extent practicable, the number of vulnerable devices or systems mitigated under the pilot program by the Agency during the preceding year.

(d) REPORT ON HARMONIZATION OF REPORTING REGULATIONS.—

(1) IN GENERAL.—Not later than 180 days after the date on which the Secretary of Homeland Security convenes the Cyber Incident Reporting Council described in section 2246 of the Homeland Security Act of 2002, as added by section 103 of this division, the Secretary of Homeland Security shall submit to the appropriate congressional committees a report that includes—

(A) a list of duplicative Federal cyber incident reporting requirements on covered entities;

(B) a description of any challenges in harmonizing the duplicative reporting requirements;

(C) any actions the Director intends to take to facilitate harmonizing the duplicative reporting requirements; and

(D) any proposed legislative changes necessary to address the duplicative reporting.

(2) RULE OF CONSTRUCTION.—Nothing in paragraph (1) shall be construed to provide any additional regulatory authority to any Federal agency.

(e) GAO REPORTS.—

(1) IMPLEMENTATION OF THIS DIVISION.—Not later than 2 years after the date of enactment of this Act, the Comptroller General of the United States shall submit to the Committee on Homeland Security and Governmental Affairs of the Senate and the Committee on Homeland Security of the House of Representatives a report on the implementation of this division and the amendments made by this division.

(2) EXEMPTIONS TO REPORTING.—Not later than 1 year after the date on which the Director issues the final rule required under section 2242(b) of the Homeland Security Act of 2002, as added by section 103 of this division, the Comptroller General of the United States shall submit to the Committee on Homeland Security and Governmental Affairs of the Senate and the Committee on Homeland Security of the House of Representatives a report on the exemptions to reporting under paragraphs (2) and (5) of section 2242(a) of the Homeland Security Act of 2002, as added by section 103 of this division, which shall include—

(A) to the extent practicable, an evaluation of the quantity of cyber incidents not reported to the Federal Government;

(B) an evaluation of the impact on impacted entities, homeland security, and the national economy due to cyber incidents, ransomware attacks, and ransom payments, including a discussion on the scope of impact of cyber incidents that were not reported to the Federal Government;

(C) an evaluation of the burden, financial and otherwise, on entities required to report cyber incidents under this division, including an analysis of entities that meet the definition of a small business concern under section 3 of the Small Business Act (15 U.S.C. 632); and

(D) a description of the consequences and effects of limiting covered cyber incident and ransom payment reporting to only covered entities.

(f) REPORT ON EFFECTIVENESS OF ENFORCEMENT MECHANISMS.—Not later than 1 year after the date on which the Director issues the final rule required under section 2242(b) of the Homeland Security Act of 2002, as added by section 103 of this division, the Director shall submit to the Committee on Homeland Security and Governmental Affairs of the Senate and the Committee on Homeland Security of the House of Representatives a report on the effectiveness of the enforcement mechanisms within section 2244 of the Homeland Security Act of 2002, as added by section 103 of this division.

FEDERAL CYBERSECURITY RESOURCES

U.S. Department of Homeland Security,
Cybersecurity and Infrastructure Security Agency
https://www.cisa.gov/cybersecurity

U.S. Department of Justice
https://www.justice.gov/usao-cdca/cybersecurity-program

Federal Bureau of Investigation, Internet Crime Complaint Center
https://www.ic3.gov

U.S. Department of Homeland Security, U.S. Secret Service
https://www.secretservice.gov/investigation/cyber

U.S. Department of Treasury, Advisory on Potential Sanctions
Risks for Facilitating Ransomware Payments
https://home.treasury.gov/system/files/126/ofac_ransomware_advisory_10012020_1.pdf

U.S. Department of Commerce,
National Institute of Standards and Technology
https://www.nist.gov/cyberframework

U.S. Department of Defense, Cyber Crime Center
https://www.dc3.mil/

Center of Internet Security (CIS),
Critical Security Controls for Effective Cyber Defense
https://www.cisecurity.org/controls/

The Open Web Application Security Project®
https://owasp.org/

The MITRE Corp, Cybersecurity Resources
https://www.mitre.org/capabilities/cybersecurity/overview/cybersecurity-resources

APPENDIX: U.S. STATE CONSUMER PROTECTION LAWS

APPENDIX 1: CALIFORNIA CONSUMER PRIVACY ACT (AMENDED BY PROP 24)

§ 1798.100. General Duties of Businesses that Collect Personal Information

(a) A business that controls the collection of a consumer's personal information shall, at or before the point of collection, inform consumers of the following:

(1) The categories of personal information to be collected and the purposes for which the categories of personal information are collected or used and whether that information is sold or shared. A business shall not collect additional categories of personal information or use personal information collected for additional purposes that are incompatible with the disclosed purpose for which the personal information was collected without providing the consumer with notice consistent with this section.

(2) If the business collects sensitive personal information, the categories of sensitive personal information to be collected and the purposes for which the categories of sensitive personal information are collected or used, and whether that information is sold or shared. A business shall not collect additional categories of sensitive personal information or use sensitive personal information collected for additional purposes that are incompatible with the disclosed purpose for which the sensitive personal information was collected without providing the consumer with notice consistent with this section.

(3) The length of time the business intends to retain each category of personal information, including sensitive personal information, or if that is not possible, the criteria used to determine that period provided that a business shall not retain a consumer's personal information or sensitive personal information for each disclosed purpose for which the personal information was collected for longer than is reasonably necessary for that disclosed purpose.

(b) A business that, acting as a third party, controls the collection of personal information about a consumer may satisfy its obligation under subdivision (a) by providing the required information prominently and conspicuously on the homepage of its internet website. In addition, if a business acting as a third party controls the collection of personal information about a consumer on its premises, including in a vehicle, then the business shall, at or before the point of collection, inform consumers as to the categories of personal information to be collected and the purposes for which the categories of personal information are used, and whether that personal information is sold, in a clear and conspicuous manner at the location.

(c) A business' collection, use, retention, and sharing of a consumer's personal information shall be reasonably necessary and proportionate to achieve the purposes for which the personal information was collected or processed, or for another disclosed purpose that is compatible with the context in which the personal information was collected, and not further processed in a manner that is incompatible with those purposes.

(d) A business that collects a consumer's personal information and that sells that personal information to, or shares it with, a third party or that discloses it to a service provider or contractor for a business purpose shall enter into an agreement with the third party, service provider, or contractor, that:

(1) Specifies that the personal information is sold or disclosed by the business only for limited and specified purposes.

(2) Obligates the third party, service provider, or contractor to comply with applicable obligations under this title and obligate those persons to provide the same level of privacy protection as is required by this title.

(3) Grants the business rights to take reasonable and appropriate steps to help ensure that the third party, service provider, or contractor uses the personal information transferred in a manner consistent with the business' obligations under this title.

(4) Requires the third party, service provider, or contractor to notify the business if it makes a determination that it can no longer meet its obligations under this title.

(5) Grants the business the right, upon notice, including under paragraph (4), to take reasonable and appropriate steps to stop and remediate unauthorized use of personal information.

(e) A business that collects a consumer's personal information shall implement reasonable security procedures and practices appropriate to the nature of the personal information to protect the personal information from unauthorized or illegal access, destruction, use, modification, or disclosure in accordance with Section 1798.81.5.

(f) Nothing in this section shall require a business to disclose trade secrets, as specified in regulations adopted pursuant to paragraph (3) of subdivision (a) of Section 1798.185.

§ 1798.105. Consumers' Right to Delete Personal Information

(a) A consumer shall have the right to request that a business delete any personal information about the consumer which the business has collected from the consumer.

(b) A business that collects personal information about consumers shall disclose, pursuant to Section 1798.130, the consumer's rights to request the deletion of the consumer's personal information.

(c) (1) A business that receives a verifiable consumer request from a consumer to delete the consumer's personal information pursuant to subdivision (a) of this section shall delete the consumer's personal information from its records, notify any service providers or contractors to delete the consumer's personal information from their records, and notify all third parties to whom the business has sold or shared the personal information to delete the consumer's personal information unless this proves impossible or involves disproportionate effort.

(2) The business may maintain a confidential record of deletion requests solely for the purpose of preventing the personal information of a consumer who has submitted a deletion request from being sold, for compliance with laws or for other purposes, solely to the extent permissible under this title.

(3) A service provider or contractor shall cooperate with the business in responding to a verifiable consumer request, and at the direction of the business, shall delete, or enable the business to delete and shall notify any of its own service providers or contractors to delete personal information about the consumer collected, used, processed, or retained by the service provider or the contractor. The service provider or contractor shall notify any service providers, contractors, or third parties who may have accessed personal information from or through the service provider or contractor, unless the information was accessed at the direction of the business, to delete the consumer's personal information unless this proves impossible or involves disproportionate effort. A service provider or contractor shall not be required to comply with a deletion request submitted by the consumer directly to the service provider or contractor to the extent that the service provider or contractor has collected, used, processed, or retained the consumer's personal information in its role as a service provider or contractor to the business.

(d) A business, or a service provider or contractor acting pursuant to its contract with the business, another service provider, or another contractor, shall not be required to comply with a consumer's request to delete the consumer's personal information if it is reasonably necessary for the business, service provider, or contractor to maintain the consumer's personal information in order to:

(1) Complete the transaction for which the personal information was collected, fulfill the terms of a written warranty or product recall conducted in accordance with federal law, provide a good or service requested by

the consumer, or reasonably anticipated by the consumer within the context of a business' ongoing business relationship with the consumer, or otherwise perform a contract between the business and the consumer.

(2) Help to ensure security and integrity to the extent the use of the consumer's personal information is reasonably necessary and proportionate for those purposes.

(3) Debug to identify and repair errors that impair existing intended functionality.

(4) Exercise free speech, ensure the right of another consumer to exercise that consumer's right of free speech, or exercise another right provided for by law.

(5) Comply with the California Electronic Communications Privacy Act pursuant to Chapter 3.6 (commencing with Section 1546) of Title 12 of Part 2 of the Penal Code.

(6) Engage in public or peer-reviewed scientific, historical, or statistical research that conforms or adheres to all other applicable ethics and privacy laws, when the business' deletion of the information is likely to render impossible or seriously impair the ability to complete such research, if the consumer has provided informed consent.

(7) To enable solely internal uses that are reasonably aligned with the expectations of the consumer based on the consumer's relationship with the business and compatible with the context in which the consumer provided the information.

(8) Comply with a legal obligation.

§ 1798.106. Consumers' Right to Correct Inaccurate Personal Information

(a) A consumer shall have the right to request a business that maintains inaccurate personal information about the consumer to correct that inaccurate personal information, taking into account the nature of the personal information and the purposes of the processing of the personal information.

(b) A business that collects personal information about consumers shall disclose, pursuant to Section 1798.130, the consumer's right to request correction of inaccurate personal information.

(c) A business that receives a verifiable consumer request to correct inaccurate personal information shall use commercially reasonable efforts to correct the inaccurate personal information as directed by the consumer, pursuant to Section 1798.130 and regulations adopted pursuant to paragraph (8) of subdivision (a) of Section 1798.185.

§ 1798.110. Consumers' Right to Know What Personal Information is Being Collected. Right to Access Personal Information

(a) A consumer shall have the right to request that a business that collects personal information about the consumer disclose to the consumer the following:

(1) The categories of personal information it has collected about that consumer.

(2) The categories of sources from which the personal information is collected.

(3) The business or commercial purpose for collecting, selling, or sharing personal information.

(4) The categories of third parties to whom the business discloses personal information.

(5) The specific pieces of personal information it has collected about that consumer.

(b) A business that collects personal information about a consumer shall disclose to the consumer, pursuant to subparagraph (B) of paragraph (3) of subdivision (a) of Section 1798.130, the information specified in subdivision (a) upon receipt of a verifiable consumer request from the consumer, provided that a business shall be deemed to be in compliance with paragraphs (1) to (4), inclusive, of subdivision (a) to the extent that the categories of information and the business or commercial purpose for collecting, selling, or sharing personal information it would be required to disclose to the consumer pursuant to paragraphs (1) to (4), inclusive, of subdivision (a) is the same as the information it has disclosed pursuant to paragraphs (1) to (4), inclusive, of subdivision (c).

(c) A business that collects personal information about consumers shall disclose, pursuant to subparagraph (B) of paragraph (5) of subdivision (a) of Section 1798.130:

(1) The categories of personal information it has collected about consumers.

(2) The categories of sources from which the personal information is collected.

(3) The business or commercial purpose for collecting, selling, or sharing personal information.

(4) The categories of third parties to whom the business discloses personal information.

(5) That a consumer has the right to request the specific pieces of personal information the business has collected about that consumer.

§ 1798.115. Consumers' Right to Know What Personal Information is Sold or Shared and to Whom

(a) A consumer shall have the right to request that a business that sells or shares the consumer's personal information, or that discloses it for a business purpose, disclose to that consumer:

(1) The categories of personal information that the business collected about the consumer.

(2) The categories of personal information that the business sold or shared about the consumer and the categories of third parties to whom the personal information was sold or shared, by category or categories of personal information for each category of third parties to whom the personal information was sold or shared.

(3) The categories of personal information that the business disclosed about the consumer for a business purpose and the categories of persons to whom it was disclosed for a business purpose.

(b) A business that sells or shares personal information about a consumer, or that discloses a consumer's personal information for a business purpose, shall disclose, pursuant to paragraph (4) of subdivision (a) of Section 1798.130, the information specified in subdivision (a) to the consumer upon receipt of a verifiable consumer request from the consumer.

(c) A business that sells or shares consumers' personal information, or that discloses consumers' personal information for a business purpose, shall disclose, pursuant to subparagraph (C) of paragraph (5) of subdivision (a) of Section 1798.130:

(1) The category or categories of consumers' personal information it has sold or shared, or if the business has not sold or shared consumers' personal information, it shall disclose that fact.

(2) The category or categories of consumers' personal information it has disclosed for a business purpose, or if the business has not disclosed consumers' personal information for a business purpose, it shall disclose that fact.

(d) A third party shall not sell or share personal information about a consumer that has been sold to, or shared with, the third party by a business unless the consumer has received explicit notice and is provided an opportunity to exercise the right to opt-out pursuant to Section 1798.120.

§ 1798.120. Consumers' Right to Opt Out of Sale or Sharing of Personal Information

(a) A consumer shall have the right, at any time, to direct a business that sells or shares personal information about the consumer to third parties not to sell or share the consumer's personal information. This right may be referred to as the right to opt-out of sale or sharing.

(b) A business that sells consumers' personal information to, or shares it with, third parties shall provide notice to consumers, pursuant to subdivision (a) of Section 1798.135, that this information may be sold or shared and that consumers have the "right to opt-out" of the sale or sharing of their personal information.

(c) Notwithstanding subdivision (a), a business shall not sell or share the personal information of consumers if the business has actual knowledge that the consumer is less than 16 years of age, unless the consumer, in the case of consumers at least 13 years of age and less than 16 years of age, or the consumer's parent or guardian, in the case of consumers who are less than 13 years of age, has affirmatively authorized the sale or sharing of the consumer's personal information. A business that willfully disregards the consumer's age shall be deemed to have had actual knowledge of the consumer's age.

(d) A business that has received direction from a consumer not to sell or share the consumer's personal information or, in the case of a minor consumer's personal information has not received consent to sell or share the minor consumer's personal information, shall be prohibited, pursuant to paragraph (4) of subdivision (c) of Section 1798.135, from selling or sharing the consumer's personal information after its receipt of the consumer's direction, unless the consumer subsequently provides consent, for the sale or sharing of the consumer's personal information.

§ 1798.121. Consumers' Right to Limit Use and Disclosure of Sensitive Personal Information

(a) A consumer shall have the right, at any time, to direct a business that collects sensitive personal information about the consumer to limit its use of the consumer's sensitive personal information to that use which is necessary to perform the services or provide the goods reasonably expected by an average consumer who requests those goods or services, to perform the services set forth in paragraphs (2), (4), (5), and (8) of subdivision (e) of Section 1798.140, and as authorized by regulations adopted pursuant to subparagraph (C) of paragraph (19) of subdivision (a) of Section 1798.185. A business that uses or discloses a consumer's sensitive personal information for purposes other than those specified in this subdivision shall provide notice to consumers, pursuant to subdivision (a) of Section 1798.135, that this information may be used, or disclosed to a service provider or contractor, for additional, specified purposes and that consumers have the right to limit the use or disclosure of their sensitive personal information.

(b) A business that has received direction from a consumer not to use or disclose the consumer's sensitive personal information, except as authorized by subdivision (a), shall be prohibited, pursuant to paragraph (4) of subdivision (c) of Section 1798.135, from using or disclosing the consumer's sensitive personal information for any other purpose after its receipt of the consumer's direction unless the consumer subsequently provides consent for the use or disclosure of the consumer's sensitive personal information for additional purposes.

(c) A service provider or contractor that assists a business in performing the purposes authorized by subdivision (a) may not use the sensitive personal information after it has received instructions from the business and to the extent it has actual knowledge that the personal information is sensitive personal information for any other purpose. A service provider or contractor is only required to limit its use of sensitive personal information received pursuant to a written contract with the business in response to instructions from the business and only with respect to its relationship with that business.

(d) Sensitive personal information that is collected or processed without the purpose of inferring characteristics about a consumer is not subject to this section, as further defined in regulations adopted pursuant to subparagraph (C) of paragraph (19) of subdivision (a) of Section 1798.185, and shall be treated as personal information for purposes of all other sections of this act, including Section 1798.100.

§ 1798.125. Consumers' Right of No Retaliation Following Opt Out or Exercise of Other Rights

(a) (1) A business shall not discriminate against a consumer because the consumer exercised any of the consumer's rights under this title, including, but not limited to, by:

(A) Denying goods or services to the consumer.

(B) Charging different prices or rates for goods or services, including through the use of discounts or other benefits or imposing penalties.

(C) Providing a different level or quality of goods or services to the consumer.

(D) Suggesting that the consumer will receive a different price or rate for goods or services or a different level or quality of goods or services.

(E) Retaliating against an employee, applicant for employment, or independent contractor, as defined in subparagraph (A) of paragraph (2) of subdivision (m) of Section 1798.145, for exercising their rights under this title.

(2) Nothing in this subdivision prohibits a business, pursuant to subdivision (b), from charging a consumer a different price or rate, or from providing a different level or quality of goods or services to the consumer, if that difference is reasonably related to the value provided to the business by the consumer's data.

(3) This subdivision does not prohibit a business from offering loyalty, rewards, premium features, discounts, or club card programs consistent with this title.

(b) (1) A business may offer financial incentives, including payments to consumers as compensation, for the collection of personal information, the sale or sharing of personal information, or the retention of personal information. A business may also offer a different price, rate, level, or quality of goods or services to the consumer if that price or difference is reasonably related to the value provided to the business by the consumer's data.

(2) A business that offers any financial incentives pursuant to this subdivision, shall notify consumers of the financial incentives pursuant to Section 1798.130.

(3) A business may enter a consumer into a financial incentive program only if the consumer gives the business prior opt-in consent pursuant to Section 1798.130 that clearly describes the material terms of the financial incentive program, and which may be revoked by the consumer at any time. If a consumer refuses to provide opt-in consent, then the business shall wait for at least 12 months before next requesting that the consumer provide opt-in consent, or as prescribed by regulations adopted pursuant to Section 1798.185.

(4) A business shall not use financial incentive practices that are unjust, unreasonable, coercive, or usurious in nature.

§ 1798.130. Notice, Disclosure, Correction, and Deletion Requirements

(a) In order to comply with Sections 1798.100, 1798.105, 1798.106, 1798.110, 1798.115, and 1798.125, a business shall, in a form that is reasonably accessible to consumers:

(1) (A) Make available to consumers two or more designated methods for submitting requests for information required to be disclosed pursuant to Sections 1798.110 and 1798.115, or requests for deletion or correction pursuant to Sections 1798.105 and 1798.106, respectively, including, at a minimum, a toll-free telephone number. A business that operates exclusively online and has a direct relationship with a consumer from whom it collects personal information shall only be required to provide an email address for submitting requests for information required to be disclosed pursuant to Sections 1798.110 and 1798.115, or for requests for deletion or correction pursuant to Sections 1798.105 and 1798.106, respectively.

(B) If the business maintains an internet website, make the internet website available to consumers to submit requests for information required to be disclosed pursuant to Sections 1798.110 and 1798.115, or requests for deletion or correction pursuant to Sections 1798.105 and 1798.106, respectively.

(2) (A) Disclose and deliver the required information to a consumer free of charge, correct inaccurate personal information, or delete a consumer's personal information, based on the consumer's request, within 45 days of receiving a verifiable consumer request from the consumer. The business shall promptly take steps to determine whether the request is a verifiable consumer request, but this shall not extend the business's duty to disclose and deliver the information, to correct inaccurate personal information, or to delete personal information within 45 days of receipt of the consumer's request. The time period to provide the required information, to correct inaccurate personal information, or to delete personal information may be extended once by an additional 45 days when reasonably necessary, provided the consumer is provided notice of the extension within the first 45-day period. The disclosure of the required information shall be made in writing and delivered through the consumer's account with the business, if the consumer maintains an account with the business, or by mail or electronically at the consumer's option if the consumer does not maintain an account with the business, in a readily useable format that allows the consumer to transmit this information from one entity to another entity without hindrance. The business may require authentication of the consumer that is reasonable in light of the nature of the personal information requested, but shall not require the consumer to create an account with the business in order to make a verifiable consumer request provided that if the consumer, has an account with the business, the business may require the consumer to use that account to submit a verifiable consumer request.

(B) The disclosure of the required information shall cover the 12-month period preceding the business' receipt of the verifiable consumer request provided that, upon the adoption of a regulation pursuant to paragraph (9) of subdivision (a) of Section 1798.185, a consumer may request that the business disclose the required information beyond the 12-month period, and the business shall be required to provide that information unless doing so proves impossible or would involve a disproportionate effort. A consumer's right to request required information beyond the 12-month period, and a business's obligation to provide that information, shall only apply to personal information collected on or after January 1, 2022. Nothing in this subparagraph shall require a business to keep personal information for any length of time.

(3) (A) A business that receives a verifiable consumer request pursuant to Section 1798.110 or 1798.115 shall disclose any personal information it has collected about a consumer, directly or indirectly, including through or by a service provider or contractor, to the consumer. A service provider or contractor shall not be required to comply with a verifiable consumer request received directly from a consumer or a consumer's authorized agent, pursuant to Section 1798.110 or 1798.115, to the extent that the service provider or contractor has collected personal information about the consumer in its role as a service provider or contractor. A service provider or contractor shall provide assistance to a business with which it has a contractual relationship with respect to the business' response to a verifiable consumer request, including, but not limited to, by providing to the business the consumer's personal information in the service provider or contractor's possession, which the service provider or contractor obtained as a result of providing services to the business, and by correcting inaccurate information or by enabling the business to do the same. A service provider or contractor that collects personal information pursuant to a written contract with a business shall be required to assist the

business through appropriate technical and organizational measures in complying with the requirements of subdivisions (d) to (f), inclusive, of Section 1798.100, taking into account the nature of the processing.

(B) For purposes of subdivision (b) of Section 1798.110:

(i) To identify the consumer, associate the information provided by the consumer in the verifiable consumer request to any personal information previously collected by the business about the consumer.

(ii) Identify by category or categories the personal information collected about the consumer for the applicable period of time by reference to the enumerated category or categories in subdivision (c) that most closely describes the personal information collected; the categories of sources from which the consumer's personal information was collected; the business or commercial purpose for collecting, selling, or sharing the consumer's personal information; and the categories of third parties to whom the business discloses the consumer's personal information.

(iii) Provide the specific pieces of personal information obtained from the consumer in a format that is easily understandable to the average consumer, and to the extent technically feasible, in a structured, commonly used, machine-readable format that may also be transmitted to another entity at the consumer's request without hindrance. "Specific pieces of information" do not include data generated to help ensure security and integrity or as prescribed by regulation. Personal information is not considered to have been disclosed by a business when a consumer instructs a business to transfer the consumer's personal information from one business to another in the context of switching services.

(4) For purposes of subdivision (b) of Section 1798.115:

(A) Identify the consumer and associate the information provided by the consumer in the verifiable consumer request to any personal information previously collected by the business about the consumer.

(B) Identify by category or categories the personal information of the consumer that the business sold or shared during the applicable period of time by reference to the enumerated category in subdivision (c) that most closely describes the personal information, and provide the categories of third parties to whom the consumer's personal information was sold or shared during the applicable period of time by reference to the enumerated category or categories in subdivision (c) that most closely describes the personal information sold or shared. The business shall disclose the information in a list that is separate from a list generated for the purposes of subparagraph (C).

(C) Identify by category or categories the personal information of the consumer that the business disclosed for a business purpose during the applicable period of time by reference to the enumerated category or categories in subdivision (c) that most closely describes the personal information, and provide the categories of persons to whom the consumer's personal information was disclosed for a business purpose during the applicable period of time by reference to the enumerated category or categories in subdivision (c) that most closely describes the personal information disclosed. The business shall disclose the information in a list that is separate from a list generated for the purposes of subparagraph (B).

(5) Disclose the following information in its online privacy policy or policies if the business has an online privacy policy or policies and in any California-specific description of consumers' privacy rights, or if the business does not maintain those policies, on its internet website, and update that information at least once every 12 months:

(A) A description of a consumer's rights pursuant to Sections 1798.100, 1798.105, 1798.106, 1798.110, 1798.115, and 1798.125 and two or more designated methods for submitting requests, except as provided in subparagraph (A) of paragraph (1) of subdivision (a).

(B) For purposes of subdivision (c) of Section 1798.110:

(i) A list of the categories of personal information it has collected about consumers in the preceding 12 months by reference to the enumerated category or categories in subdivision (c) that most closely describe the personal information collected.

(ii) The categories of sources from which consumers' personal information is collected.

(iii) The business or commercial purpose for collecting, selling, or sharing consumers' personal information.

(iv) The categories of third parties to whom the business discloses consumers' personal information.

(C) For purposes of paragraphs (1) and (2) of subdivision (c) of Section 1798.115, two separate lists:

(i) A list of the categories of personal information it has sold or shared about consumers in the preceding 12 months by reference to the enumerated category or categories in subdivision (c) that most closely describe the personal information sold or shared, or if the business has not sold or shared consumers' personal information in the preceding 12 months, the business shall prominently disclose that fact in its privacy policy.

(ii) A list of the categories of personal information it has disclosed about consumers for a business purpose in the preceding 12 months by reference to the enumerated category in subdivision (c) that most closely describes the personal information disclosed, or if the business has not disclosed consumers' personal information for a business purpose in the preceding 12 months, the business shall disclose that fact.

(6) Ensure that all individuals responsible for handling consumer inquiries about the business' privacy practices or the business' compliance with this title are informed of all requirements in Sections 1798.100, 1798.105, 1798.106, 1798.110, 1798.115, 1798.125, and this section, and how to direct consumers to exercise their rights under those sections.

(7) Use any personal information collected from the consumer in connection with the business' verification of the consumer's request solely for the purposes of verification and shall not further disclose the personal information, retain it longer than necessary for purposes of verification, or use it for unrelated purposes.

(b) A business is not obligated to provide the information required by Sections 1798.110 and 1798.115 to the same consumer more than twice in a 12-month period.

(c) The categories of personal information required to be disclosed pursuant to Sections 1798.100, 1798.110, and 1798.115 shall follow the definitions of personal information and sensitive personal information in Section 1798.140 by describing the categories of personal information using the specific terms set forth in subparagraphs (A) to (K), inclusive, of paragraph (1) of subdivision (v) of Section 1798.140 and by describing the categories of sensitive personal information using the specific terms set forth in paragraphs (1) to (9), inclusive, of subdivision (ae) of Section 1798.140.

§ 1798.135. Methods of Limiting Sale, Sharing, and Use of Personal Information and Use of Sensitive Personal Information

(a) A business that sells or shares consumers' personal information or uses or discloses consumers' sensitive personal information for purposes other than those authorized by subdivision (a) of Section 1798.121 shall, in a form that is reasonably accessible to consumers:

(1) Provide a clear and conspicuous link on the business's internet homepages, titled "Do Not Sell or Share My Personal Information," to an internet web page that enables a consumer, or a person authorized by the consumer, to opt-out of the sale or sharing of the consumer's personal information.

(2) Provide a clear and conspicuous link on the business' internet homepages, titled "Limit the Use of My Sensitive Personal Information," that enables a consumer, or a person authorized by the consumer, to limit the

use or disclosure of the consumer's sensitive personal information to those uses authorized by subdivision (a) of Section 1798.121.

(3) At the business' discretion, utilize a single, clearly labeled link on the business' internet homepages, in lieu of complying with paragraphs (1) and (2), if that link easily allows a consumer to opt out of the sale or sharing of the consumer's personal information and to limit the use or disclosure of the consumer's sensitive personal information.

(4) In the event that a business responds to opt-out requests received pursuant to paragraph (1), (2), or (3) by informing the consumer of a charge for the use of any product or service, present the terms of any financial incentive offered pursuant to subdivision (b) of Section 1798.125 for the retention, use, sale, or sharing of the consumer's personal information.

(b) (1) A business shall not be required to comply with subdivision (a) if the business allows consumers to opt out of the sale or sharing of their personal information and to limit the use of their sensitive personal information through an opt-out preference signal sent with the consumer's consent by a platform, technology, or mechanism, based on technical specifications set forth in regulations adopted pursuant to paragraph (20) of subdivision (a) of Section 1798.185, to the business indicating the consumer's intent to opt out of the business' sale or sharing of the consumer's personal information or to limit the use or disclosure of the consumer's sensitive personal information, or both.

(2) A business that allows consumers to opt out of the sale or sharing of their personal information and to limit the use of their sensitive personal information pursuant to paragraph (1) may provide a link to a web page that enables the consumer to consent to the business ignoring the opt-out preference signal with respect to that business' sale or sharing of the consumer's personal information or the use of the consumer's sensitive personal information for additional purposes provided that:

(A) The consent web page also allows the consumer or a person authorized by the consumer to revoke the consent as easily as it is affirmatively provided.

(B) The link to the web page does not degrade the consumer's experience on the web page the consumer intends to visit and has a similar look, feel, and size relative to other links on the same web page.

(C) The consent web page complies with technical specifications set forth in regulations adopted pursuant to paragraph (20) of subdivision (a) of Section 1798.185.

(3) A business that complies with subdivision (a) is not required to comply with subdivision (b). For the purposes of clarity, a business may elect whether to comply with subdivision (a) or subdivision (b).

(c) A business that is subject to this section shall:

(1) Not require a consumer to create an account or provide additional information beyond what is necessary in order to direct the business not to sell or share the consumer's personal information or to limit use or disclosure of the consumer's sensitive personal information.

(2) Include a description of a consumer's rights pursuant to Sections 1798.120 and 1798.121, along with a separate link to the "Do Not Sell or Share My Personal Information" internet web page and a separate link to the "Limit the Use of My Sensitive Personal Information" internet web page, if applicable, or a single link to both choices, or a statement that the business responds to and abides by opt-out preference signals sent by a platform, technology, or mechanism in accordance with subdivision (b), in:

(A) Its online privacy policy or policies if the business has an online privacy policy or policies.

(B) Any California-specific description of consumers' privacy rights.

(3) Ensure that all individuals responsible for handling consumer inquiries about the business's privacy practices or the business's compliance with this title are informed of all requirements in Sections 1798.120, 1798.121, and this section and how to direct consumers to exercise their rights under those sections.

(4) For consumers who exercise their right to opt-out of the sale or sharing of their personal information or limit the use or disclosure of their sensitive personal information, refrain from selling or sharing the consumer's personal information or using or disclosing the consumer's sensitive personal information and wait for at least 12 months before requesting that the consumer authorize the sale or sharing of the consumer's personal information or the use and disclosure of the consumer's sensitive personal information for additional purposes, or as authorized by regulations.

(5) For consumers under 16 years of age who do not consent to the sale or sharing of their personal information, refrain from selling or sharing the personal information of the consumer under 16 years of age and wait for at least 12 months before requesting the consumer's consent again, or as authorized by regulations or until the consumer attains 16 years of age.

(6) Use any personal information collected from the consumer in connection with the submission of the consumer's opt-out request solely for the purposes of complying with the opt-out request.

(d) Nothing in this title shall be construed to require a business to comply with the title by including the required links and text on the homepage that the business makes available to the public generally, if the business maintains a separate and additional homepage that is dedicated to California consumers and that includes the required links and text, and the business takes reasonable steps to ensure that California consumers are directed to the homepage for California consumers and not the homepage made available to the public generally.

(e) A consumer may authorize another person to opt-out of the sale or sharing of the consumer's personal information and to limit the use of the consumer's sensitive personal information on the consumer's behalf, including through an opt-out preference signal, as defined in paragraph (1) of subdivision (b), indicating the consumer's intent to opt out, and a business shall comply with an opt-out request received from a person authorized by the consumer to act on the consumer's behalf, pursuant to regulations adopted by the Attorney General regardless of whether the business has elected to comply with subdivision (a) or (b). For purposes of clarity, a business that elects to comply with subdivision (a) may respond to the consumer's opt-out consistent with Section 1798.125.

(f) If a business communicates a consumer's opt-out request to any person authorized by the business to collect personal information, the person shall thereafter only use that consumer's personal information for a business purpose specified by the business, or as otherwise permitted by this title, and shall be prohibited from:

(1) Selling or sharing the personal information.

(2) Retaining, using, or disclosing that consumer's personal information.

(A) For any purpose other than for the specific purpose of performing the services offered to the business.

(B) Outside of the direct business relationship between the person and the business.

(C) For a commercial purpose other than providing the services to the business.

(g) A business that communicates a consumer's opt-out request to a person pursuant to subdivision (f) shall not be liable under this title if the person receiving the opt-out request violates the restrictions set forth in the title provided that, at the time of communicating the opt-out request, the business does not have actual knowledge, or reason to believe, that the person intends to commit such a violation. Any provision of a contract or agreement of any kind that purports to waive or limit in any way this subdivision shall be void and unenforceable.

§ 1798.140. Definitions

For purposes of this title:

(a) “Advertising and marketing” means a communication by a business or a person acting on the business' behalf in any medium intended to induce a consumer to obtain goods, services, or employment.

(b) “Aggregate consumer information” means information that relates to a group or category of consumers, from which individual consumer identities have been removed, that is not linked or reasonably linkable to any consumer or household, including via a device. “Aggregate consumer information” does not mean one or more individual consumer records that have been deidentified.

(c) “Biometric information” means an individual's physiological, biological, or behavioral characteristics, including information pertaining to an individual's deoxyribonucleic acid (DNA), that is used or is intended to be used singly or in combination with each other or with other identifying data, to establish individual identity. Biometric information includes, but is not limited to, imagery of the iris, retina, fingerprint, face, hand, palm, vein patterns, and voice recordings, from which an identifier template, such as a faceprint, a minutiae template, or a voiceprint, can be extracted, and keystroke patterns or rhythms, gait patterns or rhythms, and sleep, health, or exercise data that contain identifying information.

(d) “Business” means:

(1) A sole proprietorship, partnership, limited liability company, corporation, association, or other legal entity that is organized or operated for the profit or financial benefit of its shareholders or other owners, that collects consumers' personal information, or on the behalf of which such information is collected and that alone, or jointly with others, determines the purposes and means of the processing of consumers' personal information, that does business in the State of California, and that satisfies one or more of the following thresholds:

(A) As of January 1 of the calendar year, had annual gross revenues in excess of twenty-five million dollars ($25,000,000) in the preceding calendar year, as adjusted pursuant to paragraph (5) of subdivision (a) of Section 1798.185.

(B) Alone or in combination, annually buys, sells, or shares the personal information of 100,000 or more consumers or households.

(C) Derives 50 percent or more of its annual revenues from selling or sharing consumers' personal information.

(2) Any entity that controls or is controlled by a business, as defined in paragraph (1), and that shares common branding with the business and with whom the business shares consumers' personal information. “Control” or “controlled” means ownership of, or the power to vote, more than 50 percent of the outstanding shares of any class of voting security of a business; control in any manner over the election of a majority of the directors, or of individuals exercising similar functions; or the power to exercise a controlling influence over the management of a company. “Common branding” means a shared name, servicemark, or trademark that the average consumer would understand that two or more entities are commonly owned.

(3) A joint venture or partnership composed of businesses in which each business has at least a 40 percent interest. For purposes of this title, the joint venture or partnership and each business that composes the joint venture or partnership shall separately be considered a single business, except that personal information in the possession of each business and disclosed to the joint venture or partnership shall not be shared with the other business.

(4) A person that does business in California, that is not covered by paragraph (1), (2), or (3), and that voluntarily certifies to the California Privacy Protection Agency that it is in compliance with, and agrees to be bound by, this title.

(e) “Business purpose” means the use of personal information for the business’ operational purposes, or other notified purposes, or for the service provider or contractor’s operational purposes, as defined by regulations adopted pursuant to paragraph (11) of subdivision (a) of Section 1798.185, provided that the use of personal information shall be reasonably necessary and proportionate to achieve the purpose for which the personal information was collected or processed or for another purpose that is compatible with the context in which the personal information was collected. Business purposes are:

(1) Auditing related to counting ad impressions to unique visitors, verifying positioning and quality of ad impressions, and auditing compliance with this specification and other standards.

(2) Helping to ensure security and integrity to the extent the use of the consumer’s personal information is reasonably necessary and proportionate for these purposes.

(3) Debugging to identify and repair errors that impair existing intended functionality.

(4) Short-term, transient use, including, but not limited to, nonpersonalized advertising shown as part of a consumer’s current interaction with the business, provided that the consumer’s personal information is not disclosed to another third party and is not used to build a profile about the consumer or otherwise alter the consumer’s experience outside the current interaction with the business.

(5) Performing services on behalf of the business, including maintaining or servicing accounts, providing customer service, processing or fulfilling orders and transactions, verifying customer information, processing payments, providing financing, providing analytic services, providing storage, or providing similar services on behalf of the business.

(6) Providing advertising and marketing services, except for cross-context behavioral advertising, to the consumer provided that, for the purpose of advertising and marketing, a service provider or contractor shall not combine the personal information of opted-out consumers that the service provider or contractor receives from, or on behalf of, the business with personal information that the service provider or contractor receives from, or on behalf of, another person or persons or collects from its own interaction with consumers.

(7) Undertaking internal research for technological development and demonstration.

(8) Undertaking activities to verify or maintain the quality or safety of a service or device that is owned, manufactured, manufactured for, or controlled by the business, and to improve, upgrade, or enhance the service or device that is owned, manufactured, manufactured for, or controlled by the business.

(f) “Collects,” “collected,” or “collection” means buying, renting, gathering, obtaining, receiving, or accessing any personal information pertaining to a consumer by any means. This includes receiving information from the consumer, either actively or passively, or by observing the consumer’s behavior.

(g) “Commercial purposes” means to advance a person’s commercial or economic interests, such as by inducing another person to buy, rent, lease, join, subscribe to, provide, or exchange products, goods, property, information, or services, or enabling or effecting, directly or indirectly, a commercial transaction.

(h) “Consent” means any freely given, specific, informed, and unambiguous indication of the consumer’s wishes by which the consumer, or the consumer’s legal guardian, a person who has power of attorney, or a person acting as a conservator for the consumer, including by a statement or by a clear affirmative action, signifies agreement to the processing of personal information relating to the consumer for a narrowly defined particular purpose. Acceptance of a general or broad terms of use, or similar document, that contains descriptions of personal information processing along with other, unrelated information, does not constitute consent. Hovering over, muting, pausing, or closing a given piece of content does not constitute consent. Likewise, agreement obtained through use of dark patterns does not constitute consent.

(i) “Consumer” means a natural person who is a California resident, as defined in Section 17014 of Title 18 of the California Code of Regulations, as that section read on September 1, 2017, however identified, including by any unique identifier.

(j) (1) “Contractor” means a person to whom the business makes available a consumer's personal information for a business purpose, pursuant to a written contract with the business, provided that the contract:

(A) Prohibits the contractor from:

(i) Selling or sharing the personal information.

(ii) Retaining, using, or disclosing the personal information for any purpose other than for the business purposes specified in the contract, including retaining, using, or disclosing the personal information for a commercial purpose other than the business purposes specified in the contract, or as otherwise permitted by this title.

(iii) Retaining, using, or disclosing the information outside of the direct business relationship between the contractor and the business.

(iv) Combining the personal information that the contractor receives pursuant to a written contract with the business with personal information that it receives from or on behalf of another person or persons, or collects from its own interaction with the consumer, provided that the contractor may combine personal information to perform any business purpose as defined in regulations adopted pursuant to paragraph (10) of subdivision (a) of Section 1798.185, except as provided for in paragraph (6) of subdivision (e) and in regulations adopted by the California Privacy Protection Agency.

(B) Includes a certification made by the contractor that the contractor understands the restrictions in subparagraph (A) and will comply with them.

(C) Permits, subject to agreement with the contractor, the business to monitor the contractor's compliance with the contract through measures, including, but not limited to, ongoing manual reviews and automated scans and regular assessments, audits, or other technical and operational testing at least once every 12 months.

(2) If a contractor engages any other person to assist it in processing personal information for a business purpose on behalf of the business, or if any other person engaged by the contractor engages another person to assist in processing personal information for that business purpose, it shall notify the business of that engagement, and the engagement shall be pursuant to a written contract binding the other person to observe all the requirements set forth in paragraph (1).

(k) “Cross-context behavioral advertising” means the targeting of advertising to a consumer based on the consumer's personal information obtained from the consumer's activity across businesses, distinctly-branded websites, applications, or services, other than the business, distinctly-branded website, application, or service with which the consumer intentionally interacts.

(l) “Dark pattern” means a user interface designed or manipulated with the substantial effect of subverting or impairing user autonomy, decisionmaking, or choice, as further defined by regulation.

(m) “Deidentified” means information that cannot reasonably be used to infer information about, or otherwise be linked to, a particular consumer provided that the business that possesses the information:

(1) Takes reasonable measures to ensure that the information cannot be associated with a consumer or

household.

(2) Publicly commits to maintain and use the information in deidentified form and not to attempt to reidentify the information, except that the business may attempt to reidentify the information solely for the purpose of determining whether its deidentification processes satisfy the requirements of this subdivision.

(3) Contractually obligates any recipients of the information to comply with all provisions of this subdivision.

(n) "Designated methods for submitting requests" means a mailing address, email address, internet web page, internet web portal, toll-free telephone number, or other applicable contact information, whereby consumers may submit a request or direction under this title, and any new, consumer-friendly means of contacting a business, as approved by the Attorney General pursuant to Section 1798.185.

(o) "Device" means any physical object that is capable of connecting to the Internet, directly or indirectly, or to another device.

(p) "Homepage" means the introductory page of an internet website and any internet web page where personal information is collected. In the case of an online service, such as a mobile application, homepage means the application's platform page or download page, a link within the application, such as from the application configuration, "About," "Information," or settings page, and any other location that allows consumers to review the notices required by this title, including, but not limited to, before downloading the application.

(q) "Household" means a group, however identified, of consumers who cohabitate with one another at the same residential address and share use of common devices or services.

(r) "Infer" or "inference" means the derivation of information, data, assumptions, or conclusions from facts, evidence, or another source of information or data.

(s) "Intentionally interacts" means when the consumer intends to interact with a person, or disclose personal information to a person, via one or more deliberate interactions, including visiting the person's website or purchasing a good or service from the person. Hovering over, muting, pausing, or closing a given piece of content does not constitute a consumer's intent to interact with a person.

(t) "Nonpersonalized advertising" means advertising and marketing that is based solely on a consumer's personal information derived from the consumer's current interaction with the business with the exception of the consumer's precise geolocation.

(u) "Person" means an individual, proprietorship, firm, partnership, joint venture, syndicate, business trust, company, corporation, limited liability company, association, committee, and any other organization or group of persons acting in concert.

(v) (1) "Personal information" means information that identifies, relates to, describes, is reasonably capable of being associated with, or could reasonably be linked, directly or indirectly, with a particular consumer or household. Personal information includes, but is not limited to, the following if it identifies, relates to, describes, is reasonably capable of being associated with, or could be reasonably linked, directly or indirectly, with a particular consumer or household:

(A) Identifiers such as a real name, alias, postal address, unique personal identifier, online identifier, Internet Protocol address, email address, account name, social security number, driver's license number, passport number, or other similar identifiers.

(B) Any personal information described in subdivision (e) of Section 1798.80.

(C) Characteristics of protected classifications under California or federal law.

(D) Commercial information, including records of personal property, products or services purchased, obtained, or considered, or other purchasing or consuming histories or tendencies.

(E) Biometric information.

(F) Internet or other electronic network activity information, including, but not limited to, browsing history, search history, and information regarding a consumer's interaction with an internet website application, or advertisement.

(G) Geolocation data.

(H) Audio, electronic, visual, thermal, olfactory, or similar information.

(I) Professional or employment-related information.

(J) Education information, defined as information that is not publicly available personally identifiable information as defined in the Family Educational Rights and Privacy Act (20 U.S.C. Sec. 1232g; 34 C.F.R. Part 99).

(K) Inferences drawn from any of the information identified in this subdivision to create a profile about a consumer reflecting the consumer's preferences, characteristics, psychological trends, predispositions, behavior, attitudes, intelligence, abilities, and aptitudes.

(L) Sensitive personal information.

(2) "Personal information" does not include publicly available information or lawfully obtained, truthful information that is a matter of public concern. For purposes of this paragraph, "publicly available" means: information that is lawfully made available from federal, state, or local government records, or information that a business has a reasonable basis to believe is lawfully made available to the general public by the consumer or from widely distributed media; or information made available by a person to whom the consumer has disclosed the information if the consumer has not restricted the information to a specific audience. "Publicly available" does not mean biometric information collected by a business about a consumer without the consumer's knowledge.

(3) "Personal information" does not include consumer information that is deidentified or aggregate consumer information.

(w) "Precise geolocation" means any data that is derived from a device and that is used or intended to be used to locate a consumer within a geographic area that is equal to or less than the area of a circle with a radius of 1,850 feet, except as prescribed by regulations.

(x) "Probabilistic identifier" means the identification of a consumer or a consumer's device to a degree of certainty of more probable than not based on any categories of personal information included in, or similar to, the categories enumerated in the definition of personal information.

(y) "Processing" means any operation or set of operations that are performed on personal information or on sets of personal information, whether or not by automated means.

(z) "Profiling" means any form of automated processing of personal information, as further defined by regulations pursuant to paragraph (16) of subdivision (a) of Section 1798.185, to evaluate certain personal aspects relating to a natural person and in particular to analyze or predict aspects concerning that natural person's performance at work, economic situation, health, personal preferences, interests, reliability, behavior, location, or movements.

(aa) "Pseudonymize" or "Pseudonymization" means the processing of personal information in a manner that renders the personal information no longer attributable to a specific consumer without the use of additional information, provided that the additional information is kept separately and is subject to technical and organizational measures to ensure that the personal information is not attributed to an identified or identifiable consumer.

(ab) "Research" means scientific analysis, systematic study, and observation, including basic research or applied research that is designed to develop or contribute to public or scientific knowledge and that adheres or otherwise conforms to all other applicable ethics and privacy laws, including, but not limited to, studies conducted in the public interest in the area of public health. Research with personal information that may have been collected from a consumer in the course of the consumer's interactions with a business' service or device for other purposes shall be:

(1) Compatible with the business purpose for which the personal information was collected.

(2) Subsequently pseudonymized and deidentified, or deidentified and in the aggregate, such that the information cannot reasonably identify, relate to, describe, be capable of being associated with, or be linked, directly or indirectly, to a particular consumer, by a business.

(3) Made subject to technical safeguards that prohibit reidentification of the consumer to whom the information may pertain, other than as needed to support the research.

(4) Subject to business processes that specifically prohibit reidentification of the information, other than as needed to support the research.

(5) Made subject to business processes to prevent inadvertent release of deidentified information.

(6) Protected from any reidentification attempts.

(7) Used solely for research purposes that are compatible with the context in which the personal information was collected.

(8) Subjected by the business conducting the research to additional security controls that limit access to the research data to only those individuals as are necessary to carry out the research purpose.

(ac) "Security and integrity" means the ability of:

(1) Networks or information systems to detect security incidents that compromise the availability, authenticity, integrity, and confidentiality of stored or transmitted personal information.

(2) Businesses to detect security incidents, resist malicious, deceptive, fraudulent, or illegal actions and to help prosecute those responsible for those actions.

(3) Businesses to ensure the physical safety of natural persons.

(ad) (1) "Sell," "selling," "sale," or "sold," means selling, renting, releasing, disclosing, disseminating, making available, transferring, or otherwise communicating orally, in writing, or by electronic or other means, a consumer's personal information by the business to a third party for monetary or other valuable consideration.

(2) For purposes of this title, a business does not sell personal information when:

(A) A consumer uses or directs the business to intentionally:

(i) Disclose personal information.

(ii) Interact with one or more third parties.

(B) The business uses or shares an identifier for a consumer who has opted out of the sale of the consumer's personal information or limited the use of the consumer's sensitive personal information for the purposes of alerting persons that the consumer has opted out of the sale of the consumer's personal information or limited the use of the consumer's sensitive personal information.

(C) The business transfers to a third party the personal information of a consumer as an asset that is part of a merger, acquisition, bankruptcy, or other transaction in which the third party assumes control of all or part of the business, provided that information is used or shared consistently with this title. If a third party materially alters how it uses or shares the personal information of a consumer in a manner that is materially inconsistent with the promises made at the time of collection, it shall provide prior notice of the new or changed practice to the consumer. The notice shall be sufficiently prominent and robust to ensure that existing consumers can easily exercise their choices consistently with this title. This subparagraph does not authorize a business to make material, retroactive privacy policy changes or make other changes in their privacy policy in a manner that would violate the Unfair and Deceptive Practices Act (Chapter 5 (commencing with Section 17200) of Part 2 of Division 7 of the Business and Professions Code).

(ae) "Sensitive personal information" means:

(1) Personal information that reveals:

(A) A consumer's social security, driver's license, state identification card, or passport number.

(B) A consumer's account log-in, financial account, debit card, or credit card number in combination with any required security or access code, password, or credentials allowing access to an account.

(C) A consumer's precise geolocation.

(D) A consumer's racial or ethnic origin, religious or philosophical beliefs, or union membership.

(E) The contents of a consumer's mail, email, and text messages unless the business is the intended recipient of the communication.

(F) A consumer's genetic data.

(2) (A) The processing of biometric information for the purpose of uniquely identifying a consumer.

(B) Personal information collected and analyzed concerning a consumer's health.

(C) Personal information collected and analyzed concerning a consumer's sex life or sexual orientation.

(3) Sensitive personal information that is "publicly available" pursuant to paragraph (2) of subdivision (v) shall not be considered sensitive personal information or personal information.

(af) "Service" or "services" means work, labor, and services, including services furnished in connection with the sale or repair of goods.

(ag) (1) "Service provider" means a person that processes personal information on behalf of a business and that receives from or on behalf of the business consumer's personal information for a business purpose pursuant to a written contract, provided that the contract prohibits the person from:

(A) Selling or sharing the personal information.

(B) Retaining, using, or disclosing the personal information for any purpose other than for the business purposes specified in the contract for the business, including retaining, using, or disclosing the personal information for a commercial purpose other than the business purposes specified in the contract with the business, or as otherwise permitted by this title.

(C) Retaining, using, or disclosing the information outside of the direct business relationship between the service provider and the business.

(D) Combining the personal information that the service provider receives from, or on behalf of, the business with personal information that it receives from, or on behalf of, another person or persons, or collects from its own interaction with the consumer, provided that the service provider may combine personal information to perform any business purpose as defined in regulations adopted pursuant to paragraph (10) of subdivision (a) of Section 1798.185, except as provided for in paragraph (6) of subdivision (e) of this section and in regulations adopted by the California Privacy Protection Agency. The contract may, subject to agreement with the service provider, permit the business to monitor the service provider's compliance with the contract through measures, including, but not limited to, ongoing manual reviews and automated scans and regular assessments, audits, or other technical and operational testing at least once every 12 months.

(2) If a service provider engages any other person to assist it in processing personal information for a business purpose on behalf of the business, or if any other person engaged by the service provider engages another person to assist in processing personal information for that business purpose, it shall notify the business of that engagement, and the engagement shall be pursuant to a written contract binding the other person to observe all the requirements set forth in paragraph (1).

(ah) (1) "Share," "shared," or "sharing" means sharing, renting, releasing, disclosing, disseminating, making available, transferring, or otherwise communicating orally, in writing, or by electronic or other means, a consumer's personal information by the business to a third party for cross-context behavioral advertising, whether or not for monetary or other valuable consideration, including transactions between a business and a third party for cross-context behavioral advertising for the benefit of a business in which no money is exchanged.

(2) For purposes of this title, a business does not share personal information when:

(A) A consumer uses or directs the business to intentionally disclose personal information or intentionally interact with one or more third parties.

(B) The business uses or shares an identifier for a consumer who has opted out of the sharing of the consumer's personal information or limited the use of the consumer's sensitive personal information for the purposes of alerting persons that the consumer has opted out of the sharing of the consumer's personal information or limited the use of the consumer's sensitive personal information.

(C) The business transfers to a third party the personal information of a consumer as an asset that is part of a merger, acquisition, bankruptcy, or other transaction in which the third party assumes control of all or part of the business, provided that information is used or shared consistently with this title. If a third party materially alters how it uses or shares the personal information of a consumer in a manner that is materially inconsistent with the promises made at the time of collection, it shall provide prior notice of the new or changed practice to the consumer. The notice shall be sufficiently prominent and robust to ensure that existing consumers can easily exercise their choices consistently with this title. This subparagraph does not authorize a business to make material, retroactive privacy policy changes or make other changes in their privacy policy in a manner that would violate the Unfair and Deceptive Practices Act (Chapter 5 (commencing with Section 17200) of Part 2 of Division 7 of the Business and Professions Code).

(ai) "Third party" means a person who is not any of the following:

(1) The business with whom the consumer intentionally interacts and that collects personal information from the consumer as part of the consumer's current interaction with the business under this title.

(2) A service provider to the business.

(3) A contractor.

(aj) “Unique identifier” or “unique personal identifier” means a persistent identifier that can be used to recognize a consumer, a family, or a device that is linked to a consumer or family, over time and across different services, including, but not limited to, a device identifier; an Internet Protocol address; cookies, beacons, pixel tags, mobile ad identifiers, or similar technology; customer number, unique pseudonym, or user alias; telephone numbers, or other forms of persistent or probabilistic identifiers that can be used to identify a particular consumer or device that is linked to a consumer or family. For purposes of this subdivision, “family” means a custodial parent or guardian and any children under 18 years of age over which the parent or guardian has custody.

(ak) “Verifiable consumer request” means a request that is made by a consumer, by a consumer on behalf of the consumer’s minor child, by a natural person or a person registered with the Secretary of State, authorized by the consumer to act on the consumer’s behalf, or by a person who has power of attorney or is acting as a conservator for the consumer, and that the business can verify, using commercially reasonable methods, pursuant to regulations adopted by the Attorney General pursuant to paragraph (7) of subdivision (a) of Section 1798.185 to be the consumer about whom the business has collected personal information. A business is not obligated to provide information to the consumer pursuant to Sections 1798.110 and 1798.115, to delete personal information pursuant to Section 1798.105, or to correct inaccurate personal information pursuant to Section 1798.106, if the business cannot verify, pursuant to this subdivision and regulations adopted by the Attorney General pursuant to paragraph (7) of subdivision (a) of Section 1798.185, that the consumer making the request is the consumer about whom the business has collected information or is a person authorized by the consumer to act on such consumer’s behalf.

§ 1798.145. Exemptions

(a) The obligations imposed on businesses by this title shall not restrict a business’ ability to:

(1) Comply with federal, state, or local laws or comply with a court order or subpoena to provide information.

(2) Comply with a civil, criminal, or regulatory inquiry, investigation, subpoena, or summons by federal, state, or local authorities. Law enforcement agencies, including police and sheriff’s departments, may direct a business pursuant to a law enforcement agency-approved investigation with an active case number not to delete a consumer’s personal information, and, upon receipt of that direction, a business shall not delete the personal information for 90 days in order to allow the law enforcement agency to obtain a court-issued subpoena, order, or warrant to obtain a consumer’s personal information. For good cause and only to the extent necessary for investigatory purposes, a law enforcement agency may direct a business not to delete the consumer’s personal information for additional 90-day periods. A business that has received direction from a law enforcement agency not to delete the personal information of a consumer who has requested deletion of the consumer’s personal information shall not use the consumer’s personal information for any purpose other than retaining it to produce to law enforcement in response to a court-issued subpoena, order, or warrant unless the consumer’s deletion request is subject to an exemption from deletion under this title.

(3) Cooperate with law enforcement agencies concerning conduct or activity that the business, service provider, or third party reasonably and in good faith believes may violate federal, state, or local law.

(4) Cooperate with a government agency request for emergency access to a consumer’s personal information if a natural person is at risk or danger of death or serious physical injury provided that:

(A) The request is approved by a high-ranking agency officer for emergency access to a consumer’s personal information.

(B) The request is based on the agency’s good faith determination that it has a lawful basis to access the information on a nonemergency basis.

(C) The agency agrees to petition a court for an appropriate order within three days and to destroy the information if that order is not granted.

(5) Exercise or defend legal claims.

(6) Collect, use, retain, sell, share, or disclose consumers' personal information that is deidentified or aggregate consumer information.

(7) Collect, sell, or share a consumer's personal information if every aspect of that commercial conduct takes place wholly outside of California. For purposes of this title, commercial conduct takes place wholly outside of California if the business collected that information while the consumer was outside of California, no part of the sale of the consumer's personal information occurred in California, and no personal information collected while the consumer was in California is sold. This paragraph shall not prohibit a business from storing, including on a device, personal information about a consumer when the consumer is in California and then collecting that personal information when the consumer and stored personal information is outside of California.

(b) The obligations imposed on businesses by Sections 1798.110, 1798.115, 1798.120, 1798.121, 1798.130, and 1798.135 shall not apply where compliance by the business with the title would violate an evidentiary privilege under California law and shall not prevent a business from providing the personal information of a consumer to a person covered by an evidentiary privilege under California law as part of a privileged communication.

(c) (1) This title shall not apply to any of the following:

(A) Medical information governed by the Confidentiality of Medical Information Act (Part 2.6 (commencing with Section 56) of Division 1) or protected health information that is collected by a covered entity or business associate governed by the privacy, security, and breach notification rules issued by the United States Department of Health and Human Services, Parts 160 and 164 of Title 45 of the Code of Federal Regulations, established pursuant to the Health Insurance Portability and Accountability Act of 1996 (Public Law 104-191) and the Health Information Technology for Economic and Clinical Health Act (Public Law 111-5).

(B) A provider of health care governed by the Confidentiality of Medical Information Act (Part 2.6 (commencing with Section 56) of Division 1) or a covered entity governed by the privacy, security, and breach notification rules issued by the United States Department of Health and Human Services, Parts 160 and 164 of Title 45 of the Code of Federal Regulations, established pursuant to the Health Insurance Portability and Accountability Act of 1996 (Public Law 104-191), to the extent the provider or covered entity maintains patient information in the same manner as medical information or protected health information as described in subparagraph (A) of this section.

(C) Personal information collected as part of a clinical trial or other biomedical research study subject to, or conducted in accordance with, the Federal Policy for the Protection of Human Subjects, also known as the Common Rule, pursuant to good clinical practice guidelines issued by the International Council for Harmonisation or pursuant to human subject protection requirements of the United States Food and Drug Administration, provided that the information is not sold or shared in a manner not permitted by this subparagraph, and, if it is inconsistent, that participants be informed of that use and provide consent.

(2) For purposes of this subdivision, the definitions of "medical information" and "provider of health care" in Section 56.05 shall apply and the definitions of "business associate," "covered entity," and "protected health information" in Section 160.103 of Title 45 of the Code of Federal Regulations shall apply.

(d) (1) This title shall not apply to an activity involving the collection, maintenance, disclosure, sale, communication, or use of any personal information bearing on a consumer's creditworthiness, credit standing, credit capacity, character, general reputation, personal characteristics, or mode of living by a consumer reporting agency, as defined in subdivision (f) of Section 1681a of Title 15 of the United States Code, by a furnisher of information, as set forth in Section 1681s-2 of Title 15 of the United States Code, who provides information for use in a consumer report, as defined in subdivision (d) of Section 1681a of Title 15 of the United States Code, and by a user of a consumer report as set forth in Section 1681b of Title 15 of the United States Code.

(2) Paragraph (1) shall apply only to the extent that such activity involving the collection, maintenance, disclosure, sale, communication, or use of such information by that agency, furnisher, or user is subject to regulation under the Fair Credit Reporting Act, Section 1681 et seq., Title 15 of the United States Code and the information is not collected, maintained, used, communicated, disclosed, or sold except as authorized by the Fair Credit Reporting Act.

(3) This subdivision shall not apply to Section 1798.150.

(e) This title shall not apply to personal information collected, processed, sold, or disclosed subject to the federal Gramm-Leach-Bliley Act (Public Law 106-102), and implementing regulations, or the California Financial Information Privacy Act (Division 1.4 (commencing with Section 4050) of the Financial Code), or the federal Farm Credit Act of 1971 (as amended in 12 U.S.C. 2001-2279cc and implementing regulations, 12 C.F.R. 600, et seq.). This subdivision shall not apply to Section 1798.150.

(f) This title shall not apply to personal information collected, processed, sold, or disclosed pursuant to the Driver's Privacy Protection Act of 1994 (18 U.S.C. Sec. 2721 et seq.). This subdivision shall not apply to Section 1798.150.

(g) (1) Section 1798.120 shall not apply to vehicle information or ownership information retained or shared between a new motor vehicle dealer, as defined in Section 426 of the Vehicle Code, and the vehicle's manufacturer, as defined in Section 672 of the Vehicle Code, if the vehicle information or ownership information is shared for the purpose of effectuating, or in anticipation of effectuating, a vehicle repair covered by a vehicle warranty or a recall conducted pursuant to Sections 30118 to 30120, inclusive, of Title 49 of the United States Code, provided that the new motor vehicle dealer or vehicle manufacturer with which that vehicle information or ownership information is shared does not sell, share, or use that information for any other purpose.

(2) Section 1798.120 shall not apply to vessel information or ownership information retained or shared between a vessel dealer and the vessel's manufacturer, as defined in Section 651 of the Harbors and Navigation Code, if the vessel information or ownership information is shared for the purpose of effectuating, or in anticipation of effectuating, a vessel repair covered by a vessel warranty or a recall conducted pursuant to Section 4310 of Title 46 of the United States Code, provided that the vessel dealer or vessel manufacturer with which that vessel information or ownership information is shared does not sell, share, or use that information for any other purpose.

(3) For purposes of this subdivision:

(A) "Ownership information" means the name or names of the registered owner or owners and the contact information for the owner or owners.

(B) "Vehicle information" means the vehicle information number, make, model, year, and odometer reading.

(C) "Vessel dealer" means a person who is engaged, wholly or in part, in the business of selling or offering for sale, buying or taking in trade for the purpose of resale, or exchanging, any vessel or vessels, as defined in Section 651 of the Harbors and Navigation Code, and receives or expects to receive money, profit, or any other thing of value.

(D) “Vessel information” means the hull identification number, model, year, month and year of production, and information describing any of the following equipment as shipped, transferred, or sold from the place of manufacture, including all attached parts and accessories:

(i) An inboard engine.

(ii) An outboard engine.

(iii) A stern drive unit.

(iv) An inflatable personal flotation device approved under Section 160.076 of Title 46 of the Code of Federal Regulations.

(h) Notwithstanding a business’ obligations to respond to and honor consumer rights requests pursuant to this title:

(1) A time period for a business to respond to a consumer for any verifiable consumer request may be extended by up to a total of 90 days where necessary, taking into account the complexity and number of the requests. The business shall inform the consumer of any such extension within 45 days of receipt of the request, together with the reasons for the delay.

(2) If the business does not take action on the request of the consumer, the business shall inform the consumer, without delay and at the latest within the time period permitted of response by this section, of the reasons for not taking action and any rights the consumer may have to appeal the decision to the business.

(3) If requests from a consumer are manifestly unfounded or excessive, in particular because of their repetitive character, a business may either charge a reasonable fee, taking into account the administrative costs of providing the information or communication or taking the action requested, or refuse to act on the request and notify the consumer of the reason for refusing the request. The business shall bear the burden of demonstrating that any verifiable consumer request is manifestly unfounded or excessive.

(i) (1) A business that discloses personal information to a service provider or contractor in compliance with this title shall not be liable under this title if the service provider or contractor receiving the personal information uses it in violation of the restrictions set forth in the title, provided that, at the time of disclosing the personal information, the business does not have actual knowledge, or reason to believe, that the service provider or contractor intends to commit such a violation. A service provider or contractor shall likewise not be liable under this title for the obligations of a business for which it provides services as set forth in this title provided that the service provider or contractor shall be liable for its own violations of this title.

(2) A business that discloses personal information of a consumer, with the exception of consumers who have exercised their right to opt out of the sale or sharing of their personal information, consumers who have limited the use or disclosure of their sensitive personal information, and minor consumers who have not opted in to the collection or sale of their personal information, to a third party pursuant to a written contract that requires the third party to provide the same level of protection of the consumer’s rights under this title as provided by the business shall not be liable under this title if the third party receiving the personal information uses it in violation of the restrictions set forth in this title provided that, at the time of disclosing the personal information, the business does not have actual knowledge, or reason to believe, that the third party intends to commit such a violation.

(j) This title shall not be construed to require a business, service provider, or contractor to:

(1) Reidentify or otherwise link information that, in the ordinary course of business, is not maintained in a manner that would be considered personal information.

(2) Retain any personal information about a consumer if, in the ordinary course of business, that information about the consumer would not be retained.

(3) Maintain information in identifiable, linkable, or associable form, or collect, obtain, retain, or access any data or technology, in order to be capable of linking or associating a verifiable consumer request with personal information.

(k) The rights afforded to consumers and the obligations imposed on the business in this title shall not adversely affect the rights and freedoms of other natural persons. A verifiable consumer request for specific pieces of personal information pursuant to Section 1798.110, to delete a consumer's personal information pursuant to Section 1798.105, or to correct inaccurate personal information pursuant to Section 1798.106, shall not extend to personal information about the consumer that belongs to, or the business maintains on behalf of, another natural person. A business may rely on representations made in a verifiable consumer request as to rights with respect to personal information and is under no legal requirement to seek out other persons that may have or claim to have rights to personal information, and a business is under no legal obligation under this title or any other provision of law to take any action under this title in the event of a dispute between or among persons claiming rights to personal information in the business' possession.

(l) The rights afforded to consumers and the obligations imposed on any business under this title shall not apply to the extent that they infringe on the noncommercial activities of a person or entity described in subdivision (b) of Section 2 of Article I of the California Constitution.

(m) (1) This title shall not apply to any of the following:

(A) Personal information that is collected by a business about a natural person in the course of the natural person acting as a job applicant to, an employee of, owner of, director of, officer of, medical staff member of, or independent contractor of, that business to the extent that the natural person's personal information is collected and used by the business solely within the context of the natural person's role or former role as a job applicant to, an employee of, owner of, director of, officer of, medical staff member of, or an independent contractor of, that business.

(B) Personal information that is collected by a business that is emergency contact information of the natural person acting as a job applicant to, an employee of, owner of, director of, officer of, medical staff member of, or independent contractor of, that business to the extent that the personal information is collected and used solely within the context of having an emergency contact on file.

(C) Personal information that is necessary for the business to retain to administer benefits for another natural person relating to the natural person acting as a job applicant to, an employee of, owner of, director of, officer of, medical staff member of, or independent contractor of, that business to the extent that the personal information is collected and used solely within the context of administering those benefits.

(2) For purposes of this subdivision:

(A) "Independent contractor" means a natural person who provides any service to a business pursuant to a written contract.

(B) "Director" means a natural person designated in the articles of incorporation as director, or elected by the incorporators and natural persons designated, elected, or appointed by any other name or title to act as directors, and their successors.

(C) "Medical staff member" means a licensed physician and surgeon, dentist, or podiatrist, licensed pursuant to Division 2 (commencing with Section 500) of the Business and Professions Code and a clinical psychologist as defined in Section 1316.5 of the Health and Safety Code.

(D) “Officer” means a natural person elected or appointed by the board of directors to manage the daily operations of a corporation, including a chief executive officer, president, secretary, or treasurer.

(E) “Owner” means a natural person who meets one of the following criteria:

(i) Has ownership of, or the power to vote, more than 50 percent of the outstanding shares of any class of voting security of a business.

(ii) Has control in any manner over the election of a majority of the directors or of individuals exercising similar functions.

(iii) Has the power to exercise a controlling influence over the management of a company.

(3) This subdivision shall not apply to subdivision (a) of Section 1798.100 or Section 1798.150.

(4) This subdivision shall become inoperative on January 1, 2023.

(n) (1) The obligations imposed on businesses by Sections 1798.100, 1798.105, 1798.106, 1798.110, 1798.115, 1798.121, 1798.130, and 1798.135 shall not apply to personal information reflecting a written or verbal communication or a transaction between the business and the consumer, where the consumer is a natural person who acted or is acting as an employee, owner, director, officer, or independent contractor of a company, partnership, sole proprietorship, nonprofit, or government agency and whose communications or transaction with the business occur solely within the context of the business conducting due diligence regarding, or providing or receiving a product or service to or from such company, partnership, sole proprietorship, nonprofit, or government agency.

(2) For purposes of this subdivision:

(A) “Independent contractor” means a natural person who provides any service to a business pursuant to a written contract.

(B) “Director” means a natural person designated in the articles of incorporation as such or elected by the incorporators and natural persons designated, elected, or appointed by any other name or title to act as directors, and their successors.

(C) “Officer” means a natural person elected or appointed by the board of directors to manage the daily operations of a corporation, such as a chief executive officer, president, secretary, or treasurer.

(D) “Owner” means a natural person who meets one of the following:

(i) Has ownership of, or the power to vote, more than 50 percent of the outstanding shares of any class of voting security of a business.

(ii) Has control in any manner over the election of a majority of the directors or of individuals exercising similar functions.

(iii) Has the power to exercise a controlling influence over the management of a company.

(3) This subdivision shall become inoperative on January 1, 2023.

(o) (1) Sections 1798.105 and 1798.120 shall not apply to a commercial credit reporting agency’s collection, processing, sale, or disclosure of business controller information to the extent the commercial credit reporting agency uses the business controller information solely to identify the relationship of a consumer to a business that the consumer owns or contact the consumer only in the consumer’s role as the owner, director, officer, or management employee of the business.

(2) For the purposes of this subdivision:

(A) “Business controller information” means the name or names of the owner or owners, director, officer, or management employee of a business and the contact information, including a business title, for the owner or owners, director, officer, or management employee.

(B) “Commercial credit reporting agency” has the meaning set forth in subdivision (b) of Section 1785.42.

(C) “Owner” means a natural person that meets one of the following:

(i) Has ownership of, or the power to vote, more than 50 percent of the outstanding shares of any class of voting security of a business.

(ii) Has control in any manner over the election of a majority of the directors or of individuals exercising similar functions.

(iii) Has the power to exercise a controlling influence over the management of a company.

(D) “Director” means a natural person designated in the articles of incorporation of a business as director, or elected by the incorporators and natural persons designated, elected, or appointed by any other name or title to act as directors, and their successors.

(E) “Officer” means a natural person elected or appointed by the board of directors of a business to manage the daily operations of a corporation, including a chief executive officer, president, secretary, or treasurer.

(F) “Management employee” means a natural person whose name and contact information is reported to or collected by a commercial credit reporting agency as the primary manager of a business and used solely within the context of the natural person’s role as the primary manager of the business.

(p) The obligations imposed on businesses in Sections 1798.105, 1798.106, 1798.110, and 1798.115 shall not apply to household data.

(q) (1) This title does not require a business to comply with a verifiable consumer request to delete a consumer’s personal information under Section 1798.105 to the extent the verifiable consumer request applies to a student’s grades, educational scores, or educational test results that the business holds on behalf of a local educational agency, as defined in subdivision (d) of Section 49073.1 of the Education Code, at which the student is currently enrolled. If a business does not comply with a request pursuant to this section, it shall notify the consumer that it is acting pursuant to this exception.

(2) This title does not require, in response to a request pursuant to Section 1798.110, that a business disclose on educational standardized assessment or educational assessment or a consumer’s specific responses to the educational standardized assessment or educational assessment if consumer access, possession, or control would jeopardize the validity and reliability of that educational standardized assessment or educational assessment. If a business does not comply with a request pursuant to this section, it shall notify the consumer that it is acting pursuant to this exception.

(3) For purposes of this subdivision:

(A) “Educational standardized assessment or educational assessment” means a standardized or nonstandardized quiz, test, or other assessment used to evaluate students in or for entry to kindergarten and grades 1 to 12, inclusive, schools, postsecondary institutions, vocational programs, and postgraduate programs that are accredited by an accrediting agency or organization recognized by the State of California or the United States Department of Education, as well as certification and licensure examinations used to determine competency and eligibility to receive certification or licensure from a government agency or government certification body.

(B) “Jeopardize the validity and reliability of that educational standardized assessment or educational assessment" means releasing information that would provide an advantage to the consumer who has submitted a verifiable consumer request or to another natural person.

(r) Sections 1798.105 and 1798.120 shall not apply to a business' use, disclosure, or sale of particular pieces of a consumer's personal information if the consumer has consented to the business' use, disclosure, or sale of that information to produce a physical item, including a school yearbook containing the consumer's photograph if:

(1) The business has incurred significant expense in reliance on the consumer's consent.

(2) Compliance with the consumer's request to opt out of the sale of the consumer's personal information or to delete the consumer's personal information would not be commercially reasonable.

(3) The business complies with the consumer's request as soon as it is commercially reasonable to do so.

§ 1798.146.

(a) This title shall not apply to any of the following:

(1) Medical information governed by the Confidentiality of Medical Information Act (Part 2.6 (commencing with Section 56) of Division 1) or protected health information that is collected by a covered entity or business associate governed by the privacy, security, and breach notification rules issued by the United States Department of Health and Human Services, Parts 160 and 164 of Title 45 of the Code of Federal Regulations, established pursuant to the Health Insurance Portability and Accountability Act of 1996 (Public Law 104-191) and the federal Health Information Technology for Economic and Clinical Health Act, Title XIII of the federal American Recovery and Reinvestment Act of 2009 (Public Law 111-5).

(2) A provider of health care governed by the Confidentiality of Medical Information Act (Part 2.6 (commencing with Section 56) of Division 1) or a covered entity governed by the privacy, security, and breach notification rules issued by the United States Department of Health and Human Services, Parts 160 and 164 of Title 45 of the Code of Federal Regulations, established pursuant to the Health Insurance Portability and Accountability Act of 1996 (Public Law 104-191), to the extent the provider or covered entity maintains, uses, and discloses patient information in the same manner as medical information or protected health information as described in paragraph (1).

(3) A business associate of a covered entity governed by the privacy, security, and data breach notification rules issued by the United States Department of Health and Human Services, Parts 160 and 164 of Title 45 of the Code of Federal Regulations, established pursuant to the Health Insurance Portability and Accountability Act of 1996 (Public Law 104-191) and the federal Health Information Technology for Economic and Clinical Health Act, Title XIII of the federal American Recovery and Reinvestment Act of 2009 (Public Law 111-5), to the extent that the business associate maintains, uses, and discloses patient information in the same manner as medical information or protected health information as described in paragraph (1).

(4) (A) Information that meets both of the following conditions:

(i) It is deidentified in accordance with the requirements for deidentification set forth in Section 164.514 of Part 164 of Title 45 of the Code of Federal Regulations.

(ii) It is derived from patient information that was originally collected, created, transmitted, or maintained by an entity regulated by the Health Insurance Portability and Accountability Act, the Confidentiality of Medical Information Act, or the Federal Policy for the Protection of Human Subjects, also known as the Common Rule.

(B) Information that met the requirements of subparagraph (A) but is subsequently reidentified shall no longer be eligible for the exemption in this paragraph, and shall be subject to applicable federal and state data privacy and security laws, including, but not limited to, the Health Insurance Portability and Accountability Act, the Confidentiality of Medical Information Act, and this title.

(5) Information that is collected, used, or disclosed in research, as defined in Section 164.501 of Title 45 of the Code of Federal Regulations, including, but not limited to, a clinical trial, and that is conducted in accordance with applicable ethics, confidentiality, privacy, and security rules of Part 164 of Title 45 of the Code of Federal Regulations, the Federal Policy for the Protection of Human Subjects, also known as the Common Rule, good clinical practice guidelines issued by the International Council for Harmonisation, or human subject protection requirements of the United States Food and Drug Administration.

(b) For purposes of this section, all of the following shall apply:

(1) "Business associate" has the same meaning as defined in Section 160.103 of Title 45 of the Code of Federal Regulations.

(2) "Covered entity" has the same meaning as defined in Section 160.103 of Title 45 of the Code of Federal Regulations.

(3) "Identifiable private information" has the same meaning as defined in Section 46.102 of Title 45 of the Code of Federal Regulations.

(4) "Individually identifiable health information" has the same meaning as defined in Section 160.103 of Title 45 of the Code of Federal Regulations.

(5) "Medical information" has the same meaning as defined in Section 56.05.

(6) "Patient information" shall mean identifiable private information, protected health information, individually identifiable health information, or medical information.

(7) "Protected health information" has the same meaning as defined in Section 160.103 of Title 45 of the Code of Federal Regulations.

(8) "Provider of health care" has the same meaning as defined in Section 56.05.

§ 1798.148.

(a) A business or other person shall not reidentify, or attempt to reidentify, information that has met the requirements of paragraph (4) of subdivision (a) of Section 1798.146, except for one or more of the following purposes:

(1) Treatment, payment, or health care operations conducted by a covered entity or business associate acting on behalf of, and at the written direction of, the covered entity. For purposes of this paragraph, "treatment," "payment," "health care operations," "covered entity," and "business associate" have the same meaning as defined in Section 164.501 of Title 45 of the Code of Federal Regulations.

(2) Public health activities or purposes as described in Section 164.512 of Title 45 of the Code of Federal Regulations.

(3) Research, as defined in Section 164.501 of Title 45 of the Code of Federal Regulations, that is conducted in accordance with Part 46 of Title 45 of the Code of Federal Regulations, the Federal Policy for the Protection of Human Subjects, also known as the Common Rule.

(4) Pursuant to a contract where the lawful holder of the deidentified information that met the requirements of paragraph (4) of subdivision (a) of Section 1798.146 expressly engages a person or entity to attempt to reidentify the deidentified information in order to conduct testing, analysis, or validation of deidentification, or

related statistical techniques, if the contract bans any other use or disclosure of the reidentified information and requires the return or destruction of the information that was reidentified upon completion of the contract.

(5) If otherwise required by law.

(b) In accordance with paragraph (4) of subdivision (a) of Section 1798.146, information reidentified pursuant this section shall be subject to applicable federal and state data privacy and security laws including, but not limited to, the Health Insurance Portability and Accountability Act, the Confidentiality of Medical Information Act, and this title.

(c) Beginning January 1, 2021, any contract for the sale or license of deidentified information that has met the requirements of paragraph (4) of subdivision (a) of Section 1798.146, where one of the parties is a person residing or doing business in the state, shall include the following, or substantially similar, provisions:

(1) A statement that the deidentified information being sold or licensed includes deidentified patient information.

(2) A statement that reidentification, and attempted reidentification, of the deidentified information by the purchaser or licensee of the information is prohibited pursuant to this section.

(3) A requirement that, unless otherwise required by law, the purchaser or licensee of the deidentified information may not further disclose the deidentified information to any third party unless the third party is contractually bound by the same or stricter restrictions and conditions.

(d) For purposes of this section, "reidentify" means the process of reversal of deidentification techniques, including, but not limited to, the addition of specific pieces of information or data elements that can, individually or in combination, be used to uniquely identify an individual or usage of any statistical method, contrivance, computer software, or other means that have the effect of associating deidentified information with a specific identifiable individual.

§ 1798.150. Personal Information Security Breaches

(a) (1) Any consumer whose nonencrypted and nonredacted personal information, as defined in subparagraph (A) of paragraph (1) of subdivision (d) of Section 1798.81.5, or whose email address in combination with a password or security question and answer that would permit access to the account is subject to an unauthorized access and exfiltration, theft, or disclosure as a result of the business's violation of the duty to implement and maintain reasonable security procedures and practices appropriate to the nature of the information to protect the personal information may institute a civil action for any of the following:

(A) To recover damages in an amount not less than one hundred dollars ($100) and not greater than seven hundred and fifty ($750) per consumer per incident or actual damages, whichever is greater.

(B) Injunctive or declaratory relief.

(C) Any other relief the court deems proper.

(2) In assessing the amount of statutory damages, the court shall consider any one or more of the relevant circumstances presented by any of the parties to the case, including, but not limited to, the nature and seriousness of the misconduct, the number of violations, the persistence of the misconduct, the length of time over which the misconduct occurred, the willfulness of the defendant's misconduct, and the defendant's assets, liabilities, and net worth.

(b) Actions pursuant to this section may be brought by a consumer if, prior to initiating any action against a business for statutory damages on an individual or class-wide basis, a consumer provides a business 30 days' written notice identifying the specific provisions of this title the consumer alleges have been or are being violated. In the event a cure is possible, if within the 30 days the business actually cures the noticed violation and provides the consumer an express written statement that the violations have been cured and that no further violations shall occur, no action for individual statutory damages or class-wide statutory damages may be initiated against the business. The implementation and maintenance of reasonable security procedures and practices pursuant to Section 1798.81.5 following a breach does not constitute a cure with respect to that breach. No notice shall be required prior to an individual consumer initiating an action solely for actual pecuniary damages suffered as a result of the alleged violations of this title. If a business continues to violate this title in breach of the express written statement provided to the consumer under this section, the consumer may initiate an action against the business to enforce the written statement and may pursue statutory damages for each breach of the express written statement, as well as any other violation of the title that postdates the written statement.

(c) The cause of action established by this section shall apply only to violations as defined in subdivision (a) and shall not be based on violations of any other section of this title. Nothing in this title shall be interpreted to serve as the basis for a private right of action under any other law. This shall not be construed to relieve any party from any duties or obligations imposed under other law or the United States or California Constitution.

§ 1798.155. Administrative Enforcement

(a) Any business, service provider, contractor, or other person that violates this title shall be liable for an administrative fine of not more than two thousand five hundred dollars ($2,500) for each violation or seven thousand five hundred dollars ($7,500) for each intentional violation or violations involving the personal information of consumers whom the business, service provider, contractor, or other person has actual knowledge are under 16 years of age, as adjusted pursuant to paragraph (5) of subdivision (a) of Section 1798.185, in an administrative enforcement action brought by the California Privacy Protection Agency.

(b) Any administrative fine assessed for a violation of this title, and the proceeds of any settlement of an action brought pursuant to subdivision (a), shall be deposited in the Consumer Privacy Fund, created within the General Fund pursuant to subdivision (a) of Section 1798.160 with the intent to fully offset any costs incurred by the state courts, the attorney general, and the California Privacy Protection Agency in connection with this title.

§ 1798.160. Consumer Privacy Fund

(a) A special fund to be known as the "Consumer Privacy Fund" is hereby created within the General Fund in the State Treasury, and is available upon appropriation by the Legislature first to offset any costs incurred by the state courts in connection with actions brought to enforce this title, the costs incurred by the attorney general in carrying out the attorney general's duties under this title, and then for the purposes of establishing an investment fund in the State Treasury, with any earnings or interest from the fund to be deposited in the General Fund, and making grants to promote and protect consumer privacy, educate children in the area of online privacy, and fund cooperative programs with international law enforcement organizations to combat fraudulent activities with respect to consumer data breaches.

(b) Funds transferred to the Consumer Privacy Fund shall be used exclusively as follows:

(1) To offset any costs incurred by the state courts and the attorney general in connection with this title.

(2) After satisfying the obligations under paragraph (1), the remaining funds shall be allocated each fiscal year as follows:

(A) Ninety-one percent shall be invested by the treasurer in financial assets with the goal of maximizing long term yields consistent with a prudent level of risk. The principal shall not be subject to transfer or appropriation, provided that any interest and earnings shall be transferred on an annual basis to the General Fund for appropriation by the Legislature for General Fund purposes.

(B) Nine percent shall be made available to the California Privacy Protection Agency for the purposes of making grants in California, with 3 percent allocated to each of the following grant recipients:

(i) Nonprofit organizations to promote and protect consumer privacy.

(ii) Nonprofit organizations and public agencies, including school districts, to educate children in the area of online privacy.

(iii) State and local law enforcement agencies to fund cooperative programs with international law enforcement organizations to combat fraudulent activities with respect to consumer data breaches.

(c) Funds in the Consumer Privacy Fund shall not be subject to appropriation or transfer by the Legislature for any other purpose.

§ 1798.175. Conflicting Provisions

This title is intended to further the constitutional right of privacy and to supplement existing laws relating to consumers' personal information, including, but not limited to, Chapter 22 (commencing with Section 22575) of Division 8 of the Business and Professions Code and Title 1.81 (commencing with Section 1798.80). The provisions of this title are not limited to information collected electronically or over the Internet, but apply to the collection and sale of all personal information collected by a business from consumers. Wherever possible, law relating to consumers' personal information should be construed to harmonize with the provisions of this title, but in the event of a conflict between other laws and the provisions of this title, the provisions of the law that afford the greatest protection for the right of privacy for consumers shall control.

§ 1798.180. Preemption

This title is a matter of statewide concern and supersedes and preempts all rules, regulations, codes, ordinances, and other laws adopted by a city, county, city and county, municipality, or local agency regarding the collection and sale of consumers' personal information by a business.

§ 1798.185. Regulations

(a) On or before July 1, 2020, the attorney general shall solicit broad public participation and adopt regulations to further the purposes of this title, including, but not limited to, the following areas:

(1) Updating or adding categories of personal information to those enumerated in subdivision (c) of Section 1798.130 and subdivision (v) of Section 1798.140, and updating or adding categories of sensitive personal information to those enumerated in subdivision (ae) of Section 1798.140 in order to address changes in technology, data collection practices, obstacles to implementation, and privacy concerns.

(2) Updating as needed the definitions of "deidentified" and "unique identifier" to address changes in technology, data collection, obstacles to implementation, and privacy concerns, and adding, modifying, or deleting categories to the definition of designated methods for submitting requests to facilitate a consumer's ability to obtain information from a business pursuant to Section 1798.130. The authority to update the definition of "deidentified" shall not apply to deidentification standards set forth in Section 164.514 of Title 45 of the Code of Federal Regulations, where such information previously was "protected health information" as defined in Section 160.103 of Title 45 of the Code of Federal Regulations.

(3) Establishing any exceptions necessary to comply with state or federal law, including, but not limited to,

those relating to trade secrets and intellectual property rights, within one year of passage of this title and as needed thereafter, with the intention that trade secrets should not be disclosed in response to a verifiable consumer request.

(4) Establishing rules and procedures for the following:

(A) To facilitate and govern the submission of a request by a consumer to opt-out of the sale or sharing of personal information pursuant to Section 1798.120 and to limit the use of a consumer's sensitive personal information pursuant to Section 1798.121 to ensure that consumers have the ability to exercise their choices without undue burden and to prevent business from engaging in deceptive or harassing conduct, including in retaliation against consumers for exercising their rights, while allowing businesses to inform consumers of the consequences of their decision to opt out of the sale or sharing of their personal information or to limit the use of their sensitive personal information.

(B) To govern business compliance with a consumer's opt-out request.

(C) For the development and use of a recognizable and uniform opt-out logo or button by all businesses to promote consumer awareness of the opportunity to opt-out of the sale of personal information.

(5) Adjusting the monetary thresholds, in January of every odd-numbered year to reflect any increase in the Consumer Price Index, in: subparagraph (A) of paragraph (1) of subdivision (d) of Section 1798.140; subparagraph (A) of paragraph (1) of subdivision (a) of Section 1798.150; subdivision (a) of Section 1798.155; Section 1798.199.25; and subdivision (a) of Section 1798.199.90.

(6) Establishing rules, procedures, and any exceptions necessary to ensure that the notices and information that businesses are required to provide pursuant to this title are provided in a manner that may be easily understood by the average consumer, are accessible to consumers with disabilities, and are available in the language primarily used to interact with the consumer, including establishing rules and guidelines regarding financial incentives within one year of passage of this title and as needed thereafter.

(7) Establishing rules and procedures to further the purposes of Sections 1798.105, 1798.106, 1798.110, and 1798.115 and to facilitate a consumer's or the consumer's authorized agent's ability to delete personal information, correct inaccurate personal information pursuant to Section 1798.106, or obtain information pursuant to Section 1798.130, with the goal of minimizing the administrative burden on consumers, taking into account available technology, security concerns, and the burden on the business, to govern a business's determination that a request for information received from a consumer is a verifiable consumer request, including treating a request submitted through a password-protected account maintained by the consumer with the business while the consumer is logged into the account as a verifiable consumer request and providing a mechanism for a consumer who does not maintain an account with the business to request information through the business's authentication of the consumer's identity, within one year of passage of this title and as needed thereafter.

(8) Establishing how often, and under what circumstances, a consumer may request a correction pursuant to Section 1798.106, including standards governing the following:

(A) How a business responds to a request for correction, including exceptions for requests to which a response is impossible or would involve disproportionate effort, and requests for correction of accurate information.

(B) How concerns regarding the accuracy of the information may be resolved.

(C) The steps a business may take to prevent fraud.

(D) If a business rejects a request to correct personal information collected and analyzed concerning a consumer's health, the right of a consumer to provide a written addendum to the business with respect to any item or statement regarding any such personal information that the consumer believes to be incomplete or incorrect. The addendum shall be limited to 250 words per alleged incomplete or incorrect item and shall clearly indicate in writing that the consumer requests the addendum to be made a part of the consumer's record.

(9) Establishing the standard to govern a business' determination, pursuant to subparagraph (B) of paragraph (2) of subdivision (a) of Section 1798.130, that providing information beyond the 12-month period in a response to a verifiable consumer request is impossible or would involve a disproportionate effort.

(10) Issuing regulations further defining and adding to the business purposes, including other notified purposes, for which businesses, service providers, and contractors may use consumers' personal information consistent with consumers' expectations, and further defining the business purposes for which service providers and contractors may combine consumers' personal information obtained from different sources, except as provided for in paragraph (6) of subdivision (e) of Section 1798.140.

(11) Issuing regulations identifying those business purposes, including other notified purposes, for which service providers and contractors may use consumers' personal information received pursuant to a written contract with a business, for the service provider or contractor's own business purposes, with the goal of maximizing consumer privacy.

(12) Issuing regulations to further define "intentionally interacts," with the goal of maximizing consumer privacy.

(13) Issuing regulations to further define "precise geolocation," including if the size defined is not sufficient to protect consumer privacy in sparsely populated areas or when the personal information is used for normal operational purposes, including billing.

(14) Issuing regulations to define the term "specific pieces of information obtained from the consumer" with the goal of maximizing a consumer's right to access relevant personal information while minimizing the delivery of information to a consumer that would not be useful to the consumer, including system log information and other technical data. For delivery of the most sensitive personal information, the regulations may require a higher standard of authentication provided that the agency shall monitor the impact of the higher standard on the right of consumers to obtain their personal information to ensure that the requirements of verification do not result in the unreasonable denial of verifiable consumer requests.

(15) Issuing regulations requiring businesses whose processing of consumers' personal information presents significant risk to consumers' privacy or security, to:

(A) Perform a cybersecurity audit on an annual basis, including defining the scope of the audit and establishing a process to ensure that audits are thorough and independent. The factors to be considered in determining when processing may result in significant risk to the security of personal information shall include the size and complexity of the business and the nature and scope of processing activities.

(B) Submit to the California Privacy Protection Agency on a regular basis a risk assessment with respect to their processing of personal information, including whether the processing involves sensitive personal information, and identifying and weighing the benefits resulting from the processing to the business, the consumer, other stakeholders, and the public, against the potential risks to the rights of the consumer associated with that processing, with the goal of restricting or prohibiting the processing if the risks to privacy of the consumer outweigh the benefits resulting from processing to the consumer, the business, other stakeholders, and the public. Nothing in this section shall require a business to divulge trade secrets.

(16) Issuing regulations governing access and opt-out rights with respect to businesses' use of automated

decisionmaking technology, including profiling and requiring businesses' response to access requests to include meaningful information about the logic involved in those decisionmaking processes, as well as a description of the likely outcome of the process with respect to the consumer.

(17) Issuing regulations to further define a "law enforcement agency-approved investigation" for purposes of the exception in paragraph (2) of subdivision (a) of Section 1798.145.

(18) Issuing regulations to define the scope and process for the exercise of the agency's audit authority, to establish criteria for selection of persons to audit, and to protect consumers' personal information from disclosure to an auditor in the absence of a court order, warrant, or subpoena.

(19) (A) Issuing regulations to define the requirements and technical specifications for an opt-out preference signal sent by a platform, technology, or mechanism, to indicate a consumer's intent to opt out of the sale or sharing of the consumer's personal information and to limit the use or disclosure of the consumer's sensitive personal information. The requirements and specifications for the opt-out preference signal should be updated from time to time to reflect the means by which consumers interact with businesses, and should:

(i) Ensure that the manufacturer of a platform or browser or device that sends the opt-out preference signal cannot unfairly disadvantage another business.

(ii) Ensure that the opt-out preference signal is consumer-friendly, clearly described, and easy to use by an average consumer and does not require that the consumer provide additional information beyond what is necessary.

(iii) Clearly represent a consumer's intent and be free of defaults constraining or presupposing that intent.

(iv) Ensure that the opt-out preference signal does not conflict with other commonly used privacy settings or tools that consumers may employ.

(v) Provide a mechanism for the consumer to selectively consent to a business' sale of the consumer's personal information, or the use or disclosure of the consumer's sensitive personal information, without affecting the consumer's preferences with respect to other businesses or disabling the opt-out preference signal globally.

(vi) State that in the case of a page or setting view that the consumer accesses to set the opt-out preference signal, the consumer should see up to three choices, including:

(I) Global opt out from sale and sharing of personal information, including a direction to limit the use of sensitive personal information.

(II) Choice to "Limit the Use of My Sensitive Personal Information."

(III) Choice titled "Do Not Sell/Do Not Share My Personal Information for Cross-Context Behavioral Advertising."

(B) Issuing regulations to establish technical specifications for an opt-out preference signal that allows the consumer, or the consumer's parent or guardian, to specify that the consumer is less than 13 years of age or at least 13 years of age and less than 16 years of age.

(C) Issuing regulations, with the goal of strengthening consumer privacy while considering the legitimate operational interests of businesses, to govern the use or disclosure of a consumer's sensitive personal information, notwithstanding the consumer's direction to limit the use or disclosure of the consumer's sensitive personal information, including:

(i) Determining any additional purposes for which a business may use or disclose a consumer's sensitive personal information.

(ii) Determining the scope of activities permitted under paragraph (8) of subdivision (e) of Section 1798.140, as authorized by subdivision (a) of Section 1798.121, to ensure that the activities do not involve health-related research.

(iii) Ensuring the functionality of the business' operations.

(iv) Ensuring that the exemption in subdivision (d) of Section 1798.121 for sensitive personal information applies to information that is collected or processed incidentally, or without the purpose of inferring characteristics about a consumer, while ensuring that businesses do not use the exemption for the purpose of evading consumers' rights to limit the use and disclosure of their sensitive personal information under Section 1798.121.

(20) Issuing regulations to govern how a business that has elected to comply with subdivision (b) of Section 1798.135 responds to the opt-out preference signal and provides consumers with the opportunity subsequently to consent to the sale or sharing of their personal information or the use and disclosure of their sensitive personal information for purposes in addition to those authorized by subdivision (a) of Section 1798.121. The regulations should:

(A) Strive to promote competition and consumer choice and be technology neutral.

(B) Ensure that the business does not respond to an opt-out preference signal by:

(i) Intentionally degrading the functionality of the consumer experience.

(ii) Charging the consumer a fee in response to the consumer's opt-out preferences.

(iii) Making any products or services not function properly or fully for the consumer, as compared to consumers who do not use the opt-out preference signal.

(iv) Attempting to coerce the consumer to opt in to the sale or sharing of the consumer's personal information, or the use or disclosure of the consumer's sensitive personal information, by stating or implying that the use of the opt-out preference signal will adversely affect the consumer as compared to consumers who do not use the opt-out preference signal, including stating or implying that the consumer will not be able to use the business' products or services or that those products or services may not function properly or fully.

(v) Displaying any notification or pop-up in response to the consumer's opt-out preference signal.

(C) Ensure that any link to a web page or its supporting content that allows the consumer to consent to opt in:

(i) Is not part of a popup, notice, banner, or other intrusive design that obscures any part of the web page the consumer intended to visit from full view or that interferes with or impedes in any way the consumer's experience visiting or browsing the web page or website the consumer intended to visit.

(ii) Does not require or imply that the consumer must click the link to receive full functionality of any products or services, including the website.

(iii) Does not make use of any dark patterns.

(iv) Applies only to the business with which the consumer intends to interact.

(D) Strive to curb coercive or deceptive practices in response to an opt-out preference signal but should not unduly restrict businesses that are trying in good faith to comply with Section 1798.135.

(21) Review existing Insurance Code provisions and regulations relating to consumer privacy, except those relating to insurance rates or pricing, to determine whether any provisions of the Insurance Code provide

greater protection to consumers than the provisions of this title. Upon completing its review, the agency shall adopt a regulation that applies only the more protective provisions of this title to insurance companies. For the purpose of clarity, the insurance commissioner shall have jurisdiction over insurance rates and pricing.

(22) Harmonizing the regulations governing opt-out mechanisms, notices to consumers, and other operational mechanisms in this title to promote clarity and the functionality of this title for consumers.

(b) The attorney general may adopt additional regulations as necessary to further the purposes of this title.

(c) The attorney general shall not bring an enforcement action under this title until six months after the publication of the final regulations issued pursuant to this section or July 1, 2020, whichever is sooner.

(d) Notwithstanding subdivision (a), the timeline for adopting final regulations required by the act adding this subdivision shall be July 1, 2022. Beginning the later of July 1, 2021, or six months after the agency provides notice to the attorney general that it is prepared to begin rulemaking under this title, the authority assigned to the attorney general to adopt regulations under this section shall be exercised by the California Privacy Protection Agency. Notwithstanding any other law, civil and administrative enforcement of the provisions of law added or amended by this act shall not commence until July 1, 2023, and shall only apply to violations occurring on or after that date. Enforcement of provisions of law contained in the California Consumer Privacy Act of 2018 amended by this act shall remain in effect and shall be enforceable until the same provisions of this act become enforceable.

§ 1798.190. Anti-Avoidance

A court or the agency shall disregard the intermediate steps or transactions for purposes of effectuating the purposes of this title:

(a) If a series of steps or transactions were component parts of a single transaction intended from the beginning to be taken with the intention of avoiding the reach of this title, including the disclosure of information by a business to a third party in order to avoid the definition of sell or share.

(b) If steps or transactions were taken to purposely avoid the definition of sell or share by eliminating any monetary or other valuable consideration, including by entering into contracts that do not include an exchange for monetary or other valuable consideration, but where a party is obtaining something of value or use.

§ 1798.192. Waiver

Any provision of a contract or agreement of any kind, including a representative action waiver, that purports to waive or limit in any way rights under this title, including, but not limited to, any right to a remedy or means of enforcement, shall be deemed contrary to public policy and shall be void and unenforceable. This section shall not prevent a consumer from declining to request information from a business, declining to opt out of a business's sale of the consumer's personal information, or authorizing a business to sell or share the consumer's personal information after previously opting out.

§ 1798.194.

This title shall be liberally construed to effectuate its purposes.

§ 1798.196.

This title is intended to supplement federal and state law, if permissible, but shall not apply if such application is preempted by, or in conflict with, federal law or the United States or California Constitution.

§ 1798.198.

(a) Subject to limitation provided in subdivision (b), and in Section 1798.199, this title shall be operative January 1, 2020.

(b) This title shall become operative only if initiative measure No. 17-0039, The Consumer Right to Privacy Act of 2018, is withdrawn from the ballot pursuant to Section 9604 of the Elections Code.

§ 1798.199.

Notwithstanding Section 1798.198, Section 1798.180 shall be operative on the effective date of the act adding this section.

§ 1798.199.10.

(a) There is hereby established in state government the California Privacy Protection Agency, which is vested with full administrative power, authority, and jurisdiction to implement and enforce the California Consumer Privacy Act of 2018. The agency shall be governed by a five-member board, including the chairperson. The chairperson and one member of the board shall be appointed by the governor. The attorney general, Senate Rules Committee, and speaker of the assembly shall each appoint one member. These appointments should be made from among Californians with expertise in the areas of privacy, technology, and consumer rights.

(b) The initial appointments to the agency shall be made within 90 days of the effective date of the act adding this section.

§ 1798.199.15.

Members of the agency board shall:

(a) Have qualifications, experience, and skills, in particular in the areas of privacy and technology, required to perform the duties of the agency and exercise its powers.

(b) Maintain the confidentiality of information which has come to their knowledge in the course of the performance of their tasks or exercise of their powers, except to the extent that disclosure is required by the Public Records Act.

(c) Remain free from external influence, whether direct or indirect, and shall neither seek nor take instructions from another.

(d) Refrain from any action incompatible with their duties and engaging in any incompatible occupation, whether gainful or not, during their term.

(e) Have the right of access to all information made available by the agency to the chairperson.

(f) Be precluded, for a period of one year after leaving office, from accepting employment with a business that was subject to an enforcement action or civil action under this title during the member's tenure or during the five-year period preceding the member's appointment.

(g) Be precluded for a period of two years after leaving office from acting, for compensation, as an agent or attorney for, or otherwise representing, any other person in a matter pending before the agency if the purpose is to influence an action of the agency.

§ 1798.199.20.

Members of the agency board, including the chairperson, shall serve at the pleasure of their appointing authority but shall serve for no longer than eight consecutive years.

§ 1798.199.25.

For each day on which they engage in official duties, members of the agency board shall be compensated at the rate of one hundred dollars ($100), adjusted biennially to reflect changes in the cost of living, and shall be reimbursed for expenses incurred in performance of their official duties.

§ 1798.199.30.

The agency board shall appoint an executive director who shall act in accordance with agency policies and regulations and with applicable law. The agency shall appoint and discharge officers, counsel, and employees, consistent with applicable civil service laws, and shall fix the compensation of employees and prescribe their duties. The agency may contract for services that cannot be provided by its employees.

§ 1798.199.35.

The agency board may delegate authority to the chairperson or the executive director to act in the name of the agency between meetings of the agency, except with respect to resolution of enforcement actions and rulemaking authority.

§ 1798.199.40.

The agency shall perform the following functions:

(a) Administer, implement, and enforce through administrative actions this title.

(b) On and after the later of July 1, 2021, or within six months of the agency providing the Attorney General with notice that it is prepared to assume rulemaking responsibilities under this title, adopt, amend, and rescind regulations pursuant to Section 1798.185 to carry out the purposes and provisions of the California Consumer Privacy Act of 2018, including regulations specifying recordkeeping requirements for businesses to ensure compliance with this title.

(c) Through the implementation of this title, protect the fundamental privacy rights of natural persons with respect to the use of their personal information.

(d) Promote public awareness and understanding of the risks, rules, responsibilities, safeguards, and rights in relation to the collection, use, sale, and disclosure of personal information, including the rights of minors with respect to their own information, and provide a public report summarizing the risk assessments filed with the agency pursuant to paragraph (15) of subdivision (a) of Section 1798.185 while ensuring that data security is not compromised.

(e) Provide guidance to consumers regarding their rights under this title.

(f) Provide guidance to businesses regarding their duties and responsibilities under this title and appoint a Chief Privacy Auditor to conduct audits of businesses to ensure compliance with this title pursuant to regulations adopted pursuant to paragraph (18) of subdivision (a) of Section 1798.185.

(g) Provide technical assistance and advice to the Legislature, upon request, with respect to privacy-related legislation.

(h) Monitor relevant developments relating to the protection of personal information and, in particular, the development of information and communication technologies and commercial practices.

(i) Cooperate with other agencies with jurisdiction over privacy laws and with data processing authorities in

California, other states, territories, and countries to ensure consistent application of privacy protections.

(j) Establish a mechanism pursuant to which persons doing business in California that do not meet the definition of business set forth in paragraph (1), (2), or (3) of subdivision (d) of Section 1798.140 may voluntarily certify that they are in compliance with this title, as set forth in paragraph (4) of subdivision (d) of Section 1798.140, and make a list of those entities available to the public.

(k) Solicit, review, and approve applications for grants to the extent funds are available pursuant to paragraph (2) of subdivision (b) of Section 1798.160.

(l) Perform all other acts necessary or appropriate in the exercise of its power, authority, and jurisdiction and seek to balance the goals of strengthening consumer privacy while giving attention to the impact on businesses.

§ 1798.199.45.

(a) Upon the sworn complaint of any person or on its own initiative, the agency may investigate possible violations of this title relating to any business, service provider, contractor, or person. The agency may decide not to investigate a complaint or decide to provide a business with a time period to cure the alleged violation. In making a decision not to investigate or provide more time to cure, the agency may consider the following:

(1) Lack of intent to violate this title.

(2) Voluntary efforts undertaken by the business, service provider, contractor, or person to cure the alleged violation prior to being notified by the agency of the complaint.

(b) The agency shall notify in writing the person who made the complaint of the action, if any, the agency has taken or plans to take on the complaint, together with the reasons for that action or nonaction.

§ 1798.199.50.

No finding of probable cause to believe this title has been violated shall be made by the agency unless, at least 30 days prior to the agency's consideration of the alleged violation, the business, service provider, contractor, or person alleged to have violated this title is notified of the violation by service of process or registered mail with return receipt requested, provided with a summary of the evidence, and informed of their right to be present in person and represented by counsel at any proceeding of the agency held for the purpose of considering whether probable cause exists for believing the person violated this title. Notice to the alleged violator shall be deemed made on the date of service, the date the registered mail receipt is signed, or if the registered mail receipt is not signed, the date returned by the post office. A proceeding held for the purpose of considering probable cause shall be private unless the alleged violator files with the agency a written request that the proceeding be public.

§ 1798.199.55.

(a) When the agency determines there is probable cause for believing this title has been violated, it shall hold a hearing to determine if a violation has or violations have occurred. Notice shall be given and the hearing conducted in accordance with the Administrative Procedure Act (Chapter 5 (commencing with Section 11500), Part 1, Division 3, Title 2, Government Code). The agency shall have all the powers granted by that chapter. If the agency determines on the basis of the hearing conducted pursuant to this subdivision that a violation or violations have occurred, it shall issue an order that may require the violator to do all or any of the following:

(1) Cease and desist violation of this title.

(2) Subject to Section 1798.155, pay an administrative fine of up to two thousand five hundred dollars ($2,500)

for each violation, or up to seven thousand five hundred dollars ($7,500) for each intentional violation and each violation involving the personal information of minor consumers to the Consumer Privacy Fund within the General Fund of the state. When the agency determines that no violation has occurred, it shall publish a declaration so stating.

(b) If two or more persons are responsible for any violation or violations, they shall be jointly and severally liable.

§ 1798.199.60.

Whenever the agency rejects the decision of an administrative law judge made pursuant to Section 11517 of the Government Code, the agency shall state the reasons in writing for rejecting the decision.

§ 1798.199.65.

The agency may subpoena witnesses, compel their attendance and testimony, administer oaths and affirmations, take evidence and require by subpoena the production of any books, papers, records, or other items material to the performance of the agency's duties or exercise of its powers, including, but not limited to, its power to audit a business' compliance with this title.

§ 1798.199.70.

No administrative action brought pursuant to this title alleging a violation of any of the provisions of this title shall be commenced more than five years after the date on which the violation occurred.

(a) The service of the probable cause hearing notice, as required by Section 1798.199.50, upon the person alleged to have violated this title shall constitute the commencement of the administrative action.

(b) If the person alleged to have violated this title engages in the fraudulent concealment of the person's acts or identity, the five-year period shall be tolled for the period of the concealment. For purposes of this subdivision, "fraudulent concealment" means the person knows of material facts related to the person's duties under this title and knowingly conceals them in performing or omitting to perform those duties for the purpose of defrauding the public of information to which it is entitled under this title.

(c) If, upon being ordered by a superior court to produce any documents sought by a subpoena in any administrative proceeding under this title, the person alleged to have violated this title fails to produce documents in response to the order by the date ordered to comply therewith, the five-year period shall be tolled for the period of the delay from the date of filing of the motion to compel until the date the documents are produced.

§ 1798.199.75.

(a) In addition to any other available remedies, the agency may bring a civil action and obtain a judgment in superior court for the purpose of collecting any unpaid administrative fines imposed pursuant to this title after exhaustion of judicial review of the agency's action. The action may be filed as a small claims, limited civil, or unlimited civil case depending on the jurisdictional amount. The venue for this action shall be in the county where the administrative fines were imposed by the agency. In order to obtain a judgment in a proceeding under this section, the agency shall show, following the procedures and rules of evidence as applied in ordinary civil actions, all of the following:

(1) That the administrative fines were imposed following the procedures set forth in this title and implementing regulations.

(2) That the defendant or defendants in the action were notified, by actual or constructive notice, of the imposition of the administrative fines.

(3) That a demand for payment has been made by the agency and full payment has not been received.

(b) A civil action brought pursuant to subdivision (a) shall be commenced within four years after the date on which the administrative fines were imposed.

§ 1798.199.80.

(a) If the time for judicial review of a final agency order or decision has lapsed, or if all means of judicial review of the order or decision have been exhausted, the agency may apply to the clerk of the court for a judgment to collect the administrative fines imposed by the order or decision, or the order as modified in accordance with a decision on judicial review.

(b) The application, which shall include a certified copy of the order or decision, or the order as modified in accordance with a decision on judicial review, and proof of service of the order or decision, constitutes a sufficient showing to warrant issuance of the judgment to collect the administrative fines. The clerk of the court shall enter the judgment immediately in conformity with the application.

(c) An application made pursuant to this section shall be made to the clerk of the superior court in the county where the administrative fines were imposed by the agency.

(d) A judgment entered in accordance with this section has the same force and effect as, and is subject to all the provisions of law relating to, a judgment in a civil action and may be enforced in the same manner as any other judgment of the court in which it is entered.

(e) The agency may bring an application pursuant to this section only within four years after the date on which all means of judicial review of the order or decision have been exhausted.

(f) The remedy available under this section is in addition to those available under any other law.

§ 1798.199.85.

Any decision of the agency with respect to a complaint or administrative fine shall be subject to judicial review in an action brought by an interested party to the complaint or administrative fine and shall be subject to an abuse of discretion standard.

§ 1798.199.90.

(a) Any business, service provider, contractor, or other person that violates this title shall be subject to an injunction and liable for a civil penalty of not more than two thousand five hundred dollars ($2,500) for each violation or seven thousand five hundred dollars ($7,500) for each intentional violation and each violation involving the personal information of minor consumers, as adjusted pursuant to paragraph (5) of subdivision (a) of Section 1798.185, which shall be assessed and recovered in a civil action brought in the name of the people of the State of California by the attorney general. The court may consider the good faith cooperation of the business, service provider, contractor, or other person in determining the amount of the civil penalty.

(b) Any civil penalty recovered by an action brought by the attorney general for a violation of this title, and the proceeds of any settlement of any said action, shall be deposited in the Consumer Privacy Fund.

(c) The agency shall, upon request by the attorney general, stay an administrative action or investigation under this title to permit the attorney general to proceed with an investigation or civil action and shall not pursue an administrative action or investigation, unless the attorney general subsequently determines not to pursue an investigation or civil action. The agency may not limit the authority of the attorney general to enforce this title.

(d) No civil action may be filed by the attorney general under this section for any violation of this title after the agency has issued a decision pursuant to Section 1798.199.85 or an order pursuant to Section 1798.199.55 against that person for the same violation.

(e) This section shall not affect the private right of action provided for in Section 1798.150.

§ 1798.199.95.

(a) There is hereby appropriated from the General Fund of the state to the agency the sum of five million dollars ($5,000,000) during the fiscal year 2020–2021, and the sum of ten million dollars ($10,000,000) adjusted for cost-of-living changes, during each fiscal year thereafter, for expenditure to support the operations of the agency pursuant to this title. The expenditure of funds under this appropriation shall be subject to the normal administrative review given to other state appropriations. The legislature shall appropriate those additional amounts to the commission and other agencies as may be necessary to carry out the provisions of this title.

(b) The department of finance, in preparing the state budget and the Budget Act bill submitted to the Legislature, shall include an item for the support of this title that shall indicate all of the following:

(1) The amounts to be appropriated to other agencies to carry out their duties under this title, which amounts shall be in augmentation of the support items of those agencies.

(2) The additional amounts required to be appropriated by the legislature to the agency to carry out the purposes of this title, as provided for in this section.

(3) In parentheses, for informational purposes, the continuing appropriation during each fiscal year of ten million dollars ($10,000,000), adjusted for cost-of-living changes made pursuant to this section.

(c) The attorney general shall provide staff support to the agency until the agency has hired its own staff. The attorney general shall be reimbursed by the agency for these services.

(Added November 3, 2020, by initiative Proposition 24, Sec. 24.18. Effective December 16, 2020. Operative December 16, 2020, pursuant to Sec. 31 of Proposition 24.)

§ 1798.199.100.

The agency and any court, as applicable, shall consider the good faith cooperation of the business, service provider, contractor, or other person in determining the amount of any administrative fine or civil penalty for a violation of this title. A business shall not be required by the agency, a court, or otherwise to pay both an administrative fine and a civil penalty for the same violation.

APPENDIX 2: COLORADO PRIVACY ACT

§ 6-1-13021. Short title.

The short title of this part 13 is the "Colorado Privacy Act".

§ 6-1-1302. Legislative declaration.

(1) The general assembly hereby:

(a) Finds that:

(i) The people of Colorado regard their privacy as a fundamental right and an essential element of their individual freedom;

(ii) Colorado's constitution explicitly provides the right to privacy under section 7 of Article II, and fundamental privacy rights have long been, and continue to be, integral to protecting Coloradans and to safeguarding our democratic republic;

(iii) Ongoing advances in technology have produced exponential growth in the volume and variety of personal data being generated, collected, stored, and analyzed and these advances present both promise and potential peril;

(iv) The ability to harness and use data in positive ways is driving innovation and brings beneficial technologies to society, but it has also created risks to privacy and freedom; and

(v) The unauthorized disclosure of personal information and loss of privacy can have devastating impacts ranging from financial fraud, identity theft, and unnecessary costs in personal time and finances to destruction of property, harassment, reputational damage, emotional distress, and physical harm;

(b) Determines that:

(i) Technological innovation and new uses of data can help solve societal problems and improve lives, and it is possible to build a world where technological innovation and privacy can coexist; and

(ii) States across the United States are looking to this part 13 and similar models to enact state-based data privacy requirements and to exercise the leadership that is lacking at the national level; and

(c) Declares that:

(i) By enacting this part 13, Colorado will be among the states that empower consumers to protect their privacy and require companies to be responsible custodians of data as they continue to innovate;

(ii) This part 13 addresses issues of statewide concern and:

(A) provides consumers the right to access, correct, and delete personal data and the right to opt out not only of the sale of personal data but also of the collection and use of personal data;

(B) Imposes an affirmative obligation upon companies to safeguard personal data; to provide clear, understandable, and transparent information to consumers about how their personal data are used; and to strengthen compliance and accountability by requiring data protection assessments in the collection and use of personal data; and

(C) Empowers the attorney general and district attorneys to access and evaluate a company's data protection assessments, to impose penalties where violations occur, and to prevent future violations.

§ 6-1-1303. Definitions.

As used in this part 13, unless the context otherwise requires:

(1) "Affiliate" means a legal entity that controls, is controlled by, or is under common control with another legal entity. As used in this subsection (1), "control" means: (a) ownership of, control of, or power to vote twenty-five percent or more of the outstanding shares of any class of voting security of the entity, directly or indirectly, or acting through one or more other persons; (b) Control in any manner over the election of a majority of the directors, trustees, or general partners of the entity or of individuals exercising similar functions; or (c) the power to exercise, directly or indirectly, a controlling influence over the management or policies of the entity as determined by the applicable prudential regulator, as that term is defined in 12 U.S.C. sec. 5481 (24), if any.

(2) "Authenticate" means to use reasonable means to determine that a request to exercise any of the rights in section 6-1-1306 (1) is being made by or on behalf of the consumer who is entitled to exercise the rights.

(3) "Business associate" has the meaning established in 45 CFR 160.103.

(4) "Child" means an individual under thirteen years of age.

(5) "Consent" means a clear, affirmative act signifying a consumer's freely given, specific, informed, and unambiguous agreement, such as by a written statement, including by electronic means, or other clear, affirmative action by which the consumer signifies agreement to the processing of personal data. The following does not constitute consent: (a) acceptance of a general or broad terms of use or similar document that contains descriptions of personal data processing along with other, unrelated information; (b) hovering over, muting, pausing, or closing a given piece of content; and (c) agreement obtained through dark patterns.

(6) "Consumer": (a) means an individual who is a Colorado resident acting only in an individual or household context; and (b) does not include an individual acting in a commercial or employment context, as a job applicant, or as a beneficiary of someone acting in an employment context.

(7) "Controller" means a person that, alone or jointly with others, determines the purposes for and means of processing personal data.

(8) "Covered Entity" has the meaning established in 45 CFR 160.103.

(9) "Dark pattern" means a user interface designed or manipulated with the substantial effect of subverting or impairing user autonomy, decision-making, or choice.

(10) "Decisions that produce legal or similarly significant effects concerning a consumer" means a decision that results in the provision or denial of financial or lending services, housing, insurance, education enrollment or opportunity, criminal justice, employment opportunities, health-care services, or access to essential goods or services.

(11) "De-identified data" means data that cannot reasonably be used to infer information about, or otherwise be linked to, an identified or identifiable individual, or a device linked to such an individual, if the controller that possesses the data: (a) takes reasonable measures to ensure that the data cannot be associated with an individual; (b) publicly commits to maintain and use the data only in a de-identified fashion and not attempt to re-identify the data; and (c) contractually obligates any recipients of the information to comply with the requirements of this subsection (11).

(12) "Health-care facility" means any entity that is licensed, certified, or otherwise authorized or permitted by law to administer medical treatment in this state.

(13) "Health-care Information" means individually identifiable information relating to the past, present, or future health status of an individual.

(14) “Health-Care Provider” means a person licensed, certified, or registered in this state to practice medicine, pharmacy, chiropractic, nursing, physical therapy, podiatry, dentistry, optometry, occupational therapy, or other healing arts under title 12.

(15) “HIPPA” means the federal “Health Insurance Portability and Accountability act of 1996”, as amended, 42 U.S.C. secs. 1320d to 1320d-9.

(16) “Identified or identifiable individual” means an individual who can be readily identified, directly or indirectly, in particular by reference to an identifier such as a name, an identification number, specific geolocation data, or an online identifier.

(17) “Personal data”: (a) means information that is linked or reasonably linkable to an identified or identifiable individual; and (b) does not include de-identified data or publicly available information. As used in this subsection (17)(b), “publicly available information” means information that is lawfully made available from federal, state, or local government records and information that a controller has a reasonable basis to believe the consumer has lawfully made available to the general public.

(18) “Process” or “processing” means the collection, use, sale, storage, disclosure, analysis, deletion, or modification of personal data and includes the actions of a controller directing a processor to process personal data.

(19) “Processor” means a person that processes personal data on behalf of a controller.

(20) “Profiling” means any form of automated processing of personal data to evaluate, analyze, or predict personal aspects concerning an identified or identifiable individual’s economic situation, health, personal preferences, interests, reliability, behavior, location, or movements.

(21) “Protected health information” has the meaning established in 45 CFR 160.03.

(22) “Pseudonymous data” means personal data that can no longer be attributed to a specific individual without the use of additional information if the additional information is kept separately and is subject to technical and organizational measures to ensure that the personal data are not attributed to a specific individual.

(23) (a) “Sale”, “sell”, or “sold” means the exchange of personal data for monetary or other valuable consideration by a controller to a third party. (b) “Sale”, “sell”, or “sold” does not include the following: (i) the disclosure of personal data to a processor that processes the personal data on behalf of a controller; (ii) the disclosure of personal data to a third party for purposes of providing a product or service requested by the consumer; (iii) the disclosure or transfer of personal data to an affiliate of the controller; (iv) the disclosure or transfer to a third party of personal data as an asset that is part of a proposed or actual merger, acquisition, bankruptcy, or other transaction in which the third party assumes control of all or part of the controller’s assets; or (v) the disclosure of personal data: (a) that a consumer directs the controller to disclose or intentionally discloses by using the controller to interact with a third party; or (b) intentionally made available by a consumer to the general public via a channel of mass media.

(24) “Sensitive data” means: (a) personal data revealing racial or ethnic origin, religious beliefs, a mental or physical health condition or diagnosis, sex life or sexual orientation, or citizenship or citizenship status; (b) genetic or biometric data that may be processed for the purpose of uniquely identifying an individual; or (c) personal data from a known child.

(25) “Targeted advertising”: (a) means displaying to a consumer an advertisement that is selected based on personal data obtained or inferred over time from the consumer’s activities across nonaffiliated websites, applications, or online services to predict consumer preferences or interests; and (b) does not include: (i) advertising to a consumer in response to the consumer’s request for information or feedback;

(ii) advertisements based on activities within a controller's own websites or online applications; (iii) advertisements based on the context of a consumer's current search query, visit to a website, or online application; or (iv) processing personal data solely for measuring or reporting advertising performance, reach, or frequency.

(26) "Third party" means a person, public authority, agency, or body other than a consumer, controller, processor, or affiliate of the processor or the controller.

§ 6-1-1304. Applicability of part.

(1) Except as specified in subsection (2) of this section, this part 13 applies to a controller that: (a) conducts business in Colorado or produces or delivers commercial products or services that are intentionally targeted to residents of Colorado; and (b) satisfies one or both of the following thresholds: (i) controls or processes the personal data of one hundred thousand consumers or more during a calendar year; or (ii) derives revenue or receives a discount on the price of goods or services from the sale of personal data and processes or controls the personal data of twenty-five thousand consumers or more.

(2) This part 13 does not apply to:

(a) Protected health information that is collected, stored, and processed by a covered entity or its business associates;

(b) Health-care information that is governed by part 8 of article 1 of title 25 solely for the purpose of access to medical records;

(c) Patient identifying information, as defined in 42 CFR 2.11, that are governed by and collected and processed pursuant to 42 CFR 2, established pursuant to 42 U.S.C. sec. 290dd-2;

(d) Identifiable private information, as defined in 45 CFR 46.102, for purposes of the federal policy for the protection of human subjects pursuant to 45 CFR 46; identifiable private information that is collected as part of human subjects research pursuant to the ICH E6 good clinical practice guideline issued by the International Council for Harmonisation of Technical Requirements for Pharmaceuticals for Human Use or the protection of human subjects under 21 CFR 50 and 56; or personal data used or shared in research conducted in accordance with one or more of the categories set forth in this subsection (2)(d);

(e) Information and documents created by a covered entity for purposes of complying with HIPAA and its implementing regulations;

(f) Patient safety work product, as defined in 42 CFR 3.20, that is created for purposes of patient safety improvement pursuant to 42 CFR 3, established pursuant to 42 U.S.C. secs. 299b-21 to 299b-26;

(g) Information that is: (i) de-identified in accordance with the requirements for de-identification set forth in 45 CFR 164; and (ii) derived from any of the health-care-related information described in this section.

(h) Information maintained in the same manner as information under subsections (2)(a) to (2)(g) of this section by: (i) a covered entity or business associate; (ii) a health-care facility or health-care provider; or (iii) a program of a qualified service organization as defined in 42 CFR 2.11;

(i) (i) Except as provided in subsection (2)(i)(ii) of this section, an activity involving the collection, maintenance, disclosure, sale, communication, or use of any personal data bearing on a consumer's creditworthiness, credit standing, credit capacity, character, general reputation, personal characteristics, or mode of living by: (a) a consumer reporting agency as defined in 15 U.S.C. sec. 1681a(f); (b) a furnisher of information as set forth in 15 U.S.C. sec. 1681s-2 that provides information for use in a consumer report, as defined in 15 U.S.C. sec. 1681a(d); or (c) a user of a consumer report as set forth in 15 U.S.C. sec. 1681b. (ii) this subsection

(2)(i) applies only to the extent that the activity is regulated by the federal "Fair Credit Reporting Act", 15 U.S.C. sec. 1681 et seq., as amended, and the personal data are not collected, maintained, disclosed, sold, communicated, or used except as authorized by the federal "Fair Credit Reporting Act", as amended.

(j) Personal data: (i) collected and maintained for purposes of article 22 of title 10; (ii) collected, processed, sold, or disclosed pursuant to the federal "Gramm-Leach-Bliley Act", 15 U.S.C. sec. 6801 et seq., as amended, and implementing regulations, if the collection, processing, sale, or disclosure is in compliance with that law; (iii) collected, processed, sold, or disclosed pursuant to the federal "Driver's Privacy Protection Act of 1994", 18 U.S.C. sec. 2721 et seq., as amended, if the collection, processing, sale, or disclosure is regulated by that law, including implementing rules, regulations, or exemptions; (iv) regulated by the federal "Children's Online Privacy Protection Act of 1998", 15 U.S.C. secs. 6501 to 6506, as amended, if collected, processed, and maintained in compliance with that law; or (v) regulated by the federal "Family Educational Rights and Privacy Act of 1974", 20 U.S.C. sec. 1232g et seq., as amended, and its implementing regulations;

(k) Data maintained for employment records purposes;

(l) An air carrier as defined in and regulated under 49 U.S.C. sec. 40101 et seq., as amended, and 49 U.S.C. sec. 41713, as amended;

(m) A national securities association registered pursuant to the federal "Securities Exchange Act of 1934", 15 U.S.C. sec. 78o-3, as amended, or implementing regulations;

(n) Customer data maintained by a public utility as defined in section 40-1-103 (1)(a)(I) or an authority as defined in section 43-4-503(1), if the data are not collected, maintained, disclosed, sold, communicated, or used except as authorized by state and federal law;

(o) Data maintained by a state institution of higher education, as defined in section 23-18-102(10), the state, the judicial department of the state, or a county, city and county, or municipality if the data is collected, maintained, disclosed, communicated, and used as authorized by state and federal law for noncommercial purposes. This subsection (2)(o) does not effect any other exemption available under this part 13.

(p) Information used and disclosed in compliance with 45 CFR 164.512; or

(q) A financial institution or an affiliate of a financial institution as defined by and that is subject to the federal "Gramm-Leach-Bliley Act", 15 U.S.C. sec. 6801 et seq., as amended, and implementing regulations, including Regulation P, 12 CFR 1016.

(3) The obligations imposed on controllers or processors under this part 13 do not:

(a) Restrict a controller's or processor's ability to: (i) comply with federal, state, or local laws, rules, or regulations; (ii) comply with a civil, criminal, or regulatory inquiry, investigation, subpoena, or summons by federal, state, local, or other governmental authorities; (iii) cooperate with law enforcement agencies concerning conduct or activity that the controller or processor reasonably and in good faith believes may violate federal, state, or local law; (iv) investigate, exercise, prepare for, or defend actual or anticipated legal claims; (v) conduct internal research to improve, repair, or develop products, services, or technology; (vi) identify and repair technical errors that impair existing or intended functionality; (vii) perform internal operations that are reasonably aligned with the expectations of the consumer based on the consumer's existing relationship with the controller; (viii) provide a product or service specifically requested by a consumer or the parent or guardian of a child, perform a contract to which the consumer is a party, or take steps at the request of the consumer prior to entering into a contract; (ix) protect the vital interests of the consumer or of another individual; (x) prevent, detect, protect against, or respond to security incidents, identity theft, fraud, harassment, or malicious, deceptive, or illegal activity; preserve the integrity or security of systems; or investigate, report, or prosecute those responsible for any such action; (xi) process personal data for reasons of public interest in the area of public health, but solely to the extent that the processing: (A) is subject to suitable and specific measures to safeguard the rights of the consumer whose personal data are processed; and (B) is under the responsibility of a professional subject to confidentiality obligations under federal, state, or local law; or (xii) assist another person with any of the activities set forth in this subsection (3);

(b) Apply where compliance by the controller or processor with this part 13 would violate an evidentiary privilege under Colorado law;

(c) Prevent a controller or processor from providing personal data concerning a consumer to a person covered by an evidentiary privilege under Colorado law as part of a privileged communication;

(d) Apply to information made available by a third party that the controller has a reasonable basis to believe is protected speech pursuant to applicable law; and

(e) Apply to the processing of personal data by an individual in the course of a purely personal or household activity.

(4) Personal data that are processed by a controller pursuant to an exception provided by this section:

(a) shall not be processed for any purpose other than a purpose expressly listed in this section or as otherwise authorized by this part 13; and

(b) shall be processed solely to the extent that the processing is necessary, reasonable, and proportionate to the specific purpose or purposes listed in this section or as otherwise authorized by this part 13.

(5) If a controller processes personal data pursuant to an exemption in this section, the controller bears the burden of demonstrating that the processing qualifies for the exemption and complies with the requirements in subsection (4) of this section.

§ 6-1-1305. Responsibility according to role.

(1) Controllers and processors shall meet their respective obligations established under this part 13.

(2) Processors shall adhere to the instructions of the controller and assist the controller to meet its obligations under this part 13. Taking into account the nature of processing and the information available to the processor, the processor shall assist the controller by:

(a) Taking appropriate technical and organizational measures, insofar as this is possible, for the fulfillment of the controller's obligation to respond to consumer requests to exercise their rights pursuant to section 6-1-1306;

(b) Helping to meet the controller's obligations in relation to the security of processing the personal data and in relation to the notification of a breach of the security of the system pursuant to section 6-1-716; and

(c) Providing information to the controller necessary to enable the controller to conduct and document any data protection assessments required by section 6-1-1309. The controller and processor are each responsible for only the measures allocated to them.

(3) Notwithstanding the instructions of the controller, a processor shall:

(a) Ensure that each person processing the personal data is subject to a duty of confidentiality with respect to the data; and

(b) Engage a subcontractor only after providing the controller with an opportunity to object and pursuant to a written contract in accordance with subsection (5) of this section that requires the subcontractor to meet the obligations of the processor with respect to the personal data.

(4) Taking into account the context of processing, the controller and the processor shall implement appropriate technical and organizational measures to ensure a level of security appropriate to the risk and establish a clear allocation of the responsibilities between them to implement the measures.

(5) Processing by a processor must be governed by a contract between the controller and the processor that is binding on both parties and that sets out:

(a) The processing instructions to which the processor is bound, including the nature and purpose of the processing;

(b) The type of personal data subject to the processing, and the duration of the processing;

(c) The requirements imposed by this subsection (5) and subsections (3) and (4) of this section; and

(d) The following requirements: (i) at the choice of the controller, the processor shall delete or return all personal data to the controller as requested at the end of the provision of services, unless retention of the personal data is required by law; (ii) (A) the processor shall make available to the controller all information necessary to demonstrate compliance with the obligations in this part 13; and (B) the processor shall allow for, and contribute to, reasonable audits and inspections by the controller or the controller's designated auditor. Alternatively, the processor may, with the controller's consent, arrange for a qualified and independent auditor to conduct, at least annually and at the processor's expense, an audit of the processor's policies and technical and organizational measures in support of the obligations under this part 13 using an appropriate and accepted control standard or framework and audit procedure for the audits as applicable. The processor shall provide a report of the audit to the controller upon request.

(6) In no event may a contract relieve a controller or a processor from the liabilities imposed on them by virtue of its role in the processing relationship as defined by this part 13.

(7) Determining whether a person is acting as a controller or processor with respect to a specific processing of data is a fact-based determination that depends upon the context in which personal data are to be processed. A person that is not limited in its processing of personal data pursuant to a controller's instructions, or that fails to adhere to the instructions, is a controller and not a processor with respect to a specific processing of data. A processor that continues to adhere to a controller's instructions with respect to a specific processing of personal data remains a processor. If a processor begins, alone or jointly with others, determining the purposes and means of the processing of personal data, it is a controller with respect to the processing.

(8) (a) A controller or processor that discloses personal data to another controller or processor in compliance with this part 13 does not violate this part 13 if the recipient processes the personal data in violation of this part 13, and, at the time of disclosing the personal data, the disclosing controller or processor did not have actual knowledge that the recipient intended to commit a violation.

(b) A controller or processor receiving personal data from a controller or processor in compliance with this part 13 as specified in subsection (8)(a) of this section does not violate this part 13 if the controller or processor from which it receives the personal data fails to comply with applicable obligations under this part 13.

§ 6-1-1306. Consumer personal data rights - repeal.

(1) Consumers may exercise the following rights by submitting a request using the methods specified by the controller in the privacy notice required under section 6-1-1308(1)(a). The method must take into account the ways in which consumers normally interact with the controller, the need for secure and reliable communication relating to the request, and the ability of the controller to authenticate the identity of the consumer making the request. Controllers shall not require a consumer to create a new account in order to exercise consumer rights pursuant to this section but may require a consumer to use an existing account. A consumer may submit a

request at any time to a controller specifying which of the following rights the consumer wishes to exercise:

(a) Right to opt out.

(i) A consumer has the right to opt out of the processing of personal data concerning the consumer for purposes of: (A) targeted advertising; (B) the sale of personal data; or (C) profiling in furtherance of decisions that produce legal or similarly significant effects concerning a consumer.

(ii) A consumer may authorize another person, acting on the consumer's behalf, to opt out of the processing of the consumer's personal data for one or more of the purposes specified in subsection (1)(a)(i) of this section, including through a technology indicating the consumer's intent to opt out such as a web link indicating a preference or browser setting, browser extension, or global device setting. A controller shall comply with an opt-out request received from a person authorized by the consumer to act on the consumer's behalf if the controller is able to authenticate, with commercially reasonable effort, the identity of the consumer and the authorized agent's authority to act on the consumer's behalf.

(iii) A controller that processes personal data for purposes of targeted advertising or the sale of personal data shall provide a clear and conspicuous method to exercise the right to opt out of the processing of personal data concerning the consumer pursuant to subsection (1)(a)(i) of this section. The controller shall provide the opt-out method clearly and conspicuously in any privacy notice required to be provided to consumers under this part 13, and in a clear, conspicuous, and readily accessible location outside the privacy notice.

(iv) (A) A controller that processes personal data for purposes of targeted advertising or the sale of personal data may allow consumers to exercise the right to opt out of the processing of personal data concerning the consumer for purposes of targeted advertising or the sale of personal data pursuant to subsections (1)(a)(i)(A) and (1)(a)(i)(B) of this section by controllers through a user-selected universal opt-out mechanism that meets the technical specifications established by the attorney general pursuant to section 6-1-1313. This subsection (1)(a)(iv)(A) is repealed, effective July 1, 2024. (B) Effective July 1, 2024, a controller that processes personal data for purposes of targeted advertising or the sale of personal data shall allow consumers to exercise the right to opt out of the processing of personal data concerning the consumer for purposes of targeted advertising or the sale of personal data pursuant to subsections (1)(a)(i)(A) and (1)(a)(i)(B) of this section by controllers through a user-selected universal opt-out mechanism that meets the technical specifications established by the attorney general pursuant to section 6-1-1313. (C) Notwithstanding a consumer's decision to exercise the right to opt out of the processing of personal data through a universal opt-out mechanism pursuant to subsection (1)(a)(iv)(B) of this section, a controller may enable the consumer to consent, through a web page, application, or a similar method, to the processing of the consumer's personal data for purposes of targeted advertising or the sale of personal data, and the consent takes precedence over any choice reflected through the universal opt-out mechanism. Before obtaining a consumer's consent to process personal data for purposes of targeted advertising or the sale of personal data pursuant to this subsection (1)(a)(iv)(C), a controller shall provide the consumer with a clear and conspicuous notice informing the consumer about the choices available under this section, describing the categories of personal data to be processed and the purposes for which they will be processed, and explaining how and where the consumer may withdraw consent. The web page, application, or other means by which a controller obtains a consumer's consent to process personal data for purposes of targeted advertising or the sale of personal data must also allow the consumer to revoke the consent as easily as it is affirmatively provided.

(b) **Right of access.** A consumer has the right to confirm whether a controller is processing personal data concerning the consumer and to access the consumer's personal data.

(c) **Right to correction.** A consumer has the right to correct inaccuracies in the consumer's personal data, taking into account the nature of the personal data and the purposes of the processing of the consumer's personal data.

(d) **Right to deletion.** A consumer has the right to delete personal data concerning the consumer.

(e) **Right to data portability.** When exercising the right to access personal data pursuant to subsection (1)(b) of this section, a consumer has the right to obtain the personal data in a portable and, to the extent technically feasible, readily usable format that allows the consumer to transmit the data to another entity without hindrance. A consumer may exercise this right no more than two times per calendar year. Nothing in this subsection (1)(e) requires a controller to provide the data to the consumer in a manner that would disclose the controller's trade secrets.

(2) **Responding to consumer requests.**

(a) a controller shall inform a consumer of any action taken on a request under subsection (1) of this section without undue delay and, in any event, within forty-five days after receipt of the request. The controller may extend the forty-five day period by forty-five additional days where reasonably necessary, taking into account the complexity and number of the requests. The controller shall inform the consumer of an extension within forty-five days after receipt of the request, together with the reasons for the delay.

(b) If a controller does not take action on the request of a consumer, the controller shall inform the consumer, without undue delay and, at the latest, within forty-five days after receipt of the request, of the reasons for not taking action and instructions for how to appeal the decision with the controller as described in subsection (3) of this section.

(c) Upon request, a controller shall provide to the consumer the information specified in this section free of charge; except that, for a second or subsequent request within a twelve-month period, the controller may charge an amount calculated in the manner specified in section 24-72-205(5)(a).

(d) A controller is not required to comply with a request to exercise any of the rights under subsection (1) of this section if the controller is unable to authenticate the request using commercially reasonable efforts, in which case the controller may request the provision of additional information reasonably necessary to authenticate the request.

(3) (a) A controller shall establish an internal process whereby consumers may appeal a refusal to take action on a request to exercise any of the rights under subsection (1) of this section within a reasonable period after the consumer's receipt of the notice sent by the controller under subsection (2)(b) of this section. The appeal process must be conspicuously available and as easy to use as the process for submitting a request under this section.

(b) Within forty-five days after receipt of an appeal, a controller shall inform the consumer of any action taken or not taken in response to the appeal, along with a written explanation of the reasons in support of the response. The controller may extend the forty-five day period by sixty additional days where reasonably necessary, taking into account the complexity and number of requests serving as the basis for the appeal. The controller shall inform the consumer of an extension within forty-five days after receipt of the appeal, together with the reasons for the delay.

(c) The controller shall inform the consumer of the consumer's ability to contact the attorney general if the consumer has concerns about the result of the appeal.

§ 6-1-1307. Processing de-identified data.

(1) This part 13 does not require a controller or processor to do any of the following solely for purposes of complying with this part 13:

(a) Reidentify de-identified data;

(b) Comply with an authenticated consumer request to access, correct, delete, or provide personal data in a portable format pursuant to section 6-1-1306(1), if all of the following are true: (i) (A) the controller is not reasonably capable of associating the request with the personal data; or (B) it would be unreasonably burdensome for the controller to associate the request with the personal data; (II) the controller does not use the personal data to recognize or respond to the specific consumer who is the subject of the personal data or associate the personal data with other personal data about the same specific consumer; and (iii) the controller does not sell the personal data to any third party or otherwise voluntarily disclose the personal data to any third party, except as otherwise authorized by the consumer; or

(c) maintain data in identifiable form or collect, obtain, retain, or access any data or technology in order to enable the controller to associate an authenticated consumer request with personal data.

(2) A controller that uses de-identified data shall exercise reasonable oversight to monitor compliance with any contractual commitments to which the de-identified data are subject and shall take appropriate steps to address any breaches of contractual commitments.

(3) The rights contained in section 6-1-1306(1)(b) to (1)(e) do not apply to pseudonymous data if the controller can demonstrate that the information necessary to identify the consumer is kept separately and is subject to effective technical and organizational controls that prevent the controller from accessing the information.

§ 6-1-1308. Duties of controllers.

(1) **Duty of Transparency.**

(a) A controller shall provide consumers with a reasonably accessible, clear, and meaningful privacy notice that includes: (i) the categories of personal data collected or processed by the controller or a processor; (ii) the purposes for which the categories of personal data are processed; (iii) how and where consumers may exercise the rights pursuant to section 6-1-1306, including the controller's contact information and how a consumer may appeal a controller's action with regard to the consumer's request; (iv) the categories of personal data that the controller shares with third parties, if any; and (v) the categories of third parties, if any, with whom the controller shares personal data.

(b) If a controller sells personal data to third parties or processes personal data for targeted advertising, the controller shall clearly and conspicuously disclose the sale or processing, as well as the manner in which a consumer may exercise the right to opt out of the sale or processing.

(c) A controller shall not: (i) require a consumer to create a new account in order to exercise a right; or (ii) based solely on the exercise of a right and unrelated to feasibility or the value of a service, increase the cost of, or decrease the availability of, the product or service.

(d) Nothing in this part 13 shall be construed to require a controller to provide a product or service that requires the personal data of a consumer that the controller does not collect or maintain or to prohibit a controller from offering a different price, rate, level, quality, or selection of goods or services to a consumer, including offering goods or services for no fee, if the offer is related to a consumer's voluntary participation in a bona fide loyalty, rewards, premium features, discount, or club card program.

(2) **Duty of purpose specification.** A controller shall specify the express purposes for which personal data are collected and processed.

(3) **Duty of data minimization.** A controller's collection of personal data must be adequate, relevant, and limited to what is reasonably necessary in relation to the specified purposes for which the data are processed.

(4) **Duty to avoid secondary use.** A controller shall not process personal data for purposes that are not reasonably necessary to or compatible with the specified purposes for which the personal data are processed, unless the controller first obtains the consumer's consent.

(5) **Duty of care.** A controller shall take reasonable measures to secure personal data during both storage and use from unauthorized acquisition. The data security practices must be appropriate to the volume, scope, and nature of the personal data processed and the nature of the business.

(6) **Duty to avoid unlawful discrimination.** A controller shall not process personal data in violation of state or federal laws that prohibit unlawful discrimination against consumers.

(7) **Duty regarding sensitive data.** A controller shall not process a consumer's sensitive data without first obtaining the consumer's consent or, in the case of the processing of personal data concerning a known child, without first obtaining consent from the child's parent or lawful guardian.

§ 6-1-1309. Data protection assessments - attorney general access and evaluation - definition.

(1) A controller shall not conduct processing that presents a heightened risk of harm to a consumer without conducting and documenting a data protection assessment of each of its processing activities that involve personal data acquired on or after the effective date of this section that present a heightened risk of harm to a consumer.

(2) For purposes of this section, "processing that presents a heightened risk of harm to a consumer" includes the following:

(a) Processing personal data for purposes of targeted advertising or for profiling if the profiling presents a reasonably foreseeable risk of: (i) unfair or deceptive treatment of, or unlawful disparate impact on, consumers; (ii) financial or physical injury to consumers; (iii) a physical or other intrusion upon the solitude or seclusion, or the private affairs or concerns, of consumers if the intrusion would be offensive to a reasonable person; or (iv) other substantial injury to consumers;

(b) Selling personal data; and

(c) Processing sensitive data.

(3) Data protection assessments must identify and weigh the benefits that may flow, directly and indirectly, from the processing to the controller, the consumer, other stakeholders, and the public against the potential risks to the rights of the consumer associated with the processing, as mitigated by safeguards that the controller can employ to reduce the risks. The controller shall factor into this assessment the use of de-identified data and the reasonable expectations of consumers, as well as the context of the processing and the relationship between the controller and the consumer whose personal data will be processed.

(4) A controller shall make the data protection assessment available to the attorney general upon request. The attorney general may evaluate the data protection assessment for compliance with the duties contained in section 6-1-1308 and with other laws, including this article 1. Data protection assessments are confidential and exempt from public inspection and copying under the "Colorado Open Records Act", part 2 of article 72 of title 24. The disclosure of a data protection assessment pursuant to a request from the attorney general under this subsection (4) does not constitute a waiver of any attorney-client privilege or work-product protection that might otherwise exist with respect to the assessment and any information contained in the assessment.

(5) A single data protection assessment may address a comparable set of processing operations that include similar activities.

(6) Data protection assessment requirements apply to processing activities created or generated after July 1,

2023, and are not retroactive.

§ 6-1-1310. Liability.

(1) Notwithstanding any provision in part 1 of this article 1, this part 13 does not authorize a private right of action for a violation of this part 13 or any other provision of law. This subsection (1) neither relieves any party from any duties or obligations imposed, nor alters any independent rights that consumers have, under other laws, including this article 1, the state constitution, or the United States Constitution.

(2) Where more than one controller or processor, or both a controller and a processor, involved in the same processing violates this part 13, the liability shall be allocated among the parties according to principles of comparative fault.

6-1-1311. Enforcement - penalties - repeal.

(1) (a) Notwithstanding any other provision of this article 1, the attorney general and district attorneys have exclusive authority to enforce this part 13 by bringing an action in the name of the state or as parens patriae on behalf of persons residing in the state to enforce this part 13 as provided in this article 1, including seeking an injunction to enjoin a violation of this part 13.

(b) Notwithstanding any other provision of this article 1, nothing in this part 13 shall be construed as providing the basis for, or being subject to, a private right of action for violations of this part 13 or any other law.

(c) For purposes only of enforcement of this part 13 by the attorney general or a district attorney, a violation of this part 13 is a deceptive trade practice.

(d) prior to any enforcement action pursuant to subsection (1)(a) of this section, the attorney general or district attorney must issue a notice of violation to the controller if a cure is deemed possible. If the controller fails to cure the violation within sixty days after receipt of the notice of violation, an action may be brought pursuant to this section. This subsection (1)(d) is repealed, effective January 1, 2025.

(2) The state treasurer shall credit all receipts from the imposition of civil penalties under this part 13 pursuant to section 24-31-108.

§ 6-1-1312. Preemption - local governments.

This part 13 supersedes and preempts laws, ordinances, resolutions, regulations, or the equivalent adopted by any statutory or home rule municipality, county, or city and county regarding the processing of personal data by controllers or processors.

§ 6-1-1313. Rules - opt-out mechanism.

(1) The attorney general may promulgate rules for the purpose of carrying out this part 13.

(2) By July 1, 2023, the attorney general shall adopt rules that detail the technical specifications for one or more universal opt-out mechanisms that clearly communicate a consumer's affirmative, freely given, and unambiguous choice to opt out of the processing of personal data for purposes of targeted advertising or the sale of personal data pursuant to section 6-1-1306(1)(a)(i)(A) or (1)(a)(i)(B). The attorney general may update the rules that detail the technical specifications for the mechanisms from time to time to reflect the means by which consumers interact with controllers. The rules must:

(a) Not permit the manufacturer of a platform, browser, device, or any other product offering a universal opt-out mechanism to unfairly disadvantage another controller;

(b) Require controllers to inform consumers about the opt-out choices available under section 6-1-1306(1)(a)(i);

(c) Not adopt a mechanism that is a default setting, but rather clearly represents the consumer's affirmative, freely given, and unambiguous choice to opt out of the processing of personal data pursuant to section 6-1-1306(1)(a)(i)(A) or (1)(a)(i)(B);

(d) Adopt a mechanism that is consumer-friendly, clearly described, and easy to use by the average consumer;

(e) Adopt a mechanism that is as consistent as possible with any other similar mechanism required by law or regulation in the United States; and

(f) Permit the controller to accurately authenticate the consumer as a resident of this state and determine that the mechanism represents a legitimate request to opt out of the processing of personal data for purposes of targeted advertising or the sale of personal data pursuant to section 6-1-1306(1)(a)(i)(A) or (1)(a)(i)(B).

(3) By January 1, 2025, the attorney general may adopt rules that govern the process of issuing opinion letters and interpretive guidance to develop an operational framework for business that includes a good faith reliance defense of an action that may otherwise constitute a violation of this part 13. The rules must become effective by July 1, 2025.

Section 2.

In Colorado Revised Statutes, amend 6-1-104 as follows:

6-1-104. Cooperative reporting. The district attorneys may cooperate in a statewide reporting system by receiving, on forms provided by the attorney general, complaints from persons concerning deceptive trade practices listed in section 6-1-105 or part 7 or 13 of this article 1 and transmitting the complaints to the attorney general.

Section 3.

In Colorado Revised Statutes, 6-1-105, add (1)(nnn) as follows:

6-1-105. Unfair or deceptive trade practices. (1) A person engages in a deceptive trade practice when, in the course of the person's business, vocation, or occupation, the person: (nnn) Violates any provision of part 13 of this article 1 as specified in section 6-1-1311(1)(c).

Section 4.

In Colorado Revised Statutes, 6-1-107, amend (1) introductory portion as follows:

6-1-107. Powers of attorney general and district attorneys. (1) When the attorney general or a district attorney has reasonable cause to believe that any person, whether in this state or elsewhere, has engaged in or is engaging in any deceptive trade practice listed in section 6-1-105 or part 7 or 13 of this article 1, the attorney general or district attorney may:

Section 5.

In Colorado Revised Statutes, 6-1-108, amend (1) as follows:

6-1-108. Subpoenas – hearings – rules. (1) When the attorney general or a district attorney has reasonable cause to believe that a person, whether in this state or elsewhere, has engaged in or is engaging in a deceptive trade practice listed in section 6-1-105 or part 7 or 13 of this article 1, the attorney general or a district attorney, in addition to other powers conferred upon the attorney general or a district attorney by this article 1, may issue subpoenas to require the attendance of witnesses or the production of documents, administer oaths, conduct hearings in aid of any investigation or inquiry, and prescribe such forms and promulgate such rules as may be necessary to administer the provisions of this article 1.

Section 6.

In Colorado Revised Statutes, 6-1-110, amend (1) and (2) as follows:

6-1-110. Restraining orders – injunctions – assurances of discontinuance. (1) Whenever the attorney general or a district attorney has cause to believe that a person has engaged in or is engaging in any deceptive trade practice listed in section 6-1-105 or part 7 or 13 of this article 1, the attorney general or district attorney may apply for and obtain, in an action in the appropriate district court of this state, a temporary restraining order or injunction, or both, pursuant to the Colorado rules of civil procedure, prohibiting the person from continuing the practices, or engaging therein, or doing any act in furtherance thereof. The court may make such orders or judgments as may be necessary to prevent the use or employment by the person of any such deceptive trade practice or that may be necessary to completely compensate or restore to the original position of any person injured by means of any such practice or to prevent any unjust enrichment by any person through the use or employment of any deceptive trade practice.

(2) Where the attorney general or a district attorney has authority to institute a civil action or other proceeding pursuant to the provisions of this article 1, the attorney general or district attorney may accept, in lieu thereof or as a part thereof, an assurance of discontinuance of any deceptive trade practice listed in section 6-1-105 or part 7 or 13 of this article 1. The assurance may include a stipulation for the voluntary payment by the alleged violator of the costs of investigation and any action or proceeding by the attorney general or a district attorney and any amount necessary to restore to any person any money or property that may have been acquired by the alleged violator by means of any such deceptive trade practice. Any such assurance of discontinuance accepted by the attorney general or a district attorney and any such stipulation filed with the court as a part of any such action or proceeding is a matter of public record unless the attorney general or the district attorney determines, at the discretion of the attorney general or the district attorney, that it will be confidential to the parties to the action or proceeding and to the court and its employees. Upon the filing of a civil action by the attorney general or a district attorney alleging that a confidential assurance of discontinuance or stipulation accepted pursuant to this subsection (2) has been violated, the assurance of discontinuance or stipulation becomes a public record and open to inspection by any person. Proof by a preponderance of the evidence of a violation of any such assurance or stipulation shall constitutes prima facie evidence of a deceptive trade practice for the purposes of any civil action or proceeding brought thereafter by the attorney general or a district attorney, whether a new action or a subsequent motion or petition in any pending action or proceeding.

Section 7. Act subject to petition – effective date – applicability. (1) This act takes effect July 1, 2023; except that, if a referendum petition is filed pursuant to section 1 (3) of article V of the state constitution against this act or an item, section, or part of this act within the ninety-day period after final adjournment of the general assembly, then the act, item, section, or part will not take effect unless approved by the people at the general election to be held in November 2022 and, in such case, will take effect July 1, 2023, or on the date of the official declaration of the vote thereon by the governor, whichever is later. (2) This act applies to conduct occurring on or after the applicable effective date of this act.

APPENDIX 3: CONNECTICUT DATA PRIVACY ACT

Section 1. (NEW) (Effective July 1, 2023)

As used in this section and sections 2 to 11, inclusive, of this act, unless the context otherwise requires:

(1) "Affiliate" means a legal entity that shares common branding with another legal entity or controls, is controlled by or is under common control with another legal entity. For the purposes of this subdivision, "control" or "controlled" means (A) ownership of, or the power to vote, more than fifty per cent of the outstanding shares of any class of voting security of a company, (B) control in any manner over the election of a majority of the directors or of individuals exercising similar functions, or (C) the power to exercise controlling influence over the management of a company.

(2) "Authenticate" means to use reasonable means to determine that a request to exercise any of the rights afforded under subdivisions (1) to (4), inclusive, of subsection (a) of section 4 of this act is being made by, or on behalf of, the consumer who is entitled to exercise such consumer rights with respect to the personal data at issue.

(3) "Biometric data" means data generated by automatic measurements of an individual's biological characteristics, such as a fingerprint, a voiceprint, eye retinas, irises or other unique biological patterns or characteristics that are used to identify a specific individual. "Biometric data" does not include (A) a digital or physical photograph, (B) an audio or video recording, or (C) any data generated from a digital or physical photograph, or an audio or video recording, unless such data is generated to identify a specific individual.

(4) "Business associate" has the same meaning as provided in HIPAA.

(5) "Child" has the same meaning as provided in COPPA.

(6) "Consent" means a clear affirmative act signifying a consumer's freely given, specific, informed and unambiguous agreement to allow the processing of personal data relating to the consumer. "Consent" may include a written statement, including by electronic means, or any other unambiguous affirmative action. "Consent" does not include (A) acceptance of a general or broad terms of use or similar document that contains descriptions of personal data processing along with other, unrelated information, (B) hovering over, muting, pausing or closing a given piece of content, or (C) agreement obtained through the use of dark patterns.

(7) "Consumer" means an individual who is a resident of this state. "Consumer" does not include an individual acting in a commercial or employment context or as an employee, owner, director, officer or contractor of a company, partnership, sole proprietorship, nonprofit or government agency whose communications or transactions with the controller occur solely within the context of that individual's role with the company, partnership, sole proprietorship, nonprofit or government agency.

(8) "Controller" means an individual who, or legal entity that, alone or jointly with others determines the purpose and means of processing personal data.

(9) "COPPA" means the Children's Online Privacy Protection Act of 1998, 15 USC 6501 et seq., and the regulations, rules, guidance and exemptions adopted pursuant to said act, as said act and such regulations, rules, guidance and exemptions may be amended from time to time.

(10) "Covered entity" has the same meaning as provided in HIPAA.

(11) "Dark pattern" (A) means a user interface designed or manipulated with the substantial effect of subverting or impairing user autonomy, decision-making or choice, and (B) includes, but is not limited to, any practice the Federal Trade Commission refers to as a "dark pattern".

(12) "Decisions that produce legal or similarly significant effects concerning the consumer" means decisions made by the controller that result in the provision or denial by the controller of financial or lending services, housing, insurance, education enrollment or opportunity, criminal justice, employment opportunities, health care services or access to essential goods or services.

(13) "De-identified data" means data that cannot reasonably be used to infer information about, or otherwise be linked to, an identified or identifiable individual, or a device linked to such individual, if the controller that possesses such data (A) takes reasonable measures to ensure that such data cannot be associated with an individual, (B) publicly commits to process such data only in a de-identified fashion and not attempt to re-identify such data, and (C) contractually obligates any recipients of such data to satisfy the criteria set forth in subparagraphs (A) and (B) of this subdivision.

(14) "HIPAA" means the Health Insurance Portability and Accountability Act of 1996, 42 USC 1320d et seq., as amended from time to time.

(15) "Identified or identifiable individual" means an individual who can be readily identified, directly or indirectly.

(16) "Institution of higher education" means any individual who, or school, board, association, limited liability company or corporation that, is licensed or accredited to offer one or more programs of higher learning leading to one or more degrees.

(17) "Nonprofit organization" means any organization that is exempt from taxation under Section 501(c)(3), 501(c)(4), 501(c)(6) or 501(c)(12) of the Internal Revenue Code of 1986, or any subsequent corresponding internal revenue code of the United States, as amended from time to time.

(18) "Personal data" means any information that is linked or reasonably linkable to an identified or identifiable individual. "Personal data" does not include de-identified data or publicly available information.

(19) "Precise geolocation data" means information derived from technology, including, but not limited to, global positioning system level latitude and longitude coordinates or other mechanisms, that directly identifies the specific location of an individual with precision and accuracy within a radius of one thousand seven hundred fifty feet. "Precise geolocation data" does not include the content of communications or any data generated by or connected to advanced utility metering infrastructure systems or equipment for use by a utility.

(20) "Process" or "processing" means any operation or set of operations performed, whether by manual or automated means, on personal data or on sets of personal data, such as the collection, use, storage, disclosure, analysis, deletion or modification of personal data.

(21) "Processor" means an individual who, or legal entity that, processes personal data on behalf of a controller.

(22) "Profiling" means any form of automated processing performed on personal data to

evaluate, analyze or predict personal aspects related to an identified or identifiable individual's economic situation, health, personal preferences, interests, reliability, behavior, location or movements.

(23) "Protected health information" has the same meaning as provided in HIPAA.

(24) Pseudonymous data" means personal data that cannot be attributed to a specific individual without the use of additional information, provided such additional information is kept separately and is subject to appropriate technical and organizational measures to ensure that the personal data is not attributed to an identified or identifiable individual.

(25) "Publicly available information" means information that (A) is lawfully made available through federal, state or municipal government records or widely distributed media, and (B) a controller has a reasonable basis to believe a consumer has lawfully made available to the general public.

(26) "Sale of personal data" means the exchange of personal data for monetary or other valuable consideration by the controller to a third party. "Sale of personal data" does not include (A) the disclosure of personal data to a processor that processes the personal data on behalf of the controller, (B) the disclosure of personal data to a third party for purposes of providing a product or service requested by the consumer, (C) the disclosure or transfer of personal data to an affiliate of the controller, (D) the disclosure of personal data where the consumer directs the controller to disclose the personal data or intentionally uses the controller to interact with a third party, (E) the disclosure of personal data that the consumer (i) intentionally made available to the general public via a channel of mass media, and (ii) did not restrict to a specific audience, or (F) the disclosure or transfer of personal data to a third party as an asset that is part of a merger, acquisition, bankruptcy or other transaction, or a proposed merger, acquisition, bankruptcy or other transaction, in which the third party assumes control of all or part of the controller's assets.

(27) "Sensitive data" means personal data that includes (A) data revealing racial or ethnic origin, religious beliefs, mental or physical health condition or diagnosis, sex life, sexual orientation or citizenship or immigration status, (B) the processing of genetic or biometric data for the purpose of uniquely identifying an individual, (C) personal data collected from a known child, or (D) precise geolocation data.

(28) "Targeted advertising" means displaying advertisements to a consumer where the advertisement is selected based on personal data obtained or inferred from that consumer's activities over time and across nonaffiliated Internet web sites or online applications to predict such consumer's preferences or interests. "Targeted advertising" does not include (A) advertisements based on activities within a controller's own Internet web sites or online applications, (B) advertisements based on the context of a consumer's current search query, visit to an Internet web site or online application, (C) advertisements directed to a consumer in response to the consumer's request for information or feedback, or (D) processing personal data solely to measure or report advertising frequency, performance or reach.

(29) "Third party" means an individual or legal entity, such as a public authority, agency or body, other than the consumer, controller or processor or an affiliate of the processor or the controller.

(30) Trade secret" has the same meaning as provided in section 35-51 of the general statutes.

Sec. 2. (NEW) (Effective July 1, 2023)

The provisions of sections 1 to 11, inclusive, of this act apply to persons that conduct business in this state or persons that produce products or services that are targeted to residents of this state and that during the preceding calendar year: (1) Controlled or processed the personal data of not less than one hundred thousand consumers, excluding personal data controlled or processed solely for the purpose of completing a payment transaction; or (2) controlled or processed the personal data of not less than twenty-five thousand consumers and derived more than twenty-five per cent of their gross revenue from the sale of personal data.

Sec. 3. (NEW) (Effective July 1, 2023)

(a) The provisions of sections 1 to 11, inclusive, of this act do not apply to any: (1) Body, authority, board, bureau, commission, district or agency of this state or of any political subdivision of this state; (2) nonprofit organization; (3) institution of higher education; (4) national securities association that is registered under 15 USC 78o-3 of the Securities Exchange Act of 1934, as amended from time to time; (5) financial institution or data subject to Title V of the Gramm-Leach-Bliley Act, 15 USC 6801 et seq.; or (6) covered entity or business associate, as defined in 45 CFR 160.103.

(b) The following information and data is exempt from the provisions of sections 1 to 11, inclusive, of this act: (1) Protected health information under HIPAA; (2) patient-identifying information for purposes of 42 USC 290dd-2; (3) identifiable private information for purposes of the federal policy for the protection of human subjects under 45 CFR 46; (4) identifiable private information that is otherwise information collected as part of human subjects research pursuant to the good clinical practice guidelines issued by the International Council for Harmonization of Technical Requirements for Pharmaceuticals for Human Use; (5) the protection of human subjects under 21 CFR Parts 6, 50 and 56, or personal data used or shared in research, as defined in 45 CFR 164.501, that is conducted in accordance with the standards set forth in this subdivision and subdivisions (3) and (4) of this subsection, or other research conducted in accordance with applicable law; (6) information and documents created for purposes of the Health Care Quality Improvement Act of 1986, 42 USC 11101 et seq.; (7) patient safety work product for purposes of section 19a-127o of the general statutes and the Patient Safety and Quality Improvement Act, 42 USC 299b-21 et seq., as amended from time to time; (8) information derived from any of the health care related information listed in this subsection that is de-identified in accordance with the requirements for de-identification pursuant to HIPAA; (9) information originating from and intermingled to be indistinguishable with, or information treated in the same manner as, information exempt under this subsection that is maintained by a covered entity or business associate, program or qualified service organization, as specified in 42 USC 290dd-2, as amended from time to time; (10) information used for public health activities and purposes as authorized by HIPAA, community health activities and population health activities; (11) the collection, maintenance, disclosure, sale, communication or use of any personal information bearing on a consumer's credit worthiness, credit standing, credit capacity, character, general reputation, personal characteristics or mode of living by a consumer reporting agency, furnisher or user that provides information for use in a consumer report, and by a user of a consumer report, but only to the extent that such activity is regulated by and authorized under the Fair Credit Reporting Act, 15 USC 1681 et seq., as amended from time to time; (12) personal data collected, processed, sold or disclosed in compliance with the Driver's

Privacy Protection Act of 1994, 18 USC 2721 et seq., as amended from time to time; (13) personal data regulated by the Family Educational Rights and Privacy Act, 20 USC 1232g et seq., as amended from time to time; (14) personal data collected, processed, sold or disclosed in compliance with the Farm Credit Act, 12 USC 2001 et seq., as amended from time to time; (15) data processed or maintained (A) in the course of an individual applying to, employed by or acting as an agent or independent contractor of a controller, processor or third party, to the extent that the data is collected and used within the context of that role, (B) as the emergency contact information of an individual under sections 1 to 11, inclusive, of this act used for emergency contact purposes, or (C) that is necessary to retain to administer benefits for another individual relating to the individual who is the subject of the information under subdivision (1) of this subsection and used for the purposes of administering such benefits; and (16) personal data collected, processed, sold or disclosed in relation to price, route or service, as such terms are used in the Airline Deregulation Act, 49 USC 40101 et seq., as amended from time to time, by an air carrier subject to said act, to the extent sections 1 to 11, inclusive, of this act are preempted by the Airline Deregulation Act, 49 USC 41713, as amended from time to time.

(c) Controllers and processors that comply with the verifiable parental consent requirements of COPPA shall be deemed compliant with any obligation to obtain parental consent pursuant to sections 1 to 11, inclusive, of this act.

Sec. 4. (NEW) (Effective July 1, 2023)

(a) A consumer shall have the right to: (1) Confirm whether or not a controller is processing the consumer's personal data and access such personal data, unless such confirmation or access would require the controller to reveal a trade secret; (2) correct inaccuracies in the consumer's personal data, taking into account the nature of the personal data and the purposes of the processing of the consumer's personal data; (3) delete personal data provided by, or obtained about, the consumer; (4) obtain a copy of the consumer's personal data processed by the controller, in a portable and, to the extent technically feasible, readily usable format that allows the consumer to transmit the data to another controller without hindrance, where the processing is carried out by automated means, provided such controller shall not be required to reveal any trade secret; and (5) opt out of the processing of the personal data for purposes of (A) targeted advertising, (B) the sale of personal data, except as provided in subsection (b) of section 6 of this act, or (C) profiling in furtherance of solely automated decisions that produce legal or similarly significant effects concerning the consumer.

(b) A consumer may exercise rights under this section by a secure and reliable means established by the controller and described to the consumer in the controller's privacy notice. A consumer may designate an authorized agent in accordance with section 5 of this act to exercise the rights of such consumer to opt out of the processing of such consumer's personal data for purposes of subdivision (5) of subsection (a) of this section on behalf of the consumer. In the case of processing personal data of a known child, the parent or legal guardian may exercise such consumer rights on the child's behalf. In the case of processing personal data concerning a consumer subject to a guardianship, conservatorship or other protective arrangement, the guardian or the conservator of the consumer may exercise such rights on the consumer's behalf.

(c) Except as otherwise provided in sections 1 to 11, inclusive, of this act, a controller shall comply with a request by a consumer to exercise the consumer rights authorized pursuant to said sections as follows:

(1) A controller shall respond to the consumer without undue delay, but not later than forty-five days after receipt of the request. The controller may extend the response period by forty-five additional days when reasonably necessary, considering the complexity and number of the consumer's requests, provided the controller informs the consumer of any such extension within the initial forty-five-day response period and of the reason for the extension.

(2) If a controller declines to take action regarding the consumer's request, the controller shall inform the consumer without undue delay, but not later than forty-five days after receipt of the request, of the justification for declining to take action and instructions for how to appeal the decision.

(3) Information provided in response to a consumer request shall be provided by a controller, free of charge, once per consumer during any twelve-month period. If requests from a consumer are manifestly unfounded, excessive or repetitive, the controller may charge the consumer a reasonable fee to cover the administrative costs of complying with the request or decline to act on the request. The controller bears the burden of demonstrating the manifestly unfounded, excessive or repetitive nature of the request.

(4) If a controller is unable to authenticate a request to exercise any of the rights afforded under subdivisions (1) to (4), inclusive, of subsection (a) of this section using commercially reasonable efforts, the controller shall not be required to comply with a request to initiate an action pursuant to this section and shall provide notice to the consumer that the controller is unable to authenticate the request to exercise such right or rights until such consumer provides additional information reasonably necessary to authenticate such consumer and such consumer's request to exercise such right or rights. A controller shall not be required to authenticate an opt-out request, but a controller may deny an opt-out request if the controller has a good faith, reasonable and documented belief that such request is fraudulent. If a controller denies an opt-out request because the controller believes such request is fraudulent, the controller shall send a notice to the person who made such request disclosing that such controller believes such request is fraudulent, why such controller believes such request is fraudulent and that such controller shall not comply with such request.

(5) A controller that has obtained personal data about a consumer from a source other than the consumer shall be deemed in compliance with a consumer's request to delete such data pursuant to subdivision (3) of subsection (a) of this section by (A) retaining a record of the deletion request and the minimum data necessary for the purpose of ensuring the consumer's personal data remains deleted from the controller's records and not using such retained data for any other purpose pursuant to the provisions of sections 1 to 11, inclusive, of this act, or (B) opting the consumer out of the processing of such personal data for any purpose except for those exempted pursuant to the provisions of sections 1 to 11, inclusive, of this act.

(d) A controller shall establish a process for a consumer to appeal the controller's refusal to take action on a request within a reasonable period of time after the consumer's receipt of the decision. The appeal process shall be conspicuously available and similar to the process for submitting requests to initiate action pursuant to this section. Not later than sixty days after receipt of an appeal, a controller shall inform the consumer in writing of any action taken or not taken in response to the appeal, including a written explanation of the reasons for the decisions. If the appeal is denied, the controller shall also provide the consumer with an online mechanism, if available, or other method through which the consumer may contact the Attorney General to submit a complaint.

Sec. 5. (NEW) (Effective July 1, 2023)

A consumer may designate another person to serve as the consumer's authorized agent, and act on such consumer's behalf, to opt out of the processing of such consumer's personal data for one or more of the purposes specified in subdivision (5) of subsection (a) of section 4 of this act. The consumer may designate such authorized agent by way of, among other things, a technology, including, but not limited to, an Internet link or a browser setting, browser extension or global device setting, indicating such consumer's intent to opt out of such processing. A controller shall comply with an opt-out request received from an authorized agent if the controller is able to verify, with commercially reasonable effort, the identity of the consumer and the authorized agent's authority to act on such consumer's behalf.

Sec. 6. (NEW) (Effective July 1, 2023)

(a) A controller shall: (1) Limit the collection of personal data to what is adequate, relevant and reasonably necessary in relation to the purposes for which such data is processed, as disclosed to the consumer; (2) except as otherwise provided in sections 1 to 11, inclusive, of this act, not process personal data for purposes that are neither reasonably necessary to, nor compatible with, the disclosed purposes for which such personal data is processed, as disclosed to the consumer, unless the controller obtains the consumer's consent; (3) establish, implement and maintain reasonable administrative, technical and physical data security practices to protect the confidentiality, integrity and accessibility of personal data appropriate to the volume and nature of the personal data at issue; (4) not process sensitive data concerning a consumer without obtaining the consumer's consent, or, in the case of the processing of sensitive data concerning a known child, without processing such data in accordance with COPPA; (5) not process personal data in violation of the laws of this state and federal laws that prohibit unlawful discrimination against consumers; (6) provide an effective mechanism for a consumer to revoke the consumer's consent under this section that is at least as easy as the mechanism by which the consumer provided the consumer's consent and, upon revocation of such consent, cease to process the data as soon as practicable, but not later than fifteen days after the receipt of such request; and (7) not process the personal data of a consumer for purposes of targeted advertising, or sell the consumer's personal data without the consumer's consent, under circumstances where a controller has actual knowledge, and wilfully disregards, that the consumer is at least thirteen years of age but younger than sixteen years of age. A controller shall not discriminate against a consumer for exercising any of the consumer rights contained in sections 1 to 11, inclusive, of this act, including denying goods or services, charging different prices or rates for goods or services or providing a different level of quality of goods or services to the consumer.

(b) Nothing in subsection (a) of this section shall be construed to require a controller to provide a product or service that requires the personal data of a consumer which the controller does not collect or maintain, or prohibit a controller from offering a different price, rate, level, quality or selection of goods or services to a consumer, including offering goods or services for no fee, if the offering is in connection with a consumer's voluntary participation in a bona fide loyalty, rewards, premium features, discounts or club card program.

(c) A controller shall provide consumers with a reasonably accessible, clear and meaningful privacy notice that includes: (1) The categories of personal data processed by the controller; (2) the purpose for processing personal data; (3) how consumers may exercise their consumer rights, including how a consumer may appeal a controller's decision with regard to the consumer's request; (4) the categories of personal data that the controller shares with third parties, if any; (5) the categories of third parties, if any, with which the controller shares personal data; and (6) an active electronic mail address or other online mechanism that the consumer may use to contact the controller.

(d) If a controller sells personal data to third parties or processes personal data for targeted advertising, the controller shall clearly and conspicuously disclose such processing, as well as the manner in which a consumer may exercise the right to opt out of such processing.

(e)

(1) A controller shall establish, and shall describe in a privacy notice, one or more secure and reliable means for consumers to submit a request to exercise their consumer rights pursuant to sections 1 to 11, inclusive, of this act. Such means shall take into account the ways in which consumers normally interact with the controller, the need for secure and reliable communication of such requests and the ability of the controller to verify the identity of the consumer making the request. A controller shall not require a consumer to create a new account in order to exercise consumer rights, but may require a consumer to use an existing account. Any such means shall include:

(A)

(i) Providing a clear and conspicuous link on the controller's Internet web site to an Internet web page that enables a consumer, or an agent of the consumer, to opt out of the targeted advertising or sale of the consumer's personal data; and

(ii) Not later than January 1, 2025, allowing a consumer to opt out of any processing of the consumer's personal data for the purposes of targeted advertising, or any sale of such personal data, through an opt-out preference signal sent, with such consumer's consent, by a platform, technology or mechanism to the controller indicating such consumer's intent to opt out of any such processing or sale. Such platform, technology or mechanism shall:

(I) Not unfairly disadvantage another controller;

(II) Not make use of a default setting, but, rather, require the consumer to make an affirmative, freely given and unambiguous choice to opt out of any processing of such consumer's personal data pursuant to sections 1 to 11, inclusive, of this act;

(III) Be consumer-friendly and easy to use by the average consumer;

(IV) Be as consistent as possible with any other similar platform, technology or mechanism required by any federal or state law or regulation; and

(V) Enable the controller to accurately determine whether the consumer is a resident of this state and whether the consumer has made a legitimate request to opt out of any sale of such consumer's personal data or targeted advertising.

(B) If a consumer's decision to opt out of any processing of the consumer's personal data for the purposes of targeted advertising, or any sale of such personal data, through an opt-out preference signal sent in accordance with the provisions of subparagraph (A) of this subdivision conflicts with the consumer's existing controller-specific privacy setting or voluntary participation in a controller's bona fide loyalty, rewards, premium features, discounts or club card program, the controller shall comply with such consumer's opt-out preference signal but may notify such consumer of such conflict and provide to such consumer the choice to confirm such controller-specific privacy setting or participation in such program.

(2) If a controller responds to consumer opt-out requests received pursuant to subparagraph (A) of subdivision (1) of this subsection by informing the consumer of a charge for the use of any product or service, the controller shall present the terms of any financial incentive offered pursuant to subsection (b) of this section for the retention, use, sale or sharing of the consumer's personal data.

Sec. 7. (NEW) (Effective July 1, 2023)

(a) A processor shall adhere to the instructions of a controller and shall assist the controller in meeting the controller's obligations under sections 1 to 11, inclusive, of this act. Such assistance shall include: (1) Taking into account the nature of processing and the information available to the processor, by appropriate technical and organizational measures, insofar as is reasonably practicable, to fulfill the controller's obligation to respond to consumer rights requests; (2) taking into account the nature of processing and the information available to the processor, by assisting the controller in meeting the controller's obligations in relation to the security of processing the personal data and in relation to the notification of a breach of security, as defined in section 36a-701b of the general statutes, of the system of the processor, in order to meet the controller's obligations; and (3) providing necessary information to enable the controller to conduct and document data protection assessments.

(b) A contract between a controller and a processor shall govern the processor's data processing procedures with respect to processing performed on behalf of the controller. The contract shall be binding and clearly set forth instructions for processing data, the nature and purpose of processing, the type of data subject to processing, the duration of processing and the rights and obligations of both parties. The contract shall also require that the processor: (1) Ensure that each person processing personal data is subject to a duty of confidentiality with respect to the data; (2) at the controller's direction, delete or return all personal data to the controller as requested at the end of the provision of services, unless retention of the personal data is required by law; (3) upon the reasonable request of the controller, make available to the controller all information in its possession necessary to demonstrate the processor's compliance with the obligations in sections 1 to 11, inclusive, of this act; (4) after providing the controller an opportunity to object, engage any subcontractor pursuant to a written contract that requires the subcontractor to meet the obligations of the processor with respect to the personal data; and (5) allow, and cooperate with, reasonable assessments by the controller or the controller's designated assessor, or the processor may arrange for a qualified and independent assessor to conduct an assessment of the processor's policies and technical and organizational measures in support of the obligations under sections 1 to 11, inclusive, of this act, using an appropriate and accepted control standard or framework and assessment procedure for such assessments. The processor shall provide a report of such assessment to the controller upon request.

(c) Nothing in this section shall be construed to relieve a controller or processor from the liabilities imposed on the controller or processor by virtue of such controller's or processor's role in the processing relationship, as described in sections 1 to 11, inclusive, of this act.

(d) Determining whether a person is acting as a controller or processor with respect to a specific processing of data is a fact-based determination that depends upon the context in which personal data is to be processed. A person who is not limited in such person's processing of personal data pursuant to a controller's instructions, or who fails to adhere to such instructions, is a controller and not a processor with respect to a specific processing of data. A processor that continues to adhere to a controller's instructions with respect to a specific processing of personal data remains a processor. If a processor begins, alone or jointly with others, determining the purposes and means of the processing of personal data, the processor is a controller with respect to such processing and may be subject to an enforcement action under section 11 of this act.

Sec. 8. (NEW) (Effective July 1, 2023)

(a) A controller shall conduct and document a data protection assessment for each of the controller's processing activities that presents a heightened risk of harm to a consumer. For the purposes of this section, processing that presents a heightened risk of harm to a consumer includes: (1) The processing of personal data for the purposes of targeted advertising; (2) the sale of personal data; (3) the processing of personal data for the purposes of profiling, where such profiling presents a reasonably foreseeable risk of (A) unfair or deceptive treatment of, or unlawful disparate impact on, consumers, (B) financial, physical or reputational injury to consumers, (C) a physical or other intrusion upon the solitude or seclusion, or the private affairs or concerns, of consumers, where such intrusion would be offensive to a reasonable person, or (D) other substantial injury to consumers; and (4) the processing of sensitive data.

(b) Data protection assessments conducted pursuant to subsection (a) of this section shall identify and weigh the benefits that may flow, directly and indirectly, from the processing to the controller, the consumer, other stakeholders and the public against the potential risks to the rights of the consumer associated with such processing, as mitigated by safeguards that can be employed by the controller to reduce such risks. The controller shall factor into any such data protection assessment the use of de-identified data and the reasonable expectations of consumers, as well as the context of the processing and the relationship between the controller and the consumer whose personal data will be processed.

(c) The Attorney General may require that a controller disclose any data protection assessment that is relevant to an investigation conducted by the Attorney General, and the controller shall make the data protection assessment available to the Attorney General. The Attorney General may evaluate the data protection assessment for compliance with the responsibilities set forth in sections 1 to 11, inclusive, of this act. Data protection assessments shall be confidential and shall be exempt from disclosure under the Freedom of Information Act, as defined in section 1-200 of the general statutes. To the extent any information contained in a data protection assessment disclosed to the Attorney General includes information subject to attorney-client privilege or work product protection, such disclosure shall not constitute a waiver of such privilege or protection.

(d) A single data protection assessment may address a comparable set of processing operations that include similar activities.

(e) If a controller conducts a data protection assessment for the purpose of complying with another applicable law or regulation, the data protection assessment shall be deemed to satisfy the requirements established in this section if such data protection assessment is reasonably similar in scope and effect to the data protection assessment that would otherwise be conducted pursuant to this section.

(f) Data protection assessment requirements shall apply to processing activities created or generated after July 1, 2023, and are not retroactive.

Sec. 9. (NEW) (Effective July 1, 2023)

(a) Any controller in possession of de-identified data shall: (1) Take reasonable measures to ensure that the data cannot be associated with an individual; (2) publicly commit to maintaining and using de-identified data without attempting to re-identify the data; and (3) contractually obligate any recipients of the de-identified data to comply with all provisions of sections 1 to 11, inclusive, of this act.

(b) Nothing in sections 1 to 11, inclusive, of this act shall be construed to: (1) Require a controller or processor to re-identify de-identified data or pseudonymous data; or (2) maintain data in identifiable form, or collect, obtain, retain or access any data or technology, in order to be capable of associating an authenticated consumer request with personal data.

(c) Nothing in sections 1 to 11, inclusive, of this act shall be construed to require a controller or processor to comply with an authenticated consumer rights request if the controller: (1) Is not reasonably capable of associating the request with the personal data or it would be unreasonably burdensome for the controller to associate the request with the personal data; (2) does not use the personal data to recognize or respond to the specific consumer who is the subject of the personal data, or associate the personal data with other personal data about the same specific consumer; and (3) does not sell the personal data to any third party or otherwise voluntarily disclose the personal data to any third party other than a processor, except as otherwise permitted in this section.

(d) The rights afforded under subdivisions (1) to (4), inclusive, of subsection (a) of section 4 of this act shall not apply to pseudonymous data in cases where the controller is able to demonstrate that any information necessary to identify the consumer is kept separately and is subject to effective technical and organizational controls that prevent the controller from accessing such information.

(e) A controller that discloses pseudonymous data or de-identified data shall exercise reasonable oversight to monitor compliance with any contractual commitments to which the pseudonymous data or de-identified data is subject and shall take appropriate steps to address any breaches of those contractual commitments.

Sec. 10. (NEW) (Effective July 1, 2023)

(a) Nothing in sections 1 to 11, inclusive, of this act shall be construed to restrict a controller's or processor's ability to: (1) Comply with federal, state or municipal ordinances or regulations; (2) comply with a civil, criminal or regulatory inquiry, investigation, subpoena or summons by federal, state, municipal or other governmental authorities; (3) cooperate with law enforcement agencies concerning conduct or activity that the controller or processor reasonably and in good faith believes may violate federal, state or municipal ordinances or regulations; (4) investigate, establish, exercise, prepare for or defend legal claims; (5) provide a product or service specifically requested by a consumer; (6) perform under a contract to which a consumer is a party, including fulfilling the terms of a written warranty; (7) take steps at the request of a consumer prior to entering into a contract; (8) take immediate steps to protect an interest that is essential for the life or physical safety of the consumer or another individual, and where the processing cannot be manifestly based on another legal basis; (9) prevent, detect, protect against or respond to security incidents, identity theft, fraud, harassment, malicious or deceptive activities or any illegal activity, preserve the integrity or security of systems or investigate, report or prosecute those responsible for any such action; (10) engage in public or peer-reviewed scientific or statistical research in the public interest that adheres to all other applicable ethics and privacy laws and is approved, monitored and governed by an institutional review board that determines, or similar independent oversight entities that determine, (A) whether the deletion of the information is likely to provide substantial benefits that do not exclusively accrue to the controller, (B) the expected benefits of the research outweigh the privacy risks, and (C) whether the controller has implemented reasonable safeguards to mitigate privacy risks associated with research, including any risks associated with re-identification; (11) assist another controller, processor or third party with any of the obligations under sections 1 to 11, inclusive, of this act; or (12) process personal data for reasons of public interest in the area of public health, community health or population health, but solely to the extent that such processing is (A) subject to suitable and specific measures to safeguard the rights of the consumer whose personal data is being processed, and (B) under the responsibility of a professional subject to confidentiality obligations under federal, state or local law.

(b) The obligations imposed on controllers or processors under sections 1 to 11, inclusive, of this act shall not restrict a controller's or processor's ability to collect, use or retain data for internal use to: (1) Conduct internal research to develop, improve or repair products, services or technology; (2) effectuate a product recall; (3) identify and repair technical errors that impair existing or intended functionality; or (4) perform internal operations that are reasonably aligned with the expectations of the consumer or reasonably anticipated based on the consumer's existing relationship with the controller, or are otherwise compatible with processing data in furtherance of the provision of a product or service specifically requested by a consumer or the performance of a contract to which the consumer is a party.

(c) The obligations imposed on controllers or processors under sections 1 to 11, inclusive, of this act shall not apply where compliance by the controller or processor with said sections would violate an evidentiary privilege under the laws of this state. Nothing in sections 1 to 11, inclusive, of this act shall be construed to prevent a controller or processor from providing personal data concerning a consumer to a person covered by an evidentiary privilege under the laws of the state as part of a privileged communication.

(d) A controller or processor that discloses personal data to a processor or third-party controller in accordance with sections 1 to 11, inclusive, of this act shall not be deemed to have violated said sections if the processor or third-party controller that receives and processes such personal data violates said sections, provided, at the time the disclosing controller or processor disclosed such personal data, the disclosing controller or processor did not have actual knowledge that the receiving processor or third-party controller would violate said sections. A third-party controller or processor receiving personal data from a controller or processor in compliance with sections 1 to 11, inclusive, of this act is likewise not in violation of said sections for the transgressions of the controller or processor from which such third-party controller or processor receives such personal data.

(e) Nothing in sections 1 to 11, inclusive, of this act shall be construed to: (1) Impose any obligation on a controller or processor that adversely affects the rights or freedoms of any person, including, but not limited to, the rights of any person (A) to freedom of speech or freedom of the press guaranteed in the First Amendment to the United States Constitution, or (B) under section 52-146t of the general statutes; or (2) apply to any person's processing of personal data in the course of such person's purely personal or household activities.

(f) Personal data processed by a controller pursuant to this section may be processed to the extent that such processing is: (1) Reasonably necessary and proportionate to the purposes listed in this section; and (2) adequate, relevant and limited to what is necessary in relation to the specific purposes listed in this section. Personal data collected, used or retained pursuant to subsection (b) of this section shall, where applicable, take into account the nature and purpose or purposes of such collection, use or retention. Such data shall be subject to reasonable administrative, technical and physical measures to protect the confidentiality, integrity and accessibility of the personal data and to reduce reasonably foreseeable risks of harm to consumers relating to such collection, use or retention of personal data.

(g) If a controller processes personal data pursuant to an exemption in this section, the controller bears the burden of demonstrating that such processing qualifies for the exemption and complies with the requirements in subsection (f) of this section.

(h) Processing personal data for the purposes expressly identified in this section shall not solely make a legal entity a controller with respect to such processing.

Sec. 11. (NEW) (Effective July 1, 2023)

(a) The Attorney General shall have exclusive authority to enforce violations of sections 1 to 10, inclusive, of this act.

(b) During the period beginning on July 1, 2023, and ending on December 31, 2024, the Attorney General shall, prior to initiating any action for a violation of any provision of sections 1 to 10, inclusive, of this act, issue a notice of violation to the controller if the Attorney General determines that a cure is possible. If the controller fails to cure such violation within sixty days of receipt of the notice of violation, the Attorney General may bring an action pursuant to this section. Not later than February 1, 2024, the Attorney General shall submit a report, in accordance with section 11-4a of the general statutes, to the joint standing committee of the General Assembly having cognizance of matters relating to general law disclosing: (1) The number of notices of violation the Attorney General has issued; (2) the nature of each violation;

(3) the number of violations that were cured during the sixty-day cure period; and (4) any other matter the Attorney General deems relevant for the purposes of such report.

(c) Beginning on January 1, 2025, the Attorney General may, in determining whether to grant a controller or processor the opportunity to cure an alleged violation described in subsection (b) of this section, consider: (1) The number of violations; (2) the size and complexity of the controller or processor; (3) the nature and extent of the controller's or processor's processing activities; (4) the substantial likelihood of injury to the public; (5) the safety of persons or property; and (6) whether such alleged violation was likely caused by human or technical error.

(d) Nothing in sections 1 to 10, inclusive, of this act shall be construed as providing the basis for, or be subject to, a private right of action for violations of said sections or any other law.

(e) A violation of the requirements of sections 1 to 10, inclusive, of this act shall constitute an unfair trade practice for purposes of section 42-110b of the general statutes and shall be enforced solely by the Attorney General, provided the provisions of section 42-110g of the general statutes shall not apply to such violation.

Sec. 12. (Effective from passage)

(a) Not later than September 1, 2022, the chairpersons of the joint standing committee of the General Assembly having cognizance of matters relating to general law shall convene a task force to study:

(1) Information sharing among health care providers and social care providers and make recommendations to eliminate health disparities and inequities across sectors, as described in subsection (a) of section 19a-133b of the general statutes;

(2) Algorithmic decision-making and make recommendations concerning the proper use of data to reduce bias in such decision-making;

(3) Possible legislation that would require an operator, as defined in the Children's Online Privacy Protection Act, 15 USC 6501 et seq., as amended from time to time, to, upon a parent's request, delete the account of a child and cease to collect, use or maintain, in retrievable form, the child's personal data on the operator's Internet web site or online service directed to children, and provide parents with an accessible, reasonable and verifiable means to make such a request;

(4) Any means available to verify the age of a child who creates a social media account;

(5) Issues concerning data colocation, including, but not limited to, the impact that the provisions of sections 1 to 11, inclusive, of this act have on third parties that provide data storage and colocation services;

(6) Possible legislation that would expand the provisions of sections 1 to 11, inclusive, of this act to include additional persons or groups; and

(7) Other topics concerning data privacy.

(b) The chairpersons of the joint standing committee of the General Assembly having cognizance of matters relating to general law shall serve as the chairpersons of the task force, and shall jointly appoint the members of the task force. Such members shall include, but need not be limited to:

(1) Representatives from business, academia, consumer advocacy groups, small and large companies and the office of the Attorney General; and

(2) Attorneys with experience in privacy law.

(c) The administrative staff of the joint standing committee of the General Assembly having cognizance of matters relating to general law shall serve as administrative staff of the task force.

(d) Not later than January 1, 2023, the task force shall submit a report on its findings and recommendations to the joint standing committee of the General Assembly having cognizance of matters relating to general law, in accordance with the provisions of section 11-4a of the general statutes. The task force shall terminate on the date that it submits such report or January 1, 2023, whichever is later.

APPENDIX 4: UTAH CONSUMER PRIVACY ACT

Section 13-61-101. Definitions.

As used in this chapter:

(1) "Account" means the Consumer Privacy Restricted Account established in Section 13-61-403.

(2) "Affiliate" means an entity that: (a) controls, is controlled by, or is under common control with another entity; or (b) shares common branding with another entity.

(3) "Aggregated data" means information that relates to a group or category of consumers: (a) from which individual consumer identities have been removed; and (b) that is not linked or reasonably linkable to any consumer.

(4) "Air carrier" means the same as that term is defined in 49 U.S.C. Sec. 40102.

(5) "Authenticate" means to use reasonable means to determine that a consumer's request to exercise the rights described in Section 13-61-201 is made by the consumer who is entitled to exercise those rights.

(6) (a) "Biometric data" means data generated by automatic measurements of an individual's unique biological characteristics. (b) "Biometric data" includes data described in Subsection (6)(a) that are generated by automatic measurements of an individual's fingerprint, voiceprint, eye retinas, irises, or any other unique biological pattern or characteristic that is used to identify a specific individual. (c) "Biometric data" does not include: (i) a physical or digital photograph; (ii) a video or audio recording; (iii) data generated from an item described in Subsection (6)(c)(i) or (ii); (iv) information captured from a patient in a health care setting; or (v) information collected, used, or stored for treatment, payment, or health care operations as those terms are defined in 45 C.F.R. Parts 160, 162, and 164.

(7) "Business associate" means the same as that term is defined in 45 C.F.R. Sec. 160.103.

(8) "Child" means an individual younger than 13 years old.

(9) "Consent" means an affirmative act by a consumer that unambiguously indicates the consumer's voluntary and informed agreement to allow a person to process personal data related to the consumer.

(10) (a) "Consumer" means an individual who is a resident of the state acting in an individual or household context.

(b) "Consumer" does not include an individual acting in an employment or commercial context.

(11) "Control" or "controlled" as used in Subsection (2) means: (a) ownership of, or the power to vote, more than 50% of the outstanding shares of any class of voting securities of an entity; (b) control in any manner over the election of a majority of the directors or of the individuals exercising similar functions; or (c) the power to exercise controlling influence of the management of an entity.

(12) "Controller" means a person doing business in the state who determines the purposes for

which and the means by which personal data are processed, regardless of whether the person makes the determination alone or with others.

(13) “Covered entity” means the same as that term is defined in 45 C.F.R. Sec. 160.103.

(14) “Deidentified data” means data that: (a) cannot reasonably be linked to an identified individual or an identifiable individual; and (b) are possessed by a controller who: (i) takes reasonable measures to ensure that a person cannot associate the data with an individual; (ii) publicly commits to maintain and use the data only in deidentified form and not attempt to reidentify the data; and (iii) contractually obligates any recipients of the data to comply with the requirements described in Subsections (14)(b)(i) and (ii).

(15) “Director” means the director of the Division of Consumer Protection.

(16) “Division” means the Division of Consumer Protection created in Section 13-2-1.

(17) “Governmental entity” means the same as that term is defined in Section 63G-2-103.

(18) “Health care facility” means the same as that term is defined in Section 26-21-2.

(19) “Health care provider” means the same as that term is defined in Section 26-21-2.

(20) “Identifiable individual” means an individual who can be readily identified, directly or indirectly.

(21) “Institution of higher education” means a public or private institution of higher education.

(22) “Local political subdivision” means the same as that term is defined in Section 11-14-102.

(23) “Nonprofit corporation” means: (a) the same as that term is defined in Section 16-6a-102; or (b) a foreign nonprofit corporation as defined in Section 16-6a-102.

(24) (a) “Personal data” means information that is linked or reasonably linkable to an identified individual or an identifiable individual. (b) “Personal data” does not include deidentified data, aggregated data, or publicly available information.

(25) “Process” means an operation or set of operations performed on personal data, including collection, use, storage, disclosure, analysis, deletion, or modification of personal data.

(26) “Processor” means a person who processes personal data on behalf of a controller.

(27) “Protected health information” means the same as that term is defined in 45 C.F.R. Sec. 160.103.

(28) “Pseudonymous data” means personal data that cannot be attributed to a specific individual without the use of additional information, if the additional information is: (a) kept separate from the consumer’s personal data; and (b) subject to appropriate technical and organizational measures to ensure that the personal data are not attributable to an identified individual or an identifiable individual.

(29) “Publicly available information” means information that a person: (a) lawfully obtains from a record of a governmental entity; (b) reasonably believes a consumer or widely distributed media has lawfully made available to the general public; or (c) if the consumer has not restricted the information to a specific audience, obtains from a person to whom the consumer disclosed the

information.

(30) “Right” means a consumer right described in Section 13-61-201.

31 (a) “Sale,” “sell,” or “sold” means the exchange of personal data for monetary consideration by a controller to a third party. (b) “Sale,” “sell,” or “sold” does not include: (i) a controller’s disclosure of personal data to a processor who processes the personal data on behalf of the controller; (ii) a controller’s disclosure of personal data to an affiliate of the controller; (iii) considering the context in which the consumer provided the personal data to the controller, a controller’s disclosure of personal data to a third party if the purpose is consistent with a consumer’s reasonable expectations; (iv) the disclosure or transfer of personal data when a consumer directs a controller to: (A) disclose the personal data; or (B) interact with one or more third parties; (v) a consumer’s disclosure of personal data to a third party for the purpose of providing a product or service requested by the consumer or a parent or legal guardian of a child; (vi) the disclosure of information that the consumer: (A) intentionally makes available to the general public via a channel of mass media; and (B) does not restrict to a specific audience; or (vii) a controller’s transfer of personal data to a third party as an asset that is part of a proposed or actual merger, an acquisition, or a bankruptcy in which the third party assumes control of all or part of the controller’s assets.

(32) “Sensitive data” means: (i) personal data that reveals: (A) an individual’s racial or ethnic origin; (B) an individual’s religious beliefs; (C) an individual’s sexual orientation; (D) an individual’s citizenship or immigration status; or (E) information regarding an individual’s medical history, mental or physical health condition, or medical treatment or diagnosis by a health care professional; (ii) the processing of genetic personal data or biometric data, if the processing is for the purpose of identifying a specific individual; or (iii) specific geolocation data. (b) “Sensitive data” does not include personal data that reveals an individual’s: (i) racial or ethnic origin, if the personal data are processed by a video communication service; or (ii) if the personal data are processed by a person licensed to provide health care under Title 26, Chapter 21, Health Care Facility Licensing and Inspection Act, or Title 58, Occupations and Professions, information regarding an individual’s medical history, mental or physical health condition, or medical treatment or diagnosis by a health care professional.

(33) (a) “Specific geolocation data” means information derived from technology, including global position system level latitude and longitude coordinates, that directly identifies an individual’s specific location, accurate within a radius of 1,750 feet or less. (b) “Specific geolocation data” does not include: (i) the content of a communication; or

(ii) any data generated by or connected to advanced utility metering infrastructure systems or equipment for use by a utility.

(34) (a) “Targeted advertising” means displaying an advertisement to a consumer where the advertisement is selected based on personal data obtained from the consumer’s activities over time and across nonaffiliated websites or online applications to predict the consumer’s preferences or interests. (b) “Targeted advertising” does not include advertising: (i) based on a consumer’s activities within a controller’s website or online application or any affiliated website or online application; (ii) based on the context of a consumer’s current search query or visit to a website or online application; (iii) directed to a consumer in response to the consumer’s request for information, product, a service, or feedback; or iv) processing personal data solely to

measure or report advertising: (A) performance; (B) reach; or (C) frequency.

(35) "Third party" means a person other than: (a) the consumer, controller, or processor; or (b) an affiliate or contractor of the controller or the processor.

(36) "Trade secret" means information, including a formula, pattern, compilation, program, device, method, technique, or process, that: (a) derives independent economic value, actual or potential, from not being generally known to, and not being readily ascertainable by proper means by, other persons who can obtain economic value from the information's disclosure or use; and (b) is the subject of efforts that are reasonable under the circumstances to maintain the information's secrecy.

Section 13-61-102. Applicability.

(1) This chapter applies to any controller or processor who: (a) (1) conducts business in the state; or

(ii) produces a product or service that is targeted to consumers who are residents of the state; (b) has annual revenue of $25,000,000 or more; and (c) satisfies one or more of the following thresholds: (i) during a calendar year, controls or processes personal data of 100,000 or more consumers; or (ii) derives over 50% of the entity's gross revenue from the sale of personal data and controls or processes personal data of 25,000 or more consumers.

(2) This chapter does not apply to: (a) a governmental entity or a third party under contract with a governmental entity when the third party is acting on behalf of the governmental entity; (b) a tribe; (c) an institution of higher education; (d) a nonprofit corporation; (e) a covered entity; (f) a business associate; (g) information that meets the definition of: (i) protected health information for purposes of the federal Health Insurance Portability and Accountability Act of 1996, 42 U.S.C. Sec. 1320d et seq., and related regulations; (ii) patient identifying information for purposes of 42 C.F.R. Part 2; (iii) identifiable private information for purposes of the Federal Policy for the Protection of Human Subjects, 45 C.F.R. Part 46; (iv) identifiable private information or personal data collected as part of human subjects research pursuant to or under the same standards as: (A) the good clinical practice guidelines issued by the International Council for Harmonisation; or (B) the Protection of Human Subjects under 21 C.F.R. Part 50 and Institutional Review Boards under 21 C.F.R. Part 56; (v) personal data used or shared in research conducted in accordance with one or more of the requirements described in Subsection (2)(g)(iv); (vi) information and documents created specifically for, and collected and maintained by, a committee listed in Section 26-1-7; (vii) information and documents created for purposes of the federal Health Care Quality Improvement Act of 1986, 42 U.S.C. Sec. 11101 et seq., and related regulations; (viii) patient safety work product for purposes of 42 C.F.R. Part 3; or (ix) information that is: (A) deidentified in accordance with the requirements for deidentification set forth in 45 C.F.R. Part 164; and (B) derived from any of the health care-related information listed in this Subsection (2)(g); (h) information originating from, and intermingled to be indistinguishable with, information under Subsection (2)(g) that is maintained by: (i) a health care facility or health care provider; or (ii) a program or a qualified service organization as defined in 42 C.F.R. Sec. 2.11; (i) information used only for public health activities and purposes as described in 45 C.F.R. Sec. 164.512; (j) (i) an activity by: (A) a consumer reporting agency, as defined in 15 U.S.C. Sec. 1681a; (B) a furnisher of information,

as set forth in 15 U.S.C. Sec. 1681s-2, who provides information for use in a consumer report, as defined in 15 U.S.C. Sec. 1681a; or (C) a user of a consumer report, as set forth in 15 U.S.C. Sec. 1681b; (ii) subject to regulation under the federal Fair Credit Reporting Act, 15 U.S.C. Sec. 1681 et seq.; and (iii) involving the collection, maintenance, disclosure, sale, communication, or use of any personal data bearing on a consumer's: (A) credit worthiness; (B) credit standing; (C) credit capacity; (D) character; (E) general reputation; (F) personal characteristics; or (G) mode of living; (k) a financial institution or an affiliate of a financial institution governed by, or personal data collected, processed, sold, or disclosed in accordance with, Title V of the Gramm-Leach-Bliley Act, 15 U.S.C. Sec. 6801 et seq., and related regulations; (i) personal data collected, processed, sold, or disclosed in accordance with the federal Driver's Privacy Protection Act of 1994, 18 U.S.C. Sec. 2721 et seq.; (m) personal data regulated by the federal Family Education Rights and Privacy Act, 20 U.S.C. Sec. 1232g, and related regulations; (n) personal data collected, processed, sold, or disclosed in accordance with the federal Farm Credit Act of 1971, 12 U.S.C. Sec. 2001 et seq.; (o) data that are processed or maintained:

(i) in the course of an individual applying to, being employed by, or acting as an agent or independent contractor of a controller, processor, or third party, to the extent the collection and use of the data are related to the individual's role;(ii) as the emergency contact information of an individual described in Subsection (2)(o)(i) and used for emergency contact purposes; or (iii) to administer benefits for another individual relating to an individual described in Subsection (2)(o)(i) and used for the purpose of administering the benefits; (p) an individual's processing of personal data for purely personal or household purposes; or (q) an air carrier.

(3) A controller is in compliance with any obligation to obtain parental consent under this chapter if the controller complies with the verifiable parental consent mechanisms under the Children's Online Privacy Protection Act, 15 U.S.C. Sec. 6501 et seq., and the act's implementing regulations and exemptions.

(4) This chapter does not require a person to take any action in conflict with the federal Health Insurance Portability and Accountability Act of 1996, 42 U.S.C. Sec. 1320d et seq., or related regulations.

Section 13-61-103. Preemption — Reference to other laws

(1) This chapter supersedes and preempts any ordinance, resolution, rule, or other regulation adopted by a local political subdivision regarding the processing of personal data by a controller or processor.

(2) Any reference to federal law in this chapter includes any rules or regulations promulgated under the federal law.

Section 13-61-201. Consumer rights — Access — Deletion — Portability — Opt out of certain processing

(1) A consumer has the right to: (a) confirm whether a controller is processing the consumer's personal data; and (b) access the consumer's personal data.

(2) A consumer has the right to delete the consumer's personal data that the consumer provided to the controller.

(3) A consumer has the right to obtain a copy of the consumer's personal data, that the consumer previously provided to the controller, in a format that: (a) to the extent technically feasible, is portable; (b) to the extent practicable, is readily usable; and (c) allows the consumer to transmit the data to another controller without impediment, where the processing is carried out by automated means.

(4) A consumer has the right to opt out of the processing of the consumer's personal data for purposes of: (a) targeted advertising; or (b) the sale of personal data.

(5) Nothing in this section requires a person to cause a breach of security system as defined in Section 13-44-102.

Section 13-61-202. Exercising consumer rights

(1) A consumer may exercise a right by submitting a request to a controller, by means prescribed by the controller, specifying the right the consumer intends to exercise.

(2) In the case of processing personal data concerning a known child, the parent or legal guardian of the known child shall exercise a right on the child's behalf.

(3) In the case of processing personal data concerning a consumer subject to guardianship, conservatorship, or other protective arrangement under Title 75, Chapter 5, Protection of Persons Under Disability and Their Property, the guardian or the conservator of the consumer shall exercise a right on the consumer's behalf.

Section 13-61-203. Controller's response to requests

(1) Subject to the other provisions of this chapter, a controller shall comply with a consumer's request under Section 13-61-202 to exercise a right.

(2) (a) Within 45 days after the day on which a controller receives a request to exercise a right, the controller shall: (i) take action on the consumer's request; and (ii) inform the consumer of any action taken on the consumer's request. (b) The controller may extend once the initial 45-day period by an additional 45 days if reasonably necessary due to the complexity of the request or the volume of the requests received by the controller. (c) If a controller extends the initial 45-day period, before the initial 45-day period expires, the controller shall: (i) inform the consumer of the extension, including the length of the extension; and (ii) provide the reasons the extension is reasonably necessary as described in Subsection (2)(b). (d) The 45-day period does not apply if the controller reasonably suspects the consumer's request is fraudulent and the controller is not able to authenticate the request before the 45-day period expires.

(3) If, in accordance with this section, a controller chooses not to take action on a consumer's request, the controller shall within 45 days after the day on which the controller receives the request, inform the consumer of the reasons for not taking action.

(4) (a) A controller may not charge a fee for information in response to a request, unless the request is the consumer's second or subsequent request during the same 12-month period. (b) (i) Notwithstanding Subsection (4)(a), a controller may charge a reasonable fee to cover the administrative costs of complying with a request or refuse to act on a request, if: (A) the request is excessive, repetitive, technically infeasible, or manifestly unfounded; (B) the controller

reasonably believes the primary purpose in submitting the request was something other than exercising a right; or (C) the request, individually or as part of an organized effort, harasses, disrupts, or imposes undue burden on the resources of the controller's business.(ii) A controller that charges a fee or refuses to act in accordance with this Subsection (4)(b) bears the burden of demonstrating the request satisfied one or more of the criteria described in Subsection (4)(b)(i).

(5) If a controller is unable to authenticate a consumer request to exercise a right described in Section 13-61-201 using commercially reasonable efforts, the controller: (a) is not required to comply with the request; and (b) may request that the consumer provide additional information reasonably necessary to authenticate the request.

Section 13-61-301. Responsibility according to role

(1) A processor shall: (a) adhere to the controller's instructions; and (b) taking into account the nature of the processing and information available to the processor, by appropriate technical and organizational measures, insofar as reasonably practicable, assist the controller in meeting the controller's obligations, including obligations related to the security of processing personal data and notification of a breach of security system described in Section 13-44-202.

(2) Before a processor performs processing on behalf of a controller, the processor and controller shall enter into a contract that: (a) clearly sets forth instructions for processing personal data, the nature and purpose of the processing, the type of data subject to processing, the duration of the processing, and the parties' rights and obligations; (b) requires the processor to ensure each person processing personal data is subject to a duty of confidentiality with respect to the personal data; and (c) requires the processor to engage any subcontractor pursuant to a written contract that requires the subcontractor to meet the same obligations as the processor with respect to the personal data.

(3) (a) Determining whether a person is acting as a controller or processor with respect to a specific processing of data is a fact-based determination that depends upon the context in which personal data are to be processed. (b) A processor that adheres to a controller's instructions with respect to a specific processing of personal data remains a processor.

Section 13-61-302. Responsibilities of controllers — Transparency — Purpose specification and data minimization — Consent for secondary use — Security — Nondiscrimination — Nonretaliation — Nonwaiver of consumer rights.

(1) (a) A controller shall provide consumers with a reasonably accessible and clear privacy notice that includes: (i) the categories of personal data processed by the controller; (ii) the purposes for which the categories of personal data are processed; (iii) how consumers may exercise a right; (iv) the categories of personal data that the controller shares with third parties, if any; and (v) the categories of third parties, if any, with whom the controller shares personal data. (b) If a controller sells a consumer's personal data to one or more third parties or engages in targeted advertising, the controller shall clearly and conspicuously disclose to the consumer the manner in which the consumer may exercise the right to opt out of the: (i) sale of the consumer's personal data; or (ii) processing for targeted advertising.

(2) (a) A controller shall establish, implement, and maintain reasonable administrative, technical, and physical data security practices designed to: (i) protect the confidentiality and integrity of

personal data; and

(ii) reduce reasonably foreseeable risks of harm to consumers relating to the processing of personal data. (b) Considering the controller's business size, scope, and type, a controller shall use data security practices that are appropriate for the volume and nature of the personal data at issue.

(3) Except as otherwise provided in this chapter, a controller may not process sensitive data collected from a consumer without: (a) first presenting the consumer with clear notice and an opportunity to opt out of the processing; or (b) in the case of the processing of personal data concerning a known child, processing the data in accordance with the federal Children's Online Privacy Protection Act, 15 U.S.C. Sec. 6501 et seq., and the act's implementing regulations and exemptions.

(4) A controller may not discriminate against a consumer for exercising a right by: (i) denying a good or service to the consumer; (ii) charging the consumer a different price or rate for a good or service; or (iii) providing the consumer a different level of quality of a good or service. (b) This Subsection (4) does not prohibit a controller from offering a different price, rate, level, quality, or selection of a good or service to a consumer, including offering a good or service for no fee or at a discount, if: (i) the consumer has opted out of targeted advertising; or (ii) the offer is related to the consumer's voluntary participation in a bona fide loyalty, rewards, premium features, discounts, or club card program.

(5) A controller is not required to provide a product, service, or functionality to a consumer if: (a) the consumer's personal data are or the processing of the consumer's personal data is reasonably necessary for the controller to provide the consumer the product, service, or functionality; and (b) the consumer does not: (i) provide the consumer's personal data to the controller; or (ii) allow the controller to process the consumer's personal data.

(6) Any provision of a contract that purports to waive or limit a consumer's right under this chapter is void.

Section 13-61-303. Processing deidentified data or pseudonymous data

(1) The provisions of this chapter do not require a controller or processor to: (a) reidentify deidentified data or pseudonymous data; (b) maintain data in identifiable form or obtain, retain, or access any data or technology for the purpose of allowing the controller or processor to associate a consumer request with personal data; or (c) comply with an authenticated consumer request to exercise a right described in Subsections 13-61-202(1) through (3), if: (1) (A) the controller is not reasonably capable of associating the request with the personal data; or (B) it would be unreasonably burdensome for the controller to associate the request with the personal data;

(ii) the controller does not: (A) use the personal data to recognize or respond to the consumer who is the subject of the personal data; or (B) associate the personal data with other personal data about the consumer; and

(iii) the controller does not sell or otherwise disclose the personal data to any third party other than a processor, except as otherwise permitted in this section.

(2) The rights described in Subsections 13-61-201(1) through (3) do not apply to pseudonymous data if a controller demonstrates that any information necessary to identify a consumer is kept: (a) separately; and (b) subject to appropriate technical and organizational measures to ensure the personal data are not attributed to an identified individual or an identifiable individual. (3) A controller who uses pseudonymous data or deidentified data shall take reasonable steps to ensure the controller: (a) complies with any contractual obligations to which the pseudonymous data or deidentified data are subject; and (b) promptly addresses any breach of a contractual obligation described in Subsection (3)(a).

Section 13-61-304. Limitations

(1) The requirements described in this chapter do not restrict a controller's or processor's ability to:(a) comply with a federal, state, or local law, rule, or regulation; (b) comply with a civil, criminal, or regulatory inquiry, investigation, subpoena, or summons by a federal, state, local, or other governmental entity; (c) cooperate with a law enforcement agency concerning activity that the controller or processor reasonably and in good faith believes may violate federal, state, or local laws, rules, or regulations; (d) investigate, establish, exercise, prepare for, or defend a legal claim; (e) provide a product or service requested by a consumer or a parent or legal guardian of a child;

(f) perform a contract to which the consumer or the parent or legal guardian of a child is a party, including fulfilling the terms of a written warranty or taking steps at the request of the consumer or parent or legal guardian before entering into the contract with the consumer; (g) take immediate steps to protect an interest that is essential for the life or physical safety of the consumer or of another individual; (h) (i) detect, prevent, protect against, or respond to a security incident, identity theft, fraud, harassment, malicious or deceptive activity, or any illegal activity; or (ii) investigate, report, or prosecute a person responsible for an action described in Subsection (1)(h)(i); (i) (i) preserve the integrity or security of systems; or (ii) investigate, report, or prosecute a person responsible for harming or threatening the integrity or security of systems, as applicable; (j) if the controller discloses the processing in a notice described in Section 13-61-302, engage in public or peer-reviewed scientific, historical, or statistical research in the public interest that adheres to all other applicable ethics and privacy laws; (k) assist another person with an obligation described in this subsection; (l) process personal data to: (i) conduct internal analytics or other research to develop, improve, or repair a controller's or processor's product, service, or technology; (ii) identify and repair technical errors that impair existing or intended functionality; or (iii) effectuate a product recall; (m) process personal data to perform an internal operation that is: (i) reasonably aligned with the consumer's expectations based on the consumer's existing relationship with the controller; or (ii) otherwise compatible with processing to aid the controller or processor in providing a product or service specifically requested by a consumer or a parent or legal guardian of a child or the performance of a contract to which the consumer or a parent or legal guardian of a child is a party; or (n) retain a consumer's email address to comply with the consumer's request to exercise a right.

(2) This chapter does not apply if a controller's or processor's compliance with this chapter: (a) violates an evidentiary privilege under Utah law; (b) as part of a privileged communication, prevents a controller or processor from providing personal data concerning a consumer to a person covered by an evidentiary privilege under Utah law; or (c) adversely affects the privacy

or other rights of any person.

(3) A controller or processor is not in violation of this chapter if: (a) the controller or processor discloses personal data to a third-party controller or processor in compliance with this chapter; (b) the third party processes the personal data in violation of this chapter; and (c) the disclosing controller or processor did not have actual knowledge of the third party's intent to commit a violation of this chapter.

(4) If a controller processes personal data under an exemption described in Subsection (1), the controller bears the burden of demonstrating that the processing qualifies for the exemption.

(5) Nothing in this chapter requires a controller, processor, third party, or consumer to disclose a trade secret.

Section 13-61-305. No private cause of action

A violation of this chapter does not provide a basis for, nor is a violation of this chapter subject to, a private right of action under this chapter or any other law.

Section 13-61-401. Investigative powers of division.

(1) The division shall establish and administer a system to receive consumer complaints regarding a controller's or processor's alleged violation of this chapter.

(2) (a) The division may investigate a consumer complaint to determine whether the controller or processor violated or is violating this chapter. (b) If the director has reasonable cause to believe that substantial evidence exists that a person identified in a consumer complaint is in violation of this chapter, the director shall refer the matter to the attorney general. (c) Upon request, the division shall provide consultation and assistance to the attorney general in enforcing this chapter.

Section 13-61-402. Enforcement powers of the attorney general

(1) The attorney general has the exclusive authority to enforce this chapter.

(2) Upon referral from the division, the attorney general may initiate an enforcement action against a controller or processor for a violation of this chapter.

(3) (a) At least 30 days before the day on which the attorney general initiates an enforcement action against a controller or processor, the attorney general shall provide the controller or processor: (i) written notice identifying each provision of this chapter the attorney general alleges the controller or processor has violated or is violating; and (ii) an explanation of the basis for each allegation. (b) The attorney general may not initiate an action if the controller or processor: (i) cures the noticed violation within 30 days after the day on which the controller or processor receives the written notice described in Subsection (3)(a); and (ii) provides the attorney general an express written statement that: (A) the violation has been cured; and(B) no further violation of the cured violation will occur.

(c)The attorney general may initiate an action against a controller or processor who: (i) fails to cure a violation after receiving the notice described in Subsection (3)(a); or (ii) after curing a noticed violation and providing a written statement in accordance with Subsection (3)(b), continues to violate this chapter. (d) In an action described in Subsection (3)(c), the attorney general may recover: (i) actual damages to the consumer; and (ii) for each violation described in Subsection (3)(c), an amount not to exceed $7,500.

(4) All money received from an action under this chapter shall be deposited into the Consumer Privacy Account established in Section 13-61-403.

(5) If more than one controller or processor are involved in the same processing in violation of this chapter, the liability for the violation shall be allocated among the controllers or processors according to the principles of comparative fault.

Section 13-61-403. Consumer Privacy Restricted Account

(1) There is created a restricted account known as the "Consumer Privacy Account."

(2) The account shall be funded by money received through civil enforcement actions under this chapter.

(3) Upon appropriation, the division or the attorney general may use money deposited into the account for:

(a) investigation and administrative costs incurred by the division in investigating consumer complaints alleging violations of this chapter; (b) recovery of costs and attorney fees accrued by the attorney general in enforcing this chapter; and (c)providing consumer and business education regarding: (i) consumer rights under this chapter; and

(ii) compliance with the provisions of this chapter for controllers and processors.

(4) If the balance in the account exceeds $4,000,000 at the close of any fiscal year, the Division of Finance shall transfer the amount that exceeds $4,000,000 into the General Fund.

Section 13-61-404. Attorney general report

(1) The attorney general and the division shall compile a report: (a) evaluating the liability and enforcement provisions of this chapter, including the effectiveness of the attorney general's and the division's efforts to enforce this chapter; and (b) summarizing the data protected and not protected by this chapter including, with reasonable detail, a list of the types of information that are publicly available from local, state, and federal government sources.

(2) The attorney general and the division may update the report as new information becomes available.

(3) The attorney general and the division shall submit the report to the Business and Labor Interim Committee before July 1, 2025.

Section 17. Effective date.

This bill takes effect on December 31, 2023.

APPENDIX 5: VIRGINIA CONSUMER DATA PROTECTION ACT

§ 59.1-571. Definitions.

As used in this chapter, unless the context requires a different meaning:

"Affiliate" means a legal entity that controls, is controlled by, or shares common control with another legal entity. For the purposes of this definition, "control" or "controlled" means (i) ownership of, or the power to vote, more than 50 percent of the outstanding shares of any class of voting security of a company; (ii) control in any manner over the election of a majority of the directors or of individuals exercising similar functions; or (iii) the power to exercise controlling influence over the management of a company.

"Authenticate" means verifying through reasonable means that the consumer entitled to exercise his consumer rights in § 59.1-573, is the same consumer exercising such consumer rights with respect to the personal data at issue.

"Business associate" means the same meaning as the term established by HIPAA.

"Child" means any natural person younger than 13 years of age.

"Consent" means clear affirmative act signifying a consumer's freely given, specific, informed, and unambiguous agreement to process personal data relating to the consumer. Consent may include a written statement, including a statement written by electronic means, or any other unambiguous affirmative action.

"Consumer" means a natural person who is a resident of the commonwealth acting only in an individual or household context. It does not include a natural person acting in a commercial or employment context.

"Controller" means the natural or legal entity that, alone or jointly with others, determines the purpose and means of processing personal data.

"Covered entity" means the same as the term is established by HIPAA.

"Decisions that produce legal or similarly significant effects concerning a consumer" means a decision made by the controller that results in the provision or denial by the controller of financial and lending services, housing, insurance, education enrollment, criminal justice, employment opportunities, health care services, or access to basic necessities, such as food and water.

"De-identified data" means data that cannot reasonably be linked to an identified or identifiable natural person, or a device linked to such person. A controller that possesses "de-identified data" shall comply with the requirements of subsection A of § 59.1-577.

"Fund" means the Consumer Privacy Fund established pursuant to § 59.1-581.

"Health record" means the same as that term is defined in § 32.1-127.1:03.

"Health care provider" means the same as that term is defined in § 32.1-276.3.

"HIPAA" means the Health Insurance Portability and Accountability Act of 1996 (42 U.S.C. § 1320d et seq.).

"Identified or identifiable natural person" means a person who can be readily identified, directly or indirectly.

"Personal data" means any information that is linked or reasonably associated to an identified or identifiable natural person. "Personal data" does not include de-identified data or publicly available information.

"Precise geolocation data" means information derived from technology, including but not limited to global positioning system level latitude and longitude coordinates or other mechanisms, that directly identifies the specific location of a natural person with precision and accuracy below 1,750 feet. "Precise geolocation data" does not include the content of communications."

"Process" or "processing" means any operation or set of operations performed, whether by manual or automated means, on personal data or on sets of personal data, such as the collection, use, storage, disclosure, analysis, deletion, or modification of personal data.

"Processor" means a natural or legal entity that processes personal data on behalf of a controller.

"Profiling" means any form of automated processing performed on personal data to evaluate, analyze, or predict personal aspects related to an identified or identifiable natural person's economic situation, health, personal preferences, interests, reliability, behavior, location, or movements.

"Protected health information" means the same as the term is established in HIPAA.

"Pseudonymous data" means personal data that cannot be attributed to a specific natural person without the use of additional information, provided that such additional information is kept separately and is subject to appropriate technical and organizational measures to ensure that the personal data is not attributed to an identified or identifiable natural person.

"Publicly available information" means information that is lawfully made available through federal, state, or local government records, or information that a business has a reasonable basis to believe is lawfully made available to the general public through widely distributed media, by the consumer, or by a person to whom the consumer has disclosed the information, unless the consumer has restricted the information to a specific audience.

"Sale of personal data" means the exchange of personal data for monetary consideration by the controller to a third party. "Sale of personal data" does not include:

1. The disclosure of personal data to a processor that processes the personal data on behalf of the controller;

2. The disclosure of personal data to a third party with whom the consumer has a direct relationship for purposes of providing a product or service requested by the consumer;

3. The disclosure or transfer of personal data to an affiliate of the controller;

4. The disclosure of information that the consumer (i) intentionally made available to the general public via a channel of mass media and (ii) did not restrict to a specific audience; or

5. The disclosure or transfer of personal data to a third party as an asset that is part of a merger, acquisition, bankruptcy, or other transaction in which the third party assumes control of all or part of the controller's assets.

"Sensitive data" means a category of personal data that includes:

1. Personal data revealing racial or ethnic origin, religious beliefs, mental or physical health diagnosis, sexual orientation, or citizenship or immigration status;

2. The processing of genetic or biometric data for the purpose of uniquely identifying a natural person;

3. The personal data collected from a known child; or

4. Precise geolocation data.

"State agency" means the same as that term is defined in § 2.2-307.

"Targeted advertising" means displaying advertisements to a consumer where the advertisement is selected based on personal data obtained from a consumer's activities over time and across nonaffiliated websites or online applications to predict such consumer's preferences or interests. "Targeted advertising" does not include:

1. Advertisements based on activities within a controller's own websites or online applications;

2. Advertisements based on the context of a consumer's current search query, visit to a website, or online application;

3. Advertisements directed to a consumer in response to the consumer's request for information or feedback; or

4. Processing personal data processed solely for measuring or reporting advertising performance, reach, or frequency.

"Third party" means a natural or legal person, public authority, agency, or body other than the consumer, controller, processor, or an affiliate of the processor or the controller.

§ 59.1-572. Scope; exemptions.

A. This chapter applies to persons that conduct business in the commonwealth or produce products or services that are targeted to residents of the commonwealth and that (i) during a calendar year, control or process personal data of at least 100,000 consumers or (ii) control or process personal data of at least 25,000 consumers and derive over 50 percent of gross revenue from the sale of personal data.

B. This chapter shall not apply to (i) any body, authority, board, bureau, commission, district, or agency of the commonwealth or of any political subdivision of the commonwealth; (ii) financial institutions or data subject to Title V of the federal Gramm-Leach-Bliley Act (15 U.S.C. § 6801 et seq.); or (iii) any covered entity or business associate governed by the privacy, security, and breach notification rules issued by the United States Department of Health and Human Services, 45 C.F.R. Parts 160 and 164 established pursuant to HIPAA, and the Health Information Technology for Economic and Clinical Health Act (Public Law 111-5).

C. The following information and data is exempt from this chapter:

1. Protected health information under HIPAA;

2. Health records for purposes of Title 32.1;

3. Patient identifying information for purposes of 42 U.S.C. § 290dd-2;

4. Identifiable private information for purposes of the federal policy for the protection of human subjects under 45 C.F.R. Part 46; identifiable private information that is otherwise information collected as part of human subjects research pursuant to the good clinical practice guidelines issued by The International Council for Harmonisation of Technical Requirements for Pharmaceuticals for Human Use; the protection of human subjects under 21 C.F.R. Parts 6, 50, and 56; or personal data used or shared in research conducted in accordance with the requirements set forth in this chapter;

5. Information and documents created for purposes of the federal Health Care Quality Improvement Act of 1986 (42 U.S.C. § 11101 et seq.);

6. Patient safety work product for purposes of the federal Patient Safety and Quality Improvement Act (42 U.S.C. § 299b-21 et seq.);

7. Information derived from any of the health care-related information listed in this subsection that is de-identified in accordance with the requirements for de-identification pursuant to HIPAA;

8. Information originating from, and intermingled to be indistinguishable with, information exempt under this subsection that is maintained by a covered entity or business associate as defined by HIPAA or a program or a qualified service organization as defined by 42 U.S.C. § 290dd-2;

9. Information used only for public health activities and purposes as authorized by HIPAA;

10. The collection, maintenance, disclosure, sale, communication, or use of any personal information bearing on a consumer's credit worthiness, credit standing, credit capacity, character, general reputation, personal characteristics, or mode of living by a consumer reporting agency, furnisher, or user that provides information for use in a consumer report, and by a user of a consumer report, but only to the extent that such activity is regulated by and authorized under the federal Fair Credit Reporting Act (15 U.S.C. § 1681 et seq.);

11. Personal data collected, processed, sold, or disclosed in compliance with the federal Driver's Privacy Protection Act of 1994 (18 U.S.C. § 2721 et seq.);

12. Personal data regulated by the federal Family Educational Rights and Privacy Act (20 U.S.C. § 1232g et seq.);

13. Personal data collected, processed, sold, or disclosed in compliance with the federal Farm Credit Act (12 U.S.C. § 2001 et seq.); and

14. Data processed by a controller, processor, or third party (i) in the course of an individual applying to, employed by, or acting as an agent of a controller, processor, or third party, to the extent that the data is collected and used within the context of that role; (ii) as the emergency contact information of an individual under this chapter used for emergency contact purposes; or (iii) that is necessary for the controller, processor, or third party to retain to administer benefits for another individual relating to the individual under clause (i) and used for the purposes of administering those benefits.

D. Controllers and processors that comply with the verifiable parental consent requirements of the Children's Online Privacy Protection Act (15 U.S.C. § 6501 et seq.) shall be deemed compliant with any obligation to obtain parental consent under this chapter.

§ 59.1-573. Personal data rights; consumers.

A. A consumer may invoke the consumer rights authorized pursuant to this subsection at any time by submitting a request to a controller specifying the consumer rights the consumer wishes to invoke. A known child's parent or legal guardian may invoke such consumer rights on behalf of the child regarding processing personal data belonging to the known child. A controller shall comply with an authenticated consumer request to exercise the right:

1. To confirm whether or not a controller is processing his personal data and to access such personal data;

2. To correct inaccuracies in his personal data, taking into account the nature of the personal data and the purposes of the processing of the personal data;

3. To delete his personal data;

4. To obtain a copy of his personal data that he previously provided to the controller in a portable and, to the extent technically feasible, readily usable format that allows the consumer to transmit the data to another controller without hindrance, where the processing is carried out by automated means; and

5. To opt out of the processing of the personal data for purposes of targeted advertising, the sale of personal data, or profiling in furtherance of decisions that produce legal or similarly significant effects concerning the consumer.

B. Except as otherwise provided in this chapter, a controller shall comply with a request by a consumer to exercise the consumer rights authorized pursuant to subsection A as follows:

1. A controller shall respond to the consumer without undue delay, but in all cases within 45 days of receipt of the request. The response period may be extended once by 45 additional days when reasonably necessary, taking into account the complexity and number of the consumer's requests, so long as the controller informs the consumer of any such extension within the initial 45-day response period, together with the reasons for the extension.

2. If a controller declines to take action regarding the consumer's request, the controller shall inform the consumer without undue delay, but in all cases and at the latest within 45 days of receipt of the request, of the justification for declining to take action and instructions for how to appeal the decision pursuant to subsection C.

3. Information provided in response to a consumer request shall be provided by a controller free of charge, up to twice annually per consumer. If requests from a consumer are manifestly unfounded, excessive, or repetitive, the controller may charge the consumer a reasonable fee to cover the administrative costs of complying with the request or decline to act on the request. The controller bears the burden of demonstrating the manifestly unfounded, excessive, or repetitive nature of the request.

4. If a controller is unable to fulfill the request using commercially reasonable efforts, the controller shall not be required to comply with a request to initiate an action under subsection A and may request that the consumer provide additional information reasonably necessary to authenticate the request.

C. A controller shall establish a process for a consumer to appeal the controller's refusal to take action on a request within a reasonable period of time after the consumer's receipt of the decision pursuant to subdivision B 2. The appeal process shall be conspicuously available and similar to the process for submitting requests to initiate action pursuant to subsection A. Within 60 days of receipt of an appeal, a controller shall inform the consumer in writing of any action taken or not taken in response to the appeal, including a written explanation of the reasons for the decisions. The controller shall also provide the consumer with an email address or other online mechanism through which the consumer may contact the attorney general to submit a complaint.

§ 59.1-574. Data controller responsibilities; transparency.

A. A controller shall:

1. Limit the collection of personal data to what is adequate, relevant, and reasonably necessary in relation to the purposes for which such data is processed, as disclosed to the consumer;

2. Except as otherwise provided in this chapter, not process personal data for purposes not reasonably necessary to, or compatible with, the disclosed purposes for which such personal data is processed, as disclosed to the consumer, unless the controller obtains the consumer's consent;

3. Establish, implement, and maintain reasonable administrative, technical, and physical data security practices to protect the confidentiality, integrity, and accessibility of personal data. Such data security practices shall be appropriate to the volume and nature of the personal data at issue;

4. Not process personal data in violation of state and federal laws that prohibit unlawful discrimination against consumers. A controller shall not discriminate against a consumer for exercising any of the consumer rights contained in this chapter, including denying goods or services, charging different prices or rates for goods or services, or providing a different level of quality of goods and services to the consumer. However, nothing in this subdivision shall be construed to prohibit a controller from offering a different price, rate, level, quality, or selection of goods or services to a consumer, including offering goods or services for no fee, if the consumer has opted out of targeted advertising or the offer is related to a consumer's voluntary participation in a bona fide loyalty, rewards, premium features, discounts, or club card program; and

5. Not process sensitive data concerning a consumer without obtaining the consumer's consent, or, in the case of the processing of sensitive data concerning a known child, without processing such data in accordance with the federal Children's Online Privacy Protection Act (15 U.S.C. § 6501 et seq.).

B. Any provision of a contract or agreement of any kind that purports to waive or limit in any way consumer rights pursuant to § 59.1-573 shall be deemed contrary to public policy and shall be void and unenforceable.

C. Controllers shall provide consumers with a reasonably accessible, clear, and meaningful privacy notice that includes:

1. The categories of personal data processed by the controller;

2. The purpose for processing personal data;

3. How consumers may exercise their consumer rights pursuant § 59.1-573, including how a consumer may appeal a controller's decision with regard to the consumer's request;

4. The categories of personal data that the controller shares with third parties, if any; and

5. The categories of third parties, if any, with whom the controller shares personal data.

D. If a controller sells personal data to third parties or processes personal data for targeted advertising, the controller shall clearly and conspicuously disclose such processing, as well as the manner in which a consumer may exercise the right to opt out of such processing.

E. A controller shall establish, and shall describe in a privacy notice, one or more secure and reliable means for consumers to submit a request to exercise their consumer rights under this chapter. Such means shall take into account the ways in which consumers normally interact with the controller, the need for secure and reliable communication of such requests, and the ability of the controller to authenticate the identity of the consumer making the request. Controllers shall not require a consumer to create a new account in order to exercise consumer rights pursuant to § 59.1-573 but may require a consumer to use an existing account.

§ 59.1-575. Responsibility according to role; controller and processor.

A. A processor shall adhere to the instructions of a controller and shall assist the controller in meeting its obligations under this chapter. Such assistance shall include:

1. Taking into account the nature of processing by appropriate technical and organizational measures, insofar as possible, to fulfill the controller's obligation to respond to consumer rights requests pursuant to § 59.1-573;

2. Securely processing personal data, taking into account the nature of processing information available to the processor, and complying with security breach notification requirements pursuant to § 18.2-186.6 in order to meet the controller's obligations; and

3. Providing necessary information to enable the controller to conduct and document data protection assessments pursuant to § 59.1-576.

B. A contract between a controller and a processor shall govern the processor's data processing procedures. The contract shall be binding and clearly set forth instructions for processing data, the nature and purpose of processing, the type of data subject to processing, the duration of processing, and the rights and obligations of both parties. The contract shall also include requirements that:

1. The processor shall ensure that each person processing personal data is subject to a duty of confidentiality with respect to the data;

2. At the controller's discretion, the processor shall delete or return all personal data to the controller as

requested at the end of the provision of services, unless retention of the personal data is required by law;

3. The processor shall make available to the controller all information in its possession necessary to demonstrate compliance with the obligations in this chapter; and

4. The processor shall allow, and contribute to, reasonable audits and inspections by the controller or the controller's designated auditor; alternatively, the processor may arrange for a qualified and independent auditor to conduct an audit of the processor's policies and technical and organizational measures in support of the obligations under this chapter using an appropriate and accepted control standard or framework and audit procedure for such audits. The processor shall provide a report of such audit to the controller upon request.

C. Nothing in this section shall be construed to relieve a controller or a processor from the liabilities imposed on it by virtue of its role in the processing relationship as defined by this chapter.

D. Determining whether a person is acting as a controller or processor with respect to a specific processing of data is a fact-based determination that depends upon the context in which personal data is to be processed. A processor that continues to adhere to a controller's instructions with respect to a specific processing of personal data remains a processor.

§ 59.1-576. Data protection assessments.

A. A controller shall conduct and document a data protection assessment of each of the following processing activities involving personal data:

1. The processing of personal data for purposes of targeted advertising;

2. The sale of personal data;

3. The processing of personal data for purposes of profiling, where such profiling presents a reasonably foreseeable risk of (i) unfair or deceptive treatment of, or unlawful disparate impact on, consumers; (ii) financial, physical, or reputational injury to consumers; (iii) a physical or other intrusion upon the solitude or seclusion, or the private affairs or concerns, of consumers, where such intrusion would be offensive to a reasonable person; or (iv) other substantial injury to consumers;

4. The processing of sensitive data; and

5. Any processing activities involving personal data that present a heightened risk of harm to consumers. A single data protection assessment may address a comparable set of processing operations that include similar activities.

Such data protection assessments shall take into account the extent to which the personal data is sensitive data and the context in which the personal data is to be processed.

B. Data protection assessments conducted pursuant to subsection A shall identify and weigh the benefits that may flow, directly and indirectly, from the processing to the controller, the consumer, other stakeholders, and the public against the potential risks to the rights of the consumer associated with such processing, as mitigated by safeguards that can be employed by the controller to reduce such risks. The use of de-identified data and the reasonable expectations of consumers, as well as the context of the processing and the relationship between the controller and the consumer whose personal data will be processed, shall be factored into this assessment by the controller.

C. The attorney general may request, in writing, that a controller disclose any data protection assessment that is relevant to an investigation conducted by the attorney general, and the controller shall make the data protection assessment available to the attorney general. The attorney general may evaluate the data protection assessment for compliance with the responsibilities set forth in § 59.1-574. Data protection assessments shall be confidential and exempt from public inspection and copying under the Virginia Freedom of Information Act (§ 2.2-3700 et seq.). The disclosure of a data protection assessment pursuant to a request from the attorney general shall not constitute a waiver of attorney-client privilege or work product protection with respect to the assessment and any information contained in the assessment.

D. Data protection assessments conducted by a controller for the purpose of compliance with other laws or regulations may comply under this section if the assessments have a reasonably comparable scope and effect.

E. Data protection assessment requirements shall apply to processing activities created or generated after January 1, 2023, and are not retroactive.

§ 59.1-577. Processing de-identified data; exemptions.

A. The controller in possession of de-identified data shall:

1. Take reasonable measures to ensure that the data cannot be associated with a natural person;

2. Publicly commit to maintaining and using de-identified data without attempting to re-identify the data; and

3. Contractually obligate any recipients of the de-identified data to comply with all provisions of this chapter.

B. Nothing in this chapter shall be construed to (i) require a controller or processor to re-identify de-identified data or (ii) maintain data in identifiable form, or collect, obtain, retain, or access any data or technology, in order to be capable of associating an authenticated consumer request with personal data.

C. Nothing in this chapter shall be construed to require a controller or processor to comply with an authenticated consumer rights request, pursuant to § 59.1-574, if all of the following are true:

1. The controller is not reasonably capable of associating the request with the personal data or it would be unreasonably burdensome for the controller to associate the request with the personal data;

2. The controller does not use the personal data to recognize or respond to the specific consumer who is the subject of the personal data, or associate the personal data with other personal data about the same specific consumer; and

3. The controller does not sell the personal data to any third party or otherwise voluntarily disclose the personal data to any third party other than a processor, except as otherwise permitted in this section.

D. The consumer rights contained in § 59.1-574 shall not apply to pseudonymous data in cases where the controller is able to demonstrate that any information necessary to identify the consumer is kept separately and is subject to effective technical and organizational controls that prevent the controller from accessing such information.

E. A controller that uses pseudonymous data or de-identified data shall exercise reasonable oversight to monitor compliance with any contractual commitments to which the pseudonymous data or de-identified data is subject and shall take appropriate steps to address any breaches of contractual commitments.

§ 59.1-578. Limitations.

A. Nothing in this section shall be construed to restrict a controller's or processor's ability to:

1. Comply with federal, state, or local laws, rules, or regulations;

2. Comply with a civil, criminal, or regulatory inquiry, investigation, subpoena, or summons by federal, state,

local, or other governmental authorities;

3. Cooperate with law-enforcement agencies concerning conduct or activity that the controller or processor reasonably and in good faith believes may violate federal, state, or local laws, rules, or regulations;

4. Investigate, establish, exercise, prepare for, or defend legal claims;

5. Provide a product or service specifically requested by a consumer, perform a contract to which the consumer is a party, or take steps at the request of the consumer prior to entering into a contract;

6. Take immediate steps to protect an interest that is essential for the life of the consumer or of another natural person, and where the processing cannot be manifestly based on another legal basis;

7. Prevent, detect, protect against, or respond to security incidents, identity theft, fraud, harassment, malicious or deceptive activities, or any illegal activity; preserve the integrity or security of systems; or investigate, report, or prosecute those responsible for any such action;

8. Engage in public- or peer-reviewed scientific, historical, or statistical research in the public interest that adheres to all other applicable ethics and privacy laws if the deletion of the information is likely to render impossible or seriously impair the achievement of the research and the consumer has provided consent; or

9. Assist another controller, processor, or third party with any of the obligations under this subsection.

B. The obligations imposed on controllers or processors under this chapter shall not restrict a controller's or processor's ability to collect, use, or retain data to:

1. Conduct internal research to improve or repair products, services, or technology;

2. Identify and repair technical errors that impair existing or intended functionality; or

3. Perform internal operations that are reasonably aligned with the expectations of the consumer based on the consumer's existing relationship with the controller or are otherwise compatible with processing data in furtherance of the provision of a product or service specifically requested by a consumer or the performance of a contract to which the consumer is a party.

C. The obligations imposed on controllers or processors under this chapter shall not apply where compliance by the controller or processor with this chapter would violate an evidentiary privilege under the laws of the commonwealth. Nothing in this chapter shall be construed to prevent a controller or processor from providing personal data concerning a consumer to a person covered by an evidentiary privilege under the laws of the commonwealth as part of a privileged communication.

D. A controller or processor that discloses personal data to a third-party controller or processor, in compliance with the requirements of this chapter, is not in violation of this chapter if the third-party controller or processor that receives and processes such personal data is in violation of this chapter, provided that, at the time of disclosing the personal data, the disclosing controller or processor did not have actual knowledge that the recipient intended to commit a violation. A third-party controller or processor receiving personal data from a controller or processor in compliance with the requirements of this chapter is likewise not in violation of this chapter for the transgressions of the controller or processor from which it receives such personal data.

E. Nothing in this chapter shall be construed as an obligation imposed on controllers and processors that adversely affects the rights or freedoms of any persons, such as exercising the right of free speech pursuant to the First Amendment to the United States Constitution, or applies to the processing of personal data by a person in the course of a purely personal or household activity.

F. Personal data processed by a controller pursuant to this section shall not be processed for any purpose other than those expressly listed in this section unless otherwise allowed by this chapter. Personal data processed by a controller pursuant to this section may be processed to the extent that such processing is:

1. Reasonably necessary and proportionate to the purposes listed in this section; and

2. Adequate, relevant, and limited to what is necessary in relation to the specific purposes listed in this section. Personal data collected, used, or retained pursuant to subsection B shall, where applicable, take into account the nature and purpose or purposes of such collection, use, or retention. Such data shall be subject to reasonable administrative, technical, and physical measures to protect the confidentiality, integrity, and accessibility of the personal data and to reduce reasonably foreseeable risks of harm to consumers relating to such collection, use, or retention of personal data.

G. If a controller processes personal data pursuant to an exemption in this section, the controller bears the burden of demonstrating that such processing qualifies for the exemption and complies with the requirements in subsection F.

H. Processing personal data for the purposes expressly identified in subdivisions A 1 through 9 shall not solely make an entity a controller with respect to such processing.

§ 59.1-579. Violations of chapter; civil penalty.

A. The attorney general shall have exclusive authority to enforce violations of this chapter.

B. Prior to initiating any action under this chapter, the attorney general shall provide a controller or processor 30 days' written notice identifying the specific provisions of this chapter the attorney general, on behalf of a consumer, alleges have been or are being violated. If within the 30 days the controller or processor cures the noticed violation and provides the consumer an express written statement that the alleged violations have been cured and that no further violations shall occur, no action for statutory damages shall be initiated against the controller or processor.

If a controller or processor continues to violate this chapter in breach of an express written statement provided to the consumer under this section, the attorney general may initiate an action and seek damages for up to $7,500 for each violation under this chapter.

C. Nothing in this chapter shall be construed as providing a private right of action to violations of this chapter.

§ 59.1-580. Enforcement; civil penalty.

A. The attorney general retains exclusive authority to enforce this chapter by bringing an action in the name of the Commonwealth, or on behalf of persons residing in the commonwealth. The attorney general may issue a civil investigative demand to any controller or processor believed to be engaged in, or about to engage in, any violation of this chapter. The provisions of § 59.1-9.10 shall apply to civil investigative demands issued under this section.

B. Any controller or processor that violates this chapter is subject to an injunction and liable for a civil penalty of not more than $7,500 for each violation.

C. The attorney general may recover reasonable expenses incurred in investigating and preparing the case, including attorney fees, of any action initiated under this chapter.

§ 59.1-581. Consumer Privacy Fund.

There is hereby created in the state treasury a special nonreverting fund to be known as the Consumer Privacy Fund. The fund shall be established on the books of the comptroller. All civil penalties collected pursuant to this chapter shall be paid into the state treasury and credited to the Fund. Interest earned on moneys in the Fund shall remain in the Fund and be credited to it. Any moneys remaining in the Fund, including interest thereon, at the end of each fiscal year shall not revert to the general fund but shall remain in the Fund. Moneys in the Fund shall be used to support the work of the Office of the Attorney General to enforce the provisions of this chapter, subject to appropriation.

2. That the provisions of this act shall become effective on January 1, 2023.

ABOUT THE AUTHOR

STEVEN G. STRANSKY is a Partner and the Co-Chair of the Privacy and Cybersecurity Practice Group at Thompson Hine LLP.

Steve is a trusted attorney, leader, and adviser on cybersecurity, data privacy, and national security issues, and he has deep experience providing legal advice and counsel to private-sector executives as well as White House and other senior government officials. In particular, Steve helps clients develop and implement data governance frameworks and internal policies and procedures to address and comply with evolving data privacy and digital marketing laws. In addition, Steve is a Data Breach Coach and frequently assists clients in responding to ransomware attacks, business email compromises, and other cybersecurity incidents. He has firsthand experience responding to multimillion-dollar ransomware demands, retaining independent digital forensic and incident response firms, negotiating ransom pricing with threat actors, coordinating incident reporting with law enforcement and regulatory authorities, and facilitating data breach notification letters and communications. In addition, Steve assists defense contractors and other private-sector businesses in satisfying cybersecurity standards issued by the federal government and in developing and maintaining insider threat programs.

Prior to joining Thompson Hine, Steve spent over 10 years serving in the federal government, including seven years with the U.S. Department of Homeland Security (DHS). While at DHS, he served as senior counsel in the Department's Intelligence Law Division in Washington, D.C., where he oversaw the Department's foreign intelligence, counterintelligence, and cybersecurity intelligence activities, including the production of cybersecurity threat assessments and data breach response recommendations for the private sector. He advised officials on Executive Order 12333 and other intelligence community directives, orders, and procedures governing the collection, retention, and dissemination of foreign and domestic intelligence and data. Steve also provided guidance on designing and implementing programs and policies regulating the storage and safeguarding of classified and unclassified information and assisted DHS in designing and implementing an insider threat program in compliance with Executive Order 13587 and other national policies and standards.

In addition, Steve was selected to serve as a deputy legal adviser to the president's National Security Council. In this role, he counseled White House officials on developing and coordinating a broad range of national security policies and programs, including on cybersecurity, intelligence and surveillance, and information sharing with foreign partners and the private sector.

Steve has earned multiple credentials from the International Association of Privacy Professionals related to government and private-sector data protection laws, statutes, regulations, and industry standards.

Also an adjunct law professor, Steve teaches courses on topics related to foreign affairs, intelligence activities, and national security law at the Frederick K. Cox International Law Center at Case Western Reserve University School of Law.

* *

THOMPSON HINE LLP
THE PRIVACY AND CYBERSECURITY PRACTICE GROUP

Thompson Hine's nationally recognized Privacy and Cybersecurity practice offers clients an interdisciplinary group of lawyers with experience in complex national and international privacy, data protection, information security, records retention, labor and employment law, consumer protection, internet law, insurance law, and intellectual property matters. Our team, which includes certified privacy professionals, former homeland security and national security officials, and former federal and state prosecutors, provides assistance and counsel to organizations with respect to complying with a broad range of federal, state, and foreign laws and regulations; designing and implementing globally compliant data privacy and information security programs; advising on the cross-border transfer of personal data; drafting and implementing internal policies related to privacy and cybersecurity; developing website, app, extranet, and computer network policies, including privacy policies and terms of use; and, developing comprehensive breach response and remediation plans.

Thompson Hine Data Breach Response Services

Thompson Hine can help you prepare for and respond to a cyberattack or the unauthorized disclosure of personal information or other sensitive data. We will work with your in-house lawyers, privacy and compliance officials, and technology teams. In addition, we will work with your other, external service providers and agents, including your information security and digital forensic consultants, cyber insurance carriers, and ransomware negotiators. We regularly lead and direct investigations into data security incidents, manage data breach response teams, and coordinate a single response process, all while working to ensure these activities are properly protected by applicable legal and evidentiary privileges. We have handled data incidents involving all 50 states, the U.S. territories, the European Union, and in several other jurisdictions around the world. Our team includes former national security officials, former federal and state prosecutors, and other highly experienced privacy and security attorneys. Thompson Hine has experience assisting clients in a broad range of industries, including manufacturing, health care, consumer goods, e-commerce, and government contractors and addressing a variety of data security events, such as complex ransomware attacks; breaches of e-commerce platforms and payment card data; unauthorized access of protected health information and other medical data; email compromises and fraudulent invoices; breaches to controlled unclassified information and government data; and insider threats.

****

If your organization has suffered a data breach or incident,
please contact us at any time (24/7) and a Thompson Hine
cybersecurity attorney will respond to you as soon as possible.

Contact us at: ThompsonHine.com/services/privacy-and-cybersecurity/contact

Made in the USA
Columbia, SC
27 January 2023

11124605R00207